D1396609

ZAGAT

Texas
Restaurants
2012

LOCAL EDITORS
Claudia Alarcón, Valerie Jarvie, Mike Riccetti and
Julia Celeste Rosenfeld

STAFF EDITOR
Michelle Golden

Published and distributed by
Zagat Survey, LLC
76 Ninth Avenue
New York, NY 10011
T: 212.977.6000
E: texas@zagat.com
www.zagat.com

ACKNOWLEDGMENTS

We thank Todd Duplechan, Whitney Francis, Larry McGuire, Mike Lima, MM Pack, Kay Winzenried and Virginia B. Wood, as well as the following members of our staff: Aynsley Karps (editor), Brian Albert, Sean Beachell, Maryanne Bertollo, Danielle Borovoy, Reni Chin, Larry Cohn, Bill Corsello, Nicole Diaz, Kelly Dobkin, Jeff Freier, Alison Gainor, Matthew Hamm, Danielle Harris, Justin Hartung, Marc Henson, Ryutaro Ishikane, Rus Kehoe, Natalie Lebert, Mike Liao, Vivian Ma, Caitlin Miehl, James Mulcahy, Polina Paley, Amanda Spurlock, Chris Walsh, Jacqueline Wasilczyk, Yoji Yamaguchi, Sharon Yates, Samantha Zalaznick, Anna Zappia and Kyle Zolner.

The reviews in this guide are based on public opinion surveys. The ratings reflect the average scores given by the survey participants who voted on each establishment. The text is based on quotes from, or paraphrasings of, the surveyors' comments. Phone numbers, addresses and other factual data were correct to the best of our knowledge when published in this guide.

Contents

Ratings & Symbols

Zagat Top Spot	Name	Symbols	Cuisine	Zagat Ratings			
				FOOD	DECOR	SERVICE	COST

Area, Address & Contact

Z Tim & Nina's ❶ *Portuguese*   ▽ 23 | 9 | 13 | $15

Downtown | 1000 E. Salinas St. (Cecilia St.) | 210-555-1234 | www.zagat.com

Review, surveyor comments in quotes

"Deep in the heart of" Downtown, this "quirky winner" may be short on decor, but it's staffed by "hardworking folks" serving a "veggie version" of Texas BBQ, including a "to-die-for beet brisket sandwich" – though insiders insist it's the "outrageously delicious chicken-fried cabbage" that's "the lone star of the menu"; P.S. remember the "à la mode" for your parsnip-tofu cream pie.

Ratings

Food, Decor & **Service** are rated on a 30-point scale.

0	–	9	poor to fair
10	–	15	fair to good
16	–	19	good to very good
20	–	25	very good to excellent
26	–	30	extraordinary to perfection
	▽		low response	less reliable

Cost

The price of dinner with a drink and tip; lunch is usually 25% to 30% less. For unrated **newcomers** or **write-ins,** the price range is as follows:

| **I** | $25 and below | **E** | $41 to $65 |
| **M** | $26 to $40 | **VE** | $66 or above |

Symbols

Z   highest ratings, popularity and importance
❶   serves after 11 PM
Ⓢ Ⓜ   closed on Sunday or Monday
⊘   no credit cards accepted

About This Survey

Here are the results of our **2012 Texas Restaurants Survey,** covering 1,431 eateries in Texas. Like all our guides, this one is based on input from avid local consumers – 3,542 all told. Our editors have synopsized this feedback, highlighting representative comments (in quotation marks within each review). To read full surveyor comments – and share your own opinions – visit **zagat.com,** where you will also find the latest restaurant news, special events, deals, reservations, menus, photos and lots more, **all for free.**

ABOUT ZAGAT: In 1979, we started asking friends to rate and review restaurants purely for fun. The term "user-generated content" had yet to be coined. That hobby grew into Zagat Survey; 33 years later, we have over 375,000 surveyors and cover airlines, bars, dining, fast food, entertaining, golf, hotels, movies, music, resorts, shopping, spas, theater and tourist attractions in over 100 countries. Along the way, we evolved from being a print publisher to a digital content provider, e.g. **zagat.com** and **Zagat To Go** mobile apps (for Android, iPad, iPhone, BlackBerry, Windows Phone 7 and Palm webOS). We also produce marketing tools for a wide range of blue-chip corporate clients. And you can find us on Google+ and just about any other social media network.

UNDERLYING PREMISES: Three simple ideas underlie our ratings and reviews. First, we believe that the collective opinions of large numbers of consumers are more accurate than those of any single person. (Consider that our surveyors bring some 705,000 annual meals' worth of experience to this survey, visiting restaurants regularly year-round, anonymously – and on their own dime.) Second, food quality is only part of the equation when choosing a restaurant, thus we ask our surveyors to rate food, decor and service separately and then report on cost. Third, since people need reliable information in an easy-to-digest, curated format, we strive to be concise and we offer our content on every platform – print, online and mobile.

THANKS: We're grateful to our local editors, Claudia Alarcón, a contributor to various Austin-area publications; Valerie Jarvie, a freelance writer specializing in culinary and dining-related articles for Dallas/Ft. Worth–based publications; Mike Riccetti, author of *Houston Dining on the Cheap* and *From the Antipasto to the Zabaglione: The Story of Italian Restaurants in America*; and Julia Celeste Rosenfeld, the dining writer for *San Antonio Magazine.* We also sincerely thank the thousands of people who participated in this survey – this guide is really "theirs."

JOIN IN: To improve our guides, we solicit your comments – positive or negative; it's vital that we hear your opinions. Just contact us at **nina-tim@zagat.com.** We also invite you to join our surveys at **zagat.com.** Do so and you'll receive a choice of rewards in exchange.

New York, NY
March 7, 2012

Nina and Tim Zagat

What's New

Texas restaurant-goers continue to lead the U.S. in dining-out frequency, with surveyors reporting an average of 3.8 meals out per week, vs. 3.1 nationally. Houston tops the list at 4.1 meals out per week, followed by Dallas/Ft. Worth (3.8), San Antonio (3.6) and Austin (3.5). The average meal cost in Texas is $32.34, comfortably below the U.S. figure of $35.62, with Austin at the low end ($29.80) and Dallas/Ft. Worth highest at $35.33. Although fine-dining destinations retain our Survey's top ratings, the past year saw a slew of new budget-friendly trucks and gussied-up comfort-fooders.

THE WINNERS: Top Food honors went to a varied lot: cutting-edge Japanese **Uchi** (Austin), classic French **Saint-Emilion** (Dallas/Ft. Worth), sophisticated Italian **Da Marco** (Houston) and low-key French **Bistro Vatel** (San Antonio). Burgers top most Best Buy lists (**Kincaid's** in Dallas/Ft. Worth, **Bellaire Broiler** in Houston and **Five Guys** in San Antonio), while Austinites are partial to fresh-Mex fave **Tacodeli.**

AUSTIN'S EDGE: Thirty-two percent of Texas surveyors patronize food trucks at least occasionally, and Austin – a pioneer in the moveable feast movement – now boasts trucks dishing all manner of eats, including serious, chef-driven fare like Raymond Tatum's Asian-inspired offerings at his **Three Little Pigs.** East Austin trailer **El Naranjo,** dispensing locally sourced Mexican fare, plans to open a brick-and-mortar site, following a path taken by trailers-turned-stationary-hits **Torchy's** and Bryce Gilmore's **Barley Swine.** But the trailer success story of the year is **Franklin Barbecue,** which started as a mobile smoker and now draws daily lines at its East Side storefront. Speaking of BBQ, Austin has serious new contenders in **Live Oak BBQ** and **JMueller,** the latter with a Taylor, Texas, pedigree. Neighborhoodwise, South First Street is enjoying a moment with **Elizabeth Street Café, Lenoir** and a yet-to-open upscale Thai from the **La Condesa** owners. Look for the North Loop district – home to Japanese **Komé** – to be the next big thing.

DALLAS/FT. WORTH DOINGS: Debuts ranged from chef-driven entries – David Uygur's **Lucia** in Oak Cliff, Tre Wilcox's **Marquee Grill** in Highland Park and Tiffany Derry's **Private Social** Uptown – to affordable eats options such as **Velvet Taco,** thin-crust pizza specialists **Cane Rosso** and **Dough,** and mobile purveyors like **Jack's Chowhound, Nammi Truck** and **Ruthie's Rolling Café.** At press time, local legend Tim Love was readying his **Woodshed** BBQer, set to open in a new complex on the Trinity River in Ft. Worth. To the west, **Blue Sushi Sake Grill** and **Shinjuku Station** expanded Ft. Worth's Japanese offerings. Finally, 64% of our surveyors say it's important that the food they eat be locally sourced, organic or sustainably raised, and restaurateurs are following suit both in veteran spots (**Bolsa, Pyramid Room**) and newcomers like **Company Café, Oddfellows** and **Texas Spice.**

HOUSTON HEADLINES: As elsewhere, food trucks were big news with entrants like **Melange Creperie** (offbeat crêpes) and **The**

Modular (Asian-inflected fare). New dining destinations include the once-forlorn Heights, now home to popular Italian **Coppa** and Lance Fegen's seafood-focused **Liberty Kitchen & Oyster Bar.** Montrose is expected to get the buzz going in 2012 with an outpost of Austin's blockbuster Japanese **Uchi** and **Underbelly,** the first solo effort from Chris Shepherd. Also drawing diners is the new mixed-use West Ave development housing the modern Indian **Pondicheri** from Anita Jaisinghani and two from Robert Del Grande: **Alto Pizzeria** and the bistro-like **Ava.**

SAN ANTONIO SCENE: With three culinary schools pumping out eager grads, San Antonio saw an influx of ambitious destinations like **Drew's, Esquire Tavern** and **Feast,** all serving grill fare and gastro-pub bites along with old-school cocktails and craft beers. **Perry's** and a new branch of **Myron's** added to the steakhouse ranks, while the city's first vegan restaurant – **Vegeria** – sprouted up to daily crowds. Though tough local vending laws mean a bumpy ride for food trucks, new ones like the pork-centric **Rolling Pig** nevertheless rolled out. Looking ahead, diners are anticipating the imminent return of Mark Bliss (**Silo**) and soon-to-open outposts for Johnny Hernandez (**La Gloria**) and Dallas' Stephan Pyles.

 SURVEY STATS: Texans tip an average of 19.0%, vs. 19.2% nationally . . . Service remains the top dining-out irritant, cited by 72% of surveyors, followed by noise (14%) . . . 75% think that restaurants should be required to post health-department letter grades in windows . . . 66% will wait no longer than 30 minutes at no-reserving places.

Austin, TX
Dallas, TX
Houston, TX
San Antonio, TX
March 7, 2012

Claudia Alarcón
Valerie Jarvie
Mike Riccetti
Julia Celeste Rosenfeld

AUSTIN AND
THE HILL COUNTRY

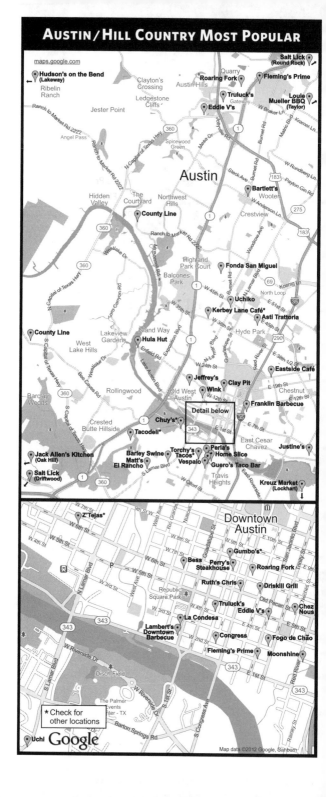

Most Popular

1	Eddie V's | *Seafood/Steak*	**23**	Truluck's* | *Seafood*
2	Uchi* | *Japanese*	**24**	Bess | *Eclectic*
3	Salt Lick | *BBQ*	**25**	Perla's* | *Seafood*
4	Uchiko | *Japanese*	**26**	Home Slice | *Pizza*
5	Wink | *American*	**27**	Barley Swine | *American*
6	Chuy's | *Tex-Mex*	**28**	Guero's Taco Bar* | *Mexican*
7	Hudson's on the Bend | *Amer.*	**29**	Ruth's Chris* | *Steak*
8	Fonda San Miguel | *Mexican*	**30**	Fleming's Prime | *Steak*
9	Congress | *American*	**31**	Matt's El Rancho* | *Tex-Mex*
10	La Condesa | *Mexican*	**32**	Moonshine* | *American*
11	County Line | *BBQ*	**33**	Tacodeli* | *Mexican*
12	Jeffrey's | *American/Continental*	**34**	Franklin Barbecue | *BBQ*
13	Clay Pit | *Indian*	**35**	Kerbey Lane Café* | *Eclectic*
14	Kreuz Market* | *BBQ*	**36**	Torchy's Tacos* | *Mexican*
15	Driskill Grill | *American*	**37**	Justine's | *French*
16	Lambert's Dtwn. | *Amer./BBQ*	**38**	Louie Mueller BBQ* | *BBQ*
17	Vespaio* | *Italian*	**39**	Asti Trattoria | *Italian*
18	Eastside Café | *American*	**40**	Chez Nous* | *French*
19	Jack Allen's Kitchen* | *American*	**41**	Fogo de Chão* | *Brazilian/Steak*
20	Roaring Fork* | *Southwestern*	**42**	Gumbo's* | *Cajun/Creole*
21	Bartlett's | *American*	**43**	Hula Hut* | *Tex-Mex*
22	Perry's Steakhouse* | *Steak*	**44**	Z'Tejas | *Southwestern*

Many of the above restaurants are among the Austin area's most expensive, but if popularity were calibrated to price, a number of other restaurants would surely join their ranks. To illustrate this, we have added two lists comprising Austin's Best Buys on page 16.

KEY NEWCOMERS

Our editors' picks among this year's arrivals. See full list at p. 66.

BC Tavern | *American* | New Bee Cave comfort-fooder

Contigo | *Eclectic* | Ranch-style cooking and open-air setting in Mueller

El Alma | *Mexican* | Mexico City cuisine in Bouldin Creek

Eleven Plates | *American* | Small plates and tipples in West Lake Hills

Elizabeth Street Café | *Fr./Viet.* | Updated Vietnamese in Bouldin Creek

JMueller | *BBQ* | Bouldin Creek mobile smoker

Komé | *Japanese* | Uchi alum serves sushi in the North Loop area

Lenoir | *Eclectic* | Inventive fare in charming Bouldin Creek bungalow

Lucy's | *Southern* | Fried chicken and pies in Bouldin Creek

Swift's Attic | *Eclectic* | Small plates and cocktails from an all-star lineup

Three Little Pigs | *Eclectic* | Asian-inflected dishes out of an East Austin trailer

* Indicates a tie with restaurant above

Top Food

| 29 | Uchi | Japanese |
| | Louie Mueller BBQ | BBQ |

28	Barley Swine	American
	Snow's BBQ	BBQ
	Carillon	American
	Franklin Barbecue*	BBQ
	Congress	American
	Uchiko*	Japanese

27	Smitty's Market	BBQ
	Hudson's on the Bend	Amer.
	City Market	BBQ
	Wink	American

26	Bartlett's	American
	Hilltop Café	Eclectic
	Perry's Steakhouse	Steak
	Home Slice	Pizza
	Perla's	Seafood
	Eddie V's	Seafood/Steak
	Tacodeli	Mexican
	Jack Allen's Kitchen	American

Vespaio | Italian
Ruth's Chris | Steak
Chez Nous | French

25	Driskill Grill	American
	Musashino	Japanese
	Backspace	Pizza
	Enoteca Vespaio*	Italian
	Eastside Café	American
	Andiamo	Italian
	Lambert's Dtwn.	Amer./BBQ
	Fonda San Miguel	Mexican
	Fogo de Chão	Brazilian/Steak
	Fleming's Prime	Steak
	Kreuz Market	BBQ
	Second Bar + Kitchen*	Amer.
	Trattoria Lisina*	Italian
	Cooper's	BBQ
	Flip Happy	Crêpes
	Olivia*	French/Italian
	Fino	Spanish

BY CUISINE

AMERICAN (NEW)

28	Barley Swine
	Carillon
	Congress
27	Hudson's on the Bend
	Wink

AMERICAN (TRAD.)

26	Bartlett's
	Jack Allen's Kitchen
25	Driskill Grill
	Eastside Café
	Lambert's Dtwn.

BARBECUE

29	Louie Mueller BBQ
28	Snow's BBQ
	Franklin Barbecue
27	Smitty's Market
	City Market

ITALIAN

26	Vespaio
25	Enoteca Vespaio
	Andiamo
	Trattoria Lisina
	Olivia

JAPANESE

29	Uchi
28	Uchiko
25	Mushashino
23	Sushi Zushi
21	Kenichi

MEXICAN

26	Tacodeli
25	Fonda San Miguel
24	Torchy's Tacos
	Azul Tequila
	Sazón

SEAFOOD

26	Perla's
	Eddie V's
24	Truluck's
23	Pappadeaux
	Parkside

SOUTHWESTERN

24	Roaring Fork
	Ranch 616
23	South Congress Café
22	Z'Tejas
21	Cool River Cafe

Excludes places with low votes, unless otherwise indicated

STEAKHOUSES

26 Perry's Steakhouse
Eddie V's
Ruth's Chris
25 Fogo de Chão
Fleming's Prime

TEX-MEX

21 Vivo▽
Chuy's
Matt's El Rancho
20 Trudy's
18 Hula Hut

BY SPECIAL FEATURE

BREAKFAST

24 El Mesón
23 Magnolia Café
Judges' Hill
21 1886 Café
20 Trudy's

BRUNCH

26 Perla's
Jack Allen's Kitchen
25 Enoteca Vespaio
Eastside Café
Lambert's Dtwn.

BUSINESS DINING

29 Uchi
28 Carillon
Congress
27 Hudson's on the Bend
26 Perry's Steakhouse

CHILD-FRIENDLY

26 Hilltop Café
25 Eastside Café
Din Ho
Salt Lick
24 El Mesón

MEET FOR A DRINK

28 Uchiko
26 Bartlett's
Perla's
Eddie V's
Jack Allen's Kitchen

OFFBEAT

28 Barley Swine
26 Hilltop Café
25 Cooper's
Flip Happy
24 Torchy's Tacos

PEOPLE-WATCHING

28 Franklin Barbecue
Uchiko
26 Perla's

23 Justine's
La Condesa

POWER SCENES

28 Carillon
Congress
26 Perry's Steakhouse
Eddie V's
24 Texas Chili Parlor

QUICK BITES

26 Perla's
Tacodeli
25 Backspace
Enoteca Vespaio*
Flip Happy

QUIET CONVERSATION

28 Carillon
26 Chez Nous
25 Driskill Grill
Eastside Café
23 Fabi + Rosi

SINGLES SCENES

26 Perla's
Eddie V's
25 Fleming's Prime
24 Sullivan's
21 Kenichi

TRENDY

29 Uchi
28 Barley Swine
Congress
Uchiko*
25 Second Bar + Kitchen

WINNING WINE LISTS

29 Uchi
28 Congress
27 Hudson's on the Bend
Wink
25 Second Bar + Kitchen

BY LOCATION

ARBORETUM

26 Eddie V's
24 Roaring Fork
   Truluck's
22 Z'Tejas
21 P.F. Chang's

CAMPUS/WEST CAMPUS

28 Carillon
25 Fino
24 Torchy's Tacos
23 Judges' Hill
20 Kerbey Lane Café

CHERRYWOOD/EAST AUSTIN

28 Franklin Barbecue
25 Eastside Café
24 Buenos Aires Café
23 Justine's
21 East Side Showroom

CLARKSVILLE/OLD WEST AUSTIN

27 Wink
24 Café Josie
   Jeffrey's
23 Magnolia Café
   Fabi + Rosi

DOWNTOWN

28 Congress
26 Perry's Steakhouse
   Eddie V's
   Ruth's Chris
   Chez Nous

NW AUSTIN/NW HILLS

26 Tacodeli
25 Musashino
   Fleming's Prime
24 Torchy's Tacos
   Jasper's

SOUTH CONGRESS (SOCO)

26 Home Slice
   Perla's
   Vespaio
25 Enoteca Vespaio
   Hopdoddy Burger Bar

WEST LAKE HILLS

24 Grove Wine Bar & Kitchen
23 Gumbo's
   360 Uno Trattoria
22 Las Palomas
21 County Line

ZILKER

29 Uchi
25 Flip Happy
24 Sazón
21 Chuy's
   Shady Grove

Top Decor

28 Green Pastures	La Condesa
Congress	25 East Side Showroom
Trattoria Lisina*	Uchi
Fonda San Miguel	Carillon
Judges' Hill	Steiner Ranch Steakhouse
Driskill Grill	Ranch 616
Uchiko	Roaring Fork
Eddie V's	Fleming's Prime
Perry's Steakhouse	24 Paggi House
Siena	Jasper's

OUTDOORS

Contigo	Salt Lick (Driftwood)
JMueller	Shady Grove
Moonshine	Takoba
Paggi House	Trattoria Lisina
Perla's	Trio

ROMANCE

Bistrot Mirabelle	Judges' Hill
Driskill Grill	Justine's
European Bistro	Lenoir
Fabi + Rosi	Sagra
Green Pastures	Siena

ROOMS

Carillon	Justine's
Congress	La Condesa
Fabi + Rosi	Lenoir
Fonda San Miguel	Peché
Judges' Hill	Vince Young Steakhouse

VIEWS

Eleven Plates	Steiner Ranch Steakhouse
Hula Hut	Trattoria Lisina
Oasis	Trio
Paggi House	219 West
Roaring Fork (Arboretum)	Upper Decks

Top Service

Best Buys

In order of Bang for the Buck rating.

OTHER GOOD VALUES

Austin and the Hill Country

Andiamo ☒ Italian
25 | 15 | 23 | $35

North Austin | 2521 Rutland Dr. (Burnet Rd.) | 512-719-3377 | www.andiamoitaliano.com

Though set in a "lackluster" North Austin strip mall, this neighborhood Italian features "fabulous" fare based on "fresh, locally sourced" ingredients and recipes "straight from" the homeland; "decor leaves a bit to be desired", but the "fantastic staff" usually makes up for it.

Annie's Café & Bar American
21 | 20 | 20 | $31

Downtown | 319 Congress Ave. (3rd St.) | 512-472-1884 | www.anniescafebar.com

"Lots of Downtown office workers" like this midpriced cafe featuring a "modestly adventurous" New American menu served from morning till late on weekends; the bistro-like atmosphere is comfy, and although the "lively" space gets hectic during the daytime rush, happy hour is relaxed with folks unwinding over nibbles and creative cocktails; P.S. don't miss "lovely patio dining" in warm weather.

Artz Rib House BBQ
21 | 11 | 18 | $21

South Lamar | 2330 S. Lamar Blvd. (Bluebonnet Ln.) | 512-442-8283 | www.artzribhouse.com

This South Lamar BBQ "hole-in-the-wall" feels like it belongs in a "small Texas town"; though some say the food's only "ok", many "rave about the ribs" as well as the "live country music" nightly.

Asti Trattoria ☒ Italian
23 | 20 | 23 | $36

Hyde Park | 408 E. 43rd St. (bet. Ave. H & Duval St.) | 512-451-1218 | www.astiaustin.com

"Unpretentious" describes this "neighborhood trattoria" in Hyde Park that always "packs them in" thanks to chef-owner Emmett Fox's "wonderful" freshly made pastas and other "excellent" midpriced Italian eats; a "witty", "accommodating" staff and "quaint" quarters inspire many to "linger till closing"; P.S. reservations are recommended, especially on weekends.

August E's Ⓜ Eclectic/Steak
24 | 23 | 25 | $51

Fredericksburg | 203 E. San Antonio St. (Llano St.) | 830-997-1585 | www.august-es.com

"It feels like New York" at this "elegant", upscale Fredericksburg bistro serving "innovative" Eclectic cuisine from steaks to sushi in "chic" digs done up with original art; add in "attentive" service and it's "a wonderful surprise" in Hill Country.

Austin Land & Cattle Co. Steak
24 | 20 | 22 | $41

Downtown | 1205 N. Lamar Blvd. (bet. Shoal Creek Blvd. & 12th St.) | 512-472-1813 | www.austinlandandcattlecompany.com

A "favorite" among beef "aficionados", this "charming", "locally owned" Downtown chophouse sears "amazing" steaks that come served by a "professional" staff in "dark", "old-fashioned" environs;

yes, it may be a tad "predictable", but factor in "prices lower than the competition", and admirers ask "who needs national chains" when you have a "quality" place like this?

Azul Tequila *Mexican*

24 | 14 | 22 | $21

South Lamar | 4211 S. Lamar Blvd. (Ben White Blvd.) | 512-416-9667 | www.azultequila.com

"Authentic" interior Mexican cooking and "potent margaritas" (with a selection of 60 tequilas) are the pull at this South Lamar eatery that's a nice changeup from the "typical Tex-Mex"; low prices are a plus, but the "nondescript" strip-mall setup is "the antithesis of a see-and-be-seen setting"; P.S. there's live mariachi on Thursday and Friday nights.

Backspace, The *Pizza*

25 | 18 | 23 | $25

Downtown | 507 San Jacinto Blvd. (6th St.) | 512-474-9899 | www.thebackspace-austin.com

This "casual, but cool" Downtown pizzeria from Shawn Cirkiel (Parkside) specializes in "thin-crust" Neapolitan pies finished with "creative" toppings and served with beer and wine; the vibe is "friendly", and if some say "overpriced" and "inconsistent", at least happy hour pleases with half-price deals.

ⓩ Barley Swine ⊠ *American*

28 | 19 | 25 | $47

South Lamar | 2024 S. Lamar Blvd. (Hether St.) | 512-394-8150 | www.barleyswine.com

One of the "hottest" places in town, this "amazing" "locavore" American in South Lamar from chef Bryce Gilmore (of the now-defunct Odd Duck trailer) provides "truly memorable" small plates all made for sharing and enjoying alongside an impressive list of beers; it's "foodie central", but the space is "hopelessly small", so "arrive early or be prepared to wait for an eternity."

Bartlett's *American*

26 | 23 | 26 | $33

(fka Houston's)

North Central | 2408 W. Anderson Ln. (Burnet Rd.) | 512-451-7333 | www.bartlettsaustin.com

Formerly a branch of Houston's, this "clubby" North Central American serves a menu "similar" to its chain predecessors with "excellent burgers, steaks" and a spinach-artichoke dip that "can't be beat"; some find it a bit "pricey", but the atmosphere's "comfort-able and cozy", service is strong and the food's always "reliable."

‖NEW‖ BC Tavern *American*

- | - | - | M

(fka Zoot)

Bee Cave | 11715 Bee Cave Rd. (Resaca Blvd.) | 512-477-6535 | www.bc-tavern.com

The dynamic duo of Stewart Scruggs and Mark Paul (Wink) have re-vamped their Zoot into this new Bee Cave tavern serving slightly dressed-up takes on American comfort food (duck nachos, pot roast) with a farm-to-table bent; the pubby space features a full bar with local beer on tap and an extensive wine selection at very affordable prices.

Berryhill Baja Grill *Mexican*

20 | 15 | 16 | $16

Northwest Hills | 3600 N. Capital of Texas Hwy. (Westlake Dr.) |
512-327-9033 | www.berryhillbajagrill.com
See review in Houston Directory.

Bess *Eclectic*

23 | 24 | 23 | $32

Downtown | 500 W. Sixth St. (San Antonio St.) | 512-477-2377 |
www.bessbistro.com
Sandra Bullock is the owner of this "cute spot" Downtown, a
"charming basement restaurant" featuring an Eclectic menu with
dishes heavy on the "southern comfort" and creative cocktails to
wash it all down; if some say it's "nothing too grand", at least the
bills are moderate, making it a favorite for dates, happy hour
and Sunday brunch.

Billy's on Burnet ● *American*

∇ 18 | 15 | 18 | $14

Rosedale | 2105 Hancock Dr. (Burnet Rd.) | 512-407-9305 |
www.billysonburnet.com
"Neighborhood bar" in Rosedale with solid burgers and other
American eats served with "refreshing, local" beers in a space that
evokes "1970s Austin"; TVs tuned to the game plus an arcade room
and a pool table increase the "fun."

Bistrot Mirabelle *French*
(fka Mirabelle)

- | - | - | M

Northwest Hills | 8127 Mesa Dr. (bet. Spicewood Springs Rd. &
Steck Ave.) | 512-346-7900 | www.mirabellerestaurant.com
A recent revamp has transformed this old Northwest Hills favorite
into a neighborhood bistro open for lunch, dinner and brunch with a
classic French menu, a thoughtful wine list and craft cocktails; a
new coat of paint in reddish tones and art deco posters add to the
casual Parisian atmosphere.

Black Star Co-op Pub & Brewery *Pub Food*

- | - | - | I

Crestview | 7020 Easy Wind Dr. (Lamar Blvd.) | 512-452-2337 |
www.blackstar.coop
One of Crestview's hottest haunts is this "unique concept" – a
member-owned co-op brewpub (also open to the public) offering local and housemade craft beers and inexpensive, "straightforward"
Texas-style pub grub; the modern, industrial space is sprawling and
frequently "packed", with a long bar and a patio with picnic tables
for sipping suds on sunny days.

Blue Star Cafeteria *American*

20 | 19 | 20 | $25

Rosedale | Rosedale Village Shopping Ctr. | 4800 Burnet Rd.
(bet. 47th & 49th Sts.) | 512-454-7827 |
www.bluestarcafeteria.com
Contrary to the name, this Rosedale New American restaurant is
"not a cafeteria", but a "bright, charming retro-modern diner"
that many surveyors find "perfect for lunch"; just be ready to
bear with a "high noise level" and service that can sometimes
border on "too casual."

FOOD | DECOR | SERVICE | COST

Braise 🅢 *American* ▽ 21 | 19 | 22 | $35

East Austin | Villas on 6th | 2121 E. Sixth St. (Robert T. Martinez St.) | 512-478-8700 | www.braiseaustin.com

Loyal followers of chef Parind Vora flock to this casual East Austin bistro for his idiosyncratic New American eats like blackened amberjack over creamy grits (in full- or half-plates) with eclectic wines; the understated "date"-worthy setting is done up in gray and burgundy and adorned in art, while unobtrusive service and moderate tabs make it a natural for a relaxed evening.

Brick Oven *Pizza* 19 | 16 | 19 | $19

Downtown | 1209 Red River St. (12th St.) | 512-477-7006
Great Hills | 10710 Research Blvd. (Braker Ln.) | 512-345-6181
Southwest Austin | 9911 Brodie Ln. (Slaughter Ln.) | 512-292-3939
www.brickovenrestaurant.com

Brick Oven on 35th *Pizza*

Brykerwoods | 1608 W. 35th St. (Glenview Ave.) | 512-453-4330 | www.brickovenon35th.com

"Thin-crust pizzas" (and even gluten-free pies) are the stars of this "popular" chainlet also churning out "strictly average" pastas; the vibe is "casual", service is "efficient" and most "never have a complaint."

Buenos Aires Café *Argentinean* 24 | 22 | 24 | $33

Bee Cave | Hill Country Galleria | 13500 Galleria Circle (Bee Cave Pkwy.) | 512-441-9000
East Austin | 1201 E. Sixth St. (Waller St.) | 512-382-1189 🅢
www.buenosairescafe.com

This Argentinean duo in East Austin and Bee Cave "hits all the right buttons" with "great" cooking (including notable gnocchi) and well-priced wines served in "warm, welcoming" surroundings; an added bonus: "you can hear yourself talk" in the dining room, and Bee Cave boasts a patio.

Cabernet Grill 🅢Ⓜ *American* ▽ 25 | 22 | 23 | $49

Fredericksburg | Cotton Gin Vill. | 2805 Hwy. 16 S. (bet. Ellebracht Dr. & Kneese Rd.) | 830-990-5734 | www.cabernetgrill.com

This "fine-dining" room within Fredericksburg's Cotton Gin Village B&B dishes out "tantalizing" American fare inspired by Hill Country with wild game and Texas wines; the beautifully landscaped patio strung with fairy lights is a highlight.

Café Blue *Eclectic* - | - | - | M

NEW **Bee Cave** | Hill Country Galleria | 12921 Hill Country Blvd. (Galleria Circle) | 512-366-5230
Volente | Sandy Creek Marina | 8714 Lime Creek Rd. (West Dr.) | 512-996-8188 🅢Ⓜ
www.cafebluetx.com

This duo takes its cues from the sea with an Eclectic fin fare menu (Redfish Louisiane, ceviche, coconut shrimp), Caribbean-inspired cocktails and a casual, island-style atmosphere; the original in Volente, set on an ample lakeside deck, opens seasonally, while the year-round Hill Country Galleria space sports blue lighting and large aquariums to complete the aquatic scene.

Café Josie 🛇 Ⓜ *Caribbean*

| 24 | 19 | 22 | $43 |

Clarksville | Pecan Sq. | 1200 W. Sixth St. (Blanco Rd.) | 512-322-9226 | www.cafejosie.com

Loyalists laud this "best-kept secret" in Clarksville, a favorite for "unusual" Caribbean creations like fish with mango-habanero butter that "don't lack for spice"; a "well-informed" staff and "attractive", colorful digs complete the "charming" package.

Cantina Laredo *Mexican*

| 21 | 19 | 20 | $26 |

Downtown | 201 W. Third St. (Colorado St.) | 512-542-9670 | www.cantinalaredo.com

See review in Dallas/Ft. Worth Directory.

🗹 Carillon, The *American*

| 28 | 25 | 26 | $55 |

Campus | AT&T Executive Education & Conference Ctr. | 1900 University Ave. (Martin Luther King Blvd.) | 512-404-3655 | www.thecarillonrestaurant.com

"Top-drawer for Austin", this "beautiful", "special-occasion" Campus-area New American in the AT&T Executive Education and Conference Center is where chef Josh Watkins "moves Texas-native materials into haute cuisine territory", yielding "exceptional" dishes; considering such "superior" quality and service, many find the prices quite "reasonable"; P.S. the lounge features a separate bar menu with small plates.

Carmelo's *Italian*

| 24 | 23 | 24 | $42 |

Downtown | 504 E. Fifth St. (Red River St.) | 512-477-7497 | www.carmelosrestaurant.com

A "little bit of the old world" can be found at these "classic" "upmarket" Italians in West Houston and Downtown Austin where "traditional" fare comes together with "gracious" service featuring "lots of flourishes" like tableside preparations and a lavish dessert cart; perhaps the "dated" looks could use a spruce-up, but most find they still "knock it out of the park" for special occasions.

Carrabba's Italian Grill *Italian*

| 23 | 20 | 22 | $29 |

North Austin | 11590 Research Blvd. (Duval Rd.) | 512-345-8232 | www.carrabbas.com

See review in Houston Directory.

Cheesecake Factory *American*

| 20 | 19 | 19 | $28 |

Arboretum | Arboretum Mall | 10000 Research Blvd. (bet. Capital of Texas Hwy. & Great Hills Trail) | 512-241-0777 | www.thecheesecakefactory.com

See review in Houston Directory.

Chez Nous Ⓜ *French*

| 26 | 18 | 23 | $35 |

Downtown | 510 Neches St. (6th St.) | 512-473-2413 | www.cheznousaustin.com

"Like a little vacation to Paris", this "cozy" Downtown bistro provides "wonderful" "truly French" fare à la carte or in a "good-value" three-course prix fixe; it may be a little "short on decor", but service is solid and overall it's "always a treat."

Chez Zee American Bistro *American*

| 22 | 20 | 22 | $26 |

Northwest Hills | 5406 Balcones Dr. (Rte. 2222) | 512-454-2666 | www.chezzee.com

The "terrific" "brunches and desserts are the raison d'être" of this "casual" Northwest Hills spot dishing up American "home cooking" in "funky", family-friendly surroundings; Sundays are usually "packed", so "go early" to beat the "church crowd."

Chinatown *Chinese*

| 23 | 19 | 21 | $24 |

Northwest Hills | 3407 Greystone Dr. (Mopac Expwy.) | 512-343-9307 | www.chinatown-mopac.com

Austinites hold a soft spot for this longtime Chinese in Northwest Hills known for its "well-prepared", "run-of-the-mill" Hunan menu, bountiful dim sum spreads (on weekends) and expansive wine list; the "pleasant" atmosphere is upscale for the genre, with fiery red accents and carved wood throughout, although prices are still easy on the wallet.

☒ Chuy's *Tex-Mex*

| 21 | 20 | 20 | $19 |

North Austin | 10520 N. Lamar Blvd. (Meadows Dr.) | 512-836-3218
North Austin | 11680 Research Blvd. (Duval Rd.) | 512-342-0011
Round Rock | 2320 I-35 N. (Old Settlers Blvd.) | 512-255-2211
South Austin | Shops at Arbor Trails | 4301 W. William Cannon Dr. (Mopac Expwy.) | 512-899-2489
Zilker | 1728 Barton Springs Rd. (Lamar Blvd.) | 512-474-4452
www.chuys.com

This longtime "Austin classic" chain "still rocks" say fans of its "tasty" Tex-Mex eats, "killer margaritas" and overall "funky", "convivial" atmosphere with decor that's a veritable "shrine to Elvis"; you get "a lot of fun for the money" and "generations of students have lived on the free chips and salsa while waiting for a table", but even so, some say it "lives off nostalgia", claiming the food's only "ok" and the "main draw is the scene."

City Market ☒⊅ *BBQ*

| 27 | 15 | 19 | $17 |

Luling | 633 E. Davis St. (Magnolia St.) | 830-875-9019

This "classic, old-time BBQ" spot in Luling is a "must-try" for its brisket, ribs and sausage served up by the pound on butcher paper and wolfed down at communal picnic tables; don't expect much in the way of decor or service, but do "expect a line."

Clay Pit:
Contemporary Indian Cuisine *Indian*

| 23 | 20 | 20 | $27 |

Downtown | 1601 Guadalupe St. (16th St.) | 512-322-5131 | www.claypit.com

"All the classic Indian dishes and some new creations" turn up at these separately owned eateries in Downtown Austin and Addison set in digs that feel "modern" and somewhat "fancy" for the genre – and service is a step up too; the "wonderful buffet" makes them a special "favorite for lunch."

	FOOD	DECOR	SERVICE	COST

☒ Congress ☒ⓂAmerican
| 28 | 28 | 27 | $90 |

Downtown | The Austonian | 200 Congress Ave. (2nd St.) | 512-827-2760 |
www.congressaustin.com

"Hands-down" among the "best" in town proclaim fans of this "up-scale" Downtown restaurant spotlighting chef David Bull's "over-the-top", "no-holds-barred" New American creations served in prix fixe feasts "fit for a foodie"; "wonderful wines", "fantastic" service (ranked No. 1 in Austin) and a "sophisticated" setting make it "worth every penny for a special occasion" – go for the "full-monty chef's tasting" "if you can afford it"; P.S. the adjacent Bar Congress has its own menu of cocktails and small bites.

NEW Contigo ❶ Eclectic
| – | – | – | I |

Mueller | 2027 Anchor Ln. (bet. Manor Rd. & Manorwood Rd.) | 512-614-2260 | www.contigotexas.com

This "rustic" find in the new Mueller development takes its inspiration from the owners' ranch in South Texas with low-cost Eclectic fare that pairs with "seasonal cocktails" and beer in a laid-back setting; a major draw is the all-weather patio strung with Christmas lights.

Cool River Cafe Southwestern/Steak
| 21 | 22 | 21 | $42 |

Northwest Austin | 4001 W. Parmer Ln. (Amherst Dr.) | 512-835-0010 | www.coolrivercafe.com

With such a "hot bar scene", "the food is almost an afterthought" at this Southwestern-styled steakhouse chainlet, although surveyors report the fare's "surprisingly good" and service "attentive" too; it's especially popular "after work", just expect a "noisy" atmosphere that's "a meat market for business folks on expense accounts."

Cooper's Old Time Pit Bar-B-Que BBQ
| 25 | 14 | 17 | $20 |

Llano | 604 W. Young St. (Ashley Ave.) | 325-247-5713 | www.coopersbbq.com

A Hill Country "must", this BBQ joint in Llano is lauded by "locals and tourists alike" for its "unbelievably delicious" brisket, pork chops and prime rib served straight "off gigantic pits" "lovingly tended" by "good ol' boys in cowboy boots"; it's certainly not fancy, so grab your grub, snag a seat at a picnic table and dig in; P.S. the New Braunfels and Ft. Worth branches are newer and perhaps "not as charming" as the original.

Corazón at Castle Hill ☒ Mexican
| 22 | 19 | 22 | $27 |

Downtown | 1101 W. Fifth St. (Baylor St.) | 512-476-0728 | www.corazonatcastlehill.com

A redo of the former Castle Hill Cafe, this midpriced Downtowner appeals to a neighborhood crowd with "innovative", "high-quality" Mexican cooking served up in a "pleasant", low-key setting.

County Line, The BBQ
| 21 | 20 | 21 | $26 |

Northwest Hills | 5204 Rte. 2222 (Capital of Texas Hwy.) | 512-346-3664
West Lake Hills | 6500 W. Bee Caves Rd. (Knollwood Dr.) | 512-327-1742
www.countyline.com

See review in San Antonio Directory.

Curra's Grill   *Mexican*

| 21 | 12 | 17 | $20 |

Travis Heights | 614 E. Oltorf St. (bet. Congress Ave. & Eastside Dr.) | 512-444-0012 | www.currasgrill.com

"Where the locals go" for breakfast, this "dependable" Travis Heights *cocina* doles out "solid interior Mexican" cooking in a colorful, art-filled setting; prices are extremely wallet-friendly, so it's "always busy" well into the night; P.S. "don't miss the avocado margaritas."

Daily Grill   *American*

| 21 | 18 | 20 | $30 |

Northwest Austin | The Domain | 11506 Century Oaks Terr. (Rogers Rd.) | 512-836-4200 | www.dailygrill.com

"Solid", "hearty" American dishes like chicken pot pie fill the menu at this "convenient" midpriced chain in Austin and Houston; though the spacious, woody setting is pleasant and service is "friendly", detractors declare it "overpriced" for "average" eats.

Din Ho Chinese BBQ   *Chinese*

| 25 | 14 | 19 | $20 |

North Austin | 8557 Research Blvd. (Fairfield Dr.) | 512-832-8788 | www.dinhochinesebbq.com

A cross between "your typical Americanized Chinese" and a joint "straight out of Chinatown", this North Austin eatery is a "favorite" for "mouthwatering" BBQ pork and other "cheap, reasonably authentic" eats; "friendly", but "harried" service matches the "basic" setup.

Dirty Martin's Kum-Bak Place   *Burgers*

| 19 | 10 | 16 | $11 |

West Campus | 2808 Guadalupe St. (Nueces St.) | 512-477-3173 | www.dirtymartins.com

"Nothing ever changes" at this University of Texas "campus classic" American putting out "great burgers" and "lots of fried food" in a "greasy-spoon" setting; "cheap" tabs, cold beer and a patio with hi-def TVs also make it a popular hangout on game day.

Driskill Grill   🖥Ⓜ️ *American*

| 25 | 26 | 25 | $61 |

Downtown | Driskill Hotel | 604 Brazos St. (6th St.) | 512-391-7162 | www.driskillgrill.com

"Tradition is the watchword" at this "sophisticated oasis" in the historic Driskill Hotel Downtown inhabiting "classy", clubby digs adorned with portraits of politicians of yore; most find the American fare – offered à la carte or in various tasting menus – "delicious" and well served at appropriately upmarket prices.

Eastside Café   *American*

| 25 | 22 | 23 | $26 |

Cherrywood | 2113 Manor Rd. (bet. Alamo & Coleto Sts.) | 512-476-5858 | www.eastsidecafeaustin.com

"They grow their own veggies" at this "charming, cozy" Cherrywood "gem" set in a "quaint, little" bungalow with a garden out back and serving an "amazing", "affordable" American menu; it's "not haute cuisine", but a "down-to-earth" staff helps keep it tried-and-true.

East Side King   ●⊄ *Asian*

| ▽ 26 | 11 | 14 | $12 |

NEW **East Austin** | Shangri-La | 1016 E. Sixth St. (Medina St.) | no phone 🖥

East Austin | Liberty Bar | 1618 E. Sixth St. (Comal St.) | no phone

(continued)

East Side King Yakitori ● ⌒ *Asian*

Downtown | The Grackle | 1700 E. Sixth St. (Chalmers Ave.) | no phone
www.eastsidekingaustin.com

Tucked in back of Austin's Liberty Bar, Shangri-La and The Grackle, these popular trailers from Uchiko chef Paul Qui specialize in "stunning" Asian fusion bar snacks like "tongue on a bun", fried chicken and beet fries; the food's cheap, "fun and different", and "adventurous" eaters find it "such a treat" late at night.

East Side Showroom ● *American*   21 | 25 | 13 | $40

East Austin | 1100 E. Sixth St. (Medina St.) | 512-467-4280 |
www.eastsideshowroom.com

"Vigorously peculiar" East Austin "steampunk" hangout with decor "trapped somewhere between burlesque house, silent-film house and roadhouse"; the "phenomenal cocktails" are a standout, although the "locally sourced" New American menu can be "hit-or-miss", and many complain about "persnickety" "hipster service."

☒ Eddie V's Prime Seafood *Seafood/Steak*   26 | 26 | 25 | $55

Arboretum | 9400 Arboretum Blvd. (Capital of Texas Hwy.) |
512-342-2642
Downtown | 301 E. Fifth St. (San Jacinto Blvd.) | 512-472-1860
www.eddiev.com

This "vibrant" chophouse chainlet – tied for Most Popular in Austin – "stands out" with "super" steaks and "excellent" "seafood without gimmicks" ("oysters as fresh as if you'd gotten them off the boat"), plus "exemplary" service and "elegant", "well-appointed" surroundings attracting a "high-rolling" crowd of "wealthy lobbyists and dealmakers"; "you pay dearly" for it all, so many seek out the half-price apps deals during happy hour; look for a "hopping" bar scene too.

1886 Café & Bakery *American*   21 | 22 | 21 | $27

Downtown | Driskill Hotel | 604 Brazos St. (6th St.) | 512-391-7066 |
www.1886cafeandbakery.com

Housed in a "beautiful" Victorian-styled space off the lobby of the Driskill Hotel, this Downtown American lures visitors and "business" types alike for "excellent" breakfasts and lunches and "wonderful" desserts served into the wee hours; dinners, however, draw less acclaim and some decry service that "needs to be better" given the prices.

NEW El Alma *Mexican*   - | - | - | I

Bouldin Creek | 1025 Barton Springs Rd. (Dawson Rd.) |
512-609-8923

Chef Alma Alcocer is behind this Bouldin Creek newcomer in the former El Chile space serving affordable specialties inspired by her Mexico City upbringing like duck mole enchiladas and a variety of chiles rellenos; white stucco walls, colorful paintings and a rock wall with trickling water create a "pleasant, casual" ambiance, as does the rooftop deck that's a fine choice for sipping cocktails.

El Chile *Mexican*

∇ 19 | 11 | 14 | $31

Cherrywood | 1809 Manor Rd. (Chicon St.) | 512-457-9900 | www.elchilecafe.com

El Chilito *Mexican*

Downtown | 2219 Manor Dr. (bet. Chestnut Ave. & Coleto St.) | 512-382-3797 | www.elchilito.com

Admirers attest you "can't go wrong with anything on the menu" at these Austin sibs showcasing "true Mexican" cooking, starring a signature "smoky salsa" and "great 'ritas"; the wallet-friendly tabs and patio-blessed settings don't disappoint either.

🆕 Eleven Plates *American*

- | - | - | M

West Lake Hills | Davenport Vill. | 3801 N. Capital of Texas Hwy., 2nd fl. (Westlake Dr.) | 512-328-0110 | www.elevenplates.com

Set on the second story of a West Lake Hills edifice, this moderately priced New American newcomer focuses on small plates and up-scale comfort-food entrees; the sleek dining room is augmented by an alfresco balcony plus an ample bar pouring craft cocktails and a large selection of wine, many available by the glass.

🆕 Elizabeth Street Café *French/Vietnamese*

- | - | - | M

Bouldin Creek | 1501 S. First St. (Elizabeth St.) | 512-291-2881

From the folks behind Lambert's and Perla's, this Bouldin Creek new-comer serves French pastries and coffee in the mornings followed by upscale takes on Vietnamese dishes like banh mi and noodle bowls for lunch and dinner; the cozy corner space is done up in a French colonial style with plants, outdoor seating and a kitchen garden blooming with herbs; P.S. be prepared to walk as parking can be a problem.

El Mesón Taqueria 🅱 *Mexican*

24 | 16 | 14 | $21

Southeast Austin | 5808 Burleson Rd. (Montopolis Dr.) | 512-416-0749

El Mesón Tequileria *Mexican*

South Lamar | 2038 S. Lamar Blvd. (Mary St.) | 512-442-4441

While the Southeast Austin taqueria specializes in counter-service snacks, its full-service South Lamar sib is set in a beautifully refur-bished space offering a diverse menu of "amazing", "authentic" in-terior Mexican fare, including regional specialties (cochinita pibil, Acapulco-style shrimp cocktail) plus "strong, cheap margaritas"; service is "friendly, but not always polished", while the big dining room with open kitchen is bright and welcoming, and the bar serves a wide variety of tequilas with small plates to match.

El Naranjo *Mexican*

- | - | - | I

Downtown | 85 Rainey St. (Driskill St.) | 512-474-2776

Chef Iliana de la Vega, who previously helmed the lauded El Naranjo in Oaxaca City – and ran a much-loved East Austin trailer – is putting the finishing touches on a brick-and-mortar eatery set to debut Downtown; she plans to cook up authentic, affordable interior Mexican fare for lunch and dinner, using as many locally sourced ingredients as possible.

	FOOD	DECOR	SERVICE	COST

El Sol y La Luna 🅼 *Mexican* — ▽ 15 | 18 | 18 | $22

Downtown | 600 E. Sixth St. (Red River St.) | 512-444-7770 |
www.elsolylalunaaustin.com

Set on bustling Sixth Street Downtown, this Mexican staple turns
out "tasty", "authentic" grub (like "great breakfast tacos") at prices
that are easy on the pocketbook; though live music on weekends
boosts the appeal, some complain the "spacious" digs lack "charm"
and can be "loud" to boot.

Enoteca Vespaio *Italian* — 25 | 19 | 23 | $32

SoCo | 1610 S. Congress Ave. (Monroe St.) | 512-441-7672 |
www.austinvespaio.com

Always "hopping", this "little-bitty" sibling to next-door Vespaio is
beloved for its "delicious" Italian cooking, snacky small plates, "fantastic" wines and Sunday brunch; prices are moderate and the
staff's "professional", but an exceedingly "intimate" setting means
it's "hard to get a table"; P.S. no reservations.

Estância Churrascaria *Brazilian/Steak* — 24 | 22 | 25 | $48

NEW Arboretum | Arboretum | 10000 Research Blvd.
(Capital of Dallas Hwy.) | 512-345-5600
Southwest Austin | 4894 US-90 W. (bet. Brodie Ln. & Gate Blvd.) |
512-892-1225
www.estanciachurrascaria.com

"Endless meats" are on parade at this Southwest Austin rodizio
where you certainly won't find any "hemp-clad vegetarians" chowing down on the all-you-can-eat feasts of skewered cuts; prices
aren't inexpensive, but insiders assure "you'll leave full"; the new
Arboretum branch is twice as big, featuring a more varied salad bar,
a wine room and an ample bar; P.S. "the [$29.50] Sunday special
will have you longing for the treadmill on Monday!"

European Bistro 🅼 *European* — - | - | - | M

Pflugerville | 111 E. Main St. (Railroad Ave.) | 512-835-1919 |
www.european-bistro.com

Eastern-European cuisine in Texas is "pretty rare", but this Pflugerville
bistro puts out "authentic" takes on all the Russian, Czech and German
classics capped by traditional desserts; a historic setting decked out
with antiques and mementos enhances the "old-world charm."

Evangeline Café 🅱 *Cajun/Creole* — 21 | 17 | 21 | $21

Southwest Austin | 8106 Brodie Ln. (bet. Alexandria & Eskew Drs.) |
512-282-2586 | www.evangelinecafe.com

"Funky" sums up this Southwest Austin "hangout" where an affable
staff rustles up "excellent" Cajun-Creole cooking like boudin and po'
boys; it's a "fun place to go with friends", thanks to cheap tabs, an
abundance of cold beer and live music most nights.

Fabi + Rosi *European* — 23 | 23 | 24 | $37

Old West Austin | 509 Hearn St. (Lake Austin Blvd.) | 512-236-0642 |
www.fabiandrosi.com

This "wonderful little hideaway" in Old West Austin serves modern
takes on European classics like escargots and housemade charcuterie

plus some of the "best schnitzel this side of the Atlantic" paired with a small but well-curated wine list; set in a "charming" rehabbed home, it's decorated in a black-and-white motif with leather banquettes, hanging votives and mirrors lending it a modern ambiance perfect for "dates."

Fino *Spanish*
25 | 23 | 23 | $38

West Campus | 2905 San Gabriel St. (29th St.) | 512-474-2905 | www.finoaustin.com

"Small plates rule" at this "upscale" West Campus eatery (and sister to Asti) where the "creative" Spanish menu "encourages experimentation" and the "fabulous cocktails" are discounted during happy hour; the locale's a bit "off the beaten path", although inside is "sophisticated" and "modern", and when the weather is warm, the place to be is out on the patio.

First Chinese BBQ *Chinese*
24 | 9 | 16 | $18

North Austin | Chinatown Ctr. | 10901 N. Lamar Blvd. (Kramer Ln.) | 512-835-8889 | www.firstchinesebbq.com
See review in Dallas/Ft. Worth Directory.

Fleming's Prime Steakhouse & Wine Bar *Steak*
25 | 25 | 25 | $56

Downtown | 320 E. Second St. (bet. San Jacinto Blvd. & Trinity St.) | 512-457-1500
Northwest Austin | The Domain | 11600 Century Oaks Terr. (Burnet Rd.) | 512-835-9463
www.flemingssteakhouse.com
See review in Houston Directory.

Flip Happy Crepes Ⓜ⇗ *Crepes*
25 | 13 | 17 | $13

Zilker | 400 Josephine St. (Butler Rd.) | 512-552-9034 | www.fliphappycrepes.blogspot.com

"Lovely" "custom crêpes" are crafted from "fresh ingredients" at this refurbished Avion trailer in Zilker, a true "Austin original" putting out an "impressively varied menu for such a tiny kitchen"; prices are low and "it's a surprisingly charming place to eat", so long as you don't mind the "quirky" hours and perpetual "lines."

Fogo de Chão *Brazilian/Steak*
25 | 23 | 26 | $55

Downtown | 309 E. Third St. (Trinity St.) | 512-472-0220 | www.fogodechao.com
See review in Houston Directory.

Ⓩ Fonda San Miguel *Mexican*
25 | 27 | 23 | $42

Highland Park | 2330 North Loop Blvd. W. (Hancock Dr.) | 512-459-4121 | www.fondasanmiguel.com

"Colorful and full of beautiful pottery", this Highland Park hacienda has long been "a treat for the eyes as well as the taste buds" with "impeccable" interior Mexican fare in a "casually elegant" setting tended by a "knowledgeable" crew; especially "memorable" is Sunday's bounteous buffet brunch – a long-standing "tradition" and quite the "event"; "don't eat all weekend" before you go.

	FOOD	DECOR	SERVICE	COST

Foreign & Domestic Ⓜ *American/European*   23 | 17 | 21 | $40

Hyde Park | 306 E. 53rd St. (Ave. H) | 512-459-1010 |
www.foodanddrinkaustin.com

Riding both the farm-to-table and nose-to-tail waves is this "inventive" Hyde Park American-European featuring an "adventurous" seasonal menu and a well-chosen array of wines and craft beers; reviews on the food are mixed ("tasty" vs. "disappointing"), although the "loud", "offbeat" setting in an old skate shop continues to draw diners in droves.

Frank *Hot Dogs*   22 | 21 | 19 | $18

Warehouse District | 407 Colorado St. (4th St.) | 512-494-6916 |
www.hotdogscoldbeer.com

This "homage to sausage" in the Warehouse District purveys an array of exotic "upscale" dogs – from Chicago-style to antelope to veggie – accompanied by creative sides and craft cocktails like the bacon-infused Bloody Mary; comfortable publike digs, an "energetic vibe" and modest tabs have gained it a loyal following; P.S. Sunday brunch is also popular.

Frank & Angie's Pizzeria *Pizza*   20 | 16 | 20 | $19

Downtown | 508 West Ave. (6th St.) | 512-472-3534 |
www.hutsfrankandangies.com

This "cute" Downtown diner is known for gently priced pizza and red-sauce classics in a red-checkered tablecloth ambiance; some shrug "nothing special", although service is "nice" and they keep Austin weird with a Russian balalaika player performing on Wednesdays.

Ⓩ Franklin Barbecue Ⓜ *BBQ*   28 | 11 | 19 | $17

East Austin | 900 E. 11th St. (Branch St.) | 512-653-1187 |
www.franklinbarbecue.com

Originally a trailer, this brick-and-mortar BBQ upstart in East Austin is "giving the big names a run for their money" with some of the "finest brisket in the entire state of Texas" plus pulled pork and other "exceptional", "simple smoked meats"; the modest space opens at 11 AM and closes whenever the eats run out, which is usually early.

NEW Full English Café Ⓜ *British*   - | - | - | I

South Austin | 2000 Southern Oaks Dr. (Manchaca Rd.) | 512-240-2748 |
www.fullenglishfood.com

English breakfasts with housemade bangers are served all day at this South Austin cheapie that also offers high tea with scones and finger sandwiches plus savory pasties, all prepared with local, organic ingredients; the funky, coffeehouse-style space features WiFi, vintage furniture, punk-rock posters and a focus on Brit musicians in the music selection.

Garrido's *Mexican*   22 | 22 | 21 | $27

Downtown | 360 Condominiums | 360 Nueces St. (3rd St.) |
512-320-8226 | www.garridosaustin.com

Longtime Jeffrey's chef David Garrido strikes out on his own with this "cool" Mexican canteen serving "a mix of traditional and fusion" items like oyster tostads and "unique" coffee-marinated rib-eye tacos; its Downtown nook in the 360 Condominiums is convenient to the Austin Music Hall, and also features a "beautiful patio" overlooking Shoal Creek.

Golden Wok *Chinese*

| 20 | 16 | 19 | $18 |

North Austin | Tech Ridge Ctr. | 500 Canyon Ridge Dr. (I-35) | 512-228-3688 | www.golden-wok.com
See review in San Antonio Directory.

Gonzales Food Market ⊠ *BBQ*

| - | - | - | I |

Gonzales | 311 St. Lawrence St. (St. James St.) | 830-672-3156
A "best-kept secret" for BBQ, this family-owned market in Gonzales – about 60 miles south of Austin – is "hard to beat" for "tasty" oak-smoked brisket, ribs and sausage on the cheap; although not as "famous" as some in Hill Country, it's been going strong since 1959 and diehards declare it "one of the best" around.

G'raj Mahal ●Ⓜ *Indian*

| 22 | 20 | 14 | $20 |

Downtown | 91 Red River St. (Willow St.) | 512-480-2255 | www.grajmahalaustin.com

Quite possibly Downtown Austin's only Indian food truck, this entry offers regional specialties with lots of vegetarian options crafted from organic ingredients; full table service is an unusual perk for the genre (although "long waits" are the norm), but otherwise the outdoor-only seating area is the definition of "funky" with colorful tapestries and mix-and-match-furniture; P.S. dinner only and BYO.

Green Mesquite *BBQ*

| 20 | 15 | 20 | $18 |

South Austin | Southpark Meadows Shopping Ctr. | 9900 I-35 S. (Brandt Rd.) | 512-282-7100
Zilker | 1400 Barton Springs Rd. (Lamar Blvd.) | 512-479-0485
www.greenmesquite.net

"Workmanlike BBQ that won't break the bank" describes this long-established South Austin and Zilker duo set in rustic digs with frequent live music; if it's "nothing to rave about", it's nothing to be disappointed by either.

🇿 Green Pastures *Continental*

| 23 | 28 | 24 | $41 |

Bouldin Creek | 811 W. Live Oak St. (3rd St.) | 512-444-4747 | www.greenpasturesrestaurant.com

"Classic dining" turns up at this "venerable" 1894 Bouldin Creek estate – ranked No. 1 for Decor in Austin – where peacocks stroll the "lovely" grounds and the "beautiful" setting is a mainstay for weddings and celebratory Sunday brunches; in comparison, some find the "expensive" Continental cuisine "ordinary", although coddling service and the signature milk punch makes it an "old Texas favorite."

Grove Wine Bar & Kitchen *American*

| 24 | 20 | 22 | $29 |

West Lake Hills | 6317 Bee Caves Rd. (Capital of Texas Hwy.) | 512-327-8822 | www.grovewinebar.com

Locals laud this "laid-back" vino-centric New American – a "welcome addition" to West Lake thanks to its "varied menu" starring "affordable wines", "wonderful" small plates and "thin-crust pizzas"; the "trendy" Napa-inspired design sports a lengthy bar and lime-green banquettes, but its "best feature" may be the oak-shaded patio where "couples", "kids" and "groups" gather on balmy evenings.

Guero's Taco Bar *Mexican* 20 | 19 | 19 | $21

SoCo | 1412 S. Congress Ave. (Elizabeth St.) | 512-447-7688 | www.guerostacobar.com

Channeling "the Austin spirit at its best", this SoCo stop attracts "masses" of locals and visitors alike for "no-nonsense" Mexican grub and "margaritas that'll take the enamel off your teeth" served inside a "grungy" old feed store or out on a covered patio; it's especially "popular" when live bands are on the bill, so "long lines" and "slow service" are to be expected.

Gumbo's *Cajun/Creole* 23 | 20 | 22 | $36

Downtown | Brown Bldg. | 710 Colorado St. (8th St.) | 512-480-8053 | www.gumbosdowntown.com 🌏

Round Rock | 901 Round Rock Ave. (Chisholm Trail) | 512-671-7925 | www.gumbosroundrock.com

West Lake Hills | 3600 N. Capital of Texas Hwy. (Westlake Dr.) | 512-328-4446 | www.gumboswestlake.com

For "a taste of New Orleans without the humidity" diners rely on these independently owned outposts offering "reliable" renditions of Cajun-Creole classics, including many "heavy on the butter"; all three boast a similar Southern panache/hospitality and upmarket pricing, but the Round Rock locale earns special nods for its "beautiful" old cottage setting on the Chisholm Trail.

Haddington's ◗ *American* 23 | 24 | 21 | $33

Downtown | 601 W. Sixth St. (Nueces St.) | 512-992-0204 | www.thehaddington.com

This moderately priced Downtown gastropub and sib of Mulberry dishes an American menu (with a standout truffled egg custard) complemented by "great beers" and specialty cocktails; the "cozy" British-inspired digs come courtesy of Michael Hsu, with work from local artists and an ample bar perfect for little bites.

Highball, The ◗ *American* ▽ 19 | 26 | 17 | $24

South Lamar | 1142 S. Lamar Blvd. (Treadwell St.) | 512-383-8309 | www.thehighball.com

From the owners of Alamo Drafthouse Cinema, this South Lamar entertainment complex serves gussied-up Traditional American favorites like "glorious" fried chicken and bison meatloaf; the kitschy space also features eight vintage bowling lanes, Skee-Ball, private karaoke rooms and a large-scale live performance venue; even if "the food is still catching up" to the surroundings, it's still "a blast."

Hilltop Café Ⓜ *Eclectic* 26 | 22 | 24 | $32

Fredericksburg | 10661 Hwy. 87 N. (Rte. 648) | 830-997-8922 | www.hilltopcafe.com

"A Hill Country treasure", this "converted 1930s gas station" near Fredericksburg is where owner and bluesman Johnny

Nicholas serves a "surprisingly fantastic" Eclectic-American menu (a "mix of Greek, Italian and Cajun" grub) and "plays most weekend nights"; it's decorated in "early garage-sale" style with "friendly" servers and modest bills adding to the warm atmosphere; P.S. reservations recommended.

Hoffbrau Steakhouse ⊠Ⓜ *Steak*

| 20 | 14 | 22 | $26 |

Downtown | 613 W. Sixth St. (Nueces St.) | 512-472-0822 | www.originalhoffbrausteaks.com

A "nongentrified slice of Austin", this historic Downtown chop shop from 1934 draws everyone from "CEOs to truck drivers" for "Texan-sized" slabs at "ridiculously cheap prices"; though service can be "hit-or-miss", the atmosphere's "comfy" and it's practically a local "tradition" to bring out-of-towners here for a beer.

Home Slice *Pizza*

| 26 | 15 | 20 | $16 |

SoCo | 1415 S. Congress Ave. (bet. Elizabeth & Gibson Sts.) | 512-444-7437 | www.homeslicepizza.com

"Real New York pizza" turns up at this SoCo parlor and take-out shop pumping out "awesome" slices and pies with a "snappy thin crust"; though a few customers carp about "crowded" conditions, admirers assure "it's always busy for a reason"; P.S. open until 3 AM on weekends.

Hoover's *Southern*

| 21 | 12 | 21 | $22 |

Cherrywood | 2002 Manor Rd. (Alamo St.) | 512-479-5006 | www.hooverscooking.com

"Comfort food at comfortable prices" sums up this Cherrywood Southern mainstay near the University of Texas campus where the "hearty" helpings mean you can "save up a week's calorie quota or share your dinner with a friend"; it's a "popular lunch spot for locals and power brokers", and "good for breakfast" and brunch on weekends too.

Hopdoddy Burger Bar *Burgers*

| 25 | 20 | 17 | $17 |

SoCo | 1400 S. Congress Ave. (Gibson St.) | 512-243-7505 | www.hopdoddy.com

It's "simple, but they really get it right" at this SoCo burger bar turning out "juicy, flavorful" patties on freshly baked buns backed by "heavenly" floats and shakes made with house-churned ice creams (with spiked versions for the grown-ups); it's "always packed" with "crazy lines" for ordering at peak hours, though most find it worth the wait.

☑ Hudson's on the Bend *American*

| 27 | 24 | 26 | $60 |

Lakeway | 3509 Ranch Rd. 620 N. (Hudson Bend Rd.) | 512-266-1369 | www.hudsononthebend.com

"Rattlesnake cakes, anyone?" – this "true Texas ranch house" in Lakeway spotlights Jeff Blank's "memorable" New American menu highlighting "elk, elk and more elk" and other "exotic" game served by a "savvy", "pleasant" staff in "romantic" digs; yes, it's "expensive", but it's truly a "unique experience" that makes any meal "feel like a special occasion"; P.S. reservations recommended.

NEW **Hugo's Restaurant y Tequila Bar** ⓩ *Nuevo Latino*

| - | - | - | - |

Zilker | 300 S. Lamar Blvd. (Toomey Rd.) | 512-474-4846 | www.hugosaustin.com

This sleek Zilker newcomer serves well-priced Nuevo Latino and South American specialties like duck flautas and empanada sliders with bacon s'mores for dessert; the bar features over 75 tequilas, while the cool patio – with entertainment on weekend nights – has become a popular spot to enjoy them.

Hula Hut *Tex-Mex*

| 18 | 23 | 18 | $22 |

Old West Austin | 3825 Lake Austin Blvd. (Enfield Rd.) | 512-476-4852 | www.hulahut.com

"A mix of Tex-Mex and Polynesian cuisines" plus "strong mixed drinks" characterize this Old West Austin "classic" set "right on the lake" with "awesome views" for out-of-towners; critics call the food "forgettable", although sitting on the deck and "sipping a cold beer while watching the boaters" is "one of the best ways to kill a Friday afternoon."

Hut's *Burgers*

| 23 | 18 | 18 | $14 |

Downtown | 807 W. Sixth St. (West Ave.) | 512-472-0693 | www.hutsfrankandangies.com

Sentimentalists swoon over this 1939 Downtown diner slinging "hangover"-busting burgers, shakes and cheese fries at a "frenetic pace"; it's nothing fancy, but it's "always packed", and prices are pleasingly "inexpensive" too; "put it on your list of 100 things to do before you die."

Hyde Park Bar & Grill *American*

| 21 | 18 | 21 | $22 |

Hyde Park | 4206 Duval St. (Park Blvd.) | 512-458-3168
Southwest Austin | 4521 W. Gate Blvd. (Lamar Blvd.) | 512-899-2700
www.hydeparkbarandgrill.com

"Neighborhood" types rely on this set of "casual" grills for "simple American fare" with "creative" touches at low rates; they're "nothing fancy" but always "crowded", especially the original Hyde Park location with its "amusing giant fork sculpture in its driveway"; the Southwest Austin branch has "more room, better parking" and a patio.

Iron Works ⓩ *BBQ*

| 22 | 17 | 17 | $18 |

Downtown | 100 Red River St. (Cesar Chavez St.) | 512-478-4855 | www.ironworksbbq.com

It's "carnivore heaven" at this practically "ancient" BBQer set in Downtown digs like "someone's backyard shed" with a "wide variety" of "bold" smoked beasts, and there's "even a salad bar, if you dare stray"; perhaps it's not up to the competition outside of the city, but "it works when you need a Hill Country fix" nearby.

Jack Allen's Kitchen *American*

| 26 | 22 | 24 | $26 |

Oak Hill | 7720 W. Hwy. 71 (bet. Chinook & Scenic Brook Drs.) | 512-852-8558 | www.jackallenskitchen.com

"Heartwarming" American fare made from local ingredients plus "imaginative drinks" keep this Oak Hill restaurant "slam packed", especially during happy hour; the earthy space includes a patio bar with a fire pit, while "delightful service" and a comfy ambiance make it "a nice date [spot] without breaking the budget"; P.S. "how do you not love a menu with a section titled 'chicken-fried anything'?"

Jasper's *American* | 24 | 24 | 23 | $43 |

Northwest Austin | The Domain | 11506 Century Oaks Terr. (Rogers Rd.) | 512-834-4111 | www.jaspers-restaurant.com

A "genuine treat", Kent Rathbun's "upscale" trio of grills turns out "wonderful", "creative" takes on "homey" Americana ("order the blue-cheese chips and thank the Lord") in "stylish", "contemporary" settings; "first-rate" service and a "friendly" bar are big draws, though a few find the bills expensive for "backyard gourmet."

Jeffrey's *American/Continental* | 24 | 21 | 24 | $57 |

Clarksville | 1204 W. Lynn St. (12th St.) | 512-477-5584 | www.jeffreysofaustin.com

"Year in, year out", this "old-school" Clarksville "fine-dining" destination since 1975 continues to turn out "top-notch" Continental-New American cuisine in a "quiet", "charming" setting; P.S. look for a complete revamp with new owners and a new menu in 2012.

NEW JMueller BBQ Ⓜ *BBQ* | - | - | - | I |

Bouldin Creek | 1502 S. First St. (Elizabeth St.) | 512-229-7366 | www.jmuellerbbq.com

A large parking lot in Bouldin Creek is the site of the long-awaited return of pit master John Mueller – of the famous Louie Mueller BBQ family in Taylor – who barbecues housemade sausage, pork chops and short ribs (along with prime rib on Fridays) and sells it from a truck; picnic tables are available for alfresco chowing, but many folks call ahead and get it to go.

❷ Judges' Hill Restaurant *American* | 23 | 27 | 21 | $48 |

West Campus | Mansion at Judges' Hill Hotel | 1900 Rio Grande St. (Martin Luther King Blvd.) | 512-495-1857 | www.judgeshillrestaurant.com

A "well-appointed historic home" – now a boutique hotel – is the setting for this "elegant" West Campus American serving braised shorts ribs at dinner and chicken and waffles at brunch in a "beautiful" room decked out with contemporary art; diners divide on the food ("average" vs. "delicious"), although most find the "romantic", "unstuffy" atmosphere well suited for "dates."

Justine's ❶ *French* | 23 | 23 | 21 | $40 |

East Austin | 4710 E. Fifth St. (bet. Shady Ln. & Springdale Rd.) | 512-385-2900 | www.justines1937.com

Set in a "seriously industrial" neighborhood in East Austin, this "hip" little bungalow serves an "all-out French" brasserie menu highlighting steak frites and duck confit plus a "strong" wine and cocktail list; the "ambiance is fab" with a light-strung patio and a turntable manned by the staff, although service can be "harried" given the perpetual "waits"; P.S. open till 1:30 AM.

	FOOD	DECOR	SERVICE	COST

Kenichi *Pan-Asian*

21	23	21	$52

Warehouse District | 419 Colorado St. (4th St.) | 512-320-8883 |
www.kenichirestaurants.com

"Sleek" and almost "over-the-top trendy", these Pan-Asian dens in
Austin and Dallas cater to a "twentysomething" "eye-candy" crowd
with "creative", "pricey" sushi, small plates and cocktails; given the
more-than-"lively" settings and "packed" houses on weekends,
"spotty" service comes as no surprise.

Kerbey Lane Café ● *Eclectic*

20	15	18	$17

Brykerwoods | 3704 Kerbey Ln. (35th St.) | 512-451-1436
Campus | 2606 Guadalupe St. (26th St.) | 512-477-5717
Northwest Austin | 13435 Research Blvd. (Anderson Mill Rd.) |
512-258-7757
South Lamar | 2700 S. Lamar Blvd. (Dickson Dr.) | 512-445-4451
Southwest Austin | Shops at Arbor Trails | 4301 W. William Cannon Dr.
(Mopac Expwy.) | 512-899-1500
www.kerbeylanecafe.com

"If you need breakfast at 3 AM", it's "hard to do better" than these
24/7 Austin-area "institutions" slinging "solid" Eclectic grub from
fajitas to "fluffy pancakes", with a handful of "healthy" "veggie-
friendly" items thrown into the mix; despite dinerlike digs and "hit-
or-miss" service from the "heavily tattooed" staff, cheap tabs make
it a "reliable" bet any time of day.

NEW Komé ⊠ *Japanese*

–	–	–	M

North Loop | 4917 Airport Blvd. (51st St.) | 512-712-5700 |
www.kome-austin.com

Také Asazu (ex Uchi) and wife Kayo – who started selling bento
boxes at the farmer's market before running the Sushi-A-Go-Go
trailer – have finally realized their dream with this newcomer in the
up-and-coming North Loop area, a favorite dining spot of local chefs
featuring sushi and homey Japanese dishes prepared with ingredients from area farms; the once-dilapidated space has been com-
pletely transformed into a contemporary yet comfortable Japanese-
style dining room featuring wood and bamboo accents, concrete
floors and modern furniture.

Kreuz Market ⊠ *BBQ*

25	14	17	$19

Lockhart | 619 N. Colorado St. (bet. Cemetery & Flores Sts.) |
512-398-2361 | www.kreuzmarket.com

There's "no forks and no sauce", but plenty to "love" at this legendary Lockhart BBQ famed for its "delicious smoked meats", "sublime
sausages" and thick-cut pork chops deemed "worth the drive from
Austin"; "cafeteria-style" service and a "cavernous" if charmless
setting suits its fan base of "old-style purists" just fine.

❷ La Condesa *Mexican*

23	26	22	$38

Second Street District | 400 W. Second St. (Guadalupe St.) |
512-499-0300 | www.lacondesaaustin.com

"Fabulous, bold" takes on Mexican street food and "wonderful margaritas" await at this Second Street District destination set in "stunning",

"sophisticated" digs with a patio; just know the "lively" atmosphere can be "a little too loud for conversation", and it's not exactly cheap, unless you "go at happy hour for deals on appetizers and drinks."

Lambert's Downtown Barbecue *American/BBQ*

25 | 23 | 23 | $37

Second Street District | Schneider Brothers Bldg. | 401 W. Second St. (Guadalupe St.) | 512-494-1500 | www.lambertsaustin.com
"Fancy barbecue" is the forte of this "classy" 'cue stop set in "gentlemanly" digs in the "historic" Schneider Brothers Building in the Second Street District; charcuterie, steaks and other Traditional American dishes round out the menu, while a "generous" brunch buffet is quite the draw on Sundays; P.S. the "cool" upstairs bar features live music most nights.

Las Palomas 🅂Ⓜ *Mexican*

22 | 16 | 19 | $25

West Lake Hills | West Woods Shopping Ctr. | 3201 Bee Caves Rd. (Walsh Tarlton Ln.) | 512-327-9889 | www.laspalomasrestaurant.com
This "hidden" Mexican in a West Lake Hills strip mall offers "generous portions" of "beautifully prepared" regional specialties, "attentive" service, modest bills and a spiffy, if low-key, setting.

La Traviata 🅂 *Italian*

23 | 20 | 23 | $35

Downtown | 314 Congress Ave. (3rd St.) | 512-479-8131 | www.latraviata.net
"Delightful, little" Downtown trattoria treasured for its "classic" Italian menu, amicable staff and "intimate", "unpretentious" setting; add in "reasonable" bills, and it almost "never disappoints."

NEW Lenoir 🅂Ⓜ *Eclectic*

- | - | - | M

Bouldin Creek | 1807 S. First St. (Annie St.) | 512-215-9778 | www.lenoirrestaurant.com
Chef Todd Duplechan (ex Trio) takes inspiration from an Eclectic array of 'hot climate' cuisines (India, Mediterranean, et al.) at this midpriced Bouldin Creek newcomer; sporting a romantic, serene blue motif, the tiny digs are bedecked with reclaimed furnishings, vintage crochet curtains and an old drugstore-style bar doling out craft beers and wines.

NEW Live Oak BBQ ❶ *BBQ*

- | - | - | I

East Austin | 2713 E. Second St. (Pleasant Valley Rd.) | 512-524-1930 | www.liveoakbbq.net
This East Austin newcomer smokes up pork steaks, ribs, crispy-skinned chicken and other BBQ, served by the pound and alongside housemade sides; the no-frills setting includes indoor and outdoor seating plus a daily midnight closing hour; P.S. 'cue hounds come for the Saturday special featuring an off-menu surprise.

❷ Louie Mueller BBQ 🅂 *BBQ*

29 | 16 | 21 | $21

Taylor | 206 W. Second St. (Talbot St.) | 512-352-6206 | www.louiemuellerbarbecue.com
The dining room itself is "charred with years of accumulating smoke" at this "real-deal" circa-1949 Taylor BBQer declared "one of

the best in Texas" thanks to its "simply divine", "thickly crusted", "flavorful" brisket that "passes the doesn't-need-sauce test"; service is "cafeteria-style" and "neon beer signs" are the only decor, but it's "well worth the drive"; P.S. it "closes when they run out of food", so "get there early."

NEW Lucy's Fried Chicken ● *Southern* | – | – | – | M |

Bouldin Creek | 2218 College Ave. (Congress Ave.) | 512-297-2423 | www.lucysfriedchicken.com

The immense popularity of Olivia chef James Holmes' brunchtime fried chicken has led to this new paean to poultry in Bouldin Creek, whose midpriced menu is filled out with gussied-up versions of Southern classics such as char-grilled oysters and homemade pies; modern yet neighborhoody, the refurbished two-story building features a covered patio and an airy upper deck.

NEW Luke's Inside Out *Sandwiches* | – | – | – | I |

Zilker | 1109 S. Lamar Blvd. (Gobson St.) | 512-589-8883 | www.lukesinsideout.com

This food truck in Zilker purveys gourmet toasted sandwiches (e.g. pulled pork, brisket and burgers) plus creative sides for cheap; neighborhood folk can eat at one of the outdoor picnic tables or take it to go, while patrons of next door's Rat Pack–inspired Gibson bar can get it delivered; P.S. it also serves weekend brunch at the Gibson.

Madam Mam's *Thai* | 19 | 14 | 16 | $16 |

Campus | 2514 Guadalupe St. (25th St.) | 512-472-8306
North Central | 2700 Anderson Ln. (bet. Burnet Rd. & Rockwood Ln.) | 512-371-9930
Southwest Austin | 4514 W. Gate Blvd. (Lamar Blvd.) | 512-899-8525
www.madammam.com

This family-owned Thai trio serves the area with an ample array of "fresh, affordable" dishes deemed "pretty good"; decor varies by location, with the spare and neat Campus branch "appealing to students", while West Gate boasts bright colors and an impressive rose garden and the North Central outpost is modern, with plenty of parking and a "child-friendly" vibe.

Madras Pavilion *Indian* | 20 | 15 | 18 | $21 |

North Austin | Colonnade Shopping Ctr. | 9025 Research Blvd. (Burnet Rd.) | 512-719-5575 | www.madraspavilionaustin.com
See review in Houston Directory.

Magnolia Café ● *American* | 23 | 17 | 21 | $17 |

Old West Austin | 2304 Lake Austin Blvd. (Veterans Dr.) | 512-478-8645
SoCo | 1920 S. Congress Ave. (bet. Johanna & Mary Sts.) | 512-445-0000
www.themagnoliacafe.com

"No matter what the hour", these "lively" twins in SoCo and Old West Austin turn out "something for everyone", from "healthy, vegetarian items" to good old-fashioned American "home cooking" and hangover-curing breakfasts, all at modest prices; though the digs are barely "a step up from a diner", "wisecracking waitresses" and a veritable "circus" of Austinites add local color.

Málaga Tapas & Bar *Spanish*

23 | 19 | 20 | $33

Second Street District | 440 W. Second St. (bet. Guadalupe & San Antonio Sts.) | 512-236-8020 | www.malagatapasbar.com

"Try a little bit of everything" at this Second Street wine and tapas bar featuring an "excellent" array of nibbles and "fun wine flights" in a "cozy", "low-lit" setting; "great" happy-hour deals bring in the crowds, and the "noise."

Mandola's Italian Market *Italian*

21 | 19 | 16 | $20

Bee Cave | Shops at The Galleria | 12815 Shops Pkwy. (Cross Town Pkwy.) | 512-600-8500

North Central | 4700 W. Guadalupe St. (Lamar Blvd.) | 512-419-9700

Southwest Austin | Arbor Trails | 4301 W. William Cannon Dr. (Mopac Expwy.) | 512-524-2222

www.mandolasmarket.com

Part market, part "homestyle" trattoria, this Italian trio from chef Damian Mandola is beloved for its "delicious", "generously portioned" fare ("meaty ragus", "outstanding antipasti", "blistery, thin-crust pizzas") served amid "salumi, breads, cheeses and gelato" all for sale; the "friendly" counter staff does its best to control the somewhat "chaotic" atmosphere, although alfresco seating and "takeout" are more sedate options.

Manuel's *Mexican*

21 | 19 | 20 | $26

Arboretum | 10201 Jollyville Rd. (Great Hills Trail) | 512-345-1042

Downtown | 310 Congress Ave. (3rd St.) | 512-472-7555

www.manuels.com

The "creative" interior Mex ("not Tex-Mex") fare is "reason enough alone" to love these Austin "reliables" also prized for their modest bills and boozy Sunday brunch with "live music"; the Downtown original is "dark and hip", while the Arboretum offshoot is more "airy" and open with an oak-lined patio that's popular for sipping "terrific cocktails" during happy hour.

Matt's El Rancho *Tex-Mex*

21 | 18 | 21 | $22

South Lamar | 2613 S. Lamar Blvd. (bet. Barton Skywy. & Bluebonnet Ln.) | 512-462-9333 | www.mattselrancho.com

"A Friday night tradition for many Austin families", this "old-time" Tex-Mexer on South Lamar has been "drawing crowds" with "solid" grub since 1952; sure, the service can be "a bit Texas slow", but budget bills and a "bustling" atmosphere compensate; P.S. "the Bob Armstrong dip is not to be missed."

Max's Wine Dive ● *Eclectic*

20 | 16 | 19 | $31

Downtown | 207 San Jacinto Blvd. (bet. 2nd & 3rd Sts.) | 512-904-0111 | www.maxswinedive.com

See review in Houston Directory.

Meyer's Elgin Smokehouse *BBQ*

- | - | - | I

Elgin | 188 Hwy. 290 E. (off Loop 109) | 512-281-3331 | www.meyerselginsausage.com

"Darned good", legendary Elgin BBQ joint famed for its "tasty" German sausages served up in "late-1970s, diner-style" digs; order at the counter and eat in or stock up "at the butcher shop to take home."

Mighty Cone Ⓜ *American*

18 | 9 | 15 | $11

SoCo | 1603 S. Congress Ave. (Monroe St.) | 512-383-9609 | www.mightycone.com

"It ain't fancy, but it is tasty", this popular SoCo trailer serves "awesome" fried chicken, shrimp and avocado packaged in a portable paper cone, plus sliders and shakes; tabs are cheap, lines can be long and picnic tables provide the seating.

Mighty Fine Burgers *Burgers*

21 | 13 | 19 | $13

NEW **Cedar Park** | 1890 Ranch Shopping Ctr. | 1335 E. Whitestone Blvd. (Rte. 183A) | 512-528-5421

North Austin | Shops at Arbor Walk | 10515 N. Mopac Expwy. (Capital of Texas Hwy.) | 512-524-2400

Round Rock | 201 University Oaks Blvd. (Oakmont Dr.) | 512-381-3310

Sunset Valley | Sunset Valley Vill. | 5601 Brodie Ln. (Ernest Robles Way) | 512-735-2800

www.mightyfineburgers.com

This Austin mini-chain with an old-fashioned vibe "hits the mark" with "solid" all-natural burgers, crinkle-cut fries and hand-dipped milkshakes made with Blue Bell ice cream; "efficient" counter service, picnic-style seating with blue checkered tablecloths and inexpensive prices are other nostalgic touches.

Monument Café *American*

23 | 19 | 20 | $18

Georgetown | 500 S. Austin Ave. (bet. 5th & 6th Sts.) | 512-930-9586 | www.themonumentcafe.com

This Georgetown diner is a mainstay for "down-home" Americana capped by "scrumptious" desserts, including an infamous deepfried pie; the cheery atmosphere is reminiscent of old-timey roadside cafes with blackboard menus and counter seating and tables facing an open kitchen; there's also a farmer's market open daily with locally sourced food meats, dairy and produce.

Moonshine *American*

24 | 22 | 23 | $27

Downtown | 303 Red River St. (3rd St.) | 512-236-9599 | www.moonshinegrill.com

Set in a "lovely historic home" Downtown right across the street from the convention center, this well-priced charmer serves "dressed-up" Southern-American cuisine with "modern" touches; "tasteful" decor, a lush patio and "busy bar" make it "pleasant" all around, not to mention a must for its "epic" Sunday brunch.

Mulberry *American*

▽ 23 | 19 | 19 | $35

Downtown | 360 Condominiums | 360 Nueces St. (3rd St.) | 512-320-0297 | www.mulberryaustin.com

"Incredibly cozy" wine bar Downtown "attracts pretty people in the know" with an "intricate" New American menu that includes snacky plates of cured meats as well as pasta, game and a rightly famous pancetta-and-egg burger; the "tiny" spot fills up fast, so "get there early" or you may end up "standing on a busy night."

Musashino Sushi Dokoro Ⓜ *Japanese*   25 | 17 | 18 | $42

Northwest Hills | 3407 Greystone Dr. (Mopac Expwy.) | 512-795-8593 |
www.musashinosushi.com

"Sit at the bar if you can" advise acolytes of this "outstanding"
Northwest Hills Japanese where the "authentic" Tokyo-style sushi
offerings are crafted from "fresh, fresh, fresh" fish flown in daily
from the Tsukiji market; despite a "laid-back" vibe, it's "often
crowded", so "come early."

North *Italian*   22 | 20 | 20 | $33

Northwest Austin | The Domain | 11506 Century Oaks Terr. (Rogers Rd.) |
512-339-4400 | www.foxrc.com

"Thin-crust pizzas" and other "light"-tasting Italian fare revive
weary shoppers at this "casual" Italian at The Domain in Northwest
Austin; the ultramodern digs can be "noisy" at peak times, luckily
there's a serene umbrella-shaded patio, perfect for a "business
lunch" or "happy hour."

Oasis, The *Tex-Mex*   11 | 24 | 13 | $27

Lakeway | 6550 Comanche Trl. (RR 620) | 512-266-2442 |
www.oasis-texas.com

The "five-star" "sunset views" are about the best thing going for this
Austin Tex-Mex "institution" with a multitude of terraces overlooking Lake Travis; with the "spectacular scenery" comes "spectacularly pricey drinks" and "spectacularly average food", though it
remains an "essential" "first stop" for "out-of-towners" seeking a
peek at the Hill Country landscape.

Olivia *French/Italian*   25 | 22 | 24 | $42

South Lamar | 2043 S. Lamar Blvd. (Oltorf St.) | 512-804-2700 |
www.olivia-austin.com

A "lovely space with good buzz", this modern South Lamar spot
"does fresh, seasonal, nice-night-out food" with an "innovative"
French-Italian menu that will "change your mind about sweetbreads, lamb tongue and other oddities"; an "extremely attentive
and knowledgeable" staff and wine list "filled with gems" help take
the sting off somewhat pricey tabs.

Opie's Barbecue *BBQ*   ▽ 23 | 13 | 20 | $18

Spicewood | 9504 Hwy. 71 E. (Texas Spur 191) | 830-693-8660 |
www.opiesbarbecue.com

'Cue buffs flock to this BYO Spicewood spot "out in the middle of nowhere" for "excellent Texas-style BBQ" including "wonderfully seasoned, tender" brisket and ribs accompanied by tater-tot casserole
and the like; just pull up to the counter and pick your meat, then take
it to go, or settle into the ample dining hall for some sports on TV.

Paggi House *American*   23 | 24 | 21 | $54

Downtown South | 200 Lee Barton Dr. (Riverside Dr.) | 512-473-3700 |
www.paggihouse.com

A revamped historic home provides the "beautiful setting" for this
New American south of Downtown where dining on the deck over-

FOOD | DECOR | SERVICE | COST

looking Lady Bird Lake and the city skyline is "simply magical"; a "stellar" menu, "unique cocktails" and a wine list that's "one of the best in town" keep it especially busy at happy hour and brunch, though some lament "tiny portions for huge prices."

Panaderia Chuy 🖼️Ⓜ️ *Mexican*

− | − | − | I

North Austin | 8716 Research Blvd. (Ohlen Rd.) | 512-374-9910
NEW **South Austin** | 801 E. William Cannon Dr. (IH-35) | 512-374-9910

CIA trained baker Chuy Guevara, a native of Mexico, stocks the cases of his namesake bakeries in North and South Austin with an impressive array of traditional pan dulce, empanadas and tres leches cake, plus gelato in tropical flavors; the in-house cafes done up with brightly colored walls and rustic furniture serve affordable Mexican street foods like tortas, breakfast tacos, quesadillas and tlacoyos made with organic blue corn masa, from breakfast till supper.

Pappadeaux *Cajun/Seafood*

23 | 20 | 21 | $32

North Austin | 6319 I-35 N. (Hwy. 290) | 512-452-9363 | www.pappadeaux.com
See review in Houston Directory.

Parkside ❶ *American*

23 | 21 | 21 | $39

Downtown | 301 E. Sixth St. (San Jacinto Blvd.) | 512-474-9898 | www.parkside-austin.com

An "oasis of sanity amid the drunken antics of Sixth Street", this moderately priced Downtown American from chef Shawn Cirkiel is known for its "innovative" small plates, "great raw bar" and "interesting cocktails" served up by an "accommodating" crew; the atmosphere's hip, and it's open late too.

Peché ❶ *French*

▽ 24 | 23 | 21 | $38

Warehouse District | 208 W. Fourth St., 2nd fl. (bet. Colorado & Lavaca Sts.) | 512-494-4011 | www.pecheaustin.com

This luxuriously retro stop in the Warehouse District is reminiscent of an "old New Orleans bistro" with "outstanding" pre-Prohibition cocktails (many made with absinthe) and seasonal French cuisine served into the wee hours; "attentive service" includes tableside visits from the owner, and manageable bills complete the picture.

Pei Wei Asian Diner *Asian*

20 | 16 | 18 | $16

Hyde Park | Hancock Shopping Ctr. | 1000 E. 41st St. (I-35) | 512-382-3860
North Austin | Shops at Tech Ridge | 12901 I-35 N. (bet. Howard & Parmer Lns.) | 512-691-3060
Northwest Austin | 13429 Hwy. 183 N. (Anderson Mill Rd.) | 512-996-0095
Round Rock | University Commons Shopping Ctr. | 200 University Blvd. (I-35) | 512-863-4087
Southwest Austin | Brodie Oaks Shopping Ctr. | 4200 S. Lamar Blvd. (Capital of Texas Hwy.) | 512-382-2990
www.peiwei.com
See review in Dallas/Ft. Worth Directory.

	FOOD	DECOR	SERVICE	COST

Perla's *Seafood* — 26 | 23 | 23 | $44

SoCo | 1400 S. Congress Ave. (Gibson St.) | 512-291-7300 |
www.perlasaustin.com

"Even Bostonians rave about the lobster roll" at this SoCo hot spot
serving a "wonderful" Cape Cod–style seafood menu featuring
"rich chowder", "fresh fish" and loads of oysters; add in a "pro" staff,
moderate bills and a "laid-back" setting with a "marvelous" deck for
"excellent people-watching" and you have a "winner"; P.S. brunch
is also popular.

Perry's Steakhouse & Grille 🗷 *Steak* — 26 | 26 | 25 | $55

Downtown | 114 W. Seventh St. (bet. Colorado St. & Congress Ave.) |
512-474-6300 | www.perryssteakhouse.com
See review in Houston Directory.

P.F. Chang's China Bistro *Chinese* — 21 | 21 | 21 | $29

Arboretum | 10114 Jollyville Rd. (Great Hills Trail) | 512-231-0208
Downtown | 201 San Jacinto Blvd. (2nd St.) | 512-457-8300
www.pfchangs.com
See review in Dallas/Ft. Worth Directory.

Piranha Killer Sushi *Japanese* — 21 | 19 | 19 | $28

Downtown | 207 San Jacinto Blvd. (bet. 2nd & 3rd Sts.) | 512-473-8775 |
www.piranhakillersushi.com
See review in Dallas/Ft. Worth Directory.

Quality Seafood Restaurant & Oyster Bar 🗷 *Seafood* — 21 | 10 | 13 | $17

North Loop | 5621 Airport Blvd. (Koenig Ln.) | 512-454-5827 |
www.qualityseafoodmarket.com

Some of the "freshest seafood in Austin" turns up at this "counter-
service" "dive" in the North Loop area near Hyde Park turning out
oysters and fried fare at a "good value"; there's also a retail shop
selling quality catch to go.

Ranch 616 *Southwestern* — 24 | 25 | 22 | $34

Downtown | 616 Nueces St. (7th St.) | 512-479-7616 |
www.theranch616.com

This Downtown "favorite" has "tons of character", from its setting
loaded with Texana oddities to its "enticing" Southwestern menu
featuring game dishes and a much-celebrated burger at lunch; most
don't mind the "loud", "crowded" environs and find that "witty service", live music (on Tuesdays and Thursdays) and a terrace only
add to the "fun"; it's "walking distance to other bars too";
P.S. Tuesday's $29.95 three-course menu with tequila is a steal.

Roaring Fork *Southwestern* — 24 | 25 | 24 | $36

Arboretum | 10850 Stonelake Blvd. (Braker Ln.) | 512-342-2700
Downtown | InterContinental Stephen F. Austin Hotel |
701 N. Congress Ave. (8th St.) | 512-583-0000
www.roaringfork.com

A "diverse" lineup of "gourmet cowboy cuisine" – from hickory-grilled
fish to slow-roasted pork – wins over the masses at this "moderately

priced" Southwestern mini-chain that's a "reliable, even superlative" choice for a "business" meal; it earns kudos for its contemporary settings with "Old West" touches and "professional" staff, while tipplers cheer the happy hour with discounted apps and drinks.

Ruby's BBQ *BBQ*

23 | 15 | 18 | $18

North Campus | 512 W. 29th St. (Guadalupe St.) | 512-477-1651 | www.rubysbbq.com

For "tender", "tasty" barbecue "within walking distance of UT", customers "queue up" at this North Campus pit stop also purveying Cajun items and plenty of "cold Shiner Bock"; inside's a bit "rundown", though outside features a "pleasant" patio populated by a motley mix of characters doing their best to "keep Austin weird"; P.S. "save some room for the peach cobbler à la mode."

Ruth's Chris Steak House *Steak*

26 | 22 | 25 | $63

Downtown | 107 W. Sixth St. (Congress Ave.) | 512-477-7884 | www.ruthschris.com

See review in San Antonio Directory.

Sagra *Italian*

∇ 19 | 22 | 23 | $30

Downtown | 1610 San Antonio St. (bet. 16th & 17th Sts.) | 512-535-5988 | www.sagrarestaurant.net

A "cozy" cottage on the outskirts of Downtown with a "nice selection" of "tasty" Italian fare – from classic osso buco to modern brick-oven pizzas – paired with wines from The Boot in a white-tablecloth setting; ask the amiable servers about their specialty cocktails and happy-hour specials.

⊠ Salt Lick *BBQ*

25 | 19 | 20 | $24

Round Rock | 3350 E. Palm Valley Blvd. (Harrell Pkwy.) | 512-386-1044
Southeast Austin | Austin-Bergstrom Int'l Airport | 3600 Presidential Blvd. (Bastrop Hwy.) | no phone
Driftwood | 18300 FM 1826 (FM 967) | 512-858-4959 ⊅
www.saltlickbbq.com

"Bring your appetite" to these "true Texas" BBQers for a "first-class orgy of meat" via "piles" of pit-smoked "fork-tender brisket", "spicy sausage" and "fall-off-the-bone ribs" served "family-style" in a "rustic" atmosphere with "great" live music on weekends; it's cash only with "looong waits" at the Driftwood original, and although it's BYO beer, you can also pick up a bottle of wine from their new tasting room to open at the picnic tables; P.S. "buy a whole brisket at the airport to carry home and your friends will love you."

ⓃⒺⓌ Santa Catarina *Mexican*

– | – | – | |

Lakeway | Lakeway Plaza | 1310 Ranch Rd. 620 S. (Lakeway Dr.) | 512-300-0946 | www.santacatarinarestaurant.com

This Lakeway newcomer from Fonda San Miguel and Manuel's alumni is "quickly becoming a favorite" for its "creative, delicious" interior Mexican cuisine served with housemade tortillas and fresh-juice margaritas, with gluten-free and vegetarian offerings; the atmosphere is low-key, but welcoming, with budget-friendly bills and a trio performing traditional music during Sunday brunch.

Sazón *Mexican*
24 | 12 | 18 | $33

Zilker | 1816 S. Lamar Blvd. (Hether St.) | 512-326-4395 |
www.sazonaustin.com

"Inexpensive interior Mexican food in a hole-in-the-wall" setting
sums up this Zilker spot lauded for its "outstanding" fish dishes and
a "huitlacoche omelet at breakfast that's worth making the trip for";
decor may be "sparse to the point of looking unfinished", but the
service is "friendly" and the covered patio is pleasant for weekend
brunches and happy-hour margaritas.

Scholz Garten *German*
19 | 21 | 18 | $17

Downtown | 1607 San Jacinto Blvd. (bet. 16th & 17th Sts.) |
512-474-1958 | www.scholzgarten.net

"A cultural touchstone [and] a major stop for politicos and University
of Texas types for more than a century", this "old-fashioned biergarten" Downtown serves more-than-"passable" German pub grub and
"good local beer" in a shaded outdoor setting that's "utter bliss" on
cool spring days; it's also a popular spot "to watch football" with a
"friendly" atmosphere that leans toward "loud."

Second Bar + Kitchen ● *American*
25 | 24 | 22 | $43

Downtown | The Austonian | 200 Congress Ave. (2nd St.) |
512-827-2750 | www.congressaustin.com

This more casual offshoot of chef David Bull's Congress specializes
in "superb", "farm-to-table" New American fare served all day in
small- and large-plates with "awesome" cocktails and wines; the
"cool" modern-industrial Downtown space sports a wraparound bar
for dining or drinks with maximum "people-watching", so the only
downsides are the lack of happy hour and no-reservations policy.

Shady Grove *American*
21 | 22 | 19 | $22

Zilker | 1624 Barton Springs Rd. (Kinney Ave.) | 512-474-9991 |
www.theshadygrove.com

Surveyors soak in the "Austin flavor" at this "comfy" Zilker "hangout" plying a "decent-enough" American menu (think cheese fries
and green-chile burgers) best enjoyed while "lolling under the trees,
listening to live music"; "inexpensive" prices and primo "people-
watching" make the only "passable" service easier to swallow.

Siena *Italian*
23 | 26 | 23 | $43

Northwest Hills | 6203 N. Capital of Texas Hwy. (Rm. 2222) |
512-349-7667 | www.sienarestaurant.com

Italophiles feel transported to "Tuscany" by this "romantic" Northwest
Hills villa rolling out seasonal Italiana like "homemade pastas and
organic meat and fowl" elevated by "excellent wines"; factor in "attentive" service and though it's not cheap, it's "always a treat."

☑ Smitty's Market ⋑ *BBQ*
27 | 14 | 15 | $18

Lockhart | 208 S. Commerce St. (bet. Market & Prairie Lea Sts.) |
512-398-9344 | www.smittysmarket.com

A "mecca" for "BBQ aficionados", this Lockhart butcher shop set in
the original site of the Kreuz Market is cherished for its "superb"

brisket, "thick pork chops" that "rock your socks" and links "to die for" (a good thing since "your arteries may never recover"); all comes served straight from the pit in an "old-time, fire-seared" setting abetted by a friendly staff and cold beer.

⊠ Snow's BBQ 🖫🅜 *BBQ*

| 28 | 15 | 22 | $18 |

Lexington | 516 Main St. (bet. 2nd & 3rd Sts.) | 979-773-4640 | www.snowsbbq.com

It's "only open on Saturday mornings" so diehards "show up at dawn and stand in line" for "melt-in-your-mouth" brisket and "tender, meaty" ribs at this Lexington smokehouse called "as close to heaven as meat eaters can get"; its "no-pretensions", "far-off-the-path" locale "down a back alley in a forgotten town" is definitely "part of the charm", and so is the "friendly" hospitality.

🆕 Sobani 🖫 *Eclectic*

| - | - | - | M |

Lakeway | 1700 N. FM 620 (Oak Grove Blvd.) | 512-266-3900 | www.sobani620.com

A nondescript strip-mall locale hides this "quaint, quiet" Lakeway newcomer flying under the radar with "unique" takes on seasonal New American dishes and Eclectic small plates (think lobster pot pie and sliders) accompanied by a selection of well-chosen wines; a "casual" yet "elegant" atmosphere and midrange tabs complete the picture.

South Congress Café *Southwestern*

| 23 | 20 | 21 | $33 |

SoCo | 1600 S. Congress Ave. (Monroe St.) | 512-447-3905 | www.southcongresscafe.com

A "local favorite" tucked "amid the hipster hangouts in trendy SoCo", this "convivial" entry serves Southwestern dishes that range from "good to very good" and "inventive cocktails" in a "snug", retro-modern space; a "charming", "tattoo-licious" staff is an added perk, and it's a "tremendous bargain to boot"; P.S. it hosts "one of the more popular brunches in town."

Southside Market & Barbecue *BBQ*

| - | - | - | I |

Elgin | 1212 Hwy. 290 E. (Hwy. 95) | 512-281-4650 | www.southsidemarket.com

This Elgin BBQ fixture born in 1882 is best known for its signature sausage, but the pitmasters also do slow-smoked brisket, ribs, chicken and even mutton, which is served cafeteria-style by the plate or by the pound; its setting is less charming than the original space in an old market, but they make up for it with ample seating and parking.

Steiner Ranch Steakhouse *Steak*

| 20 | 25 | 21 | $41 |

Steiner Ranch | 5424 Steiner Ranch Blvd. (Hwy. 620) | 512-381-0800 | www.steinersteakhouse.com

The "superb" setting with an "amazing" view of Lake Travis ("especially at sunset") is the main draw at this "upscale" steakhouse in Steiner Ranch; the food strikes some as only "ok and expensive", although many favor it for drinks and live music on the terrce with its "see-and-be-seen" scene.

FOOD | DECOR | SERVICE | COST

Stubb's *BBQ*

20 | 17 | 17 | $23

Downtown | 801 Red River St. (8th St.) | 512-480-8341 | www.stubbsaustin.com

"An icon in Austin, and rightly so", this Downtown mainstay dishes out "traditional" takes on "all the usual" 'cue with live music nightly; some say they "expected more" from the food, but at least the bands and the "charming" digs in an 1830s "old brick building" "never disappoint."

Sullivan's Steakhouse *Steak*

24 | 22 | 24 | $57

Warehouse District | 300 Colorado St. (bet. 3rd & 4th Sts.) | 512-495-6504 | www.sullivansteakhouse.com

This "big, beefy" steakhouse chain doles out "great", "but not imaginative" fare elevated by an extensive wine list and "quality service", making it a solid "expense-report" spot; digs are "dark" and "retro", while the mood is "lively", especially at the bar; P.S. the Austin branch has an adjacent lounge, Sully's Side Bar, specializing in tacos and tequilas.

Sushi Zushi *Japanese*

23 | 20 | 20 | $30

Northwest Austin | Domain II Shopping Ctr. | 3221 Feathergrass Ct. (bet. Braker Ln. & Domain Way) | 512-834-8100
Old West Austin | 5th St. Commons | 1611 W. Fifth St. (Lynn St.) | 512-474-7000
www.sushizushi.com

See review in San Antonio Directory.

🆕 Swift's Attic *Eclectic*

- | - | - | M

Downtown | 315 Congress Ave. (bet. 3rd & 4th Sts.) | no phone | www.swiftsattic.com

Slated for a winter 2012 debut, this highly anticipated Downtown New American is touting Eclectic small plates from a dream team of chefs, Mat Clouser, Zack Northcutt and Callie Speer with experience at Uchi, Mulberry and Parkside between them; set in the historic Swift Building, the space is done in a modern style with a long bar.

🇿 Tacodeli *Mexican*

26 | 12 | 20 | $11

Northwest Austin | 12001 N. Burnet Rd. (Mopac Expwy.) | 512-339-1700
Rosedale | 4200 N. Lamar Blvd. (42nd St.) | 512-419-1900
Southwest Austin | 1500 Spyglass Dr. (Mopac Expwy.) | 512-732-0303
www.tacodeli.com

"Excellence wrapped in a tortilla" is how devotees describe the "delicious", "gourmet" Mexican street eats crafted from "fresh, local and organic ingredients" at this counter-service trio that's once again ranked Austin's No. 1 for Bang for the Buck; open for breakfast and lunch only, it's always busy, but "friendly folks" keep the constant lines moving fast, and you can also call ahead to skip the wait; P.S. "the salsa doña is a true revelation."

Taco Xpress *Mexican*

∇ 20 | 14 | 18 | $15

South Lamar | 2529 S. Lamar Blvd. (bet. La Casa Dr. & Montclair St.) | 512-444-0261 | www.tacoxpress.com

"Super-friendly" South Lamar taco joint known for "no-frills" Mexican grub at "cheeeeeeeeap prices"; "cute" decor and a lively terrace hosting live music complete the "groovy Austin vibe."

Takoba ● *Mexican*

-	-	-	I

East Austin | 1411 E. Seventh St. (Onion St.) | 512-628-4466 | www.takobarestaurant.com

"See and be seen" at this "trendy" East Austin storefront turning out adventurous, affordable takes on Mexican standards with a cocktail list full of creations as playful as the atmosphere; it's too "loud" for some, while others find the food doesn't live up to the setting.

Tarka Indian Kitchen *Indian*

21	15	19	$16

NEW **Round Rock** | 201 University Blvd. (Oakmont Dr.) | 512-246-1922
Southwest Austin | 5207 Brodie Ln. (Hwy. 290) | 512-892-2008
www.tarkaindiankitchen.com

These "fast-casual" "little sisters" of the venerable Clay Pit in Southwest Austin and Round Rock pump out "flavorful", "cheap" Indian dishes like soups, naan sandwiches and "customizable" rice bowls, plus lassis, beer and wine; the "strip-mall" settings decorated in earthy tones are pleasant enough, although many opt for takeout.

Taverna Pizzeria & Risotteria *Italian*

22	21	20	$32

Second Street District | 258 W. Second St. (Lavaca St.) | 512-477-1001 | www.tavernabylombardi.com

See review in Dallas/Ft. Worth Directory.

Technique Cafe 🛇 Ⓜ *French* (fka Ventana)

-	-	-	I

North Austin | Le Cordon Bleu College | 3110 Esperanza Crossing (Domain Dr.) | 512-687-9136 | www.techniquerestaurant.com

Formerly known as Ventana, this bright, airy restaurant at Le Cordon Bleu serves modern seasonal French cuisine crafted by student chefs, who toil under instructors' guidance; three- or four-course prix fixes for an astounding $10 or $15, respectively, make it one of the best values in town; P.S. weekday lunch and dinner and wine and beer only.

Texas Chili Parlor ● *American*

24	18	18	$16

Downtown | 1409 Lavaca St. (14th St.) | 512-472-2828

Pairing "kitsch with a kick", this "old-style" parlor Downtown has long been a destination for chili cooked up in varieties "from mild to hot beyond belief" and washed down with plenty of beer; the "dark, dingy" digs suit the way-"casual" service and cheap tabs just fine.

Thai Fresh *Thai*

-	-	-	I

Bouldin Creek | 909 W. Mary St. (5th St.) | 512-494-6436 | www.thai-fresh.com

Although you still "order at the counter" and "grab a seat", this family-owned Thai in Bouldin Creek is changing up its deli-style format: the "well-made" "spicy" dishes based on fresh, local ingredients are now cooked to order; P.S. don't miss the small market on-site stocked with Asian ingredients and homemade ice creams.

Threadgill's *Southern*

20	20	20	$21

Crestview | 6416 N. Lamar Blvd. (bet. Airport Blvd. & Rte. 2222) | 512-451-5440

(continued)

(continued)

Threadgill's

Downtown South | 301 W. Riverside Dr. (Barton Springs Rd.) |
512-472-9304
www.threadgills.com

Providing "Southern comfort at its finest", this Crestview "classic" has
long been a source for "down-home" "comfort fare" "done right" in a
setting that's a veritable shrine to "local music" with "lots of memorabilia" and a stage hosting live acts most nights; it's an area "institution", even if critics call it "overhyped and overtouristed" with food
that "brings back memories of public school cafeteria lunches"; the
Downtown South spin-off features the same menu, but may be best
known for its beer garden and raucous Sunday Gospel Brunch.

III Forks *Steak*

24 | 22 | 23 | $63

Downtown | 111 Lavaca St. (Cesar Chavez St.) | 512-474-1776 |
www.3forks.com

Smitten carnivores swear by this "over-the-top" chophouse trio in
Austin, Dallas and Houston featuring "excellent" cuts and "great
wines" in "Texas-sized" "man-cave" digs; detractors dis "iffy service" and "clichéd" decor, adding "you'll need three bank accounts
to pay for it all", but ratings show they're outvoted.

NEW Three Little Pigs ⊠Ⓜ *Eclectic*

- | - | - | I

East Austin | East Side Wines | 1209 Rosewood Ct. (11th St.) |
512-653-5088 | www.3littlepigsaustin.com

Chef Raymond Tatum (ex Backstage Steakhouse) has resurfaced at
this popular trailer in the parking lot of East Side Wines, serving up
seasonal Asian-inflected Eclectic dishes; folks in the know hit the
store first for wine or beer, then eat at a picnic table under the trees.

360 Uno Trattoria *Italian*

23 | 19 | 21 | $24

West Lake Hills | Davenport Vill. | 3801 N. Capitol of Texas Hwy.
(Westlake Dr.) | 512-327-4448 | www.360uno.com

A "pleasant surprise" in West Lake Hills, this "cozy" "neighborhood"
cafe works equally well for "quick bites" like panini, pizza and gelato
as well as full Italian meals backed by housemade wines.

Thrice *Eclectic/Thai*

- | - | - | I

Bouldin Creek | 909 W. Mary St. (5th St.) | 512-447-9473 |
www.thricecafe.com

This new cozy cafe and wine bar adjacent to Thai Fresh in Bouldin
Creek (and from the same owners) serves farm-to-table Eclectic
fare for breakfast (try the Thai omelet) and lunch, with homemade
baked goods, gluten-free and vegan options rounding out the menu;
there's also a variety of coffee and tea drinks, plus local and craft
beer on tap and a small but unique wine selection.

Tomodachi Sushi ⊠ *Japanese*

- | - | - | E

Northwest Austin | Milwood Shopping Ctr. | 4101 W. Parmer Ln.
(Amherst Dr.) | 512-821-9472 | www.tomosushiaustin.com

This tiny sushi spot in a Northwest Austin strip center slices up
"unique" offerings seldom seen elsewhere, like live octopus and

monkfish liver, in addition to specialty rolls and Japanese small plates; the space is sparsely furnished, save for an eye-catching bar made of lacquered river rock, but neither that nor upper-end prices deters its committed clientele.

Torchy's Tacos *Mexican*

24 | 14 | 19 | $11

Bouldin Creek | South Austin Trailer Park & Eatery | 1311 S. First St. (bet. Elizabeth & Gibson Sts.) | 512-366-0537
Bouldin Creek | 2809 S. First St. (El Paso St.) | 512-444-0300
Brentwood | 5119 Burnet Rd. (North St.) | 512-382-0823
Campus | 2801 Guadalupe St. (bet. 28th & 29th Sts.) | 512-494-8226
Circle C | 4301 W. William Cannon Dr. (Brush Country Rd.) | 512-514-0767
Northwest Hills | 4211 Spicewood Springs Rd. (Mesa Dr.) | 512-291-7277
NEW **South Lamar** | 3005 S. Lamar Blvd. (Manchaca Rd.) | 512-614-1832
www.torchystacos.com

"Stop reading and go now!" exclaim fans of this ever-growing Mexican chain cherished for its "creative" tacos "bursting with delicious fillings" like fried avocado and "spicy" jerk chicken; "you can eat pretty well pretty cheap", so most don't mind the minimal service and settings or "lines out the door"; breakfast is popular too; P.S. the original is a trailer on 1311 South First Street in Austin.

Trace *American*

- | - | - | M

Second Street District | W Austin Hotel | 200 Lavaca St. (2nd St.) | 512-542-3660 | www.traceaustin.com

Located in the W Hotel in the burgeoning Second Street District, this "hip" New American has an of-the-moment menu of responsibly sourced fare declared "tasty, if a bit overly styled"; its minimalist look incorporates concrete and steel accents, and includes mirrored doors that open onto a sidewalk dining area; P.S. open for breakfast, lunch and dinner.

⚡ Trattoria Lisina M *Italian*

25 | 28 | 26 | $39

Driftwood | Mandola Estate Winery | 13308 FM 150 W. (FM 1826) | 512-894-3111 | www.trattorialisina.com

Just about "the prettiest restaurant in the middle of nowhere", this "romantic" Driftwood Italian inhabits a "majestic" stone building boasting a fireplace, loads of Tuscan antiques and an enclosed patio overlooking a vineyard; "downright delicious" cuisine from chef Damian Mandola, "fabulous" wines and a "charming" staff create a transporting experience deemed well "worth the drive."

Trio *American*

21 | 23 | 25 | $59

Downtown | Four Seasons Hotel | 98 San Jacinto Blvd. (1st St.) | 512-685-8300 | www.trioaustin.com

"Celebrities and power players" fill up this "expensive" New American in the Four Seasons Downtown boasting "lovely patio dining" with views of Lady Bird Lake; unfortunately, service gets mixed marks and many find the fare "not quite up to par" (it dropped five Food points this year).

	FOOD	DECOR	SERVICE	COST

Trudy's ◗ *Tex-Mex* | 20 | 17 | 19 | $21 |

North Austin | Crossroads | 8820 Burnet Rd. (Hwy. 183) | 512-454-1474
North Campus | 409 W. 30th St. (Guadalupe St.) | 512-477-2935
South Austin | 901 Little Texas Ln. (I-35) | 512-326-9899
www.trudys.com

"Students", "vegetarians" and other assorted Austinites "jump-start [their] weekend" with "migas and margaritas" at this Tex-Mex mini-chain, a "brunch mainstay" and ground zero for "weekend hangover recovery" for years; reasonable prices mean these "casual" spots "fill up fast", so "get there early" or prepare to wait.

Truluck's *Seafood* | 24 | 23 | 23 | $52 |

Arboretum | 10225 Research Blvd. (Great Hills Trail) | 512-794-8300
Warehouse District | 400 Colorado St. (4th St.) | 512-482-9000
www.trulucks.com
See review in Dallas/Ft. Worth Directory.

24 Diner ◗ *Diner* | 22 | 19 | 20 | $23 |

Downtown | 600 N. Lamar Blvd. (6th St.) | 512-472-5400 |
www.24diner.com

"Satisfying" is the word on this "hip" Downtown diner proffering "farm-to-table" takes on American "comfort food" in "T. rex-sized" helpings and "awesome beers" "at all hours of the day or night"; prices are low and the industrial space "comfortable", although some say servers have a tad too much "Austin attitude."

NEW 219 West ⊠ *American/Eclectic* | – | – | – | M |

Downtown | 612 W. Sixth St. (Rio Grande) | 512-474-2194 |
www.219west.com

Relocated to stylish new digs on West Sixth Street Downtown, this nightclubby spot still features six themed bars, each pairing a unique American-Eclectic small-plates menu with cocktails, beer, rare liqueurs and wine; the much-larger space now features outdoor dining on a sidewalk patio, intimate rooms for private dining and a massive rooftop deck with a spectacular view of the Austin skyline.

⊠ Uchi *Japanese* | 29 | 25 | 27 | $56 |

Zilker | 801 S. Lamar Blvd. (Juliet St.) | 512-916-4808 | www.uchiaustin.com
"Heaven" for sushiphiles, this Zilker jewel box presents the "finest in forward-thinking Japanese" cuisine via chef Tyson Cole – from "delish" raw fare and the signature deep-fried shag roll to "incredible" fusion plates that "make you cry tears of joy" – earning it Austin's No. 1 for Food rating and tying it for Most Popular; a "sophisticated" vibe, "outstanding" service and a "great-looking clientele" mean it "surpasses expectations" for most, just "take another hit of sake before you look at the bill"; P.S. a Houston outpost is coming soon.

⊠ Uchiko *Japanese* | 28 | 26 | 27 | $59 |

Rosedale | 4200 N. Lamar Blvd. (42nd St.) | 512-916-4808 |
www.uchikoaustin.com

"Simply brilliant", this "whimsical" Rosedale sib to Uchi features *Top Chef*'s Paul Qui's "wildly creative" Japanese fare in "beautiful" presentations capped by "dynamic" wines and "mind-blowing desserts"; service is "professional", the space is modern and while tabs are steep, that hasn't deterred the crowds.

NEW Upper Decks *American*   - | - | - | I

Downtown South | 301 Barton Springs Rd. (Riverside Dr.) | 512-291-2686 | www.upperdecksaustin.com
Just south of Downtown sits this well-priced new sports bar where the varied American menu (from burgers to short ribs) takes a backseat to the full bar with TVs broadcasting the action; although sparsely decorated, it boasts plenty of outdoor space with a ground-level patio and lower and upper decks with a view of the skyline.

Urban An American Grill *American*   - | - | - | M

Northwest Austin | Westin at The Domain | 11301 Domain Dr. (Esperanza Crossing) | 512-490-1511 | www.urbanatthedomain.com
Inside the Westin at The Domain is this contemporary canteen serving gussied-up American comfort fare emphasizing fresh, local ingredients; its lobby bar boasts live music and happy-hour specials, although the brown-and-gold dining area is more sedate.

Vespaio *Italian*   26 | 21 | 24 | $43

SoCo | 1610 S. Congress Ave. (Monroe St.) | 512-441-6100 | www.austinvespaio.com
"Long waits" are par for the course at this midpriced SoCo Italian, "hands-down one of the best in Austin" thanks to its "superb" cooking, "wonderful wines" and a warm setting that's "one of the best places to spot a movie star or politician"; an "eager" staff is "helpful" with suggestions, but it's "noisy, noisy, noisy" at prime times.

Vince Young Steakhouse *Steak*   ∇ 21 | 25 | 22 | $54

Downtown | 301 San Jacinto Blvd. (3rd St.) | 512-457-8325 | www.vinceyoungsteakhouse.com
Austin's favorite quarterback is behind this eponymous steakhouse in the heart of Downtown, where expensive meaty fare with a Southern twist is served by a staff that "really tries to please"; the "lovely" setting is done up in bronze and burnt-orange tones (of course), with dark-wood accents and iconic photographs of the Longhorn legend.

Vino Vino *American*   ∇ 20 | 19 | 18 | $32

Hyde Park | 4119 Guadalupe St. (41st St.) | 512-465-9282 | www.vinovinoaustin.com
Oenophiles flock to this "casual" Hyde Park "hangout" for its impressive wines and craft cocktails to match a snacky New American menu beefed up with a few heartier items; low lighting, live jazz and an antique wood bar add loads of charm; P.S. Paella Sundays are popular.

Vivo *Tex-Mex*   ∇ 21 | 23 | 22 | $23

Cedar Park | Lake Creek Vill. | 12233 RR 620 N. (Lake Creek Pkwy.) | 512-331-4660
Cherrywood | 2015 Manor Rd. (Poquito St.) | 512-482-0300
www.vivo-austin.com
"Affordable", "unique" Tex-Mex dishes, numerous tequilas and "fun people-watching" are the hallmarks of this Austin-area duo in

Cherrywood and Cedar Park; the "unique" decor featuring sexy nude paintings is definitely "PG-13", while happy-hour deals and DJs on weekends are other 'adult' enticements.

Whip-In Parlour Café ● *Indian*

| - | - | - | I |

South Austin | 1950 I-35 S. (Riverside Dr.) | 512-442-5337 | www.whipin.com

Inside a South Austin convenience store sits this quirky, "colorful" cafe offering "Indianish" home cooking, from "tasty" naan sandwiches to rice bowls, along with an impressive selection of beer and wine; the atmosphere gains a lift from live music, free WiFi and a patio, though takeout is also popular.

☑ Wink ☒ *American*

| 27 | 21 | 25 | $64 |

Old West Austin | 1014 N. Lamar Blvd. (11th St.) | 512-482-8868 | www.winkrestaurant.com

On the scene for a decade and still utterly "original", this Old West Austin New American delivers "highly creative", "locavore"-driven fare with a tasting menu that will "blow you away"; service is "wonderful" too, so fans only "wish the space were a little hipper", and perhaps that the check were a bit lower; P.S. "happy hour in the wine bar is a steal."

Zandunga *Mexican*

| ∇ 21 | 18 | 23 | $25 |

East Austin | 1000 E. 11th St. (Waller St.) | 512-473-4199 | www.zandungamexicanbistro.com

This family-owned Mexican in East Austin distinguishes itself with unusual, "complex" offerings like huitlacoche risotto and chile spaetzle served by an eager staff; prices are pleasantly low, while the "warm, casual" space is colorful and bright with floor-to-ceiling windows overlooking a sidewalk patio; P.S. go on Tuesdays for "$3 lobster tacos and frozen mojitos or margaritas."

NEW Zed's *American*

| - | - | - | M |

Tech Ridge | 501 Canyon Ridge Dr. (Palmer Ln.) | 512-339-9337 | www.zeds.bz

This Tech Ridge newcomer is turning heads with its "cool" "architectural design" and stunning terrace overlooking waterfalls and a pond; the "creative" American menu features twists and turns on classics like chicken pot pie and cowboy rib-eyes, while the bar serves potent potables to the after-work crowd.

Z'Tejas *Southwestern*

| 22 | 22 | 21 | $28 |

Arboretum | 9400 Arboretum Blvd. (Capital of Texas Hwy.) | 512-346-3506
Clarksville | 1110 W. Sixth St. (Lamar Blvd.) | 512-478-5355
Jollyville | 10525 W. Parmer Ln. (Avery Ranch Blvd.) | 512-388-7772
www.ztejas.com

It's one big "happy, noisy party" at these Southwestern sibs delivering "oh-so-tasty" dishes ("love the cornbread") and "great drinks" at "reasonable prices"; the Clarksville, Austin, original is the most "rambunctious" of the bunch, with live music some nights, though all branches boast "delightful" patios offering solace from the din.

AUSTIN AND THE HILL COUNTRY INDEXES

Cuisines

Includes names, locations and Food ratings.

AMERICAN

Annie's Café	**Downtown**	21
Z Barley Swine	**S Lamar**	28
Bartlett's	**N Central**	26
NEW BC Tavern	**Bee Cave**	-
Billy's/Burnet	**Rosedale**	18
Black Star Co-op	**Crestview**	-
Blue Star	**Rosedale**	20
Braise	**E Austin**	21
Cabernet Grill	**Fredericksburg**	25
Z Carillon	**Campus**	28
Cheesecake	**Arboretum**	20
Chez Zee	**NW Hills**	22
Z Congress	**Downtown**	28
Daily Grill	**NW Austin**	21
Dirty Martin's	**W Campus**	19
Driskill Grill	**Downtown**	25
Eastside Café	**Cherrywood**	25
East Side Showrm.	**E Austin**	21
1886 Café	**Downtown**	21
NEW Eleven Plates	**W Lake**	-
Foreign/Domestic	**Hyde Pk**	23
Grove Wine	**W Lake**	24
Haddington's	**Downtown**	23
Highball	**S Lamar**	19
Hilltop Café	**Fredericksburg**	26
Z Hudson's/Bend	**Lakeway**	27
Hyde Park	**multi.**	21
Jack Allen's	**Oak Hill**	26
Jasper's	**NW Austin**	24
Jeffrey's	**Clarksville**	24
Z Judges' Hill	**W Campus**	23
Lambert's Dtwn.	**Second Street District**	25
NEW Lucy's	**Bouldin Creek**	-
Magnolia Café	**multi.**	23
Mighty Cone	**SoCo**	18
Monument Café	**Georgetown**	23
Moonshine	**Downtown**	24
Mulberry	**Downtown**	23
Paggi Hse.	**Downtown S**	23
Parkside	**Downtown**	23
Second Bar	**Downtown**	25
Shady Grove	**Zilker**	21
NEW Sobani	**Lakeway**	-
Texas Chili	**Downtown**	24
Trace	**Second Street District**	-
Trio	**Downtown**	21
24 Diner	**Downtown**	22
NEW 219 West	**Downtown**	-
NEW Upper Decks	**Downtown S**	-

Urban	**NW Austin**	-
Vino Vino	**Hyde Pk**	20
Z Wink	**Old W Austin**	27
NEW Zed's	**Tech Ridge**	-

ARGENTINEAN

Buenos Aires	**multi.**	24

ASIAN

East Side King	**multi.**	26
Pei Wei	**multi.**	20

BAKERIES

1886 Café	**Downtown**	21

BARBECUE

Artz Rib Hse.	**S Lamar**	21
City Mkt.	**Luling**	27
Cooper's BBQ	**Llano**	25
County Line	**multi.**	21
Z Franklin BBQ	**E Austin**	28
Gonzales Mkt.	**Gonzales**	-
Green Mesquite	**multi.**	20
Iron Works	**Downtown**	22
NEW JMueller	**Bouldin Creek**	-
Kreuz Mkt.	**Lockhart**	25
Lambert's Dtwn.	**Second Street District**	25
NEW Live Oak	**E Austin**	-
Z Louie Mueller	**Taylor**	29
Meyer's Elgin	**Elgin**	-
Opie's BBQ	**Spicewood**	23
Ruby's	**N Campus**	23
Z Salt Lick	**multi.**	25
Z Smitty's Mkt.	**Lockhart**	27
Z Snow's BBQ	**Lexington**	28
Southside Mkt.	**Elgin**	-
Stubb's	**Downtown**	20

BRAZILIAN

Estância Churrascaria	**multi.**	24
Fogo/Chão	**Downtown**	25

BRITISH

NEW Full English	**S Austin**	-

BURGERS

Billy's/Burnet	**Rosedale**	18
Dirty Martin's	**W Campus**	19
Hopdoddy Burger	**SoCo**	25
Hut's	**Downtown**	23
Mighty Fine	**multi.**	21
Shady Grove	**Zilker**	21

CAJUN

Evangeline Café | **SW Austin** 21
Gumbo's | **multi.** 23
Pappadeaux | **N Austin** 23

CARIBBEAN

Café Josie | **Clarksville** 24

CHICKEN

NEW Lucy's | **Bouldin Creek** -

CHINESE

(* dim sum specialist)
Chinatown* | **NW Hills** 23
Din Ho | **N Austin** 25
First Chinese | **N Austin** 24
Golden Wok* | **N Austin** 20
P.F. Chang's | **multi.** 21

COFFEE SHOPS/ DINERS

24 Diner | **Downtown** 22

CONTINENTAL

Z Green Pastures | **Bouldin Creek** 23
Jeffrey's | **Clarksville** 24

CREOLE

Evangeline Café | **SW Austin** 21
Gumbo's | **multi.** 23

CRÊPES

Flip Happy | **Zilker** 25

DESSERT

Cheesecake | **Arboretum** 20
Chez Zee | **NW Hills** 22
1886 Café | **Downtown** 21
European Bistro | **Pflugerville** -

ECLECTIC

August E's | **Fredericksburg** 24
Bess | **Downtown** 23
Café Blue | **multi.** -
NEW Contigo | **Mueller** -
Hilltop Café | **Fredericksburg** 26
Kerbey Ln. | **multi.** 20
NEW Lenoir | **Bouldin Creek** -
Max's | **Downtown** 20
Second Bar | **Downtown** 25
NEW Sobani | **Lakeway** -
NEW Swift's Attic | **Downtown** -
NEW Three Little Pigs | **E Austin** -
Thrice | **Bouldin Creek** -
NEW 219 West | **Downtown** -

EUROPEAN

European Bistro | **Pflugerville** -
Fabi + Rosi | **Old W Austin** 23
Foreign/Domestic | **Hyde Pk** 23

FRENCH

Bistrot Mirabelle | **NW Hills** -
Chez Nous | **Downtown** 26
NEW Elizabeth St. | **Bouldin Creek** -
Flip Happy | **Zilker** 25
Justine's | **E Austin** 23
Olivia | **S Lamar** 25
Peché | **Warehouse Dist** 24
Technique Cafe | **N Austin** -

GERMAN

Scholz Garten | **Downtown** 19

HOT DOGS

Frank | **Warehouse Dist** 22

INDIAN

Clay Pit | **Downtown** 23
G'raj Mahal | **Downtown** 22
Madras Pavilion | **N Austin** 20
Tarka Indian | **multi.** 21
Whip-In Parlour | **S Austin** -

ITALIAN

(N=Northern)
Andiamo | **N Austin** 25
Asti Trattoria | **Hyde Pk** 23
Brick Oven | **multi.** 19
Carmelo's | **Downtown** 24
Carrabba's | **N Austin** 23
Enoteca Vespaio | **SoCo** 25
Frank & Angie's | **Downtown** 20
La Traviata | **Downtown** 23
Mandola's | **multi.** 21
North | **NW Austin** 22
Olivia | **S Lamar** 25
Sagra | **Downtown** 19
Siena | N | **NW Hills** 23
Taverna | **Second Street District** 22
360 Uno Trattoria | **W Lake** 23
Z Trattoria Lisina | **Driftwood** 25
Vespaio | **SoCo** 26

JAPANESE

(* sushi specialist)
Kenichi* | **Warehouse Dist** 21
NEW Komé* | **North Loop** -
Musashino* | **NW Hills** 25
Piranha* | **Downtown** 21
Sushi Zushi* | **multi.** 23
Tomodachi* | **NW Austin** -

Ⓩ Uchi* | **Zilker** — 29

Ⓩ Uchiko* | **Rosedale** — 28

KOSHER/ KOSHER-STYLE

Madras Pavilion | **N Austin** — 20

MEXICAN

Azul Tequila | **S Lamar** — 24

Berryhill Baja | **NW Hills** — 20

Cantina Laredo | **Downtown** — 21

Corazón | **Downtown** — 22

Curra's Grill | **Travis Hts** — 21

NEW El Alma | **Bouldin Creek** — -

El Chile/El Chilito | **multi.** — 19

El Mesón | **multi.** — 24

El Naranjo | **Downtown** — -

El Sol/La Luna | **Downtown** — 15

Ⓩ Fonda San Miguel | **Highland Pk** — 25

Garrido's | **Downtown** — 22

Guero's | **SoCo** — 20

Ⓩ La Condesa | **Second Street District** — 23

Las Palomas | **W Lake** — 22

Manuel's | **multi.** — 21

Panaderia Chuy | **multi.** — -

NEW Santa Catarina | **Lakeway** — -

Sazón | **Zilker** — 24

Ⓩ Tacodeli | **multi.** — 26

Taco Xpress | **S Lamar** — 20

Takoba | **E Austin** — -

Torchy's Tacos | **multi.** — 24

Zandunga | **E Austin** — 21

NUEVO LATINO

NEW Hugo's Rest. | **Zilker** — -

PIZZA

Backspace | **Downtown** — 25

Brick Oven | **multi.** — 19

Frank & Angie's | **Downtown** — 20

Home Slice | **SoCo** — 26

Taverna | **Second Street District** — 22

PUB FOOD

Black Star Co-op | **Crestview** — -

Scholz Garten | **Downtown** — 19

SANDWICHES

NEW Luke's Inside Out | **Zilker** — -

Mandola's | **multi.** — 21

SEAFOOD

Ⓩ Eddie V's | **multi.** — 26

Pappadeaux | **N Austin** — 23

Parkside | **Downtown** — 23

Perla's | **SoCo** — 26

Quality Seafood | **North Loop** — 21

Truluck's | **multi.** — 24

SMALL PLATES

(See also Spanish tapas specialist)

Annie's Café | Amer. | **Downtown** — 21

Ⓩ Carillon | Amer. | **Campus** — 28

NEW Contigo | Eclectic | **Mueller** — -

East Side King | Asian | **E Austin** — 26

East Side Showrm. | Amer. | **E Austin** — 21

NEW Eleven Plates | Amer. | **W Lake** — -

Enoteca Vespaio | Italian | **SoCo** — 25

Fino | Med. | **W Campus** — 25

Grove Wine | Amer. | **W Lake** — 24

Ⓩ La Condesa | Mex. | **Second Street District** — 23

Max's | Eclectic | **Downtown** — 20

Parkside | Amer. | **Downtown** — 23

Perla's | Seafood | **SoCo** — 26

Second Bar | Amer. | **Downtown** — 25

NEW Sobani | Eclectic | **Lakeway** — -

NEW Swift's Attic | Eclectic | **Downtown** — -

NEW 219 West | Amer./Eclectic | **Downtown** — -

SOUL FOOD

Hoover's | **Cherrywood** — 21

SOUTH AMERICAN

NEW Hugo's Rest. | **Zilker** — -

SOUTHERN

Hoover's | **Cherrywood** — 21

NEW Lucy's | **Bouldin Creek** — -

Moonshine | **Downtown** — 24

Threadgill's | **multi.** — 20

SOUTHWESTERN

Cool River | **NW Austin** — 21

Ranch 616 | **Downtown** — 24

Roaring Fork | **multi.** — 24

South Congress | **SoCo** — 23

Z'Tejas | **multi.** — 22

SPANISH

(* tapas specialist)

Fino* | **W Campus** — 25

Málaga* | **Second Street District** — 23

STEAKHOUSES

August E's | **Fredericksburg** — 24

Austin Land | **Downtown** — 24

Cool River | **NW Austin** — 21

Ⓩ Eddie V's | **multi.** — 26

Estância Churrascaria | **multi.** 24
Fleming's Prime | **multi.** 25
Fogo/Chão | **Downtown** 25
Hoffbrau Steakhse. | **Downtown** 20
Perry's Steak | **Downtown** 26
Ruth's Chris | **Downtown** 26
Steiner Ranch | **Steiner Rch** 20
Sullivan's | **Warehouse Dist** 24
III Forks | **Downtown** 24
Vince Young | **Downtown** 21

TEX-MEX

Z Chuy's | **multi.** 21
Hula Hut | **Old W Austin** 18
Matt's El Rancho | **S Lamar** 21

Oasis | **Lakeway** 11
Trudy's | **multi.** 20
Vivo | **multi.** 21

THAI

Madam Mam's | **multi.** 19
Thai Fresh | **Bouldin Creek** -
Thrice | **Bouldin Creek** -

VEGETARIAN

Madras Pavilion | **N Austin** 20

VIETNAMESE

NEW Elizabeth St. | -
Bouldin Creek

Locations

Includes names, cuisines and Food ratings.

Austin

ARBORETUM

Cheesecake	*Amer.*	20
Z Eddie V's	*Seafood/Steak*	26
Estância Churrascaria	*Brazilian/Steak*	24
Manuel's	*Mex.*	21
P.F. Chang's	*Chinese*	21
Roaring Fork	*SW*	24
Truluck's	*Seafood*	24
Z'Tejas	*SW*	22

BEE CAVE

NEW BC Tavern	*Amer.*	-
Buenos Aires	*Argent.*	24
Café Blue	*Eclectic*	-
Mandola's	*Italian*	21

BOULDIN CREEK

NEW El Alma	*Mex.*	-
NEW Elizabeth St.	*French/Viet.*	-
Z Green Pastures	*Continental*	23
NEW JMueller	*BBQ*	-
NEW Lenoir	*Eclectic*	-
NEW Lucy's	*Southern*	-
Thai Fresh	*Thai*	-
Thrice	*Eclectic/Thai*	-
Torchy's Tacos	*Mex.*	24

BRENTWOOD

Torchy's Tacos	*Mex.*	24

BRYKERWOODS

Brick Oven	*Pizza*	19
Kerbey Ln.	*Eclectic*	20

CAMPUS

Z Carillon	*Amer.*	28
Kerbey Ln.	*Eclectic*	20
Madam Mam's	*Thai*	19
Torchy's Tacos	*Mex.*	24

CEDAR PARK

Mighty Fine	*Burgers*	21
Vivo	*Tex-Mex*	21

CHERRYWOOD

Eastside Café	*Amer.*	25
El Chile/El Chilito	*Mex.*	19
Hoover's	*Southern*	21
Vivo	*Tex-Mex*	21

CIRCLE C

Torchy's Tacos	*Mex.*	24

CLARKSVILLE

Café Josie	*Carib.*	24
Jeffrey's	*Amer./Continental*	24
Z'Tejas	*SW*	22

CRESTVIEW

Black Star Co-op	*Pub*	-
Threadgill's	*Southern*	20

DOWNTOWN

Annie's Café	*Amer.*	21
Austin Land	*Steak*	24
Backspace	*Pizza*	25
Bess	*Eclectic*	23
Brick Oven	*Pizza*	19
Cantina Laredo	*Mex.*	21
Carmelo's	*Italian*	24
Chez Nous	*French*	26
Clay Pit	*Indian*	23
Z Congress	*Amer.*	28
Corazón	*Mex.*	22
Driskill Grill	*Amer.*	25
East Side King	*Asian*	26
Z Eddie V's	*Seafood/Steak*	26
1886 Café	*Amer.*	21
El Chile/El Chilito	*Mex.*	19
El Naranjo	*Mex.*	-
El Sol/La Luna	*Mex.*	15
Fleming's Prime	*Steak*	25
Fogo/Chão	*Brazilian/Steak*	25
Frank & Angie's	*Pizza*	20
Garrido's	*Mex.*	22
G'raj Mahal	*Indian*	22
Gumbo's	*Cajun/Creole*	23
Haddington's	*Amer.*	23
Hoffbrau Steakhse.	*Steak*	20
Hut's	*Burgers*	23
Iron Works	*BBQ*	22
La Traviata	*Italian*	23
Manuel's	*Mex.*	21
Max's	*Eclectic*	20
Moonshine	*Amer.*	24
Mulberry	*Amer.*	23
Parkside	*Amer.*	23
Perry's Steak	*Steak*	26
P.F. Chang's	*Chinese*	21
Piranha	*Japanese*	21
Ranch 616	*SW*	24
Roaring Fork	*SW*	24
Ruth's Chris	*Steak*	26
Sagra	*Italian*	19
Scholz Garten	*German*	19

Second Bar | *Amer.* 25
Stubb's | *BBQ* 20
NEW Swift's Attic | *Eclectic* -
Texas Chili | *Amer.* 24
III Forks | *Steak* 24
Trio | *Amer.* 21
24 Diner | *Diner* 22
NEW 219 West | *Amer./Eclectic* -
Vince Young | *Steak* 21

DOWNTOWN SOUTH

Paggi Hse. | *Amer.* 23
Threadgill's | *Southern* 20
NEW Upper Decks | *Amer.* -

EAST AUSTIN

Braise | *Amer.* 21
Buenos Aires | *Argent.* 24
East Side King | *Asian* 26
East Side Showrm. | *Amer.* 21
Z Franklin BBQ | *BBQ* 28
Justine's | *French* 23
NEW Live Oak | *BBQ* -
Takoba | *Mex.* -
NEW Three Little Pigs | *Eclectic* -
Zandunga | *Mex.* 21

ELGIN

Meyer's Elgin | *BBQ* -
Southside Mkt. | *BBQ* -

GEORGETOWN

Monument Café | *Amer.* 23

GONZALES

Gonzales Mkt. | *BBQ* -

GREAT HILLS

Brick Oven | *Pizza* 19

HIGHLAND PARK

Z Fonda San Miguel | *Mex.* 25

HYDE PARK

Asti Trattoria | *Italian* 23
Foreign/Domestic | *Amer./Euro.* 23
Hyde Park | *Amer.* 21
Pei Wei | *Asian* 20
Vino Vino | *Amer.* 20

JOLLYVILLE

Z'Tejas | *SW* 22

LAKEWAY

Z Hudson's/Bend | *Amer.* 27
Oasis | *Tex-Mex* 11
NEW Santa Catarina | *Mex.* -
NEW Sobani | *Eclectic* -

LEXINGTON

Z Snow's BBQ | *BBQ* 28

LOCKHART

Kreuz Mkt. | *BBQ* 25
Z Smitty's Mkt. | *BBQ* 27

LULING

City Mkt. | *BBQ* 27

MUELLER

NEW Contigo | *Eclectic* -

NORTH AUSTIN

Andiamo | *Italian* 25
Carrabba's | *Italian* 23
Z Chuy's | *Tex-Mex* 21
Din Ho | *Chinese* 25
First Chinese | *Chinese* 24
Golden Wok | *Chinese* 20
Madras Pavilion | *Indian* 20
Mighty Fine | *Burgers* 21
Panaderia Chuy | *Mex.* -
Pappadeaux | *Cajun/Seafood* 23
Pei Wei | *Asian* 20
Technique Cafe | *French* -
Trudy's | *Tex-Mex* 20

NORTH CAMPUS

Ruby's | *BBQ* 23
Trudy's | *Tex-Mex* 20

NORTH CENTRAL

Bartlett's | *Amer.* 26
Madam Mam's | *Thai* 19
Mandola's | *Italian* 21

NORTH LOOP

NEW Komé | *Japanese* -
Quality Seafood | *Seafood* 21

NORTHWEST AUSTIN

Cool River | *Steak/SW* 21
Daily Grill | *Amer.* 21
Fleming's Prime | *Steak* 25
Jasper's | *Amer.* 24
Kerbey Ln. | *Eclectic* 20
North | *Italian* 22
Pei Wei | *Asian* 20
Sushi Zushi | *Japanese* 23
Z Tacodeli | *Mex.* 26
Tomodachi | *Japanese* -
Urban | *Amer.* -

NORTHWEST HILLS

Berryhill Baja | *Mex.* 20
Bistrot Mirabelle | *French* -
Chez Zee | *Amer.* 22

Chinatown | *Chinese* 23
County Line | *BBQ* 21
Musashino | *Japanese* 25
Siena | *Italian* 23
Torchy's Tacos | *Mex.* 24

OAK HILL

Jack Allen's | *Amer.* 26

OLD WEST AUSTIN

Fabi + Rosi | *Euro.* 23
Hula Hut | *Tex-Mex* 18
Magnolia Café | *Amer.* 23
Sushi Zushi | *Japanese* 23
Ⓩ Wink | *Amer.* 27

PFLUGERVILLE

European Bistro | *Euro.* -

ROSEDALE

Billy's/Burnet | *Amer.* 18
Blue Star | *Amer.* 20
Ⓩ Tacodeli | *Mex.* 26
Ⓩ Uchiko | *Japanese* 28

ROUND ROCK

Ⓩ Chuy's | *Tex-Mex* 21
Gumbo's | *Cajun/Creole* 23
Mighty Fine | *Burgers* 21
Pei Wei | *Asian* 20
Ⓩ Salt Lick | *BBQ* 25
Tarka Indian | *Indian* 21

SECOND STREET DISTRICT

Ⓩ La Condesa | *Mex.* 23
Lambert's Dtwn. | *Amer./BBQ* 25
Málaga | *Spanish* 23
Taverna | *Italian* 22
Trace | *Amer.* -

SOCO

Enoteca Vespaio | *Italian* 25
Guero's | *Mex.* 20
Home Slice | *Pizza* 26
Hopdoddy Burger | *Burgers* 25
Magnolia Café | *Amer.* 23
Mighty Cone | *Amer.* 18
Perla's | *Seafood* 26
South Congress | *SW* 23
Vespaio | *Italian* 26

SOUTH AUSTIN

Ⓩ Chuy's | *Tex-Mex* 21
NEW Full English | *British* -
Green Mesquite | *BBQ* 20
Panaderia Chuy | *Mex.* -

Trudy's | *Tex-Mex* 20
Whip-In Parlour | *Indian* -

SOUTHEAST AUSTIN

El Mesón | *Mex.* 24
Ⓩ Salt Lick | *BBQ* 25

SOUTH LAMAR

Artz Rib Hse. | *BBQ* 21
Azul Tequila | *Mex.* 24
Ⓩ Barley Swine | *Amer.* 28
El Mesón | *Mex.* 24
Highball | *Amer.* 19
Kerbey Ln. | *Eclectic* 20
Matt's El Rancho | *Tex-Mex* 21
Olivia | *French/Italian* 25
Taco Xpress | *Mex.* 20
Torchy's Tacos | *Mex.* 24

SOUTHWEST AUSTIN

Brick Oven | *Pizza* 19
Estância Churrascaria | *Brazilian/Steak* 24
Evangeline Café | *Cajun/Creole* 21
Hyde Park | *Amer.* 21
Kerbey Ln. | *Eclectic* 20
Madam Mam's | *Thai* 19
Mandola's | *Italian* 21
Pei Wei | *Asian* 20
Ⓩ Tacodeli | *Mex.* 26
Tarka Indian | *Indian* 21

STEINER RANCH

Steiner Ranch | *Steak* 20

SUNSET VALLEY

Mighty Fine | *Burgers* 21

TAYLOR

Ⓩ Louie Mueller | *BBQ* 29

TECH RIDGE

NEW Zed's | *Amer.* -

TRAVIS HEIGHTS

Curra's Grill | *Mex.* 21

VOLENTE

Café Blue | *Eclectic* -

WAREHOUSE DISTRICT

Frank | *Hot Dogs* 22
Kenichi | *Pan-Asian* 21
Peché | *French* 24
Sullivan's | *Steak* 24
Truluck's | *Seafood* 24

WEST CAMPUS

Dirty Martin's | *Burgers* 19
Fino | *Spanish* 25
Z Judges' Hill | *Amer.* 23

WEST LAKE HILLS

County Line | *BBQ* 21
NEW Eleven Plates | *Amer.* -
Grove Wine | *Amer.* 24
Gumbo's | *Cajun/Creole* 23
Las Palomas | *Mex.* 22
360 Uno Trattoria | *Italian* 23

ZILKER

Z Chuy's | *Tex-Mex* 21
Flip Happy | *Crêpes* 25
Green Mesquite | *BBQ* 20
NEW Hugo's Rest. | *Nuevo Latino* -
NEW Luke's Inside Out | -
Sandwiches

Sazón | *Mex.* 24
Shady Grove | *Amer.* 21
Z Uchi | *Japanese* 29

Hill Country

DRIFTWOOD

Z Salt Lick | *BBQ* 25
Z Trattoria Lisina | *Italian* 25

FREDERICKSBURG

August E's | *Eclectic/Steak* 24
Cabernet Grill | *Amer.* 25
Hilltop Café | *Eclectic* 26

LLANO

Cooper's BBQ | *BBQ* 25

SPICEWOOD

Opie's BBQ | *BBQ* 23

Special Features

Listings cover the best in each category and include names, locations and Food ratings. Multi-location restaurants' features may vary by branch.

BREAKFAST

(See also Hotel Dining)

Curra's Grill | **Travis Hts**	21
El Mesón | **SE Austin**	24
El Sol/La Luna | **Downtown**	15
Guero's | **SoCo**	20
Hoover's | **Cherrywood**	21
Kerbey Ln. | **multi.**	20
Magnolia Café | **multi.**	23
Sazón | **Zilker**	24
☑ Tacodeli | **multi.**	26
Taco Xpress | **S Lamar**	20
Trudy's | **multi.**	20
24 Diner | **Downtown**	22

BRUNCH

Bess | **Downtown**	23
Bistrot Mirabelle | **NW Hills**	–
Chez Zee | **NW Hills**	22
Driskill Grill | **Downtown**	25
Eastside Café | **Cherrywood**	25
1886 Café | **Downtown**	21
Enoteca Vespaio | **SoCo**	25
☑ Fonda San Miguel | **Highland Pk**	25
Frank | **Warehouse Dist**	22
☑ Green Pastures | **Bouldin Creek**	23
Haddington's | **Downtown**	23
Hyde Park | **Hyde Pk**	21
Jack Allen's | **Oak Hill**	26
☑ La Condesa | **Second Street District**	23
Lambert's Dtwn. | **Second Street District**	25
NEW Luke's Inside Out | **Zilker**	–
Manuel's | **multi.**	21
Moonshine | **Downtown**	24
Mulberry | **Downtown**	23
Olivia | **S Lamar**	25
Paggi Hse. | **Downtown S**	23
Perla's | **SoCo**	26
South Congress | **SoCo**	23
Threadgill's | **Downtown S**	20
Trio | **Downtown**	21
Trudy's | **N Campus**	20
Urban | **NW Austin**	–
Zandunga | **E Austin**	21

BUSINESS DINING

Annie's Café | **Downtown**	21
Asti Trattoria | **Hyde Pk**	23
August E's | **Fredericksburg**	24
Backspace | **Downtown**	25
Bistrot Mirabelle | **NW Hills**	–
☑ Carillon | **Campus**	28
Carmelo's | **Downtown**	24
☑ Congress | **Downtown**	28
Corazón | **Downtown**	22
Driskill Grill | **Downtown**	25
☑ Eddie V's | **multi.**	26
1886 Café | **Downtown**	21
Fabi + Rosi | **Old W Austin**	23
Fino | **W Campus**	25
Fleming's Prime | **multi.**	25
☑ Fonda San Miguel | **Highland Pk**	25
Garrido's | **Downtown**	22
Grove Wine | **W Lake**	24
Gumbo's | **Downtown**	23
☑ Hudson's/Bend | **Lakeway**	27
Jasper's | **NW Austin**	24
Jeffrey's | **Clarksville**	24
☑ Judges' Hill | **W Campus**	23
Kenichi | **Warehouse Dist**	21
☑ La Condesa | **Second Street District**	23
Manuel's | **multi.**	21
Max's | **Downtown**	20
Musashino | **NW Hills**	25
North | **NW Austin**	22
Olivia | **S Lamar**	25
Paggi Hse. | **Downtown S**	23
Perla's | **SoCo**	26
Perry's Steak | **Downtown**	26
Piranha | **Downtown**	21
Roaring Fork | **multi.**	24
Ruth's Chris | **Downtown**	26
NEW Santa Catarina | **Lakeway**	–
Second Bar | **Downtown**	25
Siena | **NW Hills**	23
Steiner Ranch | **Steiner Rch**	20
Sullivan's | **Warehouse Dist**	24
Technique Cafe | **N Austin**	–
Trio | **Downtown**	21
Truluck's | **multi.**	24
NEW 219 West | **Downtown**	–
☑ Uchi | **Zilker**	29
NEW Upper Decks | **Downtown S**	–
Urban | **NW Austin**	–
Vince Young | **Downtown**	21
NEW Zed's | **Tech Ridge**	–

CELEBRITY CHEFS

David Bull
- Ⓩ Congress | **Downtown** 28
- Second Bar | **Downtown** 25

Shawn Cirkiel
- Backspace | **Downtown** 25
- Parkside | **Downtown** 23

Tyson Cole
- Ⓩ Uchi | **Zilker** 29
- Ⓩ Uchiko | **Rosedale** 28

David Garrido
- Garrido's | **Downtown** 22

Damian Mandola
- Mandola's | **multi.** 21
- Ⓩ Trattoria Lisina | **Driftwood** 25

Paul Qui
- East Side King | **E Austin** 26
- Ⓩ Uchiko | **Rosedale** 28

Paul Qui
- East Side King | **Downtown** 26

Kent Rathbun
- Jasper's | **NW Austin** 24

Iliana de la Vega
- El Naranjo | **Downtown** -

Josh Watkins
- Ⓩ Carillon | **Campus** 28

CHILD-FRIENDLY

(Alternatives to the usual fast-food places; * children's menu available)

- Billy's/Burnet* | **Rosedale** 18
- Brick Oven* | **multi.** 19
- Chez Zee* | **NW Hills** 22
- Ⓩ Chuy's* | **multi.** 21
- Cooper's BBQ | **Llano** 25
- County Line* | **multi.** 21
- Curra's Grill* | **Travis Hts** 21
- Din Ho | **N Austin** 25
- Eastside Café* | **Cherrywood** 25
- El Mesón | **SE Austin** 24
- El Sol/La Luna* | **Downtown** 15
- Evangeline Café* | **SW Austin** 21
- Frank & Angie's | **Downtown** 20
- Green Mesquite* | **multi.** 20
- Guero's* | **SoCo** 20
- Hilltop Café* | **Fredericksburg** 26
- Home Slice | **SoCo** 26
- Hoover's* | **Cherrywood** 21
- Hut's | **Downtown** 23
- Hyde Park* | **multi.** 21
- Iron Works | **Downtown** 22
- Kerbey Ln.* | **multi.** 20
- Las Palomas* | **W Lake** 22
- Magnolia Café* | **multi.** 23
- Matt's El Rancho* | **S Lamar** 21

- Oasis* | **Lakeway** 11
- Pei Wei* | **multi.** 20
- Ruby's* | **N Campus** 23
- Ⓩ Salt Lick | **Driftwood** 25
- Sazón* | **Zilker** 24
- Scholz Garten* | **Downtown** 19
- Shady Grove* | **Zilker** 21
- Ⓩ Smitty's Mkt. | **Lockhart** 27
- Stubb's* | **Downtown** 20
- Taco Xpress | **S Lamar** 20
- Threadgill's* | **Downtown S** 20
- Trudy's* | **S Austin** 20
- Z'Tejas* | **multi.** 22

DESSERT SPECIALISTS

- Annie's Café | **Downtown** 21
- Asti Trattoria | **Hyde Pk** 23
- Austin Land | **Downtown** 24
- Cheesecake | **Arboretum** 20
- Chez Zee | **NW Hills** 22
- Driskill Grill | **Downtown** 25
- 1886 Café | **Downtown** 21
- European Bistro | **Pflugerville** -
- Fino | **W Campus** 25
- Ⓩ La Condesa | **Second Street District** 23
- Mandola's | **multi.** 21
- Moonshine | **Downtown** 24
- Parkside | **Downtown** 23
- 360 Uno Trattoria | **W Lake** 23
- Thrice | **Bouldin Creek** -
- Ⓩ Uchi | **Zilker** 29
- Ⓩ Uchiko | **Rosedale** 28
- Ⓝ Zed's | **Tech Ridge** -

DINING ALONE

(Other than hotels and places with counter service)

- Annie's Café | **Downtown** 21
- Berryhill Baja | **NW Hills** 20
- Billy's/Burnet | **Rosedale** 18
- Chez Nous | **Downtown** 26
- Ⓝ Contigo | **Mueller** -
- East Side King | **E Austin** 26
- Ⓩ Eddie V's | **Downtown** 26
- Enoteca Vespaio | **SoCo** 25
- Fino | **W Campus** 25
- Fleming's Prime | **Downtown** 25
- Haddington's | **Downtown** 23
- Ⓝ Hugo's Rest. | **Zilker** -
- Jasper's | **NW Austin** 24
- Ⓩ La Condesa | **Second Street District** 23
- La Traviata | **Downtown** 23
- Málaga | **Second Street District** 23

Mighty Fine	**Cedar Pk**	21
Peché	**Warehouse Dist**	24
Pei Wei	**multi.**	20
Perla's	**SoCo**	26
Piranha	**Downtown**	21
Ranch 616	**Downtown**	24
Second Bar	**Downtown**	25
NEW Sobani	**Lakeway**	–
Sushi Zushi	**Old W Austin**	23
Ⓩ Tacodeli	**multi.**	26
Thrice	**Bouldin Creek**	–
Torchy's Tacos	**S Lamar**	24
Ⓩ Uchi	**Zilker**	29
Vespaio	**SoCo**	26
Vino Vino	**Hyde Pk**	20
NEW Zed's	**Tech Ridge**	–

ENTERTAINMENT

(Call for days and times of performances)

Artz Rib Hse.	live music	**S Lamar**	21
Carmelo's	accordion	**Downtown**	24
Chez Zee	pianist	**NW Hills**	22
Cool River	cover bands	**NW Austin**	21
County Line	acoustic	**NW Hills**	21
Driskill Grill	jazz/piano	**Downtown**	25
Ⓩ Eddie V's	jazz	**Downtown**	26
El Sol/La Luna	Latin	**Downtown**	15
European Bistro	varies	**Pflugerville**	–
Frank & Angie's	mandolin	**Downtown**	20
Green Mesquite	live bands	**multi.**	20
Ⓩ Green Pastures	piano	**Bouldin Creek**	23
Guero's	live bands	**SoCo**	20
Hilltop Café	blues/jazz	**Fredericksburg**	26
Las Palomas	varies	**W Lake**	22
Manuel's	jazz/Latin	**multi.**	21
Matt's El Rancho	jazz/Latin	**S Lamar**	21
Oasis	karaoke/live music	**Lakeway**	11
Ranch 616	varies	**Downtown**	24
Ⓩ Salt Lick	live bands	**Driftwood**	25
Shady Grove	live bands	**Zilker**	21
Stubb's	gospel/live bands	**Downtown**	20

Sullivan's	jazz/live bands	**Warehouse Dist**	24
Threadgill's	live music	**multi.**	20
Truluck's	piano/vocal	**Arboretum**	24
Vivo	DJs	**Cherrywood**	21
Z'Tejas	live music	**Clarksville**	22

FOOD TRUCKS

East Side King	**multi.**	26
Flip Happy	**Zilker**	25
G'raj Mahal	**Downtown**	22
NEW JMueller	**Bouldin Creek**	–
NEW Luke's Inside Out	**Zilker**	–
NEW Three Little Pigs	**E Austin**	–

HISTORIC PLACES

(Year opened; * building)

1830	Stubb's*	**Downtown**	20
1850	Moonshine*	**Downtown**	24
1866	Scholz Garten*	**Downtown**	19
1872	Carmelo's*	**Downtown**	24
1882	Southside Mkt.	**Elgin**	–
1886	Annie's Café*	**Downtown**	21
1886	Driskill Grill*	**Downtown**	25
1886	1886 Café*	**Downtown**	21
1894	Green Pastures*	**Bouldin Creek**	23
1900	Guero's*	**SoCo**	20
1900	Hudson's/Bend*	**Lakeway**	27
1900	Judges' Hill*	**W Campus**	23
1904	European Bistro*	**Pflugerville**	–
1918	Bess*	**Downtown**	23
1920	Eastside Café*	**Cherrywood**	25
1920	Green Mesquite*	**Zilker**	20
1926	Dirty Martin's*	**W Campus**	19
1930	Hyde Park*	**Hyde Pk**	21
1930	Iron Works*	**Downtown**	22
1933	Threadgill's	**Crestview**	20
1934	Hoffbrau Steakhse.*	**Downtown**	20
1939	Hut's*	**Downtown**	23
1949	Louie Mueller	**Taylor**	29
1952	Matt's El Rancho	**S Lamar**	21
1953	24 Diner*	**Downtown**	22
1957	City Mkt.	**Luling**	27
1959	Gonzales Mkt.	**Gonzales**	–
1962	Cooper's BBQ	**Llano**	25

Vote at zagat.com

HOTEL DINING

Driskill Hotel	
Driskill Grill | **Downtown**	25
1886 Café | **Downtown**	21
Four Seasons Hotel	
Trio | **Downtown**	21
InterContinental Hotel	
Roaring Fork | **Downtown**	24
Mansion at Judges' Hill	
❷ Judges' Hill | **W Campus**	23
W Austin Hotel	
Trace | **Second Street District**	⌐
Westin at The Domain	
Urban | **NW Austin**	⌐

LATE DINING

(Weekday closing hour)

Billy's/Burnet | 12 AM | **Rosedale**	18
NEW Contigo | 12 AM | **Mueller**	⌐
East Side King | varies | **multi.**	26
East Side Showrm. | varies | **E Austin**	21
G'raj Mahal | varies | **Downtown**	22
Haddington's | 1 AM | **Downtown**	23
Highball | 2 AM | **S Lamar**	19
Justine's | 1:30 AM | **E Austin**	23
Kerbey Ln. | 24 hrs. | **multi.**	20
NEW Live Oak | 12 AM | **E Austin**	⌐
NEW Lucy's | 12 AM | **Bouldin Creek**	⌐
Magnolia Café | 24 hrs. | **multi.**	23
Max's | varies | **Downtown**	20
Parkside | varies | **Downtown**	23
Peché | 1 AM | **Warehouse Dist**	24
Second Bar | 12 AM | **Downtown**	25
Takoba | varies | **E Austin**	⌐
Texas Chili | 12 AM | **Downtown**	24
Trudy's | 12 AM | **multi.**	20
24 Diner | 24 hrs. | **Downtown**	22
Whip-In Parlour | 12 AM | **S Austin**	⌐

MEET FOR A DRINK

Annie's Café | **Downtown**	21
Azul Tequila | **S Lamar**	24
Backspace | **Downtown**	25
Bartlett's | **N Central**	26
NEW BC Tavern | **Bee Cave**	⌐
Bess | **Downtown**	23
Billy's/Burnet | **Rosedale**	18
Black Star Co-op | **Crestview**	⌐
Braise | **E Austin**	21
Café Blue | **multi.**	⌐
NEW Contigo | **Mueller**	⌐
Cool River | **NW Austin**	21
Corazón | **Downtown**	22
Curra's Grill | **Travis Hts**	21
East Side Showrm. | **E Austin**	21
❷ Eddie V's | **multi.**	26
El Chile/El Chilito | **Cherrywood**	19
NEW Eleven Plates | **W Lake**	⌐
NEW Elizabeth St. | **Bouldin Creek**	⌐
El Mesón | **S Lamar**	24
Fabi + Rosi | **Old W Austin**	23
Fino | **W Campus**	25
Fleming's Prime | **multi.**	25
Fogo/Chão | **Downtown**	25
Foreign/Domestic | **Hyde Pk**	23
Garrido's | **Downtown**	22
Grove Wine | **W Lake**	24
Guero's | **SoCo**	20
Haddington's | **Downtown**	23
Highball | **S Lamar**	19
NEW Hugo's Rest. | **Zilker**	⌐
Hula Hut | **Old W Austin**	18
Jack Allen's | **Oak Hill**	26
Jasper's | **NW Austin**	24
Justine's | **E Austin**	23
La Condesa | **Second Street District**	23
NEW Lenoir | **Bouldin Creek**	⌐
NEW Lucy's | **Bouldin Creek**	⌐
Málaga | **Second Street District**	23
Manuel's | **multi.**	21
Matt's El Rancho | **S Lamar**	21
Max's | **Downtown**	20
Moonshine | **Downtown**	24
Mulberry | **Downtown**	23
North | **NW Austin**	22
Oasis | **Lakeway**	11
Olivia | **S Lamar**	25
Paggi Hse. | **Downtown S**	23
Parkside | **Downtown**	23
Peché | **Warehouse Dist**	24
Perla's | **SoCo**	26
Piranha | **Downtown**	21
Quality Seafood | **North Loop**	21
Ranch 616 | **Downtown**	24
Roaring Fork | **multi.**	24
Sagra | **Downtown**	19
NEW Santa Catarina | **Lakeway**	⌐
Sazón | **Zilker**	24
Scholz Garten | **Downtown**	19
Second Bar | **Downtown**	25
Shady Grove | **Zilker**	21
NEW Sobani | **Lakeway**	⌐
South Congress | **SoCo**	23

Sullivan's | **Warehouse Dist**	24
Sushi Zushi | **Old W Austin**	23
NEW Swift's Attic | **Downtown**	-
Takoba | **E Austin**	-
Texas Chili | **Downtown**	24
Threadgill's | **Downtown S**	20
Thrice | **Bouldin Creek**	-
Trio | **Downtown**	21
Trudy's | **multi.**	20
NEW 219 West | **Downtown**	-
Z Uchiko | **Rosedale**	28
NEW Upper Decks | **Downtown S**	-
Urban | **NW Austin**	-
Vespaio | **SoCo**	26
Vince Young | **Downtown**	21
Vino Vino | **Hyde Pk**	20
Whip-In Parlour | **S Austin**	-
Zandunga | **E Austin**	21
NEW Zed's | **Tech Ridge**	-
Z'Tejas | **multi.**	22

NEWCOMERS

BC Tavern | **Bee Cave**	-
Contigo | **Mueller**	-
El Alma | **Bouldin Creek**	-
Eleven Plates | **W Lake**	-
Elizabeth St. | **Bouldin Creek**	-
Full English | **S Austin**	-
Hugo's Rest. | **Zilker**	-
JMueller | **Bouldin Creek**	-
Komé | **North Loop**	-
Lenoir | **Bouldin Creek**	-
Live Oak | **E Austin**	-
Lucy's | **Bouldin Creek**	-
Luke's Inside Out | **Zilker**	-
Santa Catarina | **Lakeway**	-
Sobani | **Lakeway**	-
Swift's Attic | **Downtown**	-
Three Little Pigs | **E Austin**	-
219 West | **Downtown**	-
Upper Decks | **Downtown S**	-
Zed's | **Tech Ridge**	-

OFFBEAT

Z Barley Swine | **S Lamar**	28
Billy's/Burnet | **Rosedale**	18
Z Chuy's | **multi.**	21
NEW Contigo | **Mueller**	-
Cooper's BBQ | **Llano**	25
East Side King | **E Austin**	26
East Side Showrm. | **E Austin**	21
Flip Happy | **Zilker**	25
Foreign/Domestic | **Hyde Pk**	23
Frank & Angie's | **Downtown**	20
G'raj Mahal | **Downtown**	22

Guero's | **SoCo**	20
Hilltop Café | **Fredericksburg**	26
Hoffbrau Steakhse. | **Downtown**	20
Hula Hut | **Old W Austin**	18
Hut's | **Downtown**	23
NEW Lucy's | **Bouldin Creek**	-
Magnolia Café | **multi.**	23
Ranch 616 | **Downtown**	24
Shady Grove | **Zilker**	21
Taco Xpress | **S Lamar**	20
Texas Chili | **Downtown**	24
Threadgill's | **multi.**	20
Thrice | **Bouldin Creek**	-
Torchy's Tacos | **multi.**	24
Vivo | **Cherrywood**	21

OUTDOOR DINING

(G=garden; P=patio; S=sidewalk;
T=terrace; W=waterside)

Billy's/Burnet | P | **Rosedale**	18
Brick Oven | P | **multi.**	19
Cabernet Grill | P, W | **Fredericksburg**	25
Chez Zee | G | **NW Hills**	22
Z Chuy's | P | **multi.**	21
NEW Contigo | P | **Mueller**	-
Cool River | P | **NW Austin**	21
County Line | P | **W Lake**	21
Curra's Grill | P | **Travis Hts**	21
1886 Café | P | **Downtown**	21
El Chile/El Chilito | P | **Cherrywood**	19
Evangeline Café | S | **SW Austin**	21
Fino | T | **W Campus**	25
Frank & Angie's | P | **Downtown**	20
Garrido's | P, W | **Downtown**	22
G'raj Mahal | P | **Downtown**	22
Green Mesquite | P | **multi.**	20
Grove Wine | P | **W Lake**	24
Guero's | P | **SoCo**	20
Hoffbrau Steakhse. | P | **Downtown**	20
Z Hudson's/Bend | G, P | **Lakeway**	27
Hula Hut | P, W | **Old W Austin**	18
Iron Works | P | **Downtown**	22
Jack Allen's | P | **Oak Hill**	26
Jasper's | P | **NW Austin**	24
NEW JMueller | P | **Bouldin Creek**	-
Kerbey Ln. | P | **multi.**	20
Las Palomas | P | **W Lake**	22
Manuel's | P | **Arboretum**	21
Matt's El Rancho | P | **S Lamar**	21
Moonshine | G, P | **Downtown**	24
North | P | **NW Austin**	22
Oasis | P, T | **Lakeway**	11

Paggi Hse. | T | **Downtown S** | 23
Parkside | P | **Downtown** | 23
Perla's | P | **SoCo** | 26
Roaring Fork | P | **Arboretum** | 24
Ruby's | P | **N Campus** | 23
🆕 Salt Lick | P | **Driftwood** | 25
Scholz Garten | P | **Downtown** | 19
Shady Grove | P | **Zilker** | 21
Siena | P | **NW Hills** | 23
Taco Xpress | P | **S Lamar** | 20
Takoba | P | **E Austin** | -
🆕 Trattoria Lisina | P | **Driftwood** | 25
Trio | P, W | **Downtown** | 21
Trudy's | P | **multi.** | 20
Truluck's | P | **Arboretum** | 24
🆕 Upper Decks | P, T | **Downtown S** | -
Vivo | P | **Cherrywood** | 21
Z'Tejas | P | **multi.** | 22

PEOPLE-WATCHING

Annie's Café | **Downtown** | 21
Backspace | **Downtown** | 25
Bess | **Downtown** | 23
Black Star Co-op | **Crestview** | -
🆕 Contigo | **Mueller** | -
Cooper's BBQ | **Llano** | 25
East Side King | **E Austin** | 26
East Side Showrm. | **E Austin** | 21
1886 Café | **Downtown** | 21
🆕 Elizabeth St. | **Bouldin Creek** | -
Flip Happy | **Zilker** | 25
Frank & Angie's | **Downtown** | 20
🆕 Franklin BBQ | **E Austin** | 28
🆕 Full English | **S Austin** | -
Garrido's | **Downtown** | 22
G'raj Mahal | **Downtown** | 22
Grove Wine | **W Lake** | 24
Guero's | **SoCo** | 20
Highball | **S Lamar** | 19
🆕 Hugo's Rest. | **Zilker** | -
Hula Hut | **Old W Austin** | 18
🆕 JMueller | **Bouldin Creek** | -
Justine's | **E Austin** | 23
Kreuz Mkt. | **Lockhart** | 25
🆕 La Condesa | **Second Street District** | 23
🆕 Lucy's | **Bouldin Creek** | -
🆕 Luke's Inside Out | **Zilker** | -
Mighty Cone | **SoCo** | 18
North | **NW Austin** | 22
Parkside | **Downtown** | 23
Peché | **Warehouse Dist** | 24
Perla's | **SoCo** | 26
Piranha | **Downtown** | 21

Second Bar | **Downtown** | 25
Shady Grove | **Zilker** | 21
South Congress | **SoCo** | 23
🆕 Swift's Attic | **Downtown** | -
Takoba | **E Austin** | -
Texas Chili | **Downtown** | 24
Threadgill's | **multi.** | 20
🆕 Three Little Pigs | **E Austin** | -
🆕 219 West | **Downtown** | -
🆕 Upper Decks | **Downtown S** | -
Vespaio | **SoCo** | 26
Vince Young | **Downtown** | 21

POWER SCENES

August E's | **Fredericksburg** | 24
Austin Land | **Downtown** | 24
🆕 Carillon | **Campus** | 28
Carmelo's | **Downtown** | 24
Chinatown | **NW Hills** | 23
🆕 Congress | **Downtown** | 28
Cool River | **NW Austin** | 21
Driskill Grill | **Downtown** | 25
🆕 Eddie V's | **Downtown** | 26
Fleming's Prime | **multi.** | 25
Fogo/Chão | **Downtown** | 25
Garrido's | **Downtown** | 22
Jasper's | **NW Austin** | 24
🆕 La Condesa | **Second Street District** | 23
Lambert's Dtwn. | **Second Street District** | 25
Max's | **Downtown** | 20
North | **NW Austin** | 22
Olivia | **S Lamar** | 25
Paggi Hse. | **Downtown S** | 23
Parkside | **Downtown** | 23
Perry's Steak | **Downtown** | 26
Piranha | **Downtown** | 21
Roaring Fork | **multi.** | 24
Ruth's Chris | **Downtown** | 26
Second Bar | **Downtown** | 25
Steiner Ranch | **Steiner Rch** | 20
Sullivan's | **Warehouse Dist** | 24
Texas Chili | **Downtown** | 24
Trio | **Downtown** | 21
🆕 219 West | **Downtown** | -
Urban | **NW Austin** | -
Vince Young | **Downtown** | 21

QUIET CONVERSATION

August E's | **Fredericksburg** | 24
Bess | **Downtown** | 23
Bistrot Mirabelle | **NW Hills** | -

Braise | **E Austin** 21

Buenos Aires | **E Austin** 24

Cabernet Grill | **Fredericksburg** 25

Z Carillon | **Campus** 28

Carmelo's | **Downtown** 24

Chez Nous | **Downtown** 26

Chinatown | **NW Hills** 23

Driskill Grill | **Downtown** 25

Eastside Café | **Cherrywood** 25

1886 Café | **Downtown** 21

NEW Eleven Plates | **W Lake** -

European Bistro | **Pflugerville** -

Fabi + Rosi | **Old W Austin** 23

Fleming's Prime | **multi.** 25

NEW Full English | **S Austin** -

Jeffrey's | **Clarksville** 24

Z Judges' Hill | **W Campus** 23

NEW Lenoir | **Bouldin Creek** -

Madam Mam's | **N Central** 19

Mulberry | **Downtown** 23

Paggi Hse. | **Downtown S** 23

Peché | **Warehouse Dist** 24

Sagra | **Downtown** 19

NEW Santa Catarina | **Lakeway** -

Second Bar | **Downtown** 25

Siena | **NW Hills** 23

NEW Sobani | **Lakeway** -

Steiner Ranch | **Steiner Rch** 20

Sushi Zushi | **Old W Austin** 23

Technique Cafe | **N Austin** -

Thrice | **Bouldin Creek** -

Trio | **Downtown** 21

Urban | **NW Austin** -

Vince Young | **Downtown** 21

Vino Vino | **Hyde Pk** 20

Whip-In Parlour | **S Austin** -

Zandunga | **E Austin** 21

ROMANTIC PLACES

Andiamo | **N Austin** 25

August E's | **Fredericksburg** 24

Bess | **Downtown** 23

Bistrot Mirabelle | **NW Hills** -

Braise | **E Austin** 21

Buenos Aires | **E Austin** 24

Cabernet Grill | **Fredericksburg** 25

Café Blue | **Volente** -

Carmelo's | **Downtown** 24

Chez Nous | **Downtown** 26

Clay Pit | **Downtown** 23

Driskill Grill | **Downtown** 25

Eastside Café | **Cherrywood** 25

East Side Showrm. | **E Austin** 21

NEW Eleven Plates | **W Lake** -

European Bistro | **Pflugerville** -

Fabi + Rosi | **Old W Austin** 23

Fleming's Prime | **multi.** 25

Z Fonda San Miguel | **Highland Pk** 25

Foreign/Domestic | **Hyde Pk** 23

Z Green Pastures | **Bouldin Creek** 23

Z Hudson's/Bend | **Lakeway** 27

Z Judges' Hill | **W Campus** 23

Justine's | **E Austin** 23

NEW Lenoir | **Bouldin Creek** -

Olivia | **S Lamar** 25

Paggi Hse. | **Downtown S** 23

Peché | **Warehouse Dist** 24

Roaring Fork | **Arboretum** 24

Sagra | **Downtown** 19

NEW Santa Catarina | **Lakeway** -

Siena | **NW Hills** 23

Technique Cafe | **N Austin** -

Trio | **Downtown** 21

Urban | **NW Austin** -

Vince Young | **Downtown** 21

Vino Vino | **Hyde Pk** 20

SENIOR APPEAL

Andiamo | **N Austin** 25

Austin Land | **Downtown** 24

Buenos Aires | **E Austin** 24

Cabernet Grill | **Fredericksburg** 25

Z Carillon | **Campus** 28

Carmelo's | **Downtown** 24

Chez Zee | **NW Hills** 22

Chinatown | **NW Hills** 23

Cooper's BBQ | **Llano** 25

County Line | **multi.** 21

Driskill Grill | **Downtown** 25

1886 Café | **Downtown** 21

European Bistro | **Pflugerville** -

Fabi + Rosi | **Old W Austin** 23

Fleming's Prime | **multi.** 25

Gonzales Mkt. | **Gonzales** -

Z Green Pastures | **Bouldin Creek** 23

Z Hudson's/Bend | **Lakeway** 27

Hyde Park | **multi.** 21

Jasper's | **NW Austin** 24

Z Judges' Hill | **W Campus** 23

Kreuz Mkt. | **Lockhart** 25

Z Louie Mueller | **Taylor** 29

Mandola's | **multi.** 21

Perry's Steak | **Downtown** 26

Roaring Fork | **Arboretum** 24

Ruth's Chris | **Downtown** 26

Z Smitty's Mkt. | **Lockhart** 27

Technique Cafe | **N Austin** -

Threadgill's | **multi.** 20

360 Uno Trattoria | **W Lake** 23
Z Trattoria Lisina | **Driftwood** 25
Trio | **Downtown** 21
Vince Young | **Downtown** 21
Vino Vino | **Hyde Pk** 20

SINGLES SCENES

Annie's Café | **Downtown** 21
Bess | **Downtown** 23
Blue Star | **Rosedale** 20
Z Chuy's | **multi.** 21
NEW Contigo | **Mueller** –
Cool River | **NW Austin** 21
East Side King | **E Austin** 26
East Side Showrm. | **E Austin** 21
Z Eddie V's | **multi.** 26
Fleming's Prime | **multi.** 25
NEW Full English | **S Austin** –
Garrido's | **Downtown** 22
NEW Hugo's Rest. | **Zilker** –
Hula Hut | **Old W Austin** 18
Justine's | **E Austin** 23
Kenichi | **Warehouse Dist** 21
Z La Condesa | 23
    Second Street District
Málaga | **Second Street District** 23
Max's | **Downtown** 20
North | **NW Austin** 22
Paggi Hse. | **Downtown S** 23
Parkside | **Downtown** 23
Peché | **Warehouse Dist** 24
Perla's | **SoCo** 26
Piranha | **Downtown** 21
South Congress | **SoCo** 23
Sullivan's | **Warehouse Dist** 24
Takoba | **E Austin** –
Torchy's Tacos | **multi.** 24
NEW 219 West | **Downtown** –
NEW Upper Decks | –
    Downtown S
Vince Young | **Downtown** 21

TRENDY

Backspace | **Downtown** 25
Z Barley Swine | **S Lamar** 28
Z Carillon | **Campus** 28
Z Congress | **Downtown** 28
NEW Contigo | **Mueller** –
East Side Showrm. | **E Austin** 21
NEW Elizabeth St. | –
    Bouldin Creek
Fino | **W Campus** 25
Foreign/Domestic | **Hyde Pk** 23
Z Franklin BBQ | **E Austin** 28
Haddington's | **Downtown** 23
Highball | **S Lamar** 19

Justine's | **E Austin** 23
NEW Komé | **North Loop** –
Z La Condesa | 23
    Second Street District
Lambert's Dtwn. | 25
    Second Street District
NEW Lenoir | **Bouldin Creek** –
NEW Luke's Inside Out | **Zilker** –
Mulberry | **Downtown** 23
Olivia | **S Lamar** 25
Perla's | **SoCo** 26
Second Bar | **Downtown** 25
NEW Swift's Attic | **Downtown** –
NEW Three Little Pigs | **E Austin** –
Trio | **Downtown** 21
Z Uchi | **Zilker** 29
Z Uchiko | **Rosedale** 28

VIEWS

Café Blue | **Volente** –
County Line | **NW Hills** 21
Z Eddie V's | **multi.** 26
NEW Eleven Plates | **W Lake** –
Garrido's | **Downtown** 22
Hilltop Café | **Fredericksburg** 26
Hula Hut | **Old W Austin** 18
Oasis | **Lakeway** 11
Paggi Hse. | **Downtown S** 23
Roaring Fork | **Arboretum** 24
Z Salt Lick | **Driftwood** 25
Steiner Ranch | **Steiner Rch** 20
Z Trattoria Lisina | **Driftwood** 25
Trio | **Downtown** 21
NEW 219 West | **Downtown** –
NEW Upper Decks | –
    Downtown S
NEW Zed's | **Tech Ridge** –
Z'Tejas | **Arboretum** 22

VISITORS ON EXPENSE ACCOUNT

Z Carillon | **Campus** 28
Carmelo's | **Downtown** 24
Z Congress | **Downtown** 28
Cool River | **NW Austin** 21
Z Eddie V's | **multi.** 26
Fleming's Prime | **multi.** 25
Fogo/Chão | **Downtown** 25
Z Hudson's/Bend | **Lakeway** 27
Jeffrey's | **Clarksville** 24
Z Judges' Hill | **W Campus** 23
Olivia | **S Lamar** 25
Perry's Steak | **Downtown** 26
Ruth's Chris | **Downtown** 26
Steiner Ranch | **Steiner Rch** 20
Trace | **Second Street District** –

Trio | **Downtown**	21
Truluck's | **multi.**	24
☑ Uchi | **Zilker**	29
Vespaio | **SoCo**	26
Vince Young | **Downtown**	21
☑ Wink | **Old W Austin**	27

WINE BARS

Bistrot Mirabelle | **NW Hills**	-
Enoteca Vespaio | **SoCo**	25
Fleming's Prime | **multi.**	25
Grove Wine | **W Lake**	24
Málaga | **Second Street District**	23
Max's | **Downtown**	20
Thrice | **Bouldin Creek**	-
Trio | **Downtown**	21
Whip-In Parlour | **S Austin**	-
☑ Wink | **Old W Austin**	27

WINNING WINE LISTS

Asti Trattoria | **Hyde Pk**	23
August E's | **Fredericksburg**	24
NEW BC Tavern | **Bee Cave**	-
Bess | **Downtown**	23
Bistrot Mirabelle | **NW Hills**	-
Cabernet Grill | **Fredericksburg**	25
☑ Carillon | **Campus**	28
Carmelo's | **Downtown**	24
Chinatown | **NW Hills**	23
☑ Congress | **Downtown**	28
Driskill Grill | **Downtown**	25
East Side Showrm. | **E Austin**	21
NEW Eleven Plates | **W Lake**	-
Enoteca Vespaio | **SoCo**	25
Estância Churrascaria | **SW Austin**	24
Fabi + Rosi | **Old W Austin**	23
Fino | **W Campus**	25
Fleming's Prime | **multi.**	25
Fogo/Chão | **Downtown**	25
Foreign/Domestic | **Hyde Pk**	23
Haddington's | **Downtown**	23
☑ Hudson's/Bend | **Lakeway**	27
Jasper's | **NW Austin**	24

Jeffrey's | **Clarksville**	24
Justine's | **E Austin**	23
La Traviata | **Downtown**	23
NEW Lenoir | **Bouldin Creek**	-
Max's | **Downtown**	20
Mulberry | **Downtown**	23
Olivia | **S Lamar**	25
Paggi Hse. | **Downtown S**	23
Parkside | **Downtown**	23
Perla's | **SoCo**	26
Perry's Steak | **Downtown**	26
Roaring Fork | **Downtown**	24
Ruth's Chris | **Downtown**	26
Second Bar | **Downtown**	25
Siena | **NW Hills**	23
NEW Sobani | **Lakeway**	-
NEW Swift's Attic | **Downtown**	-
Technique Cafe | **N Austin**	-
Thrice | **Bouldin Creek**	-
☑ Trattoria Lisina | **Driftwood**	25
Trio | **Downtown**	21
NEW 219 West | **Downtown**	-
☑ Uchi | **Zilker**	29
☑ Uchiko | **Rosedale**	28
Urban | **NW Austin**	-
Vespaio | **SoCo**	26
Vino Vino | **Hyde Pk**	20
☑ Wink | **Old W Austin**	27

WORTH A TRIP

Driftwood	
☑ Salt Lick	25
☑ Trattoria Lisina	25
Fredericksburg	
Hilltop Café	26
Lexington	
☑ Snow's BBQ	28
Lockhart	
Kreuz Mkt.	25
☑ Smitty's Mkt.	27
Pflugerville	
European Bistro	-
Spicewood	
Opie's BBQ	23

DALLAS/FT. WORTH

FT. WORTH MOST POPULAR

maps.google.com

W McLeroy Blvd

Blue Mound

Babe's Chicken Dinner House (Roanoke)

Cromwell Marine Cr Rd

Longhorn Rd

Cantrell Sansom Rd

Marine Creek Pkwy

Old Decatur Rd

Blue Mound Rd

Mark IV Pkwy

North Fwy

Meacham Blvd

Jim Wright Fwy

Farm to Market 1220

Sansom Park

W Long Ave   E Long Ave

Karren's Diamond Hill

Bonnie Brae

Roberts Cut Off Rd

Ephriam Ave

NW 28th St   183

NE 28th St

NE 28th St

Oakhurst

N S Maria Ave

Yucca Ave

Lonesome Dove Western Bistro

Joe T. Garcia's

Jacksboro Hwy   199

NW 21st St

Belmont Terrace

NW 21st St

E Northside Dr

N Main St

287

Greenway

121

Riverside Dr

Calloway Park

River Oaks Blvd

Isbell Rd

183

Crestwood

W Northside Dr

Reading Springs Rd

White Settlement Rd   White Settlement Rd

Angelo's Barbecue

Grace   **Del Frisco's**

Saint-Emilion

Eddie V's

W 7th St

Upper West Side

35W   287

Glenwood Triangle

Burton Hills Trinity Trails

Montgomery St

Camp Bowie Blvd

377

30

8th Ave

E Hattie St

Westridge Area

30

Hulen St

377

Blue Mesa*

Forest Park Blvd

W Rosedale St

S Main St

E Rosedale St

S Riverside Dr

Fort Worth

Bryant Irvin Rd

Home St

W Vickery Blvd

S Hulen St

Park Blvd

8th Ave

W Allen Ave

Hemphill St

35W

Riverhollow

Bellaire Dr S

Alton Rd

Berry St   W Berry St

Bluebonnet Place

W Biddison St

Hemphill St

E Berry St

Morningside

Morningside Park

Riverside Dr

287

Westcliff West

Rosemont

Worth Heights

Bonnell's

W Seminary Dr

James Ave

35W

20

20

Oakmont Blvd

Granbury Rd

N Wedgwood Dr

Wedgwood East

Crowley Rd

Altamesa Blvd

Oak Grove Rd

Wedgwood

S Hulen St

McCart Ave

35W

Dirks Rd

Granbury Rd

Candleridge

Sycamore School Rd

Willow Creek

Everman Pkwy

35W

*****Check for other locations**

Google

Map data ©2012 Google, Sanborn

DALLAS MOST POPULAR

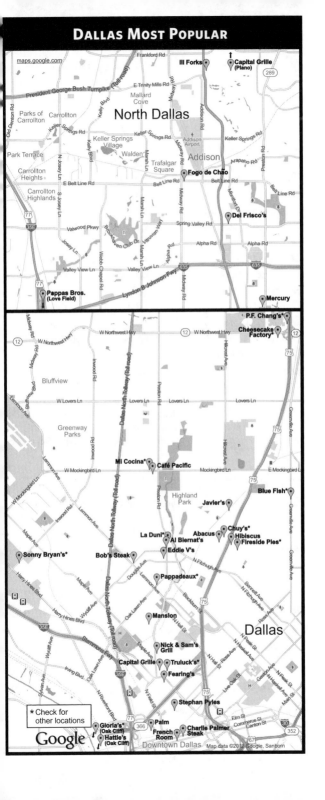

maps.google.com

Frankford Rd

III Forks

Capital Grille (Plano)

289

President George Bush Turnpike (Toll road)

E Trinity Mills Rd

Mallard Cove

Parks of Carrollton

North Dallas

Keller Springs Rd

Keller Springs Rd

Keller Springs Rd

Addison Airport

Addison

Keller Springs Village

Walden

Park Terrace

Trafalgar Square

Fogo de Chao

Carrollton Heights

E Belt Line Rd

Belt Line Rd

Belt Line Rd

Belt Line Rd

Carrollton Highlands

77

35E

Del Frisco's

Valwood Pkwy

Spring Valley Rd

Brookhaven Club Dr

Alpha Rd

Alpha Rd

Valley View Ln

Valley View Ln

635

635

Lyndon B Johnson Hwy

Pappas Bros. (Love Field)

Mercury

P.F. Chang's*

12

W Northwest Hwy

W Northwest Hwy

Cheesecake Factory*

12

75

Bluffview

W Lovers Ln

Lovers Ln

Lovers Ln

Lovers Ln

Greenway Parks

75

W Mockingbird Ln

Mi Cocina*

Café Pacific

Mockingbird Ln

E Mockingbird L

75

Blue Fish*

Highland Park

Javier's

La Duni*

Abacus

Chuy's*

Al Biernat's

Hibiscus

Fireside Pies*

Sonny Bryan's*

Bob's Steak

Eddie V's

Pappadeaux*

Mansion

Dallas

Nick & Sam's Grill

35E

Capital Grille

Truluck's*

Fearing's

75

Stephan Pyles

* Check for other locations

Gloria's* (Oak Cliff)

Palm

366

77

Charlie Palmer Steak

Google

Hattie's (Oak Cliff)

French Room

Downtown Dallas

Elm St

Commerce St

Canton St

30

352

67

Map data ©2012 Google, Sanborn

Most Popular

1. Abacus | *Eclectic*
2. Fearing's | *Southwestern*
3. Al Biernat's | *Steak*
4. Stephan Pyles | *Southwestern*
5. Del Frisco's | *Steak*
6. French Room | *Amer./French*
7. Babe's Chicken | *Southern*
8. Bob's Steak | *Steak*
9. Saint-Emilion | *French*
10. Mansion | *American*
11. Bonnell's | *Southwestern*
12. Café Pacific | *Seafood*
13. Pappadeaux | *Cajun/Seafood*
14. Lonesome Dove | *Southwestern*
15. Eddie V's | *Seafood/Steak*
16. Capital Grille | *Steak*
17. III Forks | *Steak*
18. Joe T. Garcia's* | *Tex-Mex*
19. Mi Cocina* | *Tex-Mex*
20. Gloria's | *Salvadoran/Tex-Mex*
21. Javier's* | *Mexican*
22. Charlie Palmer | *American*
23. Blue Fish | *Japanese*
24. Fogo de Chão | *Brazilian/Steak*
25. Mercury* | *American*
26. Sonny Bryan's* | *BBQ*
27. Hattie's | *American*
28. Nick & Sam's | *Seafood/Steak*
29. Pappas Bros.* | *Steak*
30. Chuy's | *Tex-Mex*
31. Hibiscus* | *American*
32. Blue Mesa | *Southwestern*
33. Cheesecake Factory | *American*
34. Fireside Pies | *Pizza*
35. La Duni* | *Pan-Latin*
36. P.F. Chang's* | *Chinese*
37. Truluck's | *Seafood*
38. Angelo's Barbecue | *BBQ*
39. Grace* | *American*
40. Palm | *Steak*

Many of the above restaurants are among the Dallas/Ft. Worth area's most expensive, but if popularity were calibrated to price, a number of other restaurants would surely join their ranks. To illustrate this, we have added two lists comprising Dallas/Ft. Worth's Best Buys on page 80.

KEY NEWCOMERS

Our editors' picks among this year's arrivals. See full list at p. 148.

Blue Sushi | *Japanese* | Stylish sushi in Ft. Worth

Company Café | *American* | Dallas duo for farm-to-table fare on a budget

Komali | *Mexican* | Uptown Modern Mex from Abraham Salum

Lucia | *Italian* | Perpetually packed Oak Cliff eatery from David Uygur

Marquee | *American* | *Top Chef*'s Tre Wilcox's Highland Park arrival

Mesa | *Mexican* | Veracruz seafood in Oak Cliff

Princi Italia | *Italian* | Wood-fired pizzas and pastas in Preston Royal

Private Social | *Eclectic* | *Top Chef*'s Tiffany Derry's sceney Uptowner

Shinjuku Station | *Japanese* | Snacks and sake in the Hospital District

Texas Spice | *American* | Locavore fare in the Omni Downtown

---

* Indicates a tie with restaurant above

Vote at zagat.com

Top Food

BY CUISINE

Excludes places with low votes, unless otherwise indicated

PIZZA

27	Cavalli Pizza
26	Grimaldi's
25	Eno's Pizza Tavern
24	Coal Vines
23	Fireside Pies

SEAFOOD

27	Nick & Sam's
	Café Pacific
26	Eddie V's
	Chamberlain's Fish
25	S & D Oyster

SOUTHWESTERN

27	Bonnell's
	Stephan Pyles

	Fearing's
	Lonesome Dove
25	Reata

STEAKHOUSES

28	Pappas Bros.
27	Nick & Sam's
	Al Biernat's
	Del Frisco's
26	Perry's Steakhouse

TEX-MEX

23	Mia's
22	Gloria's
21	Cyclone Anaya's
	Chuy's
	Mi Cocina

BY SPECIAL FEATURE

BREAKFAST

27	Esperanza's
24	La Duni
22	Kuby's
21	Main St. Bistro
20	Café Brazil

BRUNCH

27	Hattie's
	Fearing's
26	Grape
	Lawry's Prime Rib
23	Blue Mesa

BUSINESS DINING

28	Pappas Bros.
	Mercury
27	Bonnell's
	Stephan Pyles
	Al Biernat's

CHILD-FRIENDLY

25	Babe's Chicken
24	Celebration
21	Mi Cocina
20	Highland Park Soda Fountain∇
19	Zöe's Kitchen

HOTEL DINING

28	French Room (Adolphus)
27	Nana (Hilton Anatole)
	Fearing's (Ritz-Carlton)
26	Mansion (Rosewood)
25	Bob's Steak (Omni Dallas)

MEET FOR A DRINK

27	Fearing's
26	Eddie V's
	Marquee
23	Sevy's
22	Bailey's Prime

OFFBEAT

25	Babe's Chicken
	Angelo's Barbecue
22	Fred's
	Spiral Diner∇
20	Tillman's Roadhouse

PEOPLE-WATCHING

27	Fearing's
	Al Biernat's
26	Eddie V's
21	Ocean Prime
19	Dragonfly

QUIET CONVERSATION

29	Saint-Emilion
28	French Room
	Bijoux
27	Cacharel
	Suze*

TRENDY

27	Bonnell's
	Fearing's
26	Marquee
25	Bolsa
24	Nosh European Bistro

Vote at zagat.com

BY LOCATION

DALLAS

DOWNTOWN

28 French Room
25 Charlie Palmer
24 Five Sixty
Sonny Bryan's
23 Campisi's

GREENVILLE AVENUE

26 Grape
24 Woodfire Kirby's
Blue Fish
23 Campisi's
Twisted Root Burger Co.

KNOX-HENDERSON

27 Abacus
26 Hibiscus
25 Adelmo's
Neighborhood Services
Tei Tei Robata*

NORTH DALLAS

27 Del Frisco's
26 Lawry's Prime Rib
Ruth's Chris
25 Cadot
24 Sullivan's

NORTHPARK

24 La Duni
23 Blue Mesa
22 Bailey's Prime
21 P.F. Chang's
20 El Fenix

OAK LAWN

27 Al Biernat's
26 Eddie V's
25 Parigi
24 La Duni
Nosh European Bistro

UPTOWN

27 Nick & Sam's
Fearing's
26 Salum
Perry's Steakhouse
Capital Grille

WEST LOVERS LANE

28 Bijoux
25 Neighborhood Services
Shinsei*
Rise N° 1
24 Sonny Bryan's

FT. WORTH

CULTURAL DISTRICT

29 Saint-Emilion
27 Lanny's Alta Cocina

26 Eddie V's
25 Railhead Smokehouse
23 Café Modern

OTHER AREAS

ADDISON

26 Kenny's Wood Fired
Chamberlain's Fish
25 Chamberlain's Steak
Fogo de Chão
Fadi's Mediterranean

FRISCO

25 Babe's Chicken
Rudy's
Fadi's Mediterranean
22 Gloria's
Silver Fox

GRAPEVINE

25 Bob's Steak
Boi Na Braza
24 Empress of China
23 Fireside Pies
Ferrari's

PLANO

26 Bavarian Grill
Yao Fuzi Cuisine
Capital Grille
25 Bob's Steak
Roy's

Top Decor

29	French Room	
28	Mansion	
	Fearing's	
27	Nana	
	Stephan Pyles	
	Tei An	
	Café Modern	

26	Charlie Palmer
	Grace
	Saint-Emilion*
	Craft Dallas
	Komali
	Five Sixty
	Eddie V's
	Perry's Steakhouse
	Samar
	Café Pacific
25	Abacus
	Capital Grille
	Nick & Sam's

Reata*
Chamberlain's Fish
Bijoux
Nobu Dallas
Marquee
Yao Fuzi Cuisine
Pappas Bros.
Hattie's

24	Meddlesome Moth
	Lawry's Prime Rib
	Al Biernat's
	Boi Na Braza
	Jasper's
	Roy's
	Sambuca*
	Ocean Prime
	Bonnell's
	Lavendou
	Del Frisco's
	Mercury

OUTDOORS

Café Modern
Café Nasher
Fearing's
Fred's
Joe T. Garcia's

La Duni (NorthPark)
Mansion
Shinjuku Station
Texas Spice
Toulouse

ROMANCE

Bijoux
French Room
Grape
Hôtel St. Germain
Lanny's Alta Cocina

Lavendou
Mansion
Mercury
Saint-Emilion
Suze

ROOMS

Abacus
Bailey's Prime
Charlie Palmer
Fearing's
French Room

Grace
Lonesome Dove
Nana
Stephan Pyles
Tei An

VIEWS

Cacharel
Café Modern
Café Nasher
Café on the Green
Dragonfly

Five Sixty
Mi Piaci
Nana
Reata
Texas Spice

Top Service

Best Buys

In order of Bang for the Buck rating.

OTHER GOOD VALUES

Dallas/Ft. Worth

☑ **Abacus** ☒ *Eclectic*
27 | 25 | 27 | $69

Knox-Henderson | 4511 McKinney Ave. (Armstrong Ave.) | Dallas | 214-559-3111 | www.kentrathbun.com

Once again voted Most Popular in Dallas/Ft. Worth, this Knox-Henderson Eclectic is "still tops" thanks to "superstar" chef Kent Rathbun's "sublime", "innovative" cuisine ("the lobster shooters are a must") and "sophisticated" "see-and-be-seen" surroundings where you feel equally "at home whether in jeans or dressed up"; service is "smooth and polished" too, so despite a few gripes about "noise", most are "blown away" – just "bring your sense of adventure" (and your platinum card).

Aboca's Italian Grill ☒ *Italian*
▽ 23 | 15 | 21 | $18

NEW **Medical City** | 10455 N. Central Expwy. (Meadow Rd.) | Dallas | 214-364-1700
Richardson | 100 S. Central Expwy. (Belt Line Rd.) | 972-231-7500
www.abocas.com

"BYO sweetens the deal" at these "nice, neighborhood" Italians in Richardson and near Medical City featuring "huge portions" of "tasty" traditional fare; comfortable, casual digs earn them a "loyal" following.

Addison Cafe *American*
25 | 21 | 25 | $48

Addison | 5290 Belt Line Rd. (Montfort Dr.) | 972-991-8824 | www.addisoncafe.com

"Still charming" murmur fans of this "longtime" "neighborhood gem" in an Addison strip center that's still going strong with "excellent" French-inflected American cuisine offered at relatively "reasonable" rates; "dated" looks aside, an "attentive" staff makes it well suited for "business lunches" or "romantic" dinners alike – *"bon appétit!"*

Adelmo's ☒ *Italian*
25 | 20 | 25 | $43

Knox-Henderson | 4537 Cole Ave. (Knox St.) | Dallas | 214-559-0325 | www.adelmos.com

The "owner greets you at the door" at this "tiny" eponymous eatery in Knox-Henderson that recalls "NYC's Little Italy"; "stellar" cooking and a "homey ambiance" make it "perfect for a date"; P.S. wallet-watchers take note of the bargain $23.95 pre-theater dinner menu.

☑ **Al Biernat's** *Steak*
27 | 24 | 27 | $65

Oak Lawn | 4217 Oak Lawn Ave. (bet. Herschel & Wycliff Aves.) | Dallas | 214-219-2201 | www.albiernats.com

"A haven for star athletes and their fans who crave a good steak", this "loud", lively Oak Lawn "classic" "stands out" with "top-notch" fare and "supreme" service from Al himself that "makes you feel important"; all this comes at a "high price", though many find it worthwhile given the "incredible ambiance for deal-making and celebrations."

	FOOD	DECOR	SERVICE	COST

Ali Baba *Mediterranean*
23 | 15 | 19 | $18

Lakewood | 1901 Abrams Rd. (La Vista Dr.) | Dallas | 214-823-8235
Richardson | 2103 N. Central Expwy. (bet. Campbell Rd. & Fall Creek Dr.) |
972-437-1222
Las Colinas | 5910 N. MacArthur Blvd. (John W. Carpenter Frwy.) |
Irving | 972-401-3900
www.alibabamedgrill.com

"Authentic" Med-Lebanese fare in generous portions awaits at this
trio of modest eateries also attracting a "feeding frenzy" with its
lunchtime buffets; just remember, it's about "food not atmosphere."

Andiamo ⊠ *Italian*
23 | 20 | 22 | $34

Addison | 4151 Belt Line Rd. (Midway Rd.) | 972-233-1515 |
www.andiamogrill.com

This "lively" Addison Italian "hasn't changed much in years", still
providing "excellent" food in an "old-world atmosphere"; it's not inexpensive, although the dinner prix fixe ($24.95) is a bargain.

Angelo's Barbecue ⊠ *BBQ*
25 | 15 | 17 | $16

Near West | 2533 White Settlement Rd. (bet. Henderson St. &
University Dr.) | Ft. Worth | 817-332-0357 | www.angelosbbq.com

"Eat here to understand what brisket is in Texas" proclaim fans of
this BBQ "standard" in Near West Ft. Worth where "exceptional"
meat is washed down with "frosty mugs of cold beer" in an atmosphere that's "a taxidermist's delight"; in sum, it's "a guaranteed
good time for little coin."

Arcodoro & Pomodoro ⊠ *Italian*
21 | 23 | 21 | $54

Uptown | Crescent Tower | 100 Crescent Ct. (bet. Cedar Springs Rd. &
Maple Ave.) | Dallas | 214-871-1924 | www.arcodoro.com

For an "unusual twist on Italian", try Efisio Farris' "haute Sardinian"
in a relatively new location in Uptown's Crescent Hotel complex,
where the fare is "well prepared" and the "decor is serene, clean and
modern"; however, quite a few surveyors lament they "miss the ambiance" of the old Routh Street location, especially considering how
"pricey" it can be.

Artin's Grill *American*
24 | 23 | 22 | $39

West Plano | 5840 Legacy Circle (Lone Star Dr.) | Plano | 469-366-3660 |
www.artinsgrill.com

Set in the massive Shops at Legacy complex in West Plano, this
upscale-casual spot serves "creative" New Americana in a "beautiful", "comfortable" setting; diners are divided on the food ("loved it"
vs. "forgettable"), although happy hour and lunch offer good deals.

Asian Mint *Asian*
22 | 19 | 20 | $25

Medical City | 11617 N. Central Expwy. (Forest Ln.) | Dallas |
214-363-6655 | www.asianmint.com

Mint, The ⊠ *Asian*

Park Cities | Shops at Highland Park | 4246 Oak Lawn Ave. (Wycliff Ave.) |
Dallas | 214-219-6468 | www.themintdallas.com

"Out-the-door" crowds attest to the popularity of these "hip", "inexpensive" spots near Medical City and Park Cities pumping out

"modern" Pan-Asian and Thai plates with "gluten-free" and "low-carb" offerings too; both locales boast a "casual", all-white look, although "noisy", "cramped" conditions often come with the territory.

Avanti Restaurant ⊠ *Italian/Mediterranean*   23 | 21 | 22 | $42

Downtown Dallas | Fountain Pl. | 1445 Ross Ave. (Field St.) | Dallas | 214-965-0055

Avanti Ristorante *Italian/Mediterranean*

Uptown | 2720 McKinney Ave. (Worthington St.) | Dallas | 214-871-4955

www.avantirestaurants.com

The Downtown Dallas iteration of this "reasonable" white-tablecloth duo delivers "consistent" Italian-Med eats in a "sophisticated" atmosphere for lunch on weekdays only; meanwhile, the Uptown locale, which focuses on "creative, delicious" Italian cuisine, also offers seven-day dinner service and a late-night menu until 3 AM on Fridays and Saturdays, plus live music and a "frisky" bar scene that caters to an "older crowd."

Axiom Sushi Lounge *Japanese*   ∇ 26 | 23 | 21 | $32

(fka Fin Sushi Lounge)

NEW **Uptown** | 4123 Cedar Springs Rd. (Knight St.) | Dallas | 214-443-3840

Sushi Axiom *Japanese*

Knox-Henderson | 2323 N. Henderson Ave. (Capitol Ave.) | Dallas | 214-828-2288

NEW **Near West** | Montgomery Plaza | 2600 W. Seventh St. (Carroll St.) | Ft. Worth | 817-877-3331

Southwest | Chapel Hill Ctr. | 4625 Donnelly Ave. (Hulen St.) | Ft. Worth | 817-735-9100

Burleson | 12650 South Frwy. (McAlister Rd.) | 817-295-9559

www.sushiaxiom.net

"Modern takes on sushi" with a long list of colorfully named specialty maki rolls are the draw at this sleek midpriced chainlet set in sea-themed digs; enhancements include frequent DJs and sweet drink specials.

🅱 **Babe's Chicken Dinner House** *Southern*   25 | 18 | 23 | $17

Cedar Hill | 200 S. Main St. (Cedar St.) | 469-272-4500

Carrollton | 1006 W. Main St. (Broadway St.) | 972-245-7773

Frisco | 6475 Page St. (John Elliott Way Dr.) | 214-387-9500

Garland | 1456 Belt Line Rd. (Garland Ave.) | 972-496-1041

Roanoke | 104 N. Oak St. (Main St.) | 817-491-2900

Arlington | 230 N. Center St. (bet. Division & Front Sts.) | 817-801-0300

Burleson | 120 S. Main St. (Ellison St.) | 817-447-3400

www.babeschicken.com

"Craveable" fried chicken and "wonderful", "big, ol'" biscuits lead the lineup at this "affordable" Southern "home-cooking" chainlet with a "friendly" vibe and "charming" "country" decor; it's the "quintessential Texas experience" – just "don't come here if 'diet' is in your vocabulary" ("bring on the mashed potatoes!"); P.S. it's BYO.

NEW Bacon Wagon *Sandwiches*

| - | - | - | I |

Location Varies; see website | Ft. Worth | 817-691-3601 |
www.thebaconwagon.com

Smoked-pork fans flock to this cheery-orange mobile Eclectic
dispensing bacon-based items from sandwiches to desserts,
with a buttermilk-maple cupcake; service is quick, tabs are a
song and it rolls primarily around Ft. Worth, but check the website
for daily locations.

Bailey's Prime Plus *Steak*

| 22 | 23 | 21 | $57 |

NorthPark | The Shops at Park Ln. | 8160 Park Ln.
(bet. Central Expwy. & Greenville Ave.) | Dallas | 214-750-8100 ⊠
Fairview | 131 E. Stacy Rd. (Central Expwy.) | 972-363-2200
Near West | 2901 Crockett St. (Currie St.) | Ft. Worth | 817-870-1100
www.baileysprimeplus.com

This set of lavish steakhouses with an over-the-top Las Vegas–like
palatial glamor earns kudos for its "creative drinks", "fun bar scene"
with live music and dancing and "pretty" looks; however, the food
garners mixed reviews ("great" vs. "not-so-great"), and many are
left "underwhelmed" by the "pricey" eats, especially in a market
flush with beef specialists.

Baker's Ribs *BBQ*

| 22 | 12 | 18 | $15 |

Downtown Dallas | 2724 Commerce St. (Central Expwy.) | Dallas |
214-748-5433 ⊠
Greenville Avenue | 4844 Greenville Ave. (Lovers Ln.) | Dallas |
214-373-0082
Garland | 488 W. I-30 (Broadway Blvd.) | 972-226-7447
Mesquite | 2202 N. Galloway Ave. (bet. Rte. 80 & Tripp Rd.) |
972-285-4747
Rowlett | 3318 Lakeview Pkwy. (Rowlett Rd.) | 972-475-6560
www.bakersribs.com

This "no-frills" BBQ chain racks up solid scores for its "quality"
hickory-smoked meats and sides served cafeteria-style; cheap tabs
add to its "quick"-bite appeal.

Bavarian Grill ⊠ Ⓜ *German*

| 26 | 23 | 24 | $24 |

East Plano | Ruisseau Vill. | 221 W. Parker Rd. (Central Expwy.) |
Plano | 972-881-0705 | www.bavariangrill.com

"Eat, drink and be merry" at this "classic German" biergarten in an
East Plano strip mall, where a staff clad in "authentic" Deutschland
attire dispenses "well-cooked" dishes (including both classic and
vegetarian items) and a wide selection of "amazing" brews; on busy
nights it's "loud with music and revelry" with a polka band that's
"part of the fun."

NEW Bee Enchiladeria *Mexican*

| ∇ 22 | 14 | 20 | $12 |

Oak Cliff | 202 W. Davis St. (Elsbeth St.) | Dallas | 214-941-1233 |
www.bestenchiladasever.com

Customize your own enchiladas from a slew of "wonderfully tasty"
"high-quality" ingredients at this novel concept in Oak Cliff from
Monica Greene (Monica's Aca y Alla); if "decor is minimal", at least
service is "fast" and you won't pay too much, either.

Z Bijoux ☒ *French* `28` `25` `26` `$77`

West Lovers Lane | Inwood Vill. | 5450 W. Lovers Ln. (Inwood Rd.) |
Dallas | 214-350-6100 | www.bijouxrestaurant.com

"Lovely for a special occasion", this "classy, quiet" West Lovers Lane
destination features "superb" New French fare from chef Scott
Gottlich offered in five- and nine-course tasting menus; the atmosphere's a tad "too stuffy" for some, and though it's expensive",
many consider it among "Dallas' finest."

Blue Fish *Japanese* `24` `19` `21` `$34`

Greenville Avenue | 3519 Greenville Ave. (McCommas Blvd.) |
Dallas | 214-824-3474
North Dallas | 18149 N. Dallas Pkwy. (Frankford Rd.) | Dallas |
972-250-3474
Allen | Watters Creek at Montgomery Farm | 940 Garden Park Dr.
(Bethany Dr.) | 972-908-3433
Las Colinas | Las Colinas Vill. | 925 W. John Carpenter Frwy.
(MacArthur Blvd.) | Irving | 972-385-3474
www.thebluefishsushi.com

"Spanking-fresh seafood" is the specialty at this "popular" midpriced
Japanese chain fashioning "lots of creative rolls" in "hip", "lively" digs
with a "happening bar scene"; the North Dallas branch sports hibachi
tables, while other outlets feature DJs spinning on weekends.

Blue Mesa *Southwestern* `23` `20` `21` `$25`

NorthPark | Lincoln Park | 7700 W. Northwest Hwy. (Central Expwy.) |
Dallas | 214-378-8686
Addison | Village on the Pkwy. | 5100 Belt Line Rd. (Dallas N. Tollway) |
972-934-0165
West Plano | Granite Park | 8200 N. Dallas Pkwy. (Hwy. 121) |
Plano | 214-387-4407
University Area | University Park Vill. | 1600 S. University Dr.
(bet. Old University Dr. & River Run) | Ft. Worth | 817-332-6372
Southlake | Southlake Town Sq. | 1586 E. Southlake Blvd. (Carroll Ave.) |
817-416-0055
www.bluemesagrill.com

Muy "popular", this "colorful" Southwestern chain continues to
"step it up" with "addictive chips", "delicious, top-shelf margaritas"
and well-priced "quality" fare based on "locally sourced" ingredients
that's best appreciated in Sunday's "epic" brunch buffet; the service
is "reliable" too, so for many "the only complaint is the noise level";
P.S. don't miss the complimentary apps at happy hour.

NEW Blue Sushi Sake Grill *Japanese* ∇ `23` `24` `21` `$32`

Near West | 3131 W. Seventh St. (Bailey Ave.) | Ft. Worth |
817-332-2583 | www.bluesushisakegrill.com

An "energetic" crowd rocks this high-style Japanese in Ft. Worth's
Near West development offering cocktails, "a huge list of sakes" and
traditional and Americanized sushi and cooked items; the dramatic
space juxtaposes a red-hued lounge and a blue dining room divided
by a massive aquarium, while a DJ on weekends and streaming
Japanese movies and anime add to the overall "great vibe"; P.S. there's
also a bargain happy hour.

	FOOD	DECOR	SERVICE	COST

☑ Bob's Steak & Chop House ☒ *Steak* — 25 | 22 | 24 | $62

NEW Downtown Dallas | Omni Dallas Hotel | 555 S. Lamar St. (Young St.) | Dallas | 214-652-4800
Lemmon Avenue | 4300 Lemmon Ave. (Wycliff Ave.) | Dallas | 214-528-9446
West Plano | Shops at Legacy | 5760 Legacy Dr. (Bishop Rd.) | Plano | 972-608-2627
Downtown Ft. Worth | Omni Ft. Worth Hotel | 1300 Houston St. (Lancaster Ave.) | Ft. Worth | 817-350-4100
Grapevine | 1255 S. Main St. (Hwy. 114) | 817-481-5555
www.bobs-steakandchop.com

Like "a private club without the monthly dues", this "old-guard steakhouse" chain pampers power brokers and sports stars with "polished" service and "succulent", "well-aged" steaks plated alongside "the biggest carrot you've ever seen" (a signature) in über-masculine digs; outvoted critics claim it's "coasting on its former reputation" with "lackluster", "overpriced" eats, but it's nevertheless "the place to be seen" on an expense account.

Boi Na Braza *Brazilian/Steak* — 25 | 24 | 26 | $59

Grapevine | 4025 William D. Tate Ave. (Hall Johnson Rd.) | 817-251-9881 | www.boinabraza.com

"Bring your desire to eat a ton of meat" to this "fun" Grapevine Brazilian churrascaria where diners "get their money's worth" via an endless array of skewered cuts and an ample salad bar; a banquet-hall setting and "courteous" service cap an experience dubbed "a must-stop before joining Overeaters Anonymous."

Bolla *American* — - | - | - | E

Uptown | Stoneleigh Hotel | 2927 Maple Ave. (bet. Randall & Wolf Sts.) | Dallas | 214-871-7111 | www.stoneleighhotel.com

Uptown's aristocratic Stoneleigh Hotel – done up in the art deco style of its glamorous heyday – is the setting for this dining room, showcasing the "wonderful" New American cuisine of Cesar Gallegos; his modern menu is served in an elegant dining room with dark-wood floors, luxe leather banquettes and museum-worthy artwork throughout; P.S. a $40 four-course tasting menu is also available.

Bolsa *American* — 25 | 21 | 21 | $35

Oak Cliff | 614 W. Davis St. (Cedar Hill Ave.) | Dallas | 214-367-9367 | www.bolsadallas.com

It can be a "mob scene" at this "foodie delight" in Oak Cliff cooking up an "exciting", ever-"changing" seasonal New American menu backed by "awesome drinks" crafted by some of the "best mixologists in Dallas"; look for an "energetic" vibe, "casual but attentive service" and a "fun" patio packed with "hipsters"; P.S. Bolsa Mercado is a separate market vending local meats, charcuterie and cheeses.

Bonnell's ☒ ☒ *Southwestern* — 27 | 24 | 27 | $53

Southwest | 4259 Bryant Irvin Rd. (Southwest Blvd.) | Ft. Worth | 817-738-5489 | www.bonnellstexas.com

"Where else can you get elk, ostrich, bison, antelope and boar?" but at this Southwest Ft. Worth "treasure" specializing in Jon Bonnell's own brand of "unique" "upscale" "cowboy cuisine" that's "always a treat"; it's not inexpensive, but add in "top-notch" service and "casually elegant" surroundings and it's a "pleasure on every level."

Brio Tuscan Grille *Italian*   22 | 23 | 22 | $33

Allen | Watters Creek at Montgomery Farm | 810 Central Expwy. (Bethany Dr.) | 214-383-5556

Southlake | Southlake Town Sq. | 1431 Plaza Pl. (Hwy. 114) | 817-310-3136 www.brioitalian.com

The 'burbs benefit from this "unchainlike" collection of Italians in Dallas and Houston proffering "dependable", "affordable" fare in villa-style settings; though it's a favorite for "soccer moms" (thanks in part to a standout "kids' menu"), "spotty" service is a sore spot, and some can't fathom why they're always "packed."

Brownstone Ⓜ *American*   21 | 23 | 22 | $40

Near West | 840 Currie St. (bet. Crockett & 7th Sts.) | Ft. Worth | 817-332-1555 | www.brownstonerestaurants.com

This stylish New American in Ft. Worth's West 7th development features Southern-inflected fare from sliders to strip steak with an emphasis on "fresh, local" ingredients; the "welcoming" patio-blessed space has the familiar feel of a well-put-together home, with gracious service, moderate prices and a "vibrant bar scene" adding to its warm glow.

Bubba's *Southern*   23 | 12 | 20 | $13

Park Cities | Snider Plaza | 6617 Hillcrest Ave. (bet. Daniel & Rosedale Aves.) | Dallas | 214-373-6527 | www.bubbascatering.org

"If you like it fried", head to this Snider Plaza comfort-fooder (and sib of Babe's) featuring "memorable" chicken as well as "biscuits and gravy the way grandma used to make them" and "breakfasts that shine" zipped via order-at-the-counter and drive-thru service; way-"reasonable" prices keep it tried-and-true.

Buffet at the Kimbell Ⓜ *American*   ▽ 22 | 19 | 18 | $18

Cultural District | Kimbell Art Museum | 3333 Camp Bowie Blvd. (Arch Adams St.) | Ft. Worth | 817-332-8451 | www.kimbellart.org

"Perfect for lunch in the Cultural District", this cafe within the Louis Kahn–designed Kimbell Museum building offers pleasant outdoor courtyard seating for a "nice, but limited" lunch buffet of salads, sandwiches, quiches and desserts; P.S. it's also open for early supper Friday nights.

Buttons *American*   23 | 20 | 21 | $29

NEW DeSoto | 209 E. Pleasant Run Rd. (Hilltop Circle) | 972-503-2888

Addison | 15207 Addison Rd. (Belt Line Rd.) | 972-503-2888

Southwest | 4701 West Fwy. (Hulen St.) | Ft. Worth | 817-735-4900 www.buttonsrestaurant.com

"Soul food" and jazz come together at these "funky" sibs known for "generous" helpings of fried chicken and waffles, live music nightly and a "to-die-for" Sunday brunch; prices are manageable, but look out for acoustics "so loud you can't even hear the person sitting next to you."

	FOOD	DECOR	SERVICE	COST

Buzzbrews Kitchen ❶ *Coffeehouse* — 20 | 17 | 21 | $15

NEW **Deep Ellum** | 2801 Commerce St. (Crowdus St.) | Dallas | 214-741-2801
Knox-Henderson | 4154 N. Central Expwy. (Fitzhugh Ave.) | Dallas | 214-826-7100
Lemmon Avenue | 4334 Lemmon Ave. (Herschel Ave.) | Dallas | 214-521-4334
www.buzzbrews.com

One of the "best places to cure a hangover", this Pop Art-themed trio of coffee shops slings "greasy-spoon breakfasts" and unlimited coffee all day and into the wee hours; service is spotty, but there's free WiFi and the tab's cheap too.

Byblos Lebanese ❶🖾 *Lebanese* — ▽ 27 | 19 | 23 | $21

North Side | 1406 N. Main St. (Central Ave.) | Ft. Worth | 817-625-9667 | www.byblostx.com

"A nice change of pace", this North Side Ft. Worth Lebanese offers "unique", well-priced fare (with a bargain buffet at lunch) plus hookahs and belly dancing on weekends.

❷ Cacharel 🖾 *French* — 27 | 23 | 27 | $50

Arlington | Brookhollow Tower Two | 2221 E. Lamar Blvd., 9th fl. (Ballpark Way) | 817-640-9981 | www.cacharel.net

Set in an Arlington office tower "overlooking the Cowboys Stadium dome", this upscale entry delivers true "French fine dining" including "wonderful" Grand Marnier soufflés; it's "a little old-fashioned" and not inexpensive, but with "charming" service and a "spectacular view", it's "perfect" for a business lunch or "romantic dinner."

Cadot 🖾 *French* — 25 | 20 | 22 | $44

North Dallas | 18111 Preston Rd. (Frankford Rd.) | Dallas | 972-267-5700 | www.cadotrestaurant.com

Francophiles fawn over this "casually elegant" North Dallas venue from Jean-Marie Cadot (ex Lavendou) featuring "beautifully executed" preparations of Dover sole, coq au vin and other traditional recipes; "knowledgeable" service "without pretension" and relatively fair prices fairly further its rep as a "charming" player in the local dining scene.

Café Brazil *Coffeehouse* — 20 | 15 | 18 | $17

Deep Ellum | 2815 Elm St. (Malcolm X Blvd.) | Dallas | 214-747-2730 ❶
Greenville Avenue | 2900 Greenville Ave. (Goodwin Ave.) | Dallas | 214-841-0900
Park Cities | 6420 N. Central Expwy. (Fondren Dr.) | Dallas | 214-691-7791 ❶
Oak Lawn | 3847 Cedar Springs Rd. (Oak Lawn Ave.) | Dallas | 214-461-8762 ❶
Addison | Quorum II Plaza | 4930 Belt Line Rd. (Addison Rd.) | 972-386-7966
Richardson | 2071 N. Central Expwy. (Campbell Rd.) | 972-783-9011 ❶
McKinney | 3190 S. Central Expwy. (Eldorado Pkwy.) | 972-984-1259
Carrollton | 2510 N. Josey Ln. (Trinity Mills Rd.) | 972-242-8228

(continued)

Café Brazil

East Plano | 200 Coit Rd. (President George Bush Tpke.) | Plano | 469-229-9140

NEW **University Area** | 2880 W. Berry St. (Greene Ave.) | Ft. Worth | 817-923-7777 ●

www.cafebrazil.com

Additional locations throughout the Dallas/Ft. Worth area

"Get your caffeine buzz going" at this "funky" coffeehouse chain, a "regular weekend breakfast hangout" with "filling" fare and "nothing fancy, but comfortable" digs; "wildly inconsistent" service is a drawback, although some branches redeem with 24/7 hours, making them "a beacon of hope" late at night; P.S. it's kid-friendly too.

Café Express *Eclectic*

20 | 16 | 16 | $16

Mockingbird Station | Mockingbird Station | 5307 E. Mockingbird Ln. (I-75) | Dallas | 214-841-9444

West Lovers Lane | Pavilion Ctr. | 5600 W. Lovers Ln. (Inwood Rd.) | Dallas | 214-352-2211

Uptown | 3230 McKinney Ave. (Bowen St.) | Dallas | 214-999-9444

West Plano | Shops at Legacy | 5800 Legacy Dr. (Bishop Rd.) | Plano | 972-378-9444

Southlake | Southlake Town Sq. | 1472 Main St. (Carroll Ave.) | 817-251-0063

www.cafe-express.com

See review in Houston Directory.

Café Istanbul *Turkish*

23 | 19 | 22 | $31

West Lovers Lane | Inwood Vill. | 5450 W. Lovers Ln. (Inwood Rd.) | Dallas | 214-902-0919

West Plano | Shops at Legacy | 7300 Lone Star Dr. (Legacy Circle) | Plano | 972-398-2020

www.cafe-istanbul.net

For "authentic Turkish" on West Lovers Lane or in Plano, hit this "real treat" where the food's "reliable", the staff is "friendly" and the decor is "appropriate" to the theme; weekend belly dancers add to the "fun."

Café Madrid 🗷 *Spanish*

23 | 17 | 20 | $28

Knox-Henderson | 4501 Travis St. (Armstrong Ave.) | Dallas | 214-528-1731 | www.cafemadrid-dallas.com

Iberiaphiles insist it's "worth seeking out" this "lively" tapas stop in Knox-Henderson for "authentic" (if a bit "run-of-the-mill") Spanish nibbles supported by an "extensive" array of vinos and sherries; occasional live flamenco boosts the appeal, even if the unimpressed label the fare and service "spotty."

Café Modern ⊠ *Eclectic*

23 | 27 | 22 | $30

Cultural District | Modern Art Museum | 3200 Darnell St. (University Dr.) | Ft. Worth | 817-840-2157 | www.thecafemodern.com

The "inspired" Eclectic fare is the "perfect complement" to the "magnificent" setting at this "stylish" daytime cafe ensconced in the Tadao Ando-designed Modern Art Museum in Ft. Worth's Cultural District; midlevel prices, solid service and a view of a reflecting pool cap a "relaxing" meal; P.S. dinner is served on Fridays.

	FOOD	DECOR	SERVICE	COST

Café Nasher by Wolfgang Puck ⓜ *American*

▽ 25 | 27 | 20 | $30

Arts District | Nasher Sculpture Ctr. | 2001 Flora St. (Olive St.) | Dallas | 214-242-5118 | www.nashersculpturecenter.org

"Artful food in an artful location" sums up this eatery on the grounds of the "stunning" Nasher Sculpture Center, where a "high-quality light lunch" of New American fare in a "lovely setting" can be found at "reasonable" cost; just note, it's only accessible with museum admission.

Café on the Green *American*

▽ 24 | 24 | 25 | $49

Las Colinas | Four Seasons Resort & Club | 4150 N. MacArthur Blvd. (Byron Nelson Way) | Irving | 972-717-2420 | www.fourseasons.com

"Far too beautiful to be called a cafe", this ritzy "retreat" in the Four Seasons Las Colinas features an elegant Zen-like ambiance with terrace seating overlooking the pool; seasonal American cuisine and servers that "know what they're talking about" make for a pleasant time, whether for brunch or a glass of wine from the ample cellar.

Café Pacific *Seafood*

27 | 26 | 26 | $57

Park Cities | 24 Highland Park Vill. (Preston Rd.) | Dallas | 214-526-1170 | www.cafepacificdallas.com

A "high-roller crowd" favors this "old-school" Park Cities "tradition" putting out "top-notch" seafood and "generous cocktails" in "plush" digs; the "formal" setting isn't for everyone ("proper dress required"), nor are the prices; P.S. don't miss the "last meal"–worthy pecan balls.

Campisi's *Pizza*

23 | 16 | 21 | $20

Downtown Dallas | Stone Street Gdns. | 1520 Elm St. (bet. Akard & Ervay Sts.) | Dallas | 214-752-0141 🖪

West Lovers Lane | Inwood Vill. | 5405 W. Lovers Ln. (Inwood Rd.) | Dallas | 214-350-2595

North Dallas | 7632 W. Campbell Rd. (Coit Rd.) | Dallas | 972-931-2267

West Plano | 3115 W. Parker Rd. (Independence Pkwy.) | Plano | 972-612-1177

West Plano | 8100 N. Dallas Pkwy. (Granite Pkwy.) | Plano | 214-387-0233

Campisi's Egyptian *Pizza*

Greenville Avenue | 5610 E. Mockingbird Ln. (Greenville Ave.) | Dallas | 214-827-0355
www.campisis.us

Sentimental surveyors swoon over this "old-school" Italian "throwback" near Greenville Avenue – a "Dallas institution" since 1946 frequented by a colorful mix of customers from "Jack Ruby" to "Frank Sinatra" with decor "unchanged for decades"; the newer satellites with thin-crust pizzas are fallbacks for "takeout", with hit-or-miss service but always a wallet-friendly check.

Cane Rosso 🖪 *Pizza*
(fka Il Cane Rosso)

– | – | – | M

Deep Ellum | 2612 Commerce St. (Henry St.) | Dallas | 214-741-1188 | www.ilcanerosso.com

Certified-authentic Neapolitan pizza comes to Dallas via this Deep Ellum parlor where a Naples-born pizzaiolo puts out "one of the best" pies in town plus beer and wine for not a lot of dough; popular from day one, it's already expanding its contemporary space whose centerpiece is a bright-red wood-burning oven imported from Italy; P.S. a mobile oven makes the food truck rounds too.

Cane Rosso Mobile Oven 🗷 *Pizza* — | — | — | I

Location varies; see website | Dallas | 214-741-1188 | www.ilcanerosso.com

This mobile offshoot of Cane Rosso brings its Neapolitan pizza to grateful diners all over the metroplex; it makes regular stops at Green Spot Market, Veritas Wine Room and Times Ten Cellars in Ft. Worth, but check Twitter or Facebook for more locations.

Cantina Laredo *Mexican* 21 | 19 | 20 | $26

Lakewood | 2031 Abrams Rd. (Gaston Ave.) | Dallas | 214-821-5785
Preston Royal | 6025 Royal Ln. (Preston Rd.) | Dallas | 214-265-1610
West Lovers Lane | 165 Inwood Vill. (Lovers Ln.) | Dallas | 214-350-5227
Addison | 4546 Belt Line Rd. (Beltway Dr.) | 972-458-0962
North Dallas | 17808 Dallas Pkwy. (Briargrove Ln.) | Dallas | 469-828-4818
Frisco | 1125 Legacy Dr. (Hwy. 121) | 214-618-9860
Sundance Square | 530 Throckmorton St. (bet. 4th & 5th Sts.) | Ft. Worth | 817-810-0773
Lewisville | 2225 S. Stemmons Frwy. (bet. Corporate Dr. & Hebron Pkwy.) | 972-315-8100
Grapevine | 4020 William D. Tate Ave. (Hall Johnson Rd.) | 817-358-0505
www.cantinalaredo.com

Fans count on "consistently well-prepared" fare and "fast, attentive service" at this "upscale" Mexican chain where the "tableside guacamole is a must", as are the "excellent margaritas"; true, it may be "a bit more pricey" than some competitors, but "one taste of the food, and you'll see why."

Capital Grille *Steak* 26 | 25 | 26 | $61

Uptown | Crescent Shops & Galleries | 500 Crescent Ct. (bet. Cedar Springs Rd. & Maple Ave.) | Dallas | 214-303-0500
NEW West Plano | The Shops at Legacy | 7300 Dallas Pkwy. (Legacy Circle) | Plano | 972-398-2221
www.thecapitalgrille.com

"Great" dry-aged steaks and "strong drinks" are the hallmarks of this "fine" chophouse chain that follows through with "polished, professional" service and "attractive" settings chock-full of "good, old boys"; it's certainly not cheap, but it's "never a disappointment" either.

Carrabba's Italian Grill *Italian* 23 | 20 | 22 | $29

North Dallas | 17548 Dallas Pkwy. (Trinity Mills Rd.) | Dallas | 972-732-7752
East Plano | 3400 N. Central Expwy. (Parker Rd.) | Plano | 972-516-9900
Hurst | Northeast Mall | 1101 Melbourne Rd. (bet. Bedford Euless & Pipeline Rds.) | 817-595-3345
Grapevine | 1701 Crossroads Dr. (Hwy. 114) | 817-410-8461
www.carrabbas.com

See review in Houston Directory.

	FOOD	DECOR	SERVICE	COST

Cat City Grill *American*   ▽ 21 | 18 | 22 | $32

Hospital District | 1208 W. Magnolia Ave. (5th Ave.) | Ft. Worth | 817-916-5333 | www.catcitygrill.com

It's "biz-lunch" central by day and hot spot for the "happy-hour" crowd" come nightfall at this stylish Hospital District bistro and spin-off of neighboring Lili's Bistro; a "good variety" of "delicious" New American dishes, "friendly" service and "moderate" pricing make it "an easy place to come back to" anytime; P.S. a full brunch and a kids' menu are added perks.

Cattlemen's Steakhouse *Steak*   23 | 19 | 20 | $41

Stockyards | 2458 N. Main St. (Exchange Ave.) | Ft. Worth | 817-624-3945 | www.cattlemenssteakhouse.com

"Wear your jeans, spurs and hat" when moseying into this "super" steakhouse near the Stockyards in Old Ft. Worth, serving up "con-sistent" beef in cow-centric digs since 1947; "service is fun and courteous", another reason why it's just the ticket when you need to entertain "visitors" and "don't want to spend a lot of dough."

Cavalli Pizza Napoletana *Pizza*   27 | 16 | 22 | $15

NEW **McKinney** | 6851 Virginia Pkwy. (Stonebridge Dr.) | 972-540-1449

Irving | 3601 Regent Blvd. (Belt Line Rd.) | 972-915-0001 www.cavallipizza.com

Some of the "best pizza" "outside of Rome" with "chewy crusts" and "interesting" toppings turns up at this Neapolitan twosome in Irving (quick-bite) and McKinney (full service); "reasonable" prices and a BYO policy keep it "crowded" but "worth the wait."

NEW Cedars Social ❶ *American*   ▽ 20 | 18 | 19 | $34

Downtown Dallas | 1326 S. Lamar St. (Belleview St.) | Dallas | 214-928-7700 | www.thecedarssocial.com

Always "hopping", this cocktail den near the Southside on Lamar complex Downtown is best-known for its "excellent" drinks with a seasonal bent shaken up in a 1970s retro setting; foodwise, there's New American snacks and meals that run the gamut from home-made hot dogs and sliders to chicken and waffles, all priced to move.

Celebration *American*   24 | 18 | 23 | $22

Love Field | 4503 W. Lovers Ln. (bet. Elsby Ave. & Thelma St.) | Dallas | 214-351-5681 | www.celebrationrestaurant.com

"Cooking almost as good as grandma's" awaits at this Love Field American where seconds are available on the "homestyle", "farm-fresh" dishes like pot roast and fried chicken; perhaps the setting "needs a face-lift", but "wonderful service" and "fair" prices com-pensate; P.S. look for the farmer's market in the parking lot on Saturday mornings in season.

Central 214 *American*   19 | 24 | 21 | $52

Park Cities | Hotel Palomar | 5680 N. Central Expwy. (Mockingbird Ln.) | Dallas | 214-443-9339 | www.central214.com

This slick, midpriced enclave in Park Cities' Hotel Palomar serves up "innovative" American fare with Southern touches like chicken-fried

Kobe steak and cheddar grits; though the reviews are mixed on the food, it's a "hip" place with a "spirited" bar scene boasting both impressive cocktails and "people-watching."

Chamberlain's Fish Market Grill *Seafood* | 26 | 25 | 26 | $51 |

Addison | 4525 Belt Line Rd. (bet. Beltway Dr. & Midway Rd.) | 972-503-3474 | www.chamberlainsrestaurant.com

This Addison seafooder – and sister to Chamberlain's Steak & Chop House down the street – reels 'em in with "great", "fresh" fish and "generous" drinks, all "attentively served" by an "outgoing" staff; an "elegant" setting helps justify "the splurge"; P.S. "check out the lounge" for happy-hour specials.

Chamberlain's Steak & Chop House *Steak* | 25 | 23 | 24 | $60 |

Addison | 5330 Belt Line Rd. (bet. Montfort & Oaks North Drs.) | 972-934-2467 | www.chamberlainsrestaurant.com

"Forget all of the big chains" instruct fans, and head to this Addison steakhouse, a "local favorite" for "perfectly tender" prime meats plus stone crabs in season served in "warm", "masculine" surroundings with a cigar lounge; a "top-notch" staff "makes you feel valued", but watch out for a tab that tallies on the "expensive" end.

Charleston's *American* | 21 | 20 | 20 | $24 |

Southwest | 3020 S. Hulen St. (Bellaire Dr.) | Ft. Worth | 817-735-8900 | www.charlestons.com

Whether for lunch or a "quick dinner with family", you'll find "consistently good" American fare and service at this "casual" Southwest link in a small chain; the "pleasant" Victorian-themed atmosphere is a draw, but it's the reasonable prices that keep it "always crowded."

Charlie Palmer Steak *American* | 25 | 26 | 25 | $68 |
(fka Charlie Palmer at the Joule)

Downtown Dallas | Joule Hotel | 1530 Main St. (bet. Akard & Ervay Sts.) | Dallas | 214-261-4600 | www.charliepalmer.com

A "jewel" in the "luxury" Joule Hotel Downtown, this glitzy showcase from celeb chef Charlie Palmer "pampers" guests with "excellent" New American fare, "impressive" wines and "gracious" service in an "elegant" room brimming with "business types"; "it's definitely a wow locale", even if a few find the fare "hit-or-miss" given the prices.

Cheesecake Factory *American* | 20 | 19 | 19 | $28 |

NorthPark | Lincoln Park | 7700 W. Northwest Hwy. (Central Expwy.) | Dallas | 214-373-4844

Allen | Watters Creek at Montgomery Farm | 820 Central Expwy. (Bethany Dr.) | 972-908-3900

Frisco | Stonebriar Ctr. | 2601 Preston Rd. (bet. Gaylord Pkwy. & Rte. 121) | 972-731-7799

Arlington | Parks at Arlington Mall | 3811 S. Cooper St. (Arbrook Blvd.) | 817-465-2211

Southlake | Southlake Town Sq. | 1440 Plaza Pl. (Grand Ave.) | 817-310-0050

www.thecheesecakefactory.com

See review in Houston Directory.

	FOOD	DECOR	SERVICE	COST

Chef Point Café *Southern* ▽ 24 | 7 | 19 | $19

Watauga | 5901 Watauga Rd. (Whitley Rd.) | 817-656-0080 |
www.chefpointcafe.org

Set in a Conoco gas station, this offbeat Watauga spot serves up
"good" Southern grub including a rightly famous bread pudding in a
low-key setting with a full bar; service is "friendly" and tabs are inexpensive, and as a bonus, you can still "fill up your car" at the pumps.

Chuy's *Tex-Mex*   21 | 20 | 20 | $19

Knox-Henderson | 4544 McKinney Ave. (bet. Armstrong Ave. &
Knox St.) | Dallas | 214-559-2489
East Plano | 3408 Central Expwy. (Parker Rd.) | Plano | 469-241-9393
West Plano | 3908 Dallas Pkwy. (Parker Rd.) | Plano |
469-467-2489
Arlington | Arlington Highlands | 4001 Bagpiper Way
(bet. Curtis Mathes & Partners Ways) | 817-557-2489
www.chuys.com
See review in Austin and the Hill Country Directory.

Cindi's New York Delicatessen *Deli*   21 | 13 | 21 | $16

Downtown Dallas | 306 S. Houston St. (Jackson St.) | Dallas |
214-744-4745
Medical City | 11111 N. Central Expwy. (bet. Forest & Royal Lns.) |
Dallas | 214-739-0918
Preston Hollow | 3565 Forest Ln. (bet. Marsh Ln. & Webb Chapel Rd.) |
Dallas | 972-241-9204
Richardson | 7522 Campbell Rd. (Coit Rd.) | 972-248-0608
Carrollton | 2001 Midway Rd. (bet. Keller Springs Rd. & Lindbergh Dr.) |
972-458-7740
www.cindisnydeli.com

"It's not New York, but it'll do" pronounce patrons of this "old-
school" deli-diner chain with a "wide selection of the classics", from
matzo-ball soup to smoked fish and pastrami; the settings are spare
and service ranges from "quick" to "downright mean", but at least
prices are "reasonable."

City Café *American*   21 | 15 | 20 | $42

West Lovers Lane | 5757 W. Lovers Ln. (Dallas N. Tollway) | Dallas |
214-351-2233 | www.thecitycafedallas.com

Park Cities patrons are charmed by this white-tablecloth neighborhood bistro, a "quiet", "comfortable" "place to linger" over "very
good" New American fare that's well priced too; those in the know
insist it's "best for lunch", and an adjacent take-out shop makes it
convenient for those on the run.

Clay Pit:
Contemporary Indian Cuisine *Indian*   23 | 20 | 20 | $27

Addison | 4460 Belt Line Rd. (Midway Rd.) | 972-233-0111 |
www.claypitdallas.com
See review in Austin and the Hill Country Directory.

Coal Vines *Italian*   24 | 20 | 23 | $23

Uptown | 2404 Cedar Springs Rd. (Maple Ave.) | Dallas |
214-855-4999

(continued)

Coal Vines

NEW **West Plano** | 7300 Lone Star Dr. (Legacy Circle) | Plano | 972-943-1339

Southlake | 1251 E. Southlake Blvd. (Carroll Ave.) | 817-310-0850
www.coalvines.com

Lithe twentysomethings in "little black dresses" fill this "swanky" Uptown Italian specializing in "crisp", "Greenwich Village–style" pizzas and "incredible", "reasonably priced" wines; "get there early" because the brick-lined interior and patio tend to overflow, especially "after theater and sporting events"; P.S. the Southlake and Plano sibs bring equally good pie to the 'burbs.

NEW Company Café *American*

| - | - | - | I |

Greenville Avenue | 2217 Greenville Ave. (Belmont Ave.) | Dallas | 214-827-2233

Uptown | 3136 Routh St. (Cedar Springs Rd.) | Dallas | 214-468-8721
www.companycafe.net

New to Greenville Avenue and Uptown, this American duo serves three squares daily with a focus on healthy preparations and organic, farm-to-table ingredients like cage-free eggs, grass-fed beef and smoked-in-house poultry; vegetarian, vegan and gluten-free options are also available, and while the settings are strictly no-frills, they're commensurate with the inexpensive prices.

Cool River Cafe *Southwestern/Steak*

| 21 | 22 | 21 | $42 |

Las Colinas | 1045 Hidden Ridge (MacArthur Blvd.) | Irving | 972-871-8881 | www.coolrivercafe.com

See review in Austin and the Hill Country Directory.

Cooper's Old Time Pit Bar-B-Que *BBQ*

| 25 | 14 | 17 | $20 |

Stockyards | 301 Stockyards Blvd. (Main St.) | Ft. Worth | 817-626-6464 | www.coopersbbq.com

See review in Austin and the Hill Country Directory.

Cosmic Café *Eclectic/Vegetarian*

| - | - | - | I |

Oak Lawn | 2912 Oak Lawn Ave. (Congress Ave.) | Dallas | 214-521-6157 | www.cosmiccafedallas.com

Even "certified carnivores" commend the "imaginative" meat-free eats at this "hip and healthy" Oak Lawn Eclectic veggie venue set in "whimsical" digs with yoga and meditation offered on-site; a "kooky" staff adds to the "groovy" vibe, and it all comes at a cost that's not out of this world either; P.S. on a sunny day, try the patio.

Cousin's Bar-B-Q *BBQ*

| 22 | 15 | 19 | $16 |

Airport | Dallas Ft. Worth Int'l Airport | 3200 Airfield Dr., Terminal B (Gate 27) | Dallas | 972-973-2271

Airport | Dallas Ft. Worth Int'l Airport | 3200 Airfield Dr., Terminal D (Gate 28) | Dallas | 972-973-2271

Southwest | 5125 Bryant Irvin Rd. (bet. Overton Ridge Blvd. & Trailview Dr.) | Ft. Worth | 817-346-3999

South Side | 6262 McCart Ave. (Westcreek Dr.) | Ft. Worth | 817-346-2511 🅢

(continued)

(continued)

Cousin's Bar-B-Q

Alliance | 9560 Feather Grass Ln. (bet. Heritage Trace Pkwy. & I-35) | Ft. Worth | 817-750-2020
Crowley | 910 S. Crowley Rd. (bet. Harris & Mesa Vista Drs.) | 817-297-0557 🖪
www.cousinsbbq.com

BBQ buffs line up "self serve"-style at these modest joints in Ft. Worth proffering "terrific" smoked meats, "tasty" sides and an especially noteworthy peach cobbler; "quick" service and honest prices complete the package; P.S. the food's available to go at two outposts inside the DFW airport.

Craft Dallas *American*

24 | 26 | 24 | $65

Victory Park | W Hotel | 2440 Victory Park Ln. (Olive St.) | Dallas | 214-397-4111 | www.craftdallas.com

Top Chef host Tom Colicchio's "swanky" outpost in the W Hotel in Victory Park features his "top-notch" New American cuisine based on "fresh", seasonal ingredients and brought by a "spot-on" staff; though it earns nods as a "spectacular special-occasion destination", a few find it "disappointing", especially given the "expensive" bills.

Cyclone Anaya's *Tex-Mex*

21 | 20 | 20 | $26

Lemmon Avenue | 3211 Oak Lawn Ave. (bet. Cedar Springs Rd. & Hall St.) | Dallas | 214-420-0030
NEW **Fairview** | 241 Stacy Rd. (I-75) | 972-549-0040
www.cycloneanaya.com

See review in Houston Directory.

🆉 Del Frisco's Double Eagle Steak House *Steak*

27 | 24 | 26 | $67

North Dallas | 5251 Spring Valley Rd. (Dallas N. Tollway) | Dallas | 972-490-9000
Downtown Ft. Worth | 812 Main St. (8th St.) | Ft. Worth | 817-877-3999
www.delfriscos.com

NEW Del Frisco's Grille *American*

Uptown | 3232 McKinney Ave. (Hall St.) | Dallas | 972-807-6152 | www.delfriscosgrille.com

You might just "need two stomachs" for the "outrageous", "buttery" steaks "cooked to perfection" at this high-end chophouse chain catering to an "expense-account" clientele with its "extensive wine list", "fine" service and setting akin to a "chic Western saloon"; it's especially "great for a special occasion" "if money is no object"; P.S. the Uptown Dallas Grille offers a lighter menu with a focus on cocktails, apps and burgers plus brunch in a more relaxed setting.

Deli News *Deli*

22 | 9 | 16 | $19

North Dallas | 17062 Preston Rd. (Campbell Rd.) | Dallas | 972-733-3354 | www.delinewsdallas.com

This "New York–style" deli in North Dallas is a nexus for "classic", "kosher-style" goodies like chopped liver, overstuffed sandwiches and bagels; you get "good value for your money", but watch out for occasionally "rude" service that's a bit too "authentic" for some.

Dimassi's Mediterranean Buffet *Mideastern*

| 19 | 12 | 16 | $16 |

Richardson | 180 W. Campbell Rd. (bet. Alamo Rd. & Lakeside Blvd.) | 972-250-2000 | www.dimassisbuffet.com

See review in Houston Directory.

Dish ●Ⓜ *American*

| 20 | 21 | 20 | $46 |

Oak Lawn | Ilume | 4123 Cedar Springs Rd. (Douglas Ave.) | Dallas | 214-522-3474 | www.dish-dallas.com

This "cool" enclave anchors Ilume, the trendy Oak Lawn residential complex, thus ensuring the LED-illuminated space ensures some "great people-watching"; its "creative", midpriced American menu and glammed-up bar fare go down well with the lengthy list of Cosmos, peartinis and such; P.S. Drag Brunch Sundays draw an especially lively crowd.

Dixie House *Southern*

| ▽ 23 | 15 | 22 | $17 |

Lakewood | 6400 Gaston Ave. (Abrams Pkwy.) | Dallas | 214-826-2412 | www.theblackeyedpea.com

"Good" Southern "home cooking" – especially breakfasts and "country fried chicken" – is the forte of this Lakewood longtimer; "basic" digs, budget bills and servers who call you "honey" help explain its staying power.

NEW Dough ⓍⓂ *Pizza*

| 27 | 21 | 24 | $26 |

Preston Forest | Preston Forest Sq. | 11909 Preston Rd. (Forest Ln.) | Dallas | 972-788-4600 | www.doughpizzeria.com

See review in San Antonio Directory.

Dragonfly *American*

| 19 | 21 | 18 | $56 |

Uptown | Hotel ZaZa | 2332 Leonard St. (McKinney Ave.) | Dallas | 214-468-8399 | www.hotelzaza.com

There's "people-watching" galore ("especially in summer when the pool is open") at this "hip" Uptown eatery in the Hotel ZaZa; critics claim "inconsistency" is an issue with service and the premium-priced New American cuisine, but that doesn't deter the "twentysomething" clientele – it's really about the scene here; P.S. ratings don't reflect the post-Survey addition of chef Dan Landsberg (ex Tillman's Roadhouse).

Dream Café *American*

| 23 | 15 | 19 | $21 |

Uptown | Quadrangle | 2800 Routh St. (Howell St.) | Dallas | 214-954-0486

Addison | Village on the Pkwy. | 5100 Belt Line Rd. (Dallas N. Tollway) | 972-503-7326

www.thedreamcafe.com

"Wear your Birkenstocks" to fit in at these "hippie" havens in Uptown and Addison, where "free spirits" gather for "tasty", inexpensive American eats with a "healthy" bent; "laid-back" service and "pleasant" patios make them a natural for an "easy brunch", and dogs are welcome at both venues too; P.S. Addison is open for breakfast and lunch only.

Dutch's *Burgers*
22 | 16 | 18 | $15

University Area | 3009 S. University Dr. (bet. Berry & Bowie Sts.) | Ft. Worth | 817-927-5522 | www.dutchshamburgers.com

Collegiate types cram into this Ft. Worth University Area "hangout" named after one of TCU's legendary football coaches, and turning out "terrific", "juicy" burgers in tons of varieties; "hand-cut fries", a "nice choice of draft beers" and shakes ice the cake, so no one minds the worn-looking retro digs and prices that can feel a tad high for the genre.

Eddie V's Prime Seafood *Seafood/Steak*
26 | 26 | 25 | $55

Oak Lawn | 4023 Oak Lawn Ave. (Avondale Ave.) | Dallas | 214-890-1500
Cultural District | 3100 W. Seventh St. (Bailey Ave.) | Ft. Worth | 214-890-1500
www.eddiev.com

See review in Austin and the Hill Country Directory.

Eden *American*
- | - | - | M

West Lovers Lane | 4416 W. Lovers Ln. (Taos Rd.) | Dallas | 972-267-3336 | www.eden-dallas.com

A quaint little house on West Lovers Lane provides the setting for this New American serving up crowd-pleasing dinners, brunch and high tea; a BYO policy (with $5 corkage) keeps the cost down.

El Fenix *Tex-Mex*
20 | 18 | 21 | $20

Lake Highlands | 255 Casa Linda Plaza (Garland Rd.) | Dallas | 214-327-6173
Lake Highlands | 9090 Skillman St. (Audelia Rd.) | Dallas | 214-349-3815
Lemmon Avenue | 5622 Lemmon Ave. (Inwood Rd.) | Dallas | 214-521-5166
NorthPark | 6811 W. Northwest Hwy. (Hillcrest Rd.) | Dallas | 214-363-5279
Uptown | 1601 McKinney Ave. (Broom St.) | Dallas | 214-747-1121
Oak Cliff | 120 E. Colorado Blvd. (Beckley Ave.) | Dallas | 214-941-4050
Addison | 5280 Belt Line Rd. (Addison Rd.) | 972-387-2533
North Dallas | 3128 Forest Ln. (Webb Chapel Rd.) | Dallas | 972-241-3248
Irving | 3911 W. Airport Frwy. (Belt Line Rd.) | 972-573-3980
West | 6391 Camp Bowie Blvd. (Hilldale Rd.) | Ft. Worth | 817-732-5584
www.elfenix.com
Additional locations throughout the Dallas/Ft. Worth area

After more than 90 years, this "tried-and-true" chain of Tex-Mex (aka "Velveeta Mex") cantinas is "still cranking out" "solid" grub in "huge" portions with "fun drinks to wash it down"; service varies, but "moderate prices" and a casual vibe keep it "popular"; P.S. expect crowds on specials nights.

Ellerbe Fine Food 🗷 Ⓜ *American*
26 | 22 | 26 | $46

Hospital District | 1501 W. Magnolia Ave. (7th Ave.) | Ft. Worth | 817-926-3663 | www.ellerbefinefoods.com

"Foodies adore" this "fantastic" restaurant from chef/co-owner Molly McCook set in a former gas station in Ft. Worth's "hip"

Hospital District; the Southern-influenced American menu "swings from nouvelle to rustic", while "helpful" service and a "gracious", "homey" atmosphere help cement its standing as "one of the best" in the area.

Empress of China *Chinese*
24 | 18 | 22 | $20

Las Colinas | Grande Shopping Ctr. | 2648 N. Belt Line Rd. (Grande Bulevar Blvd.) | Irving | 972-252-7677
Flower Mound | 1913 Justin Rd. (Highland Village Rd.) | 972-691-1628
Grapevine | 2030 Glade Rd. (Hwy. 121) | 817-442-0088
www.eocrestaurant.com

Regulars rely on this trio of suburban eateries out of the Howard Wang dynasty for "consistently well-prepared" traditional Chinese cooking; service and surroundings vary by locale, but the ambiance is "pleasant" enough, and it works for takeout too.

Eno's Pizza Tavern Ⓜ *Italian/Pizza*
25 | 21 | 24 | $26

Oak Cliff | 407 N. Bishop Ave. (bet. 7th & 8th Sts.) | Dallas | 214-943-9200 | www.enospizza.com

"Amazing", "über-thin" pizzas with "fancy toppings", "fresh salads" and an "impressive" wine and microbrew list keep customers coming to this "cool" Oak Cliff spot; "affordable" bills make the frequent "long waits" easier to handle.

Esperanza's Mexican Bakery & Café *Mexican*
27 | 17 | 23 | $16

Hospital District | 1601 Park Place Ave. (8th Ave.) | Ft. Worth | 817-923-1992
North Side | 2122 N. Main St. (21st St.) | Ft. Worth | 817-626-5770
www.joets.com

The "wow factor" is high at this Ft. Worth Mexican duo from descendents of the Joe T. Garcia–Lancarte family serving "superb" takes on the classics in "homey" surroundings; expect long lines, especially for the "unbeatable" Sunday brunch; P.S. the on-site bakeries vending pan dulce are "not to be missed on the way out."

Fadi's Mediterranean *Mideastern*
25 | 16 | 18 | $16

Knox-Henderson | 3001 Knox St. (I-75) | Dallas | 214-528-1800
Addison | 14902 Preston Rd. (Belt Line Rd.) | 972-934-8500
Frisco | 2787 Preston Rd. (Gaylord Pkwy.) | 972-712-1600
www.fadiscuisine.com

See review in Houston Directory.

☑ Fearing's *Southwestern*
27 | 28 | 27 | $75

Uptown | Ritz-Carlton Hotel | 2121 McKinney Ave. (Pearl St.) | Dallas | 214-922-4848 | www.fearingsrestaurant.com

Smitten fans say it "doesn't get any better" than Dean Fearing's eponymous "fine-dining" venue in Uptown's Ritz-Carlton Hotel featuring his "spectacular", "sophisticated" Southwestern cooking that's "just plain awesome"; it follows through with "warm" service (Dean himself often "works the room") and a glitzy setting that's a total "scene", so even if some sniff "overrated", the "overall event" is "quite an experience."

Ferrari's Italian Villa *Italian* | 23 | 22 | 23 | $43 |

Addison | 14831 Midway Rd. (bet. Belt Line & Spring Valley Rds.) | 972-980-9898
Grapevine | 1200 William D. Tate Ave. (Ira E. Woods Ave.) | 817-251-2525
www.ferrarisrestaurant.com

A "date-night" kind of place, this Sardinian-themed eatery in Addison (and its Grapevine offshoot) presents "very good" Italiana in a "relaxed", low-lit setting centered around a wood-burning oven; "gracious" service and moderate costs keep guests coming "back often."

Ferre Ristorante e Bar 🅂🅼 *Italian* | ▽ 18 | 21 | 20 | $36 |

Sundance Square | Sundance Sq. | 215 E. Fourth St. (bet. Calhoun & Commerce Sts.) | Ft. Worth | 817-332-0033 | www.ferrerestaurant.com

"Location" is a virtue for this contemporary Italian on Ft. Worth's Sundance Square whose proximity to "Bass Hall" makes it well-suited for a "romantic" "pre-theater" meal; yet, despite a "wide variety" of Tuscan dishes on the menu, the "unimpressed" say that "for the price, it should be better."

Fireside Pies *Pizza* | 23 | 20 | 21 | $24 |

Knox-Henderson | 2820 N. Henderson Ave. (Milam St.) | Dallas | 214-370-3916
West Lovers Lane | 7709 Inwood Rd. (bet. Newmore Ave. & W. Lovers Ln.) | Dallas | 214-357-3800
West Plano | Shops at Legacy | 5717 Legacy Dr. (bet. Dallas N. Tollway & Parkwood Blvd.) | Plano | 972-398-2700
Near West | 2949 Crockett St. (bet. Currie St. & Norwood St.) | Ft. Worth | 817-769-3590
Grapevine | 1285 S. Main St. (Hwy. 114) | 817-416-1285
www.firesidepies.com

"Wonderful artisanal pizzas" bring in the masses to these "upscale" pizzerias dotted around Dallas sending out pies with "trendy" toppings, "innovative" salads and "great beers and wines"; they're "hugely popular" and the spaces are "small", so a "frat-party crush and deafening noise levels" come with the territory.

First Chinese BBQ ⊅ *Chinese* | 24 | 9 | 16 | $18 |

Richardson | 111 S. Greenville Ave. (Belt Line Rd.) | 972-680-8216
Carrollton | 1927 E. Belt Line Rd. (Metrocrest Dr.) | 972-478-7228
East Plano | 3304 Coit Rd. (Parker Rd.) | Plano | 972-758-2988
Garland | 3405 W. Walnut St. (Jupiter Rd.) | 972-494-3430
Arlington | 2214 S. Collins St. (Pioneer Pkwy.) | 817-469-8876
Haltom City | 5310 E. Belknap St. (Midway Rd.) | 817-834-1888
www.firstchinesebbq.com

The "roast pork and lacquered duck" are the "clear stars" of this Chinese chainlet, also churning out "a broad spectrum" of Cantonese fare, from noodle soups to stir-fries; "no-frills" digs and "language barriers" with the staff aside, its "bargain-basement prices" keep it "popular", especially for "takeout."

	FOOD	DECOR	SERVICE	COST

Five Sixty Wolfgang Puck 🖂 *American* | 24 | 26 | 24 | $69 |

Downtown Dallas | Reunion Tower | 300 E. Reunion Blvd. (Houston St.) | Dallas | 214-741-5560 | www.wolfgangpuck.com

A "perfect spot to take out-of-town guests", this New American from celeb chef Wolfgang Puck offers "spectacular" 360-degree vistas from a revolving room atop Downtown's Reunion Tower, "fabulous" Asian-accented cuisine and "top-notch" service; some prefer to "stick with drinks and appetizers", because "you pay for the view" dearly.

Fogo de Chão *Brazilian/Steak* | 25 | 23 | 26 | $55 |

Addison | 4300 Belt Line Rd. (Midway Rd.) | 972-503-7300 | www.fogodechao.com

See review in Houston Directory.

Fred's ◑Ⓜ *Burgers* | 22 | 15 | 17 | $16 |

Near West | 915 Currie St. (bet. Lancaster Ave. & 7th St.) | Ft. Worth | 817-332-0083

Fred's North ◑ *Burgers*

NEW **Far North** | 2730 Wester Ctr. (Old Denton Rd.) | Ft. Worth | 817-232-0111
www.fredstexascafe.com

They're "cheap" and "nothing fancy", and "that's the charm" of these hamburger "dives" dishing out "perfectly cooked" patties, diner fare and "cold beer" to a cool crowd; throw in outdoor patios at both locations and nightly live music at the Near West original, and you see why some fans exclaim "this is Texas."

🛛 French Room 🖂Ⓜ *American/French* | 28 | 29 | 29 | $90 |

Downtown Dallas | Hotel Adolphus | 1321 Commerce St. (Field St.) | Dallas | 214-742-8200 | www.hoteladolphus.com

"For a splurge night", fans tout this "top-flight" haute French inside the historic Hotel Adolphus, voted Dallas' No. 1 for Decor and Service thanks to its "breathtaking", "rococo" interior and "impeccable" hospitality; "creative", "perfectly executed" cuisine and "marvelous wines" round out a "superior dining experience" that's "memorable in every way"; P.S. jackets required.

Fuel City Tacos ◑⇼ *Mexican* | – | – | – | I |

Downtown Dallas | 801 S. Riverfront Blvd. (I-35) | Dallas | 214-426-0011 | www.fuelcity-tacos.com

Folks from all walks of life trek to this quirky truck stop and beer barn south of Downtown's Reunion Tower to snag tall boys, cheap gas and *muy authentico* tacos handcrafted in the tiny kitchen within; there's no indoor seating, but picnic benches on a patio and lawn makes for comfortable munching in fine weather; P.S. it's open 24/7.

Gloria's *Salvadoran/Tex-Mex* | 22 | 20 | 21 | $23 |

Greenville Avenue | 3715 Greenville Ave. (bet. Martel & Matalee Aves.) | Dallas | 214-874-0088
Lemmon Avenue | 4140 Lemmon Ave. (Douglas Ave.) | Dallas | 214-521-7576

(continued)

(continued)

Gloria's

Uptown | 3223 Lemmon Ave. (Cole Ave.) | Dallas | 214-303-1166

Oak Cliff | 600 W. Davis St. (bet. Bishop Ave. & Tyler St.) | Dallas | 214-948-3672

Addison | Village on the Pkwy. | 5100 Belt Line Rd. (Dallas N. Tollway) | 972-387-8442

Frisco | 8600 Gaylord Pkwy. (Preston Rd.) | 972-668-1555

Garland | Firewheel Town Ctr. | 360 Coneflower Dr. (Town Center Blvd.) | 972-526-5290

Rockwall | 2079 Summer Lee Dr. (Horizon Rd.) | 972-772-4088

Near West | Montgomery Plaza | 2600 W. Seventh St. (Carroll St.) | Ft. Worth | 817-332-8800

Arlington | Arlington Highlands | 3901 Arlington Highlands Blvd. (Curtis Mathes Ways) | 817-701-2981

www.gloriasrestaurants.com

Additional locations throughout the Dallas/Ft. Worth area

An "original" mix of Salvadoran and Tex-Mex mainstays make up the menu at these "lively" cantinas "worth visiting for the warm black-bean dip" and cut-rate mojitos alone; service is "fast", but be fore-warned they're "impossibly noisy" on weekends.

Grace ☒ *American*

25 | 26 | 25 | $60

Downtown Ft. Worth | 777 Main St. (7th St.) | Ft. Worth | 817-877-3388 | www.gracefortworth.com

A "contemporary, chic setting", "perfectly prepared" steaks and "imaginative" New American dishes, a wine list that's "worth a night's reading" and "stellar" service – these are the reasons this Downtown eatery is considered one of the "best places for a special evening in Ft. Worth"; though some wince at "expense-account" prices, most concur it's "well worth it."

Grape, The *American*

26 | 21 | 24 | $41

Greenville Avenue | 2808 Greenville Ave. (Vickery Blvd.) | Dallas | 214-828-1981 | www.thegraperestaurant.com

"More than just a neighborhood restaurant", this "cozy" Greenville Avenue bistro/wine bar has been pleasing guests "for over 30 years" with its "innovative" New American cuisine that "never disappoints"; though the mood is "romantic", tables are a tad "tight", making seats at Sunday brunch (starring their famous burger) hard to come by.

Green House Food

– | – | – | I

Truck *American/Vegetarian*

Location varies; see website | Dallas | no phone | www.greenhousetruck.com

Look for this health-conscious mobile unit in the environs of the Arts District in Dallas where it appeases a loyal lunch crowd with salads, sandwiches and rice bowls topped with miso flank steak, lemon chicken and the like plus vegetarian items too; customers find nearby perches on which to nosh or hot-foot it back to their desk having given up only about 10 bucks and 10 minutes for this grab and go spot.

	FOOD	DECOR	SERVICE	COST

Green Papaya *Vietnamese*

24 | 13 | 21 | $20

Oak Lawn | 3211 Oak Lawn Ave. (Cedar Springs Rd.) | Dallas |
214-521-4811 | www.greenpapayadallas.com

"Super-fresh" Vietnamese fare pleases the masses at this modern Oak Lawn entry offering fusion plates and fruity cocktails; it works equally well for a "quick, tasty lunch" or happy hour with "great people-watching."

Greenz *American*

▽ 23 | 13 | 16 | $14

Park Cities | Equinox Fitness Ctr. | 4023 Oak Lawn Ave. (Avondale Ave.) |
Dallas | 214-559-4102

Uptown | 2808 McKinney Ave. (Worthington St.) | Dallas |
214-720-7788 Ⓢ

Addison | 5290 Belt Line Rd. (Montfort Dr.) | 972-385-7721 Ⓢ
www.greenzsalads.com

This affordable American trio offers a menu of "tasty" salads and sandwiches that's "suitable for vegetarians, vegans and meat eaters" (with gluten-free options too); it's counter-service only in the fast-casual settings, although there are patios at the Addison and Uptown locations, while the Park Cities branch is housed in the swanky Highland Park Equinox.

Grimaldi's *Pizza*

26 | 20 | 21 | $21

West Village | West Vill. | 3636 McKinney Ave. (Lemmon Ave.) |
Dallas | 214-559-4611

🆕 **North Dallas** | The Shops at Park Ln. | 8060 Park Ln. (Service Rd.) |
Dallas | 214-987-1173

Allen | Watters Creek at Montgomery Farm | 836 Market St.
(Bethany Dr.) | 214-383-9703
www.grimaldispizzeria.com

"Fantastic" coal-fired pies "hot out of the oven" are the draw at these Texas spin-offs of the venerable New York City pizzeria that "compare favorably to the original"; with "kitschy" settings trimmed in old photos and memorabilia, it's just like "Brooklyn" only with shorter lines and "nicer" service.

Hacienda on Henderson *Mexican*

▽ 23 | 21 | 20 | $24

Knox-Henderson | 2326 N. Henderson Ave. (Capitol Ave.) | Dallas |
214-515-9990 | www.haciendaonhenderson.com

"Hipster hangout" in the Knox-Henderson area with infused tequilas and Mexican snacks like tamales and such; more of a bar than a restaurant, some say it's "strictly for the kids partying."

Hard Eight BBQ *BBQ*

25 | 19 | 17 | $20

Coppell | 688 Freeport Pkwy. (Bethel Rd.) | 972-471-5462 |
www.hardeightbbq.com

It's a "meatfest" of "true central Texas–style BBQ" at this Coppell pit stop just minutes from DFW Airport, where you "order your meat right off the smoker", then choose your sides and drinks in the "cafeteria-style" setup; the digs are "spotless", though you may "reek of smoke" afterwards, and while some report "long lines", most agree the "wonderful" 'cue is "well worth the wait"; P.S. it's priced by the pound, so "be careful not to over-order."

Hattie's *American*

27 | 25 | 24 | $39

Oak Cliff | 418 N. Bishop Ave. (8th St.) | Dallas | 214-942-7400 | www.hatties.net

"Charleston comes to Dallas" via this American "gem" in a "buzzy area" of Oak Cliff turning out "contemporary", "fancified" takes on Low Country fare ("superb" shrimp and grits, chicken and waffles "to die for"), plus a standout Sunday brunch, in a "modern, civilized" setting; "impeccable" service, a "casual atmosphere" and moderate prices all "soothe the soul."

Hibiscus *American*

26 | 23 | 24 | $56

Knox-Henderson | 2927 N. Henderson Ave. (Miller Ave.) | Dallas | 214-827-2927 | www.hibiscusdallas.com

"In-the-know locals" head to this "upscale" Knox-Henderson eatery for "sophisticated" New American fare, including "fresh" seafood, and a "high-end" wine list, all served in a "California woody" space with a "hip" vibe; though some question the "price-to-reward ratio", most agree it's nearly "top-notch in all respects."

Highland Park Soda Fountain *American*

▽ 20 | 14 | 26 | $10

Knox-Henderson | 3229 Knox St. (Travis St.) | Dallas | 214-521-2126

"A blast from the past", this "original" "soda fountain" from 1912 caters to generations of Knox-Henderson regulars with "real-deal" Americana like malts, grilled cheese and the like served up fast and "cheap" at the counter (with a side of "local gossip"); although most marvel at the "nostalgic" vibe, some sigh "it's not what it used to be."

Holy Grail Pub ● *European/Pub Food*

- | - | - | I

West Plano | 8240 Preston Rd. (bet. Rasor Blvd. & Town Square Dr.) | Plano | 972-377-6633 | www.holygrailpub.com

A "fantastic brewpub" in West Plano, this two-year-old European provides food "well above what you would expect" plus a stellar selection of whiskeys and suds (43 on tap, 170 total); the staff "makes an effort to know your name" and prices are easy on the wallet too; P.S. it also hosts a notable weekend brunch.

Hôtel St. Germain 🅱 Ⓜ *Continental/French*

▽ 26 | 27 | 26 | $111

Uptown | Hôtel St. Germain | 2516 Maple Ave. (bet. Cedar Springs Rd. & McKinney Ave.) | Dallas | 214-871-2516 | www.hotelstgermain.com

"For a special night out", fans recommend this "romantic getaway" located in a "beautiful" Uptown boutique hotel, offering seven-course prix fixe dinners of French-Continental cuisine and white-glove service in a candlelit setting; the "extraordinary, classic" fare "tends to be very rich", as are the prices; P.S. jacket and tie required.

Houston's *American*

24 | 22 | 24 | $37

Addison | 5318 Belt Line Rd. (Dallas N. Tollway) | 972-960-1752

Hillstone *American*

Preston Center | Plaza at Preston Ctr. | 8300 Preston Rd. (Northwest Hwy.) | Dallas | 214-691-8991
www.hillstone.com

See review in Houston Directory.

I Fratelli Ristorante & Wine Bar *Italian* | 23 | 20 | 23 | $23 |

Irving | 7701 N. MacArthur Blvd. (Lyndon B. Johnson Frwy.) |
972-501-9700 | www.ifratelli.net

This "fabulous" "family-run" "neighborhood hangout" in Irving offers
"old-school" Italiana – including "excellent" pizza – "that will fill you up
without draining your wallet"; P.S. there's a nice wine list too.

India Palace *Indian* | 22 | 19 | 21 | $26 |

Preston Forest | Preston Valley | 12817 Preston Rd.
(Lyndon B. Johnson Frwy.) | Dallas | 972-392-0190 |
www.indiapalacedallas.com

Loyal subjects seeking a "saag paneer fix" say this Preston Forest
Indian delivers with "authentic", "well-balanced" specialties, including a wide array of vegetarian options; the "comfortable" space
may be "limited" in the looks department, but the staff "treats you
like royalty" and the tab doesn't require a king's ransom either.

NEW Jack's Chowhound | – | – | – | I |
Food Truck ●🖫Ⓜ *American*

Location varies; see website | Dallas | 817-421-3270 |
www.jackschowhound.com

Jack Mooney's four-wheeled retro-themed kitchen proffers
Americana like pulled-pork grilled-cheese sandwiches, meatball
sliders, hot dogs and Cajun fries, along with old-time root beer
floats to wash it down; all comes served with a smile and cheap at
various Dallas locations.

Jasper's *American* | 24 | 24 | 23 | $43 |

West Plano | Shops at Legacy | 7161 Bishop Rd. (bet. Legacy Dr. &
Tennyson Pkwy.) | Plano | 469-229-9111 | www.jaspers-restaurant.com
See review in Austin and the Hill Country Directory.

Javier's *Mexican* | 24 | 24 | 24 | E |

Knox-Henderson | 4912 Cole Ave. (Harvard Ave.) | Dallas |
214-521-4211 | www.javiers.net

If you "see the Bentleys out front, you'll know you're at the right
place" quip aficionados of this Knox-Henderson hacienda where
"you're treated well" while enjoying "excellent, high-end" Mexican
fare in a "dark", "old-school" setting complete with a cigar room
"full of trophy mounts" that's "pure Texas"; it's "always crowded",
but "fun" people-watching (including occasional celebrity sight-
ings) and "fantastic" margaritas take the edge off the wait.

Jinbeh *Japanese* | 22 | 15 | 19 | $33 |

Frisco | Shafer Plaza | 2693 Preston Rd. (bet. Gaylord Pkwy. & Rte. 121) |
214-619-1000
Las Colinas | 301 E. Las Colinas Blvd. (O'Connor Blvd.) | Irving |
972-869-4011
Lewisville | 2440 S. Stemmons Frwy. (bet. Hebron Pkwy. & Rte. 121) |
214-488-2224
www.jinbeh.com

"Kids love" this lively Japanese chainlet centered around "watching
your own personal chef at the hibachi table"; prices are "decent",

and it's "fun for special occasions", but critics call the food "nothing special", claiming "there are better places for sushi."

Joe T. Garcia's ⊅ *Tex-Mex*   20 | 23 | 21 | $24

North Side | 2201 N. Commerce St. (22nd St.) | Ft. Worth | 817-626-4356 | www.joets.com

Devotees dub this "iconic" Ft. Worth "institution" on the North Side the "Holy Grail of Tex-Mex", offering a "solidly good", "no-surprises" menu in the "huge" dining room or on the "massive", "beautiful" patio and poolside garden; some critics find the fare "routine" and contend its appeal is strictly the "scene that it offers" and the "fab" margaritas; P.S. cash only.

Kenichi *Pan-Asian*   21 | 23 | 21 | $52

Victory Park | 2400 Victory Park Ln. (Museum Way) | Dallas | 214-871-8883 | www.kenichirestaurants.com

See review in Austin and the Hill Country Directory.

Kenny's Burger Joint *Burgers*   ▽ 22 | 18 | 21 | $17

Frisco | Stonebriar Commons Shopping Ctr. | 1377 Legacy Dr. (Town & Country Blvd.) | 214-618-8001 | www.kennysburgerjoint.com

"Fresh, juicy and cooked-to-perfection" "gourmet" burgers are the main attraction at this Frisco offshoot of Kenny's Wood Fired Grill also putting out french fries full of "crispy goodness"; it's not fancy, but a "friendly" vibe, a full bar and cheap tabs compensate.

Kenny's Wood Fired Grill ❶ *American*   26 | 21 | 25 | $39

Addison | Addison Walk Shopping Ctr. | 5000 Belt Line Rd. (Dallas N. Tollway) | 972-392-9663 | www.kennyswoodfiredgrill.com

Loyalists "love" this "clubby" "neighborhood" grill in Addison with "excellent" American fare, "generous cocktails" and an "active bar scene" all overseen by an "accommodating" crew; the decor has the "feel of a good steakhouse", and though acoustics are a little "loud", it's "enjoyable" nonetheless.

🄩 Kincaid's Hamburgers *Burgers*   25 | 16 | 19 | $12

Southwest | 4825 Overton Ridge Blvd. (Hulen St.) | Ft. Worth | 817-370-6400

West | 4901 Camp Bowie Blvd. (Eldridge St.) | Ft. Worth | 817-732-2881

Arlington | 3900 Arlington Highlands Blvd. (Merchants Row Dr.) | 817-466-4211

Alliance | 3124 Texas Sage Trail (Heritage Trace Pkwy.) | Ft. Worth | 817-750-3200

Southlake | 100 N. Kimball Ave. (Southlake Blvd.) | 817-416-2573

www.kincaidshamburgers.com

For burger buffs it "doesn't get any better" than the "juicy", "hand-made" patties at this circa-1946 "institution" off Camp Bowie and its spin-offs, which deliver the Dallas/Ft. Worth area's Best Bang for the Buck; many surveyors swear that the "original is still the best", housed in an "old grocery store" with "decor from days past", where you serve yourself and sit at communal picnic tables.

	FOOD	DECOR	SERVICE	COST

Kirby's Steakhouse *Steak*

24 | 22 | 23 | $52

Southlake | 3305 E. Hwy. 114 (Southlake Blvd.) | 817-410-2221 | www.kirbyssteakhouse.com

Woodfire Kirby's *Steak*
(fka Kirby's Greenville Avenue)

Greenville Avenue | 3525 Greenville Ave. (McCommas Blvd.) | Dallas | 214-821-2122 | www.woodfirekirbys.com

Enjoy "high-quality steaks", "great wines", stiff drinks and "excellent" service from a dedicated staff at this classic chophouse micro-chain born in Dallas in 1954; handsome woody decor gives it the feel of an old supper club, especially at the branches with piano on weekends.

NEW Komali *Mexican*

24 | 26 | 24 | $40

Uptown | 4152 Cole Ave. (Fitzhugh Ave.) | Dallas | 214-252-0200 | www.komalirestaurant.com

A "bright, cheery", "modern" space with a long bar and a mosaic fireplace is the backdrop for chef Abraham Salum's "exciting" "interior Mexican" cuisine at this Uptown sibling (and next-door neighbor) of Salum; "fabulous" margs and a "good selection of mezcals" help fuel a lively scene that "can redefine 'loud' on weekend nights."

Kuby's Sausage House *German*

22 | 14 | 19 | $19

Park Cities | Snider Plaza | 6601 Snider Plaza (Daniel Ave.) | Dallas | 214-363-2231 | www.kubys.com

"Genuine" German sausage, schnitzel and other *essen* are the hallmarks of this affordable Park Cities stalwart that's adjacent to a "super" meat market/deli, offering breakfast, brunch and lunch in an old-world, beer-hall setting, where the staff goes "above and beyond" to please; it also serves dinner Fridays and Saturdays, complete with live accordion music.

La Calle Doce *Mexican*

∇ 25 | 21 | 23 | $22

Lakewood | 1925 Skillman St. (La Vista Dr.) | Dallas | 214-824-9900
Oak Cliff | 415 W. 12th St. (Bishop Ave.) | Dallas | 214-941-4304
www.lacalledoce-dallas.com

"What Mexican food is supposed to be" is how fans describe this family-owned duo specializing in Veracruz-style cuisine featuring "fresh, spicy" seafood as well as "classic" Tex-Mex, warmly served in an old house in Oak Cliff and a recently remodeled strip-mall space in Lakewood; affordable prices, outdoor patios and strolling musicians on weekend nights add to the charm.

La Duni Latin Cafe *Pan-Latin*

24 | 21 | 21 | $29

Knox-Henderson | 4620 McKinney Ave. (Knox St.) | Dallas | 214-520-7300

La Duni Latin Kitchen *Pan-Latin*

Oak Lawn | 4264 Oak Lawn Ave. (Herschel Ave.) | Dallas | 214-520-6888

La Duni Latin Kitchen & Coffee Studio *Pan-Latin*

NorthPark | NorthPark Ctr. | 8687 N. Central Expwy. (bet. Northwest Hwy. & Parkview Pl.) | Dallas | 214-987-2260
www.laduni.com

The "desserts are from another world" and the "South American comfort food" is "always excellent" at these contemporary Pan-

Latin bistros from husband and wife Espartaco and Dunia Borga; the settings are "casual" with a "cool", "festive" vibe, but some gripe about "spotty" service and a no-reservations policy that can mean "excruciatingly long waits."

La Familia ☒ *Mexican* ▽ 25 | 21 | 26 | $22

Near West | 841 Foch St. (7th St.) | Ft. Worth | 817-870-2002 | www.lafamilia-fw.com

Loyal fans feel like they're "going home to mama" at this "home-grown, family-owned" Mexican restaurant, a Ft. Worth "must" for "fresh, top-quality" cooking and "friendly" service in "comfortable", if sometimes "noisy", environs; most agree you "can't beat it" for the price.

Lambert's *Steak* ▽ 24 | 20 | 21 | $40

Near West | 2731 White Settlement Rd. (Foch St.) | Ft. Worth | 817-882-1161 | www.lambertsfortworth.com

A spin-off of Lou Lambert's Austin original, this Near West Ft. Worth steakhouse trades in "delicious" fare like oak-grilled, all-natural meats and "Southwestern-style" entrees; an "unobtrusive" staff and gussied-up rustic decor create an ambiance that's upmarket without feeling "overdone or fussy."

L'Ancestral ☒ *French* ▽ 25 | 17 | 25 | $45

Knox-Henderson | Travis Walk | 4514 Travis St. (Knox St.) | Dallas | 214-528-1081 | www.restauranteur.com/lancestral

"Even the portraits are of people long past" at this Knox-Henderson veteran that attracts a largely patrician following with "consistently fine", "authentic country French" cuisine at "decent prices", expertly delivered by a "longtime" staff; another plus: "you can always get a table" in the "quiet", "pleasant" room.

Lanny's Alta Cocina Mexicana ☒ Ⓜ *Eclectic* 27 | 23 | 25 | $52

Cultural District | 3405 W. Seventh St. (Boland St.) | Ft. Worth | 817-850-9996 | www.lannyskitchen.com

"A special-occasion place" that's "matured perfectly in sync with its chef", this upscale Eclectic in the Cultural District "shines" with an "excellent" "creative" menu of Mexican-inspired cuisine from chef-owner Lanny Lancarte (of the Joe T. Garcia's dynasty), backed by a "terrific selection of wines and beers"; the mood is "romantic" in the contemporary space, but some balk at the prices unless they can "dine on someone else's tab."

Lavendou ☒ *French* 24 | 24 | 24 | $50

North Dallas | 19009 Preston Rd. (bet. Frankford Rd. & President George Bush Tpke.) | Dallas | 972-248-1911 | www.lavendou.com

Gallic groupies skip "the hassle of flying to France" by dropping into Pascal Cayet's "inviting" North Dallas French offering "perfectly prepared" Provençal specialties and "warm" service in a "charming" brick-accented space; although the "prices are a little steep", it "always pleases."

	FOOD	DECOR	SERVICE	COST

Lawry's The Prime Rib *Steak*   26 | 24 | 27 | $55

North Dallas | 14655 Dallas Pkwy. (Spring Valley Rd.) | Dallas | 972-503-6688 | www.lawrysonline.com

"The place to go for a big hunk of beef and a dose of nostalgia", this North Dallas steakhouse chain link has stood as the "longtime standard" for prime rib carved tableside by "well-trained", toque-wearing servers in a "formal" setting (with a "less-stuffy" bar area); it's "pricey and worth it" for special occasions and expense-account dining.

Lefty's Lobster Chowder House *Seafood*   ▽ 22 | 16 | 26 | $33

Addison | 4021 Belt Line Rd. (Runyon Rd.) | 972-774-9518 | www.leftyslobster.com

"It doesn't look like much", but fans aren't fooled by the "kitschy" New England atmosphere at this "simple, charming" Addison seafooder where "everything is very good" and the prices are reasonable; you also get a "warm welcome" from the family that runs the place.

Lili's Bistro 🗷 *Eclectic*   ▽ 26 | 21 | 21 | $31

South Side | 1310 W. Magnolia Ave. (bet. Lake St. & 6th Ave.) | Ft. Worth | 817-877-0700 | www.lilisbistro.com

"Please don't give away the secret" of this South Side Eclectic beg Ft. Worthians, who want the moderately priced, "flavorful" casual lunch fare and "imaginative" Mediterranean-influenced dinners to themselves; "friendly service" is another plus, and the addition of a "new piano and wine bar makes it easier to get seated" in the "cozy" space.

Local 🗷🅜 *American*   26 | 21 | 24 | $62

Deep Ellum | 2936 Elm St. (Hall St.) | Dallas | 214-752-7500 | www.localdallas.com

There's a real "SoHo feel" at chef Tracy Miller's "cool" "little secret" in the old Boyd Hotel in Deep Ellum done up in a "groovy", "minimalist" style with Eames furnishings; "welcoming service" is an added perk, but admirers insist it's really the "fabulous", if "expensive", market-driven New American menu prepared "with care and attention to every detail" that makes it a "memorable" experience.

🆕 Lockhart Smokehouse *BBQ*   ▽ 21 | 13 | 15 | $18

Oak Cliff | 400 W. Davis St. (Bishop Ave.) | Dallas | 214-944-5521 | www.lockhartsmokehouse.com

Founded by kin of the legendary Kreuz Market's pitmaster, this hip new Oak Cliff smokehouse in the historic Spoetzl Brewery building serves up signature sausages (from Kreuz) plus other "over-the-top" BBQ straight out of the smoker, sliced to order and served from the counter on butcher paper sans sauce or fork; early fans are "confident" it will "be just as good" as the original.

Lonesome Dove Western
Bistro 🗷 *Southwestern*   27 | 24 | 26 | $55

Stockyards | 2406 N. Main St. (24th St.) | Ft. Worth | 817-740-8810 | www.lonesomedovebistro.com

Celeb chef Tim Love's "signature cowboy cuisine" "shines" in a "Western-themed" setting "with a touch of elegance" at his flagship in the Ft. Worth Stockyards, where "innovative" takes on "game, pork and anything else you'd find on a ranch" are served by an "outstanding" staff amid a "cool", if "loud" scene; "extremely reasonable" lunch specials offset otherwise "high-end" prices.

Love Shack *Burgers*   23 | 16 | 15 | $15

Near West | So7 | 817 Matisse (7th St.) | Ft. Worth | 817-348-9655
Stockyards | 110 E. Exchange Ave. (Main St.) | Ft. Worth | 817-740-8812 ⊘
www.shakeyourloveshack.com

There's almost "no service or decor", just "incredible gourmet" burgers and "excellent" shakes from celeb chef Tim Love's Lonesome Dove team, turned out counter-side in the Stockyards, where open-air seating and live music on weekends make it a "fun", if "noisy", place to sit outside in nice weather; the Near West outpost offers some indoor space plus a full American menu padded out with cocktails and apps.

Ⓩ NEW Lucia Ⓢ Ⓜ *Italian*   29 | 21 | 25 | $58

Oak Cliff | 408 W. Eighth St. (Bishop Ave.) | Dallas | 214-948-4998 | www.luciadallas.com

"It takes weeks to get in" to chef David Uygur's tiny Oak Cliff Italian, but his "awesomely creative" cuisine that's "executed to perfection" is "worth the effort"; led by the chef's wife and co-owner, Jennifer, the front-of-house staff "treats you like beloved family" in the rustic 36-seat space, which is housed in a historic building dating back to the '20s.

Lucky's Cafe *American*   ▽ 21 | 18 | 22 | $16

Oak Lawn | 3531 Oak Lawn Ave. (Lemmon Ave.) | Dallas | 214-522-3500 | www.luckysdallas.com

"After too long a night", many head to this retro diner in Oak Lawn serving "generous" portions of American "comfort food", including standout breakfasts and weekend brunches, delivered by a "friendly", "colorful" staff in black-and-chrome retro surroundings; affordable prices make it an "easy" choice.

Madras Pavilion *Indian*   20 | 15 | 18 | $21

Richardson | Dalrich Shopping Ctr. | 101 S. Coit Rd. (Belt Line Rd.) | 972-671-3672
See review in Houston Directory.

Maguire's *American*   23 | 21 | 24 | $38

North Dallas | 17552 Dallas Pkwy. (Trinity Mills Rd.) | Dallas | 972-818-0068 | www.maguiresdallas.com

"Always dependable", this North Dallas American is a "habit" "locals call home" thanks to "generous" portions of "creative" steakhouse-style fare, an "owner who cares" about his customers and a "pleasant", "unpretentious" bistro ambiance; with a bar scene and "fair prices", it's no wonder it's a "neighborhood fave."

Main Street Bistro & Bakery *French*   21 | 16 | 18 | $22

Richardson | Shire | 3600 Shire Blvd. (Jupiter Rd.) | 972-578-0294

(continued)

Main Street Bistro & Bakery

West Plano | Shops at Legacy | 7200 Bishop Rd. (Legacy Dr.) | Plano | 972-309-0404
Grapevine | 316 S. Main St. (Northwest Hwy.) | 817-424-4333
www.themainbakery.com

Sweet-toothed surveyors "love" this trio of "little French bakeries" where pastries, crêpes, "flaky croissants" and galettes get top billing, and salads, sandwiches and other French standards (some "hit-or-miss") round out the offerings; all thrive in digs so "cute" "you feel like you're at a bistro in Paris" with a favorable exchange rate.

Malai *Thai/Vietnamese*

| – | – | – | M |

West Village | West Vill. | 3699 McKinney Ave. (Blackburn St.) | Dallas | 214-599-7857 | www.malaikitchen.com

Young and beautiful folks are drawn to this midrange West Village bistro whose Thai–Vietnamese fusion fare (rife with small-plate and vegetarian options) is complemented by cocktails by mixologist Jason Kosmas; the dark and trendy, tropical-feeling interior matches the menu, while a high-visibility patio bolsters the scene.

Mama's Daughters' Diner *Diner*

| 19 | 7 | 19 | $14 |

Market Center | 2014 Irving Blvd. (Market Center Blvd.) | Dallas | 214-742-8646
Love Field | 2610 Royal Ln. (Harry Hines Blvd.) | Dallas | 972-241-8646 ⑤
NEW **West Plano** | 6509 W. Park Blvd. (bet. Midway Rd. & Plano Pkwy.) | Plano | 972-473-8877
Irving | 2412 W. Shady Grove Rd. (Story Rd.) | 972-790-2778
Lewisville | 1288 W. Main St. (Old Orchard Ln.) | 972-353-5955 ⑤
www.mamasdaughtersdiner.com

"You'll think you're in your mama's kitchen" indulging in the "down-home" Southern-style cooking at this family-owned mini-chain of "truck stop cafes with saucy waitresses in abundance" scattered throughout the Metroplex; the Market Center flagship's Food scores rate well-ahead of its sibs', but the staff is "friendly" and the price is right throughout; P.S. limited evening and weekend hours at some locations.

Mango Thai *Thai*

| ▽ 24 | 20 | 20 | $19 |

Park Cities | 4448 E. Lovers Ln. (Dallas N. Tollway) | Dallas | 214-265-9996
West Plano | Berkley Sq. | 4701 W. Park Blvd. (Ohio Dr.) | Plano | 972-599-0289
www.mangothaicuisine.com

For "novel modern Thai" cooking, fans tout these "moderately priced" twins in Park Cities and Plano plying "well-prepared" "variations on old classics"; "funky", "nontraditional" interiors make up for their strip-center locations; they're popular for take-out too.

☑ Mansion, The *American*

| 26 | 28 | 27 | $89 |

Uptown | Rosewood Mansion on Turtle Creek | 2821 Turtle Creek Blvd. (Gillespie St.) | Dallas | 214-559-2100 | www.mansiononturtlecreek.com

"Divine as it's always been", this Uptown icon showcases chef Bruno Davaillon's "impeccable" French-influenced New American cuisine, served by a staff that "couldn't be kinder" in "elegant" environs in a historic boutique luxury hotel; while a few feel "it's not what it used to be", most "highly recommend" it when you want to "pamper yourself and a loved one", though all agree "it helps if the oil wells are still producing when the check arrives."

Maple & Motor *Burgers*

25 | 14 | 19 | $14

Love Field | 4810 Maple Ave. (Denton Dr.) | Dallas | 214-522-4400 | www.mapleandmotor.com

"Be ready for a line" because "the word is out" about what fans are calling the "coolest burger joint around", this budget burgertory in a renovated Love Field gas station slinging "greasy, cheesy, amazing burgers", "must-try" onion rings and "tater tots that make you think you're back in elementary school"; it's counter service only, and even though it's "mega-busy at lunchtime", all agree the wait is "worth it."

NEW Marquee Grill & Bar ❶ *American*

26 | 25 | 24 | $53

Highland Park Village | Highland Park Vill. | 33 Highland Park Vill. (Douglas Ave.) | Dallas | 214-522-6035 | www.marqueegrill.com

Top Chef alum Tre Wilcox stars in the kitchen and mixologist Jason Kosmas crafts cocktails in the lounge at this "hip, happening" "place to be seen", located adjacent to the Highland Park Village Theatre and presenting "excellent", "innovative" New Americana in a glam 1930s Hollywood setting; "attentive service" and "people-watching" galore, especially the "scene at the bar", add to the "delight."

Meddlesome Moth *American*

22 | 24 | 21 | $32

Market Center | 1621 Oak Lawn Ave. (Hi Line Dr.) | Dallas | 214-628-7900 | www.mothinthe.net

A "zymurgist's dream", this "hip" Design District gastropub features an "incredible" beer selection (40 draft, 100 bottles), plus weekly tastings of rare brews, and a "fun" New American menu that offers some "fantastic pairings" with a cold one; a stained-glass triptych of Chuck Berry, Elvis and Jerry Lee Lewis dominates the dark-wood space, where the staff is "good at helping you make your selection."

☑ Mercury, The ⓈⒷ *American*

28 | 24 | 25 | $62

Preston Forest | Preston Forest Vill. | 11909 Preston Rd. (Forest Ln.) | Dallas | 972-960-7774 | www.themercurydallas.com

Chef Chris Ward "blends tastes like a harmonious work of art" in his "exceptional" French- and Mediterranean-influenced New American cuisine, served "without attitude" by an "attentive" staff at this up-scale sophisticate in Preston Forest; "don't be fooled by the strip-mall location", for it's "beautiful inside", with a "cool, New Yorkish" ambiance and "lively" lounge scene, making it a "must visit" for many, including former President George W. Bush.

NEW Mesa *Mexican*

- | - | - | M

Oak Cliff | 118 W. Jefferson Blvd. (Zang Blvd.) | Dallas | 214-941-4246 | www.mesadallas.com

Mexican-style seafood stars at this Oak Cliff charmer where husband-and-wife team Raul and Olga Reyes turn out authentic coastal dishes from their native Veracruz and family staffers dote on

| | FOOD | DECOR | SERVICE | COST |

patrons in a simple space with reclaimed wood crafted by Raul himself; it owes its loyal following thanks in part to its moderate bills.

NEW Meso Maya *Mexican*

| - | - | - | M |

Preston Forest | 11909 Preston Rd. (Forest Ln.) | Dallas | 469-726-4390 |
www.mesomaya.com

A modern, resortlike setting belies the Preston Forest shopping center location of this interior Mexican (read: not Tex-Mex) eatery; it's
popular with hipsters who plant themselves on cushy seats under
arty lighting to partake of moderately priced Oaxaca- and Puebla-
inspired fare chased with top-shelf margaritas.

Mia's *Tex-Mex*

| 23 | 13 | 19 | $22 |

Lemmon Avenue | 4322 Lemmon Ave. (Wycliff Ave.) | Dallas |
214-526-1020 | www.miastexmex.com

"Two words: brisket tacos" sum up much of the appeal of this Lemmon
Avenue *cocina*, a "longtime favorite" for "wonderful", "no-fuss" Tex-
Mex, as evidenced by the perpetual "lines" out front; no, there's "not
much decor" or "elbow room" either, but bargain prices compensate.

Mi Cocina *Tex-Mex*

| 21 | 19 | 20 | $25 |

Lake Highlands | 7201 Skillman St. (Walnut Hill Ln.) | Dallas |
214-503-6426
Park Cities | Highland Park Vill. | 77 Highland Park Vill. (Douglas Ave.) |
Dallas | 214-521-6426
Preston Forest | Preston Forest Vill. | 11661 Preston Rd. (bet. Forest Ln. &
Preston Haven Dr.) | Dallas | 214-265-7704
West Village | West Vill. | 3699 McKinney Ave. (bet. Blackburn St. &
Lemmon Ave.) | Dallas | 469-533-5663
North Dallas | 18352 N. Dallas Pkwy. (Frankford Rd.) | Dallas |
972-250-6426
West Plano | Lakeside Mkt. | 4001 Preston Rd. (Lorimar Dr.) | Plano |
469-467-8655
West Plano | Shops at Legacy | 5760 Legacy Dr. (Bishop Rd.) | Plano |
972-473-8745
Las Colinas | 7750 N. MacArthur Blvd. (I-635) | Irving | 469-621-0452
Sundance Square | Sundance Sq. | 509 Main St. (bet. 4th & 5th Sts.) |
Ft. Worth | 817-877-3600
Southlake | Southlake Town Sq. | 1276 Main St. (Carroll Ave.) |
817-410-6426
www.mcrowd.com
Additional locations throughout the Dallas/Ft. Worth area

It's "always a scene" at these "smartly designed" Tex-Mex cantinas
favored by the "young and beautiful" for "well-prepared" "lighter alternatives" and "killer" Mambo Taxi 'ritas ("after two you'll want to
mambo and need a taxi"); though a few critics find them "overrated"
and "overpriced" for what they are with "spotty" service, defenders
insist "these guys know how to run a restaurant."

Mi Piaci Ristorante *Italian*

| ▽ 26 | 24 | 23 | $54 |

Addison | 14854 Montfort Dr. (bet. Belt Line Rd. & Verde Valley Ln.) |
972-934-8424 | www.mipiaci-dallas.com

Popular among "those who understand Italian food", this upscale
Addison destination offers "excellent" Northern Italian cuisine in a

"sophisticated", modern setting with an inviting bar and a soothing view of a pond; it's run by "nice people", and while it's pricey, most agree you "can't go wrong" here.

Morton's The Steakhouse *Steak*

26 | 24 | 25 | $67

Uptown | 2222 McKinney Ave. (bet. McKinney Ave. & N. Pearl St.) | Dallas | 214-741-2277 | www.mortons.com
See review in Houston Directory.

🆕 Nammi Truck *Vietnamese*

- | - | - | I

Location varies; see website | Dallas | 972-252-2052 | www.nammitruck.com

'Cruisin' Vietnamese fusion' is the tagline of this colorful food truck doling out banh mi, rice bowls and tacos along with basil-mint lemonade and iced coffee; prices on par with local ethnic dives ensure lines of hungry snackers wherever in Dallas and the surrounding suburbs it roams.

🇿 Nana *American*

27 | 27 | 27 | $74

Market Center | Hilton Anatole Hotel | 2201 Stemmons Frwy., 27th fl. (Market Center Blvd.) | Dallas | 214-761-7470 | www.nanarestaurant.com
"Go for the view, but stay for the food" at this New American destination on the 27th floor of the Market Center's Hilton Anatole Hotel, showcasing chef Anthony Bombaci's "amazing", "creative" cuisine; "superb, friendly" service and a "beautiful" interior graced with Asian art from the Crow Collection round out the "top-dollar" experience.

Neighborhood Services ☒ *American*

25 | 22 | 23 | $41

West Lovers Lane | 5027 W. Lovers Ln. (Inwood Rd.) | Dallas | 214-350-5027

Neighborhood Services Bar & Grill ☒ *American*
Preston Royal | 10720 Preston Rd. (Royal Ln.) | Dallas | 214-368-1101

Neighborhood Services Tavern ☒ *American*
Knox-Henderson | 2405 N. Henderson Ave. (Capital Ave.) | Dallas | 214-827-2405
www.neighborhoodservicesdallas.com

"Haute blue-plate specials" headline chef Nick Badovinus' "ingredient-driven" New American menu delivering "creative twists on home-style food" at these "hip" "favorites"; the servers are "impressive", and while some critics cite "extremely long waits" (due to a no-reservations policy), others take the opportunity for a little "social networking" at the "trendy bar", or "call ahead and get your name on the list"; P.S. the Tavern on Henderson is a "scaled down, more casual" version of the original.

Nick & Sam's *Seafood/Steak*

27 | 25 | 25 | $75

Uptown | 3008 Maple Ave. (bet. Carlisle & Wolf Sts.) | Dallas | 214-871-7444 | www.nick-sams.com
Imagine, a "New York steakhouse in the middle of Texas" exclaim fans of this Uptown meatery, the "place to be seen" over "excellent" prime beef and seafood in "dark", "attractive" digs highlighted by a grand piano player in the kitchen; whether you're seated in the "gor-

geous" dining room or "less formal, action-packed bar", you'll find "eye candy", "top-notch" service" and "Texas-size tabs."

Nick & Sam's Grill *American*

25 | 23 | 22 | $36

Uptown | 2816 Fairmount St. (Cedar Springs Rd.) | Dallas | 214-303-1880 | www.nick-samsgrill.com

This contemporary Uptown offshoot of the vaunted steakhouse delivers a more afforable American menu that works for a "quick lunch" or casual "first-date" dinner; it's "always buzzing" and there's "lots to watch" at the bar and on the patio, though some feel it "falls short" compared to its namesake.

Nicola's *Italian*

22 | 22 | 20 | $45

West Plano | Shops at Legacy | 5800 Legacy Dr. (Bishop Rd.) | Plano | 972-608-4455 | www.nicolaslegacy.com

Ristorante Nicola *Italian*

Preston Center | 8111 Preston Rd. (Weldon Howell Pkwy.) | Dallas | 214-379-1111 | www.nicoladallas.com

"Loyal patrons" fill the "attractive" bar and dome-topped dining room at this slightly "upscale" Northern Italian in West Plano (with a Preston Center offshoot) serving "well-executed" staples; the atmosphere is refreshingly "unstuffy", and since it's inside the tony Shops at Legacy complex, it's "convenient to the Angelika" for a movie.

Nobu Dallas *Japanese*

26 | 25 | 24 | $75

Uptown | Rosewood Crescent Hotel | 400 Crescent Ct. (bet. Cedar Springs Rd. & Maple Ave.) | Dallas | 214-252-7000 | www.noburestaurants.com

"Far beyond typical sushi or Japanese", Nobu Matsuhisa's "phenomenal" fusion of Japanese and Peruvian cuisine is showcased at this Dallas outpost of his "deservedly famous" chain, located within the Hotel Crescent complex Uptown; "superb" service and a "fantastic", serene ambiance help ease some of the "sticker shock when the bill arrives."

Nonna 🗷 *Italian*

25 | 19 | 23 | $53

Lemmon Avenue | 4115 Lomo Alto Dr. (bet. Bowser & Lemmon Aves.) | Dallas | 214-521-1800 | www.nonnadallas.com

Chef Julian Barsotti's "sophisticated", "upscale" Northern Italian cuisine "reigns supreme" at this cozy "bit of heaven" off Lemmon Avenue; a wood-burning oven highlights the "small" contemporary space, and while some grouse about "terrible acoustics", many others insist "it's worth the wait", which may be unavoidable "even with reservations."

Nonna Tata 🗷Ⓜ⇗ *Italian*

27 | 15 | 20 | $27

Hospital District | 1400 W. Magnolia Ave. (6th Ave.) | Ft. Worth | 817-332-0250

"Lines form quickly" at this BYO Italian "gem" in the Hospital District, where chef-owner Donatella Trotti creates "incredible" "Italian home cooking, done just right" at modest prices; while the "tiny", "cafe"-style setting is "not too comfortable" "unless you're able to eat outside" (some even advise "bringing your own chair"), the "authentic" experience is a "bucket-list" item for many; P.S. cash only.

	FOOD	DECOR	SERVICE	COST

Nosh Euro Bistro *American*
24 | **19** | **20** | **$49**

Oak Lawn | 4216 Oak Lawn Ave. (Wycliff Ave.) | Dallas | 214-528-9400 ☒
NEW **West Plano** | 4701 W. Park Blvd. (Ohio Dr.) | Plano | 972-612-3200
www.nosheurobistro.com

Its roots may be in classic Gallic cuisine, but the attitude is anything but stuffy at prolific chef-restaurateur Avner Samuel's "lively" enclave in Oak Lawn; the crowd is chock-a-block with business types and luncheonistas tucking into "creative" French-influenced riffs on New American fare – including plenty of noshes from pâté to escargot fritters – that's served at a "brisk" pace and priced well for the times; P.S. the Plano offshoot is new and unrated.

Oceanaire Seafood Room *Seafood*
23 | **23** | **23** | **$59**

Galleria | Westin Galleria Hotel | 13340 N. Dallas Pkwy.
(Lyndon B. Johnson Frwy.) | Dallas | 972-759-2277 |
www.theoceanaire.com
See review in Houston Directory.

Ocean Prime *Seafood/Steak*
21 | **24** | **21** | **$63**

Uptown | 2101 Cedar Springs Rd. (Moody St.) | Dallas | 214-965-0440 |
www.oceanprimedallas.com

This "upscale" Uptown surf 'n' turf specialist near the Crescent Hotel dazzles with a "quieter", "refined" dining space, "stunning outdoor bar" and a lounge with live music and "people-watching"; "attentive" service is another plus, but to some, the "incredible" digs and "expense-account" tabs make the fare seem relatively "average."

NEW Oddfellows *American/Coffeehouse*
– | **–** | **–** | **M**

Oak Cliff | 316 W. Seventh St. (Madison Ave.) | Dallas | 214-944-5958 |
www.oddfellowsdallas.com

"Comfort-food classics with a twist" and premium coffees are the focus of this sophisticated Oak Cliff diner serving an "excellent" menu of Americana featuring locally sourced ingredients from breakfast to dinner, plus cocktails and a rotating selection of beers; it's set in a pleasant vintage storefront, which "gets packed on weekends, so be prepared to wait."

Off the Bone Barbeque *BBQ*
– | **–** | **–** | **I**

Downtown Dallas | 1734 S. Lamar St. (bet. Alexander Ave. & McKee St.) |
Dallas | 214-565-9551 | www.offthebonebarbeque.com

All walks of Dallasites swing by this converted gas station Downtown for gourmet riffs on 'cue like pecan-smoked ribs and brisket dished out with gussied-up sides; the staff is friendly and tabs are a song, although given the modest digs, many opt for takeout.

Olenjack's Grille *American*
25 | **18** | **23** | **$36**

Arlington | Lincoln Sq. | 770 E. Road to Six Flags (Collins St.) |
817-226-2600 | www.olenjacksgrille.com

Fans cheer the "affordable", "creative and well-prepared" American cuisine at this Arlington "surprise", calling staples like babyback ribs and shrimp and grits "as good as it gets"; proximity to Cowboys Stadium and the ballpark guarantees a crowd on game day when the tailgate party kicks into high gear, while "hands-on" chef-owner

Brian Olenjack maintains the kind of "quality and service you'd expect in a much higher-end restaurant."

Olivella's *Pizza* ▽ 24 | 17 | 21 | $20

Park Cities | 3406 McFarlin Blvd. (Hillcrest Rd.) | Dallas | 214-528-7070 | www.olivellas.com

Piezani proclaim "heaven is a rectangular pizza" at this "wonderful hole-in-the-wall" in Park Cities near SMU plying "crispy crust" Neapolitan pies; there are "not many tables" in the "small" space with an old-world motif, but there's always takeout.

Palm, The *Steak* 25 | 20 | 24 | $64

West End | 701 Ross Ave. (Market St.) | Dallas | 214-698-0470 | www.thepalm.com

See review in San Antonio Directory.

Pappadeaux *Cajun/Seafood* 23 | 20 | 21 | $32

Oak Lawn | 3520 Oak Lawn Ave. (Lemmon Ave.) | Dallas | 214-521-4700
Duncanville | 800 E. Hwy. 67 (Cockrell Hill Rd.) | 972-572-0580
North Dallas | 10428 Lombardy Ln. (Northwest Hwy.) | Dallas | 214-358-1912
North Dallas | 18349 N. Dallas Pkwy. (Frankford Rd.) | Dallas | 972-447-9616
Richardson | 725 S. Central Expwy. (bet. Belt Line & Spring Valley Rds.) | 972-235-1181
Forest Park | 2708 West Frwy. (Parkview Dr.) | Ft. Worth | 817-877-8843
Arlington | 1304 Copeland Rd. (bet. Collins St. & Nolan Ryan Expwy.) | 817-543-0545
Bedford | 2121 Airport Frwy. (Central Dr.) | 817-571-4696
www.pappadeaux.com

See review in Houston Directory.

Pappas Bar-B-Q *BBQ* 21 | 16 | 19 | $17

Love Field | 2231 W. Northwest Hwy. (Technology Blvd.) | Dallas | 214-956-9038 | www.pappas.com

See review in Houston Directory.

☒ Pappas Bros. Steakhouse ☒ *Steak* 28 | 25 | 27 | $71

Love Field | 10477 Lombardy Ln. (Stemmons Frwy.) | Dallas | 214-366-2000 | www.pappasbros.com

See review in Houston Directory.

Pappas Burgers *Burgers* 24 | 17 | 18 | $19

Sundance Square | 2700 West Frwy. (Kirby Dr.) | Ft. Worth | 817-870-9736 | www.pappasburger.com

See review in Houston Directory.

Parigi *American* 25 | 23 | 24 | $44

Oak Lawn | 3311 Oak Lawn Ave. (Hall St.) | Dallas | 214-521-0295 | www.parigidallas.com

Despite the "unpretentious" vibe at this longtime "neighborhood bistro" in Oak Lawn, regulars report a "rather sophisticated dining experience" replete with "exciting" New American cuisine with French and Italian accents; housed in a "size-seven shoebox", it has the "heart of a size-18 Dallas Mavericks player", thanks to a dedicated chef/co-owner and "friendly" staff.

Paris Coffee Shop ⓢ *Coffeeshop* ▽ 23 | 14 | 24 | $13

Hospital District | 704 W. Magnolia Ave. (Hemphill St.) | Ft. Worth | 817-335-2041 | www.pariscoffeeshop.net

Ft. Worth's "legendary" coffee shop in the Hospital District dishes up affordable, "old-fashioned" American "home cooking", including "well-known" pies that "live up to their reputation", served by a staff so "friendly", you'll "feel like you've been going there for years"; "long lines" are a sign that "locals love it"; P.S. it closes at 2:30 PM weekdays, 11 AM Saturdays.

Peggy Sue BBQ *BBQ* 21 | 12 | 19 | $20

Park Cities | Snider Plaza | 6600 Snider Plaza (Daniel Ave.) | Dallas | 214-987-9188 | www.peggysuebbq.com

Park Cities denizens and their offspring rely on this "unpretentious" Snider Plaza institution, a "fine choice" for Texas 'cue and "luscious fried pies" clad in "down-home" 1950s-style furnishings; service is basic, but at this price no one's complaining – in fact they're coming back for more and double parking for takeout.

Pei Wei Asian Diner *Asian* 20 | 16 | 18 | $16

Knox-Henderson | 3001 Knox St. (I-75) | Dallas | 214-219-0000
Preston Center | Preston Center Pavilion | 8305 Westchester Dr. (Luther Ln.) | Dallas | 214-765-9911
Addison | 4801 Belt Line Rd. (Addison Rd.) | 972-764-0844
North Dallas | 18204 Preston Rd. (Frankford Rd.) | Dallas | 972-985-0090
Allen | 1008 W. McDermott Dr. (Watters Rd.) | 469-675-2266
Irving | 7600 N. MacArthur Blvd. (bet. I-635 & Kinwest Pkwy.) | 972-373-8000
Cultural District | Montgomery Plaza | 2600 W. Seventh St. (Carroll St.) | Ft. Worth | 817-806-9950
Southwest | 5900 Overton Ridge Rd. (Bryant Irvin Rd.) | Ft. Worth | 817-294-0808
Arlington | Village by the Parks | 4133 E. Cooper St. (Pleasant Ridge Rd.) | 817-466-4545
Southlake | 1582 E. Southlake Blvd. (bet. Central Ave. & Village Center Dr.) | 817-722-0070
www.peiwei.com
Additional locations throughout the Dallas/Ft. Worth area

"Stir-fry chefs tame the flames" at this fast-casual Asian chain (P.F. Chang's "less-expensive" little sibling) serving "quick, flavorful" and "dependable" eats; while some critics find the fare "formulaic", many regard it as a "good value for your money."

Perry's Steakhouse & Grille ⓢ *Steak* 26 | 26 | 25 | $55

Uptown | 2000 McKinney Ave. (Olive St.) | Dallas | 214-855-5151 | www.perryssteakhouse.com
See review in Houston Directory.

P.F. Chang's China Bistro *Chinese* 21 | 21 | 21 | $29

NorthPark | NorthPark Ctr. | 225 NorthPark Ctr. (Northwest Hwy.) | Dallas | 214-265-8669

(continued)

P.F. Chang's China Bistro

North Dallas | 18323 N. Dallas Pkwy. (Frankford Rd.) | Dallas | 972-818-3336

Allen | Watters Creek at Montgomery Farm | 915 W. Bethany Dr. (Market St.) | 972-390-1040

Sundance Square | Bank One Bldg. | 400 Throckmorton St. (3rd St.) | Ft. Worth | 817-840-2450

Arlington | Arlington Highlands | 215 I-20 E. (bet. Collins St. & Matlock Rd.) | 817-375-8690

Grapevine | 650 Hwy. 114 (bet. Main St. & William D. Tate Ave.) | 817-421-6658

www.pfchangs.com

A "vast" menu of "reliable" "American-Chinese" standards with a range of tastes "from bland to bam" (including gluten-free options) makes this chain a "safe choice" for "big groups" and "families with children"; fans find the relatively "upscale" settings "impressive", and while critics decry it as "loud", "crowded" and "overrated", defenders counter that as chains go, "this one is well run."

Piccolo Mondo *Italian*　　▽ 24 | 20 | 24 | $48

Arlington | Parkway Central Ctr. | 829 E. Lamar Blvd. (bet. Collins St. & Madison Dr.) | 817-265-9174 | www.piccolomondo.com

"Don't let the strip-mall location fool you", this Arlington mainstay boasts a "lovely" interior with a piano bar that's a welcoming stop for a drink; admirers would "eat there every week if [they] could", thanks to a "dependable" "old-school" Italian menu, "gracious" service and reasonable prices; P.S. located midway between Dallas and Ft. Worth, it's also ideal for a business lunch.

Piranha Killer Sushi *Japanese*　　21 | 19 | 19 | $28

Sundance Square | 335 W. Third St. (Throckmorton St.) | Ft. Worth | 817-348-0200

NEW **Flower Mound** | 5801 Long Prairie Rd. (Dixon Ln.) | 972-539-6052

Arlington | 309 Curtis Mathes Way (bet. Five Points & Highlander Blvds.) | 817-465-6455

Arlington | 851 NE Green Oaks Blvd. (Collins St.) | 817-261-1636

www.piranhakillersushi.com

Admirers applaud the "never boring" sushi combos at this moderately priced Japanese mini-chain where raw plates, tempura and spicy starters abound; antagonists argue it "tries to be too cute" with "quite average" results, but the "great ambiance", particularly at the colorful Sundance Square locale, goes a long way; P.S. most locations are open late on weekends too.

NEW Platia Greek Kouzina Ⓜ *Greek*　　- | - | - | M

Frisco | 2995 Preston Rd. (Gaylord Pkwy.) | 972-334-0031 | www.platiagreek.com

Tucked away in a Frisco strip center, this family-owned BYO newcomer is attracting attention with "excellent", well-priced Greek fare served in a "cozy" space supplemented by a pleasant patio; dancing and a flaming tableside cheese service add to the festive vibe.

FOOD DECOR SERVICE COST

Porch, The *Pub Food*   22 | 19 | 21 | $29

Knox-Henderson | 2912 N. Henderson Ave. (bet. Miller & Willis Aves.) | Dallas | 214-828-2916 | www.theporchrestaurant.com

"Rich" short-rib stroganoff and an "evil" burger with a "foie-buttered bun" lead the amped-up pub-grub menu at this "hip" Knox-Henderson American that sees "lots of action from the young crowd"; with a "massive bar" pouring "creative cocktails", it's a "casual" place to "meet friends", especially on the patio.

NEW Princi Italia *Italian*   - | - | - | M

Preston Royal | 5959 Royal Ln. (Preston Rd.) | Dallas | 214-739-5959 | www.princiitalia.com

One of Preston Royal's long-standing Italians has been revamped by chef Kevin Ascolese and restaurateur Patrick Colombo, who augment wood-fired pizzas, pasta dishes and the like with nightly specials; a smartly turned-out crowd can often be spied in the newly snappy setting, but everyday prices keep the mood casual.

NEW Private Social ⊠ *Eclectic*   - | - | - | M

Uptown | 3232 McKinney Ave. (Hall St.) | Dallas | 214-754-4744 | www.privatesocial.com

Two-time *Top Chef*-testant Tiffany Derry is at the helm of this Uptown arrival proffering two moderately priced Eclectic menus – 'private', comprising large plates for one, and 'social', filled with tapas meant for grazing and sharing; the venue's already a hit with foodies and scenesters who vie for prime placement in the pearl-colored booths.

Pyramid Restaurant & Bar *American*   ▽ 29 | 27 | 29 | $56

Arts District | Fairmont Dallas | 1717 N. Akard St. (Ross Ave.) | Dallas | 214-720-5249 | www.pyramidrestaurant.com

Chef André Natera restores this Arts District stalwart anchoring the Fairmont Hotel to pinnacle status with an "excellent" New American menu emphasizing fresh, seasonal ingredients enhanced by herbs and vegetables from the rooftop garden; sleek decor, well-"synchronized" service, a winning wine list and somewhat more reasonable prices than in years past make it a "must-try."

R+D Kitchen *American*   24 | 21 | 21 | $35

Preston Center | Plaza at Preston Ctr. | 8300 Preston Center Plaza (Wentwood Dr.) | Dallas | 214-890-7900 | www.hillstone.com

There's a "slick, California feel" to this "Frank Lloyd Wright–style" canteen and patio in Preston Center where a "straightforward" if somewhat "limited" American menu is "executed with flair" and delivered by an "eager" staff; prices are moderate, but best of all, "unlike Houston's" (its sib across the parking lot), it takes reservations.

Rafain Brazilian Steakhouse *Brazilian/Steak*   - | - | - | E

North Dallas | 18010 Dallas Pkwy. (Frankford Rd.) | Dallas | 972-733-1110 | www.rafain.com

"Meat, meat and more meat" is the specialty of the house at this spacious North Dallas churrascaria, where gauchos brandish swordlike skewers of charcoal-grilled viands tableside; for non-carnivores, there's an ample salad and appetizer buffet, making it "worthwhile" even if you're "not so crazy" about churrasco.

Railhead Smokehouse ☒ BBQ | 25 | 19 | 18 | $21

Cultural District | 2900 Montgomery St. (I-30) | Ft. Worth |
817-738-9808 | www.railheadonline.com
You "can't get more Texan" than this "old-style" BBQ "landmark" in the Cultural District, dishing out "amazing" "fall-off-the-bones" ribs and "the coldest beer in town"; you "wait in line to order" at the counter, and insiders caution "beware the crowds" during the "January stock show" and on TCU game days, when it's really "the place to go."

Ranch at Las Colinas, The ☒ Southern | ▽ 26 | 25 | 25 | $25

Las Colinas | 857 W. John Carpenter Frwy. (bet. MacArthur Blvd. & Walnut Hill Ln.) | Irving | 972-506-7262 | www.theranchlc.com
Offering a "great spin on Texas ingredients, without being hokey", this midpriced "sleeper" in Las Colinas dishes out locally sourced American fare; set in a modern, "Western-style" ranch house complex, it boasts a bar, a porch with live music and a quieter dining room, making it suitable for "happy hour", a "date night" or "business dinner."

Rathbun's Blue Plate Kitchen American | 22 | 19 | 21 | $36

Preston Center | Plaza at Preston Ctr. | 6130 Luther Ln. (Kate St.) | Dallas | 214-890-1103 | www.kentrathbun.com
The "sophisticated" yet "comforting" "homestyle" Southern cuisine from celebrity chef Kent Rathbun is "spot-on" at this Preston Center sibling of Abacus and Jasper's, where a staff that "knows its craft" makes surveyors feel "welcome" in the "cool" contemporary space; an uptick in the Food score suggests it's finally "hit [its] stride."

Reata Southwestern | 25 | 25 | 24 | $46

Sundance Square | 310 Houston St. (3rd St.) | Ft. Worth | 817-336-1009 | www.reata.net
Recommended as a "first stop for visitors" "without being too touristy", this "hot spot" in Sundance Square hits a "home run" with "great" Southwestern "ranch-style" cuisine and "outstanding" service; while a few find the Texas-size, Western-themed setting "overwhelming", the "romantic rooftop" offers a "great view of Ft. Worth" and helps justify the "expensive" tab.

Rick's Chophouse ☒ Southern/Steak | - | - | - | E

McKinney | Grand Hotel | 107 N. Kentucky St. (Louisiana St.) |
214-726-9251 | www.rickschophouse.com
"Excellent in every way" rave respondents of this upscale steakhouse lodged in McKinney's historic Grand Hotel with "fantastic" Southern-leaning fare (like shrimp and grits and porterhouse for two) and "lovely" decor featuring a pressed-tin ceiling, gas lamps and vintage mahogany; P.S. live music on weekends makes it a special-occasion hot spot.

	FOOD	DECOR	SERVICE	COST

Rise N° 1 *French*

25 | 22 | 22 | $39

West Lovers Lane | Inwood Vill. | 5360 W. Lovers Ln. (Inwood Rd.) |
Dallas | 214-366-9900 | www.risesouffle.com

"*Allez-vous* straight to France" via this "quirky" soufflé specialist in a
shopping center off West Lovers Lane, whipping up "adventurous"
yet "satisfying" "savory pillows of joy" (plus sweet varieties) that
"aim for heaven", offered with "perfect" soups and an extensive
wine selection at wide-ranging price points; "cute" vintage-style decor featuring birch trees enhances its appeal, plus most of the furnishings are for sale.

Royal China *Chinese*

26 | 19 | 22 | $30

Preston Royal | Preston Royal Vill. | 6025 Royal Ln. (Preston Rd.) |
Dallas | 214-361-1771 | www.royalchinadallas.com

"Not your usual Chinese restaurant", this "long-standing" Preston
Royal charmer offers an entertaining view of "melt-in-your-mouth
noodles and dumplings made before your eyes" in the open kitchen;
"large portions" suitable for "family-style" dining, moderate prices
and "friendly" servers who "remember you when you come back"
make it a "keeper" for many.

Roy's *Hawaiian*

25 | 24 | 23 | $50

West Plano | 2840 Dallas Pkwy. (bet. Park Blvd. & Parker Rd.) |
Plano | 972-473-6263 | www.roysrestaurant.com

There are "no hula skirts" at this West Plano outpost of Roy
Yamaguchi's global chain, just "wonderfully inspired and executed"
Hawaiian cuisine from the exhibition kitchen; the staff provides
"outstanding" service in the space graced with paintings of tropical
flowers, and while a few quip it "might be cheaper to go to Hawaii",
others insist it's "worth a visit."

Rudy's *BBQ*

25 | 16 | 20 | $16

NEW Allen | 1790 N. Central Expwy. (Cabela Dr.) | 214-383-5353
NEW Frisco | 9828 Dallas Pkwy. (Technology Dr.) | 972-712-7839
Arlington | 451 I-20 E. (5 Points Blvd.) | 817-465-7839
www.rudys.com

See review in San Antonio Directory.

NEW Ruthie's Rolling Café *Sandwiches*

– | – | – | I

Location varies; see website | Dallas | 972-380-4233 |
www.ruthiesrollingcafe.com

The classic grilled-cheese sandwich is elevated to gourmet levels thanks to artisanal breads, cheeses, meats and sauces at this
bright-blue food truck whose pleasing prices extend to the sides
and sodas; click on its website for daily locations at various
venues throughout Dallas.

Ruth's Chris Steak House *Steak*

26 | 22 | 25 | $63

North Dallas | 17840 Dallas Pkwy. (bet. Frankford & Trinity Mills Rds.) |
Dallas | 972-250-2244
Downtown Ft. Worth | 813 Main St. (7th St.) | Ft. Worth | 817-348-0080
www.ruthschris.com

See review in San Antonio Directory.

	FOOD	DECOR	SERVICE	COST

☑ Saint-Emilion ☒Ⓜ *French*   29 | 26 | 28 | $57

Cultural District | 3617 W. Seventh St. (Montgomery St.) | Ft. Worth | 817-737-2781 | www.saint-emilionrestaurant.com

Bernard Tronche's "*fantastique*" "jewel" in the Cultural District is "always tops" proclaim fans who vote it No. 1 for Food in Dallas/Ft. Worth, a tribute to the daily blackboard menu of "exquisite" fare from the south of France complemented by a "fabulous" wine list; "impeccable" service and a "quaint old house" setting are more reasons why it's a "favorite destination" of many.

Salum ☒ *American*   26 | 24 | 25 | $54

Uptown | 4152 Cole Ave. (Fitzhugh Ave.) | Dallas | 214-252-9604 | www.salumrestaurant.com

Though it's hidden in an unassuming Uptown strip center, chef-owner Abraham Salum's upscale "culinary haven" "takes its rightful place in the upper echelon" of the Dallas dining scene thanks to his "superb", "eclectic" New American menu, which changes monthly and is "attentively" served by a "caring" staff; the "simple", "elegant" venue is adjacent to sibling Komali.

Samar ☒ *Eclectic*   26 | 26 | 25 | $51

Arts District | 2100 Ross Ave. (Pearl St.) | Dallas | 214-922-9922 | www.samarrestaurant.com

"Perfect for pre-performance", Stephan Pyles' Arts District Eclectic is a "global gastric experience", offering "original takes on classic ethnic small plates" and main courses from Spain, India and the Mediterranean in an "exotic", "intimate" setting complete with patio hookah lounge; "impeccable" service makes it all the more "special", and while most find the prices "reasonable", a few caution that "small plates can equal big checks."

Sambuca *Eclectic*   22 | 24 | 21 | $38

Uptown | 2120 McKinney Ave. (Pearl St.) | Dallas | 214-744-0820
Sambuca 360 *Eclectic*
West Plano | 7200 Bishop Rd. (Legacy Dr.) | Plano | 469-467-3393
www.sambucarestaurant.com

This jazz/supper club trio in Dallas and Houston offers an Eclectic menu of "respectable", but slightly "pricey", dishes (ranging from small plates to full meals) served by a "pleasant" staff, but many say it's the nightly "live bands" that really lure the "hip", music-centric crowd; with "trendy" digs and a "cool" vibe, it's a "singles' paradise", and also well-suited for "birthday and bachelorette parties."

S & D Oyster Company ☒ *Seafood*   25 | 19 | 26 | $26

Uptown | 2701 McKinney Ave. (Boll St.) | Dallas | 214-880-0111 | www.sdoyster.com

A Dallas "treasure", this "venerable" Uptown seafood "stalwart" is always "packed with local business folk" savoring "fabulous" "New Orleans-style" fried shrimp, oysters and hushpuppies, delivered by a "friendly", "time-tested staff" in a "casual", "old-fashioned" setting; aficionados advise "go early, because there are no reservations."

| | FOOD | DECOR | SERVICE | COST |

Screen Door *Southern*

| 23 | 23 | 19 | $42 |

Arts District | One Arts Plaza | 1722 Routh St. (bet. Flora St. & Ross Ave.) | Dallas | 214-720-9111 | www.screendoordallas.com

Guests indulge in a "gourmet taste of the South" at this "inventive" One Arts Plaza belle whose "posh" modernized plantation furnishings set the stage for "delicious" "comfort food deluxe (desserts are the best part)"; though "a little pricey", pre-theater packages help ease the cost, and the bar attracts a "young neighborhoody scene."

Seasons 52 *American*

| 24 | 24 | 25 | $41 |

West Plano | Shops at Legacy | 7300 Lone Star Dr. (Legacy Dr.) | Plano | 972-312-8852 | www.seasons52.com

This "moderately expensive" West Plano chain link "draws crowds" of "foodies" and "health nuts" alike with its seasonal, "low-cal" menu of "healthy", "imaginative" New American dishes (all less than 475 calories), "nice" international wine list and "not-to-be-missed" mini-desserts; it "doesn't feel like a chain", thanks to "friendly, accommodating" service and a "romantic", "comfortable" modern setting with soft lighting and live music nightly.

Sevy's Grill *American*

| 23 | 23 | 23 | $46 |

Preston Center | 8201 Preston Rd. (Sherry Ln.) | Dallas | 214-265-7389 | www.sevys.com

Chef/co-owner Jim Severson sets a "relaxed" tone working the room and the kitchen in "spikeless golf shoes" (there's a ready-to-play putting green outside), turning out "fantastic" American fare at this Preston Center clubhouse; "knowledgeable" service and a "pleasant" Frank Lloyd Wright–inspired interior also set it apart for "business lunches" and "special dinners that won't break the bank."

NEW Shinjuku Station ☒ *Japanese*

| - | - | - | M |

Hospital District | 711. W. Magnolia Ave. (Hemphill St.) | Ft. Worth | 817-923-2695 | www.shinjuku-station.com

Sushi and other Japanese specialties are artfully presented at this cozy izakaya lodged in a '30s-era bank in the Hospital District; well-priced bento boxes are lunchtime lures, small plates, sake and exotic libations are draws in the evening, while the cool vibe and pretty patio attract at all times.

Shinsei ☒ *Asian*

| 25 | 24 | 26 | $51 |

West Lovers Lane | 7713 Inwood Rd. (bet. Newmore Ave. & W. Lovers Ln.) | Dallas | 214-352-0005 | www.shinseirestaurant.com

In the luxe West Lovers Lane area, this "people-watching place" from Lynae Fearing and Tracy Rathbun offers an "original menu" of "awesome Asian fusion" fare and the "artistry" of Elvis the sushi chef in the form of "gorgeous, fresh" nigiri and rolls; a 400-year-old carving of Buddha watches over the space with "fabulous", loungey decor that makes it a "favorite" spot for "romance."

Silver Fox Steakhouse ☒ *Steak*

| 22 | 22 | 24 | $53 |

Richardson | 3650 Shire Blvd. (President George Bush Tpke.) | 972-423-8121

(continued)

Silver Fox Steakhouse

Frisco | 1303 Legacy Dr. (Hwy. 121) | 214-618-5220
University Area | 1651 S. University Dr. (I-30) | Ft. Worth | 817-332-9060
Grapevine | 1235 William D. Tate Ave. (Hwy. 114) | 817-329-6995
www.silverfoxsteakhouse.com

This relatively "upscale" Texas steakhouse chain features "well-prepared" cuts along with satisfying if "familiar" sides (like potatoes "actually included in the price" of the entree); the "special-occasion" destination in Ft. Worth's University Area earns the most kudos, although "underwhelmed" critics call the eats "mediocre" "for the price."

Smoke *BBQ*

24 | 20 | 21 | $35

Oak Cliff | Belmont Hotel | 901 Ft. Worth Ave. (Sylvan Blvd.) |
Dallas | 214-393-4141 | www.smokerestaurant.com

So hot it's practically smoldering, this "quirky" BBQer adjacent to the Belmont Hotel takes its inspiration from the smokehouses of yore, with oak floors, "comfortable" leather banquettes and a mid-priced 'farm-to-fork' menu that runs the gamut from grass-fed steaks to pickled beet salad and other "complex", "gourmet" dishes; of course there's also "amazing" 'cue galore.

Snuffer's Restaurant & Bar *Burgers*

19 | 13 | 17 | $18

Greenville Avenue | 3526 Greenville Ave. (bet. Longview St. &
McCommas Blvd.) | Dallas | 214-826-6850 ●
Preston Center | 8411 Preston Rd. (Northwest Hwy.) | Dallas |
214-265-9911
Addison | 14910 Midway Rd. (Beltway Dr.) | 972-991-8811
West Plano | 2408 Preston Rd. (Highland Dr.) | Plano | 469-467-9911
Rockwall | 2901 Village Dr. (I-30) | 972-722-9811
Highland Village | Shops at Highland Vill. | 4050 Barton Creek
(bet. Chinn Chapel Rd. & Village Pkwy.) | 972-317-9111
Southlake | 431 Grand Ave. E. (bet. Hwy. 114 & Southlake Blvd.) |
817-410-9811
www.snuffers.com

"Go on your diet 'cheat' day" to devour a "huge, juicy" burger accompanied by "hot, gooey" cheddar fries at this growing local chain whose "never dull" Greenville Avenue "original" opened in 1978; a "young, swarming" staff delivers the budget-friendly baskets of goodies, and the "sports-bar" feel is just right for the "jeans-and-beer" crowd.

Sonny Bryan's Smokehouse *BBQ*

24 | 14 | 19 | $17

Downtown Dallas | Republic Center Tunnel | 325 N. St. Paul St.
(Pacific Ave.) | Dallas | 214-979-0102 🖪
West End | 302 N. Market St. (Pacific Ave.) | Dallas | 214-744-1610
Galleria | Macy's | 13375 Noel Rd. (bet. Alpha Rd. & Lyndon B.
Johnson Frwy.) | Dallas | 214-295-1497 🖪
Love Field | 2202 Inwood Rd. (Harry Hines Blvd.) | Dallas | 214-357-7120
Preston Forest | Preston Forest Vill. | 11661 Preston Rd. (bet. Forest Ln. &
Preston Haven Dr.) | Dallas | 214-234-0888

(continued)

(continued)

Sonny Bryan's Smokehouse

West Lovers Lane | 5519 W. Lovers Ln. (Inwood Rd.) | Dallas | 214-351-2024

Richardson | Pavilion Park Ctr. | 1251 W. Campbell Rd. (bet. Lake Park Blvd. & Mimosa Dr.) | 972-664-9494

Las Colinas | Las Colinas Plaza | 4030 N. MacArthur Blvd. (Northgate Dr.) | Irving | 972-650-9564

Alliance | Alliance Ctr. | 2421 Westport Pkwy. (I-35) | Ft. Worth | 817-224-9191

www.sonnybryans.com

Sure, it's a chain, but it feels like "an old pal's backyard" cookout at this BBQ "standard"-bearer, serving "awesome" smoked meats and "outstanding" onion rings at "reasonable" prices; the consensus is that the "original shack" on Inwood Road is "still the best" (the "smell of savory 'cue permeating every inch" of it), with some nay-sayers lamenting that "franchising has taken its toll", but for many it remains a quintessential "Texas experience."

Spiral Diner & Bakery Ⓜ *Diner/Vegetarian*   ▽ 22 | 12 | 18 | $16

Oak Cliff | 1101 N. Beckley Ave. (Zang Blvd.) | Dallas | 214-948-4747

Hospital District | 1314 W. Magnolia Ave. (bet. Lake St. & 6th Ave.) | Ft. Worth | 817-332-8834

www.spiraldiner.com

Even non-vegetarians give "props" to this organic vegan diner duo in Fort Worth and Oak Cliff for its "creative, tasty" fare; "tattooed, pierced" staffers bring out your food in the classic '50s-style setting, and affordable prices are one more reason fans find it "worth the trip."

Square Burger *Burgers*   - | - | - | M

McKinney | 115 N. Kentucky St. (Virginia St.) | 972-542-0185

Grass-fed beef burgers and other American items made from locally sourced ingredients fill out the menu at this upscale spot in McKinney, its handsome setting in an art deco building with tin ceilings and a bamboo bar pouring interesting wines and cocktails help distinguish it from the competition.

Steel *Japanese/Vietnamese*   23 | 23 | 20 | $46

Oak Lawn | Centrum Plaza | 3102 Oak Lawn Ave. (Cedar Springs Rd.) | Dallas | 214-219-9908 | www.steeldallas.com

"Even in an economic slump there are Ferraris parked out front" at this Oak Lawn trendsetter whose "excellent", pricey Japanese-Vietnamese fare (including "great-quality" sushi) accompanies a nightly "scene"; an "attractive" (if "noisy") art-filled backdrop completes the picture for the high-powered crowd.

☑ Stephan Pyles Ⓢ *Southwestern*   27 | 27 | 27 | $69

Arts District | 1807 Ross Ave. (St. Paul St.) | Dallas | 214-580-7000 | www.stephanpyles.com

The "master of New Texas cuisine", Stephan Pyles "reigns" at his "classy, modern" Arts District Southwestern where diners can watch chefs create his "amazing", "constantly evolving" globally influenced fare in the glass-enclosed display kitchen; with "outstanding" service and a "cosmopolitan vibe", it's the "perfect place to take out-of-towners" – "particularly if they're paying."

Steve Fields Steak & Lobster Lounge *Seafood/Steak*

▽ 28 | 24 | 27 | $62

West Plano | 5013 W. Park Blvd. (Preston Rd.) | Plano | 972-596-7100 | www.stevefieldsrestaurant.com

In a "steak-driven state", this West Plano meatery stands out with "superb" surf 'n' turf at "reasonable" prices and an "owner who comes by to make sure everything is going right"; it's "fine dining" all the way in the white-tablecloth setting with live entertainment nightly in the lounge, making it a popular spot to "celebrate special occasions."

Sullivan's Steakhouse *Steak*

24 | 22 | 24 | $57

North Dallas | 17795 Dallas Pkwy. (Briargrove Ln.) | Dallas | 972-267-9393 | www.sullivansteakhouse.com

See review in Austin and the Hill Country Directory.

Sushi Sake ⓈⒽ *Japanese*

27 | 22 | 21 | $40

Richardson | 2150 N. Collins Blvd. (Campbell Rd.) | 972-470-0722 | www.sushi-sake.com

You feel like "you're in Japan" at this discreet, "authentic" Richardson hideaway serving "generous" portions of "amazing sushi" and plentiful sake choices; though critics say the "decor doesn't quite live up to the phenomenal fish" and grouse over "indifferent" service, "excellent" cuisine at "reasonable prices" makes up for most glitches.

Sushi Zushi *Japanese*

23 | 20 | 20 | $30

Oak Lawn | Turtle Creek Shopping Ctr. | 3858 Oak Lawn Ave. (Blackburn St.) | Dallas | 214-522-7253 | www.sushizushi.com

See review in San Antonio Directory.

Suze ⓈⓂ *Mediterranean*

27 | 20 | 25 | $53

Preston Hollow | Villages of Preston Hollow | 4345 W. Northwest Hwy. (Midway Rd.) | Dallas | 214-350-6135 | www.suzedallas.com

"Unpretentious and friendly", Gilbert Garza's "hidden gem" in Preston Hollow is a "high-end neighborhood place" offering "beautifully presented" Mediterranean fare, an "excellent wine list" and "perfect" service in an "intimate, quiet" setting; given its "reasonable prices", it's no surprise that it's "always booked."

Szechuan Chinese *Chinese*

▽ 24 | 16 | 21 | $20

Southwest | 4750 Bryant Irvin Rd. (I-20) | Ft. Worth | 817-346-6111

West | 5712 Locke Ave. (bet. Camp Bowie Blvd. & Horne St.) | Ft. Worth | 817-738-7300

This "neighborhood" Chinese duo in Ft. Worth's Southwest and West neighborhoods has a "long track record" for "reliable" crowd-pleasing fare in a "quiet" setting, delivered by a "wonderful" staff; it's not "cutting-edge", but the price is "reasonable", especially for lunch.

Taco Diner *Mexican* | 21 | 17 | 18 | $21 |

Preston Center | 4011 Villanova St. (Preston Rd.) | Dallas | 214-696-4944
West Village | West Vill. | 3699 McKinney Ave. (bet. Blackburn St. & Lemmon Ave.) | Dallas | 214-521-3669
Addison | 4933 Belt Line Rd. (Quorum Dr.) | 972-702-6426
West Plano | Shops at Legacy | 7201 Bishop Rd. (Legacy Dr.) | Plano | 469-241-9945
Las Colinas | 5904 N. MacArthur Blvd. (Hwy. 114) | Irving | 972-401-2691
Southlake | Southlake Town Sq. | 432 Grand Ave. W. (bet. Division St. & Federal Way) | 817-488-6995
www.mcrowd.com

These "trendy" Mexican diners from the M Crowd (Mi Cocina, Mercury Grill) "elevate the lowly taco to chic" with a "straight formula" that's "simple and focused", augmented by "addictive" green salsa, "luscious" Mambo Taxi frappes and fruity "aguas frescas" (in case you're driving the taxi); a "bright spot for lunch" or dinner, it's definitely an affordable choice if you want to "ogle or be ogled."

Taverna Pizzeria & Risotteria *Italian* | 22 | 21 | 20 | $32 |

Knox-Henderson | 3210 Armstrong Ave. (bet. Cole Ave. & Travis St.) | Dallas | 214-520-9933
Sundance Square | Sundance Sq. | 450 Throckmorton St. (4th St.) | Ft. Worth | 817-885-7502
www.tavernabylombardi.com

Customers compliment the "kitchen that seems to care" in preparing "fabulous" risotto, "delicious" pizzas and other "dependable" Italian food at this Austin-Metroplex chainlet from the Lombardi family; it also gets "kudos for Euro-style" settings, "knowledgeable" service and "reasonable prices", so many "recommend" it for a casual night.

Tei An Ⓜ *Japanese* | 26 | 27 | 24 | $59 |

Arts District | One Arts Plaza | 1722 Routh St. (bet. Flora St. & Ross Ave.) | Dallas | 214-220-2828 | www.tei-an.com

Foodies "feel transported to Japan" by chef-owner Teiichi Sakurai's "brilliant" cuisine at this "cutting-edge" Japanese atelier in the Arts District showcasing "amazing" handmade soba, sushi and more "esoteric" specials, all "flawlessly served" in an "elegant" "Zen-like" interior ("like a spa"); it's a splurge, yes, but the "price is right for the product"; P.S. there's also a rooftop cocktail bar.

Tei Tei Robata Bar Ⓜ *Japanese* | 25 | 20 | 21 | $56 |

Knox-Henderson | 2906 N. Henderson Ave. (Willis Ave.) | Dallas | 214-828-2400 | www.teiteirobata.com

A "very Dallas" crowd exalts the "uncompromising quality" of the "top-notch" sushi, "Tokyo"-style robata and "fantastic sake" at this Japanese "marvel" in Knox-Henderson; "everything is served elegantly and simply" in a contemporary, warmly lit space, though a few aren't so keen on the "scene", the "long wait" and the price/portion ratio.

Texas de Brazil *Brazilian/Steak* | 24 | 22 | 22 | $50 |

Uptown | 2727 Cedar Springs Rd. (bet. Carlisle & Woodrow Sts.) | Dallas | 214-720-1414
Addison | 15101 Addison Rd. (Belt Line Rd.) | 972-385-1000

Vote at zagat.com

(continued)

Texas de Brazil

Downtown Ft. Worth | 101 N. Houston St. (Weatherford St.) |
Ft. Worth | 817-882-9500
www.texasdebrazil.com

A "must for any hard-core meat eater", this "Texas take on Brazilian churrascarias" offers "quality" cuts carved tableside by "excellent" servers in gaucho garb, along with an "awesome salad bar"; red-hued, Brazilian-themed decor adds to the "entertaining" vibe, though some balk at the cost and recommend going for a more "affordable" lunch.

NEW Texas Spice *American*

- | - | - | M

Downtown Dallas | Omni Hotel | 555 S. Lamar St. (Young St.) |
Dallas | 214-652-4810 | www.omnihotels.com

Jason Weaver, of French Room acclaim, has co-created an American menu with locavore leanings and regional inspiration at this debut in the Omni Hotel Downtown with a stylish setting featuring repurposed wood, brick walls and views of the skyline; prices are midrange, with the under-$20 express lunch a particular bargain.

III Forks *Steak*

24 | 22 | 23 | $63

North Dallas | 17776 Dallas Pkwy. (bet. Frankford & Trinity Mills Rds.) |
Dallas | 972-267-1776 | www.3forks.com

See review in Austin and the Hill Country Directory.

Tillman's Roadhouse Ⓜ *American*

20 | 21 | 19 | $33

Oak Cliff | 324 W. Seventh St. (Bishop Ave.) | Dallas | 214-942-0988
Near West | 2933 Crockett St. (Currie St.) | Ft. Worth | 817-850-9255
www.tillmansroadhouse.com

"Metrosexuals meet cowboys" at this "unique" "Western-chic" venue in Oak Cliff and its Ft. Worth offshoot, where "faux deer heads, chandeliers" and "old black-and-white movies in the lounge", plus the warm personality of "queen-of-the-place" owner Sara Tillman, set a "playful" tone for feasting on "gourmeted-up roadhouse" cuisine topped off by "tableside s'mores"; a few call the cooking "inconsistent", though moderate bills are a plus.

Torchy's Tacos *Mexican*

24 | 14 | 19 | $11

Preston Forest | Preston Forest Vill. | 5921 Forest Ln. (bet. Jamestown Rd. & Preston Rd.) | Dallas | 972-720-9200 | www.torchystacos.com

See review in Austin and the Hill Country Directory.

Toulouse Café & Bar *French*

22 | 23 | 22 | $38

Knox-Henderson | 3314 Knox St. (Travis St.) | Dallas | 214-520-8999 |
www.toulousecafeandbar.com

"Delicious" French food and "generous" drinks are complemented by "people-watching almost as good as the Champs-Elysées" at Alberto Lombardi's "friendly little bistro" in Knox-Henderson with a patio looking out to the Katy Trail; "pleasant" service adds to the "delight."

Truluck's *Seafood*

24 | 23 | 23 | $52

Uptown | 2401 McKinney Ave. (Maple Ave.) | Dallas | 214-220-2401
Addison | 5001 Belt Line Rd. (Quorum Dr.) | 972-503-3079

(continued)

FOOD · DECOR · SERVICE · COST

(continued)

Truluck's

Southlake | Southlake Town Sq. | 1420 Plaza Pl. (Grand Ave.) |
817-912-0500
www.trulucks.com

"If you want steak or stone crab, proceed directly to" this "quality" surf
'n' turf chain with "excellent" fare in portions "big enough to share";
service is "attentive" and the "dressy" setting is "enjoyable" with a "fun
bar", so what's "not to love, except the bill"?

Twisted Root Burger Co. *Burgers*   23 | 18 | 17 | $16

Deep Ellum | 2615 Commerce St. (bet. Canton & Main Sts.) |
Dallas | 214-741-7668
Greenville Avenue | 5609 SMU Blvd. (Prentice St.) | Dallas |
214-361-2910 ◗
Richardson | 730 E. Campbell Rd. (bet. Central Expwy. & Lakeside Blvd.) |
214-570-9999
NEW **West Plano** | Shops at Legacy | 7300 Lone Star Dr. (Legacy Circle) |
Plano | 972-312-0011
NEW **Fairview** | Village at Fairview | 232 Town Pl. (Indian Springs Rd.) |
972-886-4045
Roanoke | Oak St. Plaza | 101 S. Oak St. (bet. Bowie & Main Sts.) |
817-490-6628
NEW **Arlington** | 310 E. Abram St. (bet. East & Elm Sts.) |
817-201-9669
www.twistedrootburgerco.com

"Messy, juicy burgers" made from "lots of unique meats like elk, buffalo and ostrich" fill out the menu at this "popular" Dallas-bred chain
also offering "enough fried sides to please anyone" and spiked milkshakes for cheap; an "energetic" staff matches the "quirky" digs.

Urban Crust *Pizza*   ▽ 23 | 22 | 20 | $21

East Plano | 1006 E. 15th St. (K Ave.) | Plano | 972-509-1400 |
www.urbancrust.com

"Wonderful" "unique" pizza and a "cool" vibe are the draws at this frequently "packed" Plano spot set in a historic building and known for its
rooftop bar; "service suffers when it's crowded", but most don't mind.

Urban Taco *Mexican*   20 | 18 | 17 | $20

Mockingbird Station | Mockingbird Station | 5331 E. Mockingbird Ln.
(I-75) | Dallas | 214-823-4723
Uptown | 3411 McKinney Ave. (bet. Hall St. & Lemmon Ave.) |
Dallas | 214-922-7080
www.urban-taco.com

Presenting a "refreshing" take on Mexican, these taquerias in Dallas
and San Antonio specialize in "healthy" street fare that's a "cut above";
thanks to the "reasonable prices" and upbeat digs, the "hip, young"
crowd doesn't mind if food and service are sometimes "hit-or-miss."

NEW Velvet Taco *Mexican*   - | - | - | I

Knox-Henderson | 3012 N. Henderson Ave. (I-75) | Dallas |
214-823-8358 | www.velvettaco.com

Tacos with global flavor inspirations (Asian, Indian, etc.) are the
main attractions at this Knox-Henderson Mexican that also offers a

FOOD | DECOR | SERVICE | COST

selection of boutique sodas and beers, late hours on Saturdays and modest prices; indeed, the hipsters who converge here don't seem to mind the converted-fast-food-joint setting featuring cramped communal tables inside and a patio with views of the expressway.

Veracruz Café *Mexican*

26 | 19 | 22 | $26

Cedar Hill | Ranch at Cedar Hill | 1427 Hwy. 67 S. (Mt. Lebanon Rd.) | 972-293-8926
Oak Cliff | 408 N. Bishop Ave. (8th St.) | Dallas | 214-948-4746
www.veracruzcafedallas.com

"Unique spins" on "traditional" interior Mexican dishes – including some of the "best mole in Dallas" – keep customers coming to this low-key duo in Cedar Hill and Oak Cliff.

Via Reál *Mexican*

23 | 23 | 24 | $36

Las Colinas | Las Colinas Plaza | 4020 N. MacArthur Blvd. (Byron Nelson Way) | Irving | 972-650-9001 | www.viareal.com

"Well run" since 1985, this Las Colinas Mex is a pick for "solid" fare and Southwestern offerings in a "pleasant" adobe-clad setting with a Santa Fe feel; moderate tabs are another reason it's "worth a visit."

NEW Whiskey Cake *American*

20 | 20 | 20 | $26

West Plano | 3601 Dallas Pkwy. (Parker Rd.) | Plano | 972-993-2253 | www.whiskey-cake.com

"Grab a couple of beers" at this "neighborhood hot spot" in West Plano pairing "well-executed" New American bar bites with interesting brews (and whiskey cocktails, natch) in contemporary, industrial surroundings; given the buzz, expect acoustics on the "loud" side; P.S. you can also order its namesake whiskey-glazed dessert to go.

NEW Wild Salsa Ⓩ *Mexican*

- | - | - | M

Downtown Dallas | Mercantile Pl. | 1800 Main St. (Ervay St.) | Dallas | 214-741-9453 | www.wildsalsarestaurant.com

Warm, cantinalike environs with reclaimed wood and Day of the Dead–themed decorations set the stage for sophisticated Mexico City-style *comida* at this venture in Downtown's Mercantile Place; the moderate prices, which extend to the broad tequila selection, are even better during happy hour, which often boasts extended hours.

Yao Fuzi Cuisine *Chinese*

26 | 25 | 24 | $39

West Plano | 4757 W. Park Blvd. (bet. Ohio Dr. & Preston Rd.) | Plano | 214-473-9267 | www.yaofuzi.com

"Inspired", "high-end" Chinese cooking "with panache" draws fans to this "fine" West Plano Shanghainese famed for its soup dumplings, soft-shell crab and specialty martinis; it's a "feast for the senses", with an "upscale" setting and pricing reflecting the quality.

Yucatan Taco Stand *Mexican*

22 | 16 | 14 | $18

Hospital District | 909 W. Magnolia Ave. (Alston Ave.) | Ft. Worth | 817-924-8646
www.yucatantacostand1.com

This fast-casual Mexican chainlet attracts a "hip" crowd tucking into "twists on classic dishes" including "killer" nachos and Latin fusion plates with "bargain" margaritas and a huge tequila selection to chase it all down; with "fast, friendly" table service and frequent live music, it's "great for groups."

Yutaka Sushi Bistro ⑤ *Japanese* ▽ 28 | 22 | 25 | $46

Uptown | 2633 McKinney Ave. (Boll St.) | Dallas | 214-969-5533 | www.yutakasushibistro.com

"Perfection in execution and presentation" sets apart this "popular" Uptown Japanese where "freaking genius" chef-owner Yutaka Yamato "makes everything look effortless" as he prepares the "finest" sushi and small plates; "warm service" and an adjacent izakaya lounge help ease the "waits" inside the "Lilliputian setting", and help the "pricey" tabs go down easier too.

Ziziki's Restaurant & Bar *Greek* 24 | 19 | 23 | $32

Knox-Henderson | Travis Walk | 4514 Travis St. (Knox St.) | Dallas | 214-521-2233

Preston Forest | Preston Forest Vill. | 11661 Preston Rd. (bet. Forest Ln. & Preston Haven Dr.) | Dallas | 469-232-9922

West Plano | Lakeside Mkt. | 5809 Preston Rd. (bet. Lorimar Dr. & Spring Creek Pkwy.) | Plano | 972-943-8090
www.zizikis.com

Ziziki's Taverna *Greek*

Addison | 5000 Belt Line Rd. (bet. Inwood Rd. & Montfort Dr.) | Dallas | 972-233-1199 | www.zizikistaverna.com

A "pilgrimage" to this temple to Greek cuisine (with locations in Addison, Knox-Henderson, Preston Forest and West Plano) "will make you a believer" assert acolytes who savor its "always tasty" fare accompanied by "good wines"; sunny Mediterranean-inspired settings, pleasant service and moderate prices are pluses, leaving many "looking for their next excuse to go."

Zodiac, The ⑤ *American* ▽ 24 | 24 | 23 | $38

Downtown Dallas | Neiman Marcus | 1618 Main St. (Ervay St.) | Dallas | 214-573-5800 | www.neimanmarcus.com

"Lunch à la *Mad Men*" is yours at this "Dallas tradition" set in Downtown's landmark Neiman Marcus department store in operation since 1957; expect "old-school" Traditional American fare, "attentive" service and moderate tabs; "long may she live!"

Zoë's Kitchen *American* 19 | 14 | 16 | $14

Park Cities | Snider Plaza | 6800 Snider Plaza (Milton Ave.) | Dallas | 214-987-1020

West Lovers Lane | 5710 Lovers Ln. (Dallas N. Tollway) | Dallas | 214-357-0100

West Plano | 1901 Preston Rd. (Park Blvd.) | Plano | 972-248-1010

University Area | 1601 S. University Dr. (Rosedale St.) | Ft. Worth | 817-885-8965
www.zoeskitchen.com

"Light, fresh and healthy" are the watchwords at this fast-casual American chain inhabiting modern digs so "cute and kid-friendly, it almost feels like an Ikea ad"; "quick" counter service and "good value" make it a magnet for families.

DALLAS/FT. WORTH
INDEXES

Cuisines

Includes names, locations and Food ratings.

AMERICAN

Addison Cafe | **Addison**	25
Artin's Grill | **West Plano**	24
☑ Babe's Chicken | **multi.**	25
NEW Bacon Wagon | **Location Varies**	-
Bolla | **Uptown**	-
Bolsa | **Oak Cliff**	25
Brownstone | **Near W**	21
Buffet/Kimbell | **Cultural Dist**	22
Buzzbrews Kitchen | **multi.**	20
Café Nasher | **Arts Dist**	25
Café/Green | **Las Colinas**	24
Cat City Grill | **Hospital Dist**	21
NEW Cedars Social | **Downtown D**	20
Celebration | **Love Field**	24
Central 214 | **Park Cities**	19
Charleston's | **SW**	21
Charlie Palmer Steak | **Downtown D**	25
Cheesecake | **multi.**	20
Cindi's Deli | **multi.**	21
City Café | **W Lovers Ln**	21
NEW Company Café | **multi.**	-
Craft Dallas | **Victory Pk**	24
Del Frisco's | **Uptown**	27
Deli News | **N Dallas**	22
Dish | **Oak Lawn**	20
Dragonfly | **Uptown**	19
Dream Café | **multi.**	23
Eden | **W Lovers Ln**	-
Ellerbe | **Hospital Dist**	26
Five Sixty | **Downtown D**	24
☑ French Rm. | **Downtown D**	28
Grace | **Downtown FW**	25
Grape | **Greenville Ave**	26
Green House | **Location Varies**	-
Greenz | **multi.**	23
Hattie's | **Oak Cliff**	27
Hibiscus | **Knox-Henderson**	26
Highland Pk. Soda | **Knox-Henderson**	20
Houston's/Hillstone | **multi.**	24
NEW Jack's Chowhound | **Location Varies**	-
Jasper's | **West Plano**	24
Kenny's Wood Fired | **Addison**	26
Local | **Deep Ellum**	26
Love Shack | **multi.**	23
Lucky's Cafe | **Oak Lawn**	21
Maguire's | **N Dallas**	23

Mama's Daughters' | **multi.**	19
☑ Mansion | **Uptown**	26
NEW Marquee | **Highland Pk Vill**	26
Meddlesome Moth | **Market Ctr**	22
☑ Mercury | **Preston Forest**	28
☑ Nana | **Market Ctr**	27
Neighborhood Services | **multi.**	25
Nick/Sam's Grill | **Uptown**	25
Nosh Euro | **multi.**	24
NEW Oddfellows | **Oak Cliff**	-
Olenjack's | **Arlington**	25
Parigi | **Oak Lawn**	25
Paris Coffee | **Hospital Dist**	23
Porch | **Knox-Henderson**	22
Pyramid | **Arts Dist**	29
R+D Kitchen | **Preston Ctr**	24
Ranch/Las Colinas | **Las Colinas**	26
Rathbun's Blue | **Preston Ctr**	22
Salum | **Uptown**	26
Seasons 52 | **West Plano**	24
Sevy's | **Preston Ctr**	23
NEW Texas Spice | **Downtown D**	-
Tillman's | **multi.**	20
NEW Whiskey Cake | **West Plano**	20
Kirby's | **Greenville Ave**	24
Zodiac | **Downtown D**	24
Zoë's Kitchen | **multi.**	19

ASIAN

Pei Wei | **multi.**	20

BAKERIES

Eden | **W Lovers Ln**	-
Esperanza's | **multi.**	27
La Duni | **multi.**	24
Main St. Bistro | **multi.**	21

BARBECUE

Angelo's | **Near W**	25
Baker's Ribs | **multi.**	22
Cooper's BBQ | **Stockyards**	25
Cousin's | **multi.**	22
Hard Eight BBQ | **Coppell**	25
NEW Lockhart | **Oak Cliff**	21
Off the Bone | **Downtown D**	-
Pappas BBQ | **Love Field**	21
Peggy Sue BBQ | **Park Cities**	21
Railhead | **Cultural Dist**	25
Rudy's | **multi.**	25
Smoke | **Oak Cliff**	24
Sonny Bryan's | **multi.**	24

BRAZILIAN

Boi Na Braza | **Grapevine**	25
Fogo/Chão | **Addison**	25
Rafain Brazilian | **N Dallas**	-
Texas/Brazil | **multi.**	24

BURGERS

Dutch's | **University Area**	22
Fred's | **multi.**	22
NEW Jack's Chowhound | **Location Varies**	-
Kenny's Burger | **Frisco**	22
Z Kincaid's | **multi.**	25
Love Shack | **multi.**	23
Maple/Motor | **Love Field**	25
Pappas Burgers | **Sundance Sq**	24
Snuffer's | **multi.**	19
Square Burger | **McKinney**	-
Twisted Root | **multi.**	23

CAJUN

Pappadeaux | **multi.**	23

CHINESE

Empress/China | **multi.**	24
First Chinese | **multi.**	24
P.F. Chang's | **multi.**	21
Royal China | **Preston Royal**	26
Szechuan Chinese | **multi.**	24
Yao Fuzi | **West Plano**	26

COFFEEHOUSES

Buzzbrews Kitchen | **multi.**	20
Café Brazil | **multi.**	20

COFFEE SHOPS/ DINERS

Lucky's Cafe | **Oak Lawn**	21
Mama's Daughters' | **multi.**	19
NEW Oddfellows | **Oak Cliff**	-
Paris Coffee | **Hospital Dist**	23
Spiral Diner | **multi.**	22

CONTINENTAL

Hôtel St. Germain | **Uptown**	26

DELIS

Cindi's Deli | **multi.**	21
Deli News | **N Dallas**	22

DESSERT

Cheesecake | **multi.**	20
Eden | **W Lovers Ln**	-
La Duni | **multi.**	24
Main St. Bistro | **multi.**	21

ECLECTIC

Z Abacus | **Knox-Henderson**	27
Café Express | **multi.**	20
Café Modern | **Cultural Dist**	23
Cosmic Café | **Oak Lawn**	-
Lanny's Alta | **Cultural Dist**	27
Lili's Bistro | **S Side**	26
NEW Private Social | **Uptown**	-
Samar | **Arts Dist**	26
Sambuca | **multi.**	22

EUROPEAN

Holy Grail Pub | **West Plano**	-

FRENCH

Z Bijoux | **W Lovers Ln**	28
Z Cacharel | **Arlington**	27
Cadot | **N Dallas**	25
Z French Rm. | **Downtown D**	28
Hôtel St. Germain | **Uptown**	26
L'Ancestral | **Knox-Henderson**	25
Lavendou | **N Dallas**	24
Main St. Bistro | **multi.**	21
Rise Nº 1 | **W Lovers Ln**	25
Z Saint-Emilion | **Cultural Dist**	29
Toulouse | **Knox-Henderson**	22

GERMAN

Bavarian Grill | **East Plano**	26
Kuby's | **Park Cities**	22

GREEK

NEW Platia Greek | **Frisco**	-
Ziziki's | **multi.**	24

HAWAIIAN

Roy's | **West Plano**	25

HEALTH FOOD

(See also Vegetarian)

Dream Café | **multi.**	23
Seasons 52 | **West Plano**	24
Zoë's Kitchen | **multi.**	19

ICE CREAM PARLORS

Highland Pk. Soda | **Knox-Henderson**	20

INDIAN

Clay Pit | **Addison**	23
India Palace | **Preston Forest**	22
Madras Pavilion | **Richardson**	20

ITALIAN

(N=Northern; S=Southern)

Aboca's | **multi.**	23
Adelmo's | **Knox-Henderson**	25
Andiamo | **Addison**	23
Arcodoro/Pomodoro | S | **Uptown**	21
Avanti | **multi.**	23
Brio | **multi.**	22

Campisi's | **multi.**	23
Cane Rosso | S | **Deep Ellum**	-
Cane Rosso Mobile | S | **Location Varies**	-
Carrabba's | **multi.**	23
Coal Vines | **multi.**	24
Eno's Pizza | **Oak Cliff**	25
Ferrari's | **multi.**	23
Ferre | N | **Sundance Sq**	18
Z NEW Lucia | **Oak Cliff**	29
Mi Piaci | N | **Addison**	26
Nicola's/Rest. Nicola | N | **multi.**	22
Nonna | **Lemmon Ave**	25
Nonna Tata | **Hospital Dist**	27
Piccolo Mondo | **Arlington**	24
NEW Princi Italia | **Preston Royal**	-
Taverna | **multi.**	22

JAPANESE

(* sushi specialist)

Sushi Axiom* | **multi.**	26
Blue Fish* | **multi.**	24
NEW Blue Sushi* | **Near W**	23
Jinbeh* | **multi.**	22
Kenichi* | **Victory Pk**	21
Nobu* | **Uptown**	26
Piranha* | **multi.**	21
NEW Shinjuku Station | **Hospital Dist**	-
Shinsei* | **W Lovers Ln**	25
Steel | **Oak Lawn**	23
Sushi Sake* | **Richardson**	27
Sushi Zushi* | **Oak Lawn**	23
Tei An* | **Arts Dist**	26
Tei Tei Robata* | **Knox-Henderson**	25
Yutaka* | **Uptown**	28

KOSHER/ KOSHER-STYLE

Deli News | **N Dallas**	22
Madras Pavilion | **Richardson**	20

LEBANESE

Ali Baba | **multi.**	23
Byblos | **N Side**	27

MEDITERRANEAN

Ali Baba | **multi.**	23
Avanti | **multi.**	23
Suze | **Preston Hollow**	27

MEXICAN

NEW Bee Enchiladeria | **Oak Cliff**	22
Cantina Laredo | **multi.**	21
El Fenix | **multi.**	20
Esperanza's | **multi.**	27
Fuel City Tacos | **Downtown D**	-
Hacienda | **Knox-Henderson**	23
Javier's | **Knox-Henderson**	24

NEW Komali | **Uptown**	24
La Calle Doce | **multi.**	25
La Familia | **Near W**	25
NEW Mesa | **Oak Cliff**	-
NEW Meso Maya | **Preston Forest**	-
Taco Diner | **multi.**	21
Torchy's Tacos | **Preston Forest**	24
Urban Taco | **multi.**	20
NEW Velvet Taco | **Knox-Henderson**	-
Veracruz | **multi.**	26
Via Reál | **Las Colinas**	23
NEW Wild Salsa | **Downtown D**	-
Yucatan Taco | **Hospital Dist**	22

MIDDLE EASTERN

Dimassi's Med. | **Richardson**	19
Fadi's | **multi.**	25

PAN-LATIN

La Duni | **multi.**	24

PIZZA

Arcodoro/Pomodoro | **Uptown**	21
Campisi's | **multi.**	23
Cane Rosso | **Deep Ellum**	-
Cane Rosso Mobile | **Location Varies**	-
Cavalli Pizza | **multi.**	27
Coal Vines | **multi.**	24
Dough | **Preston Forest**	27
Eno's Pizza | **Oak Cliff**	25
Fireside Pies | **multi.**	23
Grimaldi's | **multi.**	26
I Fratelli | **Irving**	23
Olivella's | **Park Cities**	24
Taverna | **multi.**	22
Urban Crust | **East Plano**	23

PUB FOOD

Holy Grail Pub | **West Plano**	-
Porch | **Knox-Henderson**	22

SALVADORAN

Gloria's | **multi.**	22

SANDWICHES

(See also Delis)

NEW Bacon Wagon | **Location Varies**	-
NEW Jack's Chowhound | **Location Varies**	-
NEW Ruthie's | **Location Varies**	-

SEAFOOD

Café Pacific | **Park Cities**	27
Chamberlain's Fish | **Addison**	26

Eddie V's | **multi.**	26
La Calle Doce | **multi.**	25
Lefty's Lobster | **Addison**	22
NEW Mesa | **Oak Cliff**	–
Nick & Sam's | **Uptown**	27
Oceanaire | **Galleria**	23
Ocean Prime | **Uptown**	21
Pappadeaux | **multi.**	23
S&D Oyster | **Uptown**	25
Steve Fields | **West Plano**	28
Truluck's | **multi.**	24

SMALL PLATES

(See also Spanish tapas specialist)

Cat City Grill | Amer. | **Hospital Dist**	21
Del Frisco's | Amer. | **Uptown**	27
Dish | Amer. | **Oak Lawn**	20
Lili's Bistro | Eclectic | **S Side**	26
NEW Marquee | Amer. | **Highland Pk Vill**	26
NEW Private Social | Eclectic | **Uptown**	–
Rathbun's Blue | Amer. | **Preston Ctr**	22
Samar | Eclectic | **Arts Dist**	26
Sambuca | Eclectic | **multi.**	22
NEW Shinjuku Station | Japanese | **Hospital Dist**	–

SOUTHERN

☑ Babe's Chicken | **multi.**	25
Bubba's | **Park Cities**	23
Buttons | **multi.**	23
Chef Point Café | **Watauga**	24
Dixie Hse. | **Lakewood**	23
Rathbun's Blue | **Preston Ctr**	22
Rick's Chophse. | **McKinney**	–
Screen Door | **Arts Dist**	23

SOUTHWESTERN

Blue Mesa | **multi.**	23
Bonnell's | **SW**	27
Cool River | **Las Colinas**	21
☑ Fearing's | **Uptown**	27
Lonesome Dove | **Stockyards**	27
Reata | **Sundance Sq**	25
☑ Stephan Pyles | **Arts Dist**	27
Via Reál | **Las Colinas**	23

SPANISH

(* tapas specialist)

Café Madrid* | **Knox-Henderson**	23

STEAKHOUSES

☑ Al Biernat's | **Oak Lawn**	27
Bailey's | **multi.**	22
☑ Bob's | **multi.**	25
Boi Na Braza | **Grapevine**	25
Capital Grille | **multi.**	26
Cattlemen's | **Stockyards**	23
Chamberlain's Steak | **Addison**	25
Cool River | **Las Colinas**	21
☑ Del Frisco's | **multi.**	27
Eddie V's | **multi.**	26
Fogo/Chão | **Addison**	25
Kirby's | **Southlake**	24
Lambert's | **Near W**	24
Lawry's | **N Dallas**	26
Morton's | **Uptown**	26
Nick & Sam's | **Uptown**	27
Palm | **W End**	25
☑ Pappas Bros. | **Love Field**	28
Rafain Brazilian | **N Dallas**	–
Rick's Chophse. | **McKinney**	–
Ruth's Chris | **multi.**	26
Silver Fox | **multi.**	22
Steve Fields | **West Plano**	28
Sullivan's | **N Dallas**	24
Texas/Brazil | **multi.**	24
III Forks | **N Dallas**	24

TEX-MEX

Chuy's | **multi.**	21
Cyclone Anaya's | **multi.**	21
El Fenix | **multi.**	20
Gloria's | **multi.**	22
Joe T. Garcia's | **N Side**	20
Mia's | **Lemmon Ave**	23
Mi Cocina | **multi.**	21

THAI

Asian Mint/Mint | **multi.**	22
Malai | **W Vill**	–
Mango | **multi.**	24

TURKISH

Café Istanbul | **multi.**	23

VEGETARIAN

(* vegan)

NEW Company Café | **multi.**	–
Cosmic Café | **Oak Lawn**	–
Green House | **Location Varies**	–
Madras Pavilion | **Richardson**	20
Spiral Diner* | **multi.**	22

VIETNAMESE

Green Papaya | **Oak Lawn**	24
Malai | **W Vill**	–
NEW Nammi Truck | **Location Varies**	–
Steel | **Oak Lawn**	23

Locations

Includes names, cuisines and Food ratings.

Dallas

ARTS DISTRICT

Café Nasher	Amer.	25
Pyramid	Amer.	29
Samar	Eclectic	26
Screen Door	Southern	23
☑ Stephan Pyles	SW	27
Tei An	Japanese	26

DEEP ELLUM/ DOWNTOWN/ MARKET CENTER/ WEST END

Avanti	Italian/Med.	23
Baker's Ribs	BBQ	22
☑ Bob's	Steak	25
Buzzbrews Kitchen	Coffee	20
Café Brazil	Coffee	20
Campisi's	Pizza	23
Cane Rosso	Pizza	–
NEW Cedars Social	Amer.	20
Charlie Palmer Steak	Amer.	25
Cindi's Deli	Deli	21
Five Sixty	Amer.	24
☑ French Rm.	Amer./French	28
Fuel City Tacos	Mex.	–
Local	Amer.	26
Mama's Daughters'	Diner	19
Meddlesome Moth	Amer.	22
☑ Nana	Amer.	27
Off the Bone	BBQ	–
Palm	Steak	25
Sonny Bryan's	BBQ	24
NEW Texas Spice	Amer.	–
Twisted Root	Burgers	23
NEW Wild Salsa	Mex.	–
Zodiac	Amer.	24

GALLERIA

Oceanaire	Seafood	23
Sonny Bryan's	BBQ	24

GREENVILLE AVE./ LAKE HIGHLANDS/ LAKEWOOD

Ali Baba	Med.	23
Baker's Ribs	BBQ	22
Blue Fish	Japanese	24
Café Brazil	Coffee	20
Campisi's	Pizza	23
Cantina Laredo	Mex.	21

NEW Company Café	Amer.	–
Dixie Hse.	Southern	23
El Fenix	Tex-Mex	20
Gloria's	Salvadoran/Tex-Mex	22
Grape	Amer.	26
La Calle Doce	Mex.	25
Mi Cocina	Tex-Mex	21
Snuffer's	Burgers	19
Twisted Root	Burgers	23
Kirby's	Steak	24

HIGHLAND PARK VILL./MOCKINGBIRD STA./PARK CITIES

Bubba's	Southern	23
Café Brazil	Coffee	20
Café Express	Eclectic	20
Café Pacific	Seafood	27
Central 214	Amer.	19
Greenz	Amer.	23
Kuby's	German	22
Mango	Thai	24
NEW Marquee	Amer.	26
Mi Cocina	Tex-Mex	21
Asian Mint/Mint	Asian	22
Olivella's	Pizza	24
Peggy Sue BBQ	BBQ	21
Urban Taco	Mex.	20
Zoë's Kitchen	Amer.	19

KNOX-HENDERSON

☑ Abacus	Eclectic	27
Adelmo's	Italian	25
Buzzbrews Kitchen	Coffee	20
Café Madrid	Spanish	23
Chuy's	Tex-Mex	21
Fadi's	Mideast.	25
Fireside Pies	Pizza	23
Hacienda	Mex.	23
Hibiscus	Amer.	26
Highland Pk. Soda	Amer.	20
Javier's	Mex.	24
La Duni	Pan-Latin	24
L'Ancestral	French	25
Neighborhood Services	Amer.	25
Pei Wei	Asian	20
Porch	Pub	22
Sushi Axiom	Japanese	26
Taverna	Italian	22
Tei Tei Robata	Japanese	25
Toulouse	French	22

Vote at zagat.com

NEW Velvet Taco	*Mex.*	–
Ziziki's	*Greek*	24

LEMMON AVE./ OAK LAWN

Ⓩ Al Biernat's	*Steak*	27
Ⓩ Bob's	*Steak*	25
Buzzbrews Kitchen	*Coffee*	20
Café Brazil	*Coffee*	20
Cosmic Café	*Eclectic/Veg.*	–
Cyclone Anaya's	*Tex-Mex*	21
Dish	*Amer.*	20
Eddie V's	*Seafood/Steak*	26
El Fenix	*Tex-Mex*	20
Gloria's	*Salvadoran/Tex-Mex*	22
Green Papaya	*Viet.*	24
La Duni	*Pan-Latin*	24
Lucky's Cafe	*Amer.*	21
Mia's	*Tex-Mex*	23
Nonna	*Italian*	25
Nosh Euro	*Amer.*	24
Pappadeaux	*Cajun/Seafood*	23
Parigi	*Amer.*	25
Steel	*Japanese/Viet.*	23
Sushi Zushi	*Japanese*	23

LOVE FIELD AREA/ NORTHPARK/ PRESTON/ WEST LOVERS LN.

Aboca's	*Italian*	23
Asian Mint/Mint	*Asian*	22
Bailey's	*Steak*	22
Ⓩ Bijoux	*French*	28
Blue Mesa	*SW*	23
Café Express	*Eclectic*	20
Café Istanbul	*Turkish*	23
Campisi's	*Pizza*	23
Cantina Laredo	*Mex.*	21
Celebration	*Amer.*	24
Cheesecake	*Amer.*	20
Cindi's Deli	*Deli*	21
City Café	*Amer.*	21
Dough	*Pizza*	27
Eden	*Amer.*	–
El Fenix	*Tex-Mex*	20
Fireside Pies	*Pizza*	23
Hillstone	*Amer.*	24
India Palace	*Indian*	22
La Duni	*Pan-Latin*	24
Mama's Daughters'	*Diner*	19
Maple/Motor	*Burgers*	25
Ⓩ Mercury	*Amer.*	28
NEW Meso Maya	*Mex.*	–
Mi Cocina	*Tex-Mex*	21
Neighborhood Services	*Amer.*	25

Pappas BBQ	*BBQ*	21
Ⓩ Pappas Bros.	*Steak*	28
Pei Wei	*Asian*	20
P.F. Chang's	*Chinese*	21
NEW Princi Italia	*Italian*	–
R+D Kitchen	*Amer.*	24
Rathbun's Blue	*Amer.*	22
Rise N° 1	*French*	25
Nicola's/Rest. Nicola	*Italian*	22
Royal China	*Chinese*	26
Sevy's	*Amer.*	23
Shinsei	*Asian*	25
Snuffer's	*Burgers*	19
Sonny Bryan's	*BBQ*	24
Taco Diner	*Mex.*	21
Torchy's Tacos	*Mex.*	24
Ziziki's	*Greek*	24
Zoë's Kitchen	*Amer.*	19

MCKINNEY AVE./ QUADRANGLE/ UPTOWN/WEST VILLAGE (NORTH OF DOWNTOWN)

Arcodoro/Pomodoro	*Italian*	21
Avanti	*Italian/Med.*	23
Sushi Axiom	*Japanese*	26
Bolla	*Amer.*	–
Café Express	*Eclectic*	20
Capital Grille	*Steak*	26
Coal Vines	*Italian*	24
NEW Company Café	*Amer.*	–
Del Frisco's	*Amer.*	27
Dragonfly	*Amer.*	19
Dream Café	*Amer.*	23
El Fenix	*Tex-Mex*	20
Ⓩ Fearing's	*SW*	27
Gloria's	*Salvadoran/Tex-Mex*	22
Greenz	*Amer.*	23
Grimaldi's	*Pizza*	26
Hôtel St. Germain	*Continental/French*	26
NEW Komali	*Mex.*	24
Malai	*Thai/Viet.*	–
Ⓩ Mansion	*Amer.*	26
Mi Cocina	*Tex-Mex*	21
Morton's	*Steak*	26
Nick & Sam's	*Seafood/Steak*	27
Nick/Sam's Grill	*Amer.*	25
Nobu	*Japanese*	26
Ocean Prime	*Seafood/Steak*	21
Perry's Steak	*Steak*	26
NEW Private Social	*Eclectic*	–
Salum	*Amer.*	26
Sambuca	*Eclectic*	22
S&D Oyster	*Seafood*	25

Taco Diner | *Mex.*	21
Texas/Brazil | *Brazilian/Steak*	24
Truluck's | *Seafood*	24
Urban Taco | *Mex.*	20
Yutaka | *Japanese*	28

PRESTON HOLLOW

Cindi's Deli | *Deli*	21
Suze | *Med.*	27

VICTORY PARK

Craft Dallas | *Amer.*	24
Kenichi | *Pan-Asian*	21

South Dallas

CEDAR HILL

Z Babe's Chicken | *Southern*	25
Veracruz | *Mex.*	26

DESOTO

Buttons | *Amer.*	23

DUNCANVILLE

Pappadeaux | *Cajun/Seafood*	23

OAK CLIFF

NEW Bee Enchiladeria | *Mex.*	22
Bolsa | *Amer.*	25
El Fenix | *Tex-Mex*	20
Eno's Pizza | *Italian/Pizza*	25
Gloria's | *Salvadoran/Tex-Mex*	22
Hattie's | *Amer.*	27
La Calle Doce | *Mex.*	25
NEW Lockhart | *BBQ*	21
Z NEW Lucia | *Italian*	29
NEW Mesa | *Mex.*	-
NEW Oddfellows | *Amer./Coffee*	-
Smoke | *BBQ*	24
Spiral Diner | *Diner/Veg.*	22
Tillman's | *Amer.*	20
Veracruz | *Mex.*	26

Outlying Dallas

ADDISON/ NORTH DALLAS/ RICHARDSON

Aboca's | *Italian*	23
Addison Cafe | *Amer.*	25
Ali Baba | *Med.*	23
Andiamo | *Italian*	23
Blue Fish | *Japanese*	24
Blue Mesa | *SW*	23
Buttons | *Amer.*	23
Cadot | *French*	25
Café Brazil | *Coffee*	20

Campisi's | *Pizza*	23
Cantina Laredo | *Mex.*	21
Carrabba's | *Italian*	23
Chamberlain's Fish | *Seafood*	26
Chamberlain's Steak | *Steak*	25
Cindi's Deli | *Deli*	21
Clay Pit | *Indian*	23
Z Del Frisco's | *Steak*	27
Deli News | *Deli*	22
Dimassi's Med. | *Mideast.*	19
Dream Café | *Amer.*	23
El Fenix | *Tex-Mex*	20
Fadi's | *Mideast.*	25
Ferrari's | *Italian*	23
First Chinese | *Chinese*	24
Fogo/Chão | *Brazilian/Steak*	25
Gloria's | *Salvadoran/Tex-Mex*	22
Greenz | *Amer.*	23
Grimaldi's | *Pizza*	26
Houston's/Hillstone | *Amer.*	24
Kenny's Wood Fired | *Amer.*	26
Lavendou | *French*	24
Lawry's | *Steak*	26
Lefty's Lobster | *Seafood*	22
Madras Pavilion | *Indian*	20
Maguire's | *Amer.*	23
Main St. Bistro | *French*	21
Mi Cocina | *Tex-Mex*	21
Mi Piaci | *Italian*	26
Pappadeaux | *Cajun/Seafood*	23
Pei Wei | *Asian*	20
P.F. Chang's | *Chinese*	21
Rafain Brazilian | *Brazilian/Steak*	-
Ruth's Chris | *Steak*	26
Silver Fox | *Steak*	22
Snuffer's | *Burgers*	19
Sonny Bryan's | *BBQ*	24
Sullivan's | *Steak*	24
Sushi Sake | *Japanese*	27
Taco Diner | *Mex.*	21
Texas/Brazil | *Brazilian/Steak*	24
III Forks | *Steak*	24
Truluck's | *Seafood*	24
Twisted Root | *Burgers*	23
Ziziki's | *Greek*	24

AIRPORT

Cousin's | *BBQ*	22

ALLEN/MCKINNEY

Blue Fish | *Japanese*	24
Brio | *Italian*	22
Café Brazil | *Coffee*	20
Cavalli Pizza | *Pizza*	27
Cheesecake | *Amer.*	20

Grimaldi's | *Pizza* — 26
Pei Wei | *Asian* — 20
P.F. Chang's | *Chinese* — 21
Rick's Chophse. | *Southern/Steak* — -
Rudy's | *BBQ* — 25
Square Burger | *Burgers* — -

CARROLLTON/ FARMERS BRANCH

🛿 Babe's Chicken | *Southern* — 25
Café Brazil | *Coffee* — 20
Cindi's Deli | *Deli* — 21
First Chinese | *Chinese* — 24

EAST PLANO/ WEST PLANO

Artin's Grill | *Amer.* — 24
Bavarian Grill | *German* — 26
Blue Mesa | *SW* — 23
🛿 Bob's | *Steak* — 25
Café Brazil | *Coffee* — 20
Café Express | *Eclectic* — 20
Café Istanbul | *Turkish* — 23
Campisi's | *Pizza* — 23
Capital Grille | *Steak* — 26
Carrabba's | *Italian* — 23
Chuy's | *Tex-Mex* — 21
Coal Vines | *Italian* — 24
Fireside Pies | *Pizza* — 23
First Chinese | *Chinese* — 24
Holy Grail Pub | *Euro./Pub* — -
Jasper's | *Amer.* — 24
Main St. Bistro | *French* — 21
Mama's Daughters' | *Diner* — 19
Mango | *Thai* — 24
Mi Cocina | *Tex-Mex* — 21
Nicola's/Rest. Nicola | *Italian* — 22
Nosh Euro | *Amer.* — 24
Roy's | *Hawaiian* — 25
Sambuca | *Eclectic* — 22
Seasons 52 | *Amer.* — 24
Snuffer's | *Burgers* — 19
Steve Fields | *Seafood/Steak* — 28
Taco Diner | *Mex.* — 21
Twisted Root | *Burgers* — 23
Urban Crust | *Pizza* — 23
🆕 Whiskey Cake | *Amer.* — 20
Yao Fuzi | *Chinese* — 26
Ziziki's | *Greek* — 24
Zoë's Kitchen | *Amer.* — 19

FAIRVIEW

Bailey's | *Steak* — 22
Cyclone Anaya's | *Tex-Mex* — 21
Twisted Root | *Burgers* — 23

FRISCO

🛿 Babe's Chicken | *Southern* — 25
Cantina Laredo | *Mex.* — 21
Cheesecake | *Amer.* — 20
Fadi's | *Mideast.* — 25
Gloria's | *Salvadoran/Tex-Mex* — 22
Jinbeh | *Japanese* — 22
Kenny's Burger | *Burgers* — 22
🆕 Platia Greek | *Greek* — -
Rudy's | *BBQ* — 25
Silver Fox | *Steak* — 22

GARLAND/ MESQUITE

🛿 Babe's Chicken | *Southern* — 25
Baker's Ribs | *BBQ* — 22
First Chinese | *Chinese* — 24
Gloria's | *Salvadoran/Tex-Mex* — 22

IRVING/ LAS COLINAS

Ali Baba | *Med.* — 23
Blue Fish | *Japanese* — 24
Café/Green | *Amer.* — 24
Cavalli Pizza | *Pizza* — 27
Cool River | *Steak/SW* — 21
El Fenix | *Tex-Mex* — 20
Empress/China | *Chinese* — 24
I Fratelli | *Italian* — 23
Jinbeh | *Japanese* — 22
Mama's Daughters' | *Diner* — 19
Mi Cocina | *Tex-Mex* — 21
Pei Wei | *Asian* — 20
Ranch/Las Colinas | *Southern* — 26
Sonny Bryan's | *BBQ* — 24
Taco Diner | *Mex.* — 21
Via Reál | *Mex.* — 23

ROCKWALL

Gloria's | *Salvadoran/Tex-Mex* — 22
Snuffer's | *Burgers* — 19

ROWLETT

Baker's Ribs | *BBQ* — 22

Ft. Worth

CULTURAL DISTRICT/ NEAR WEST/ SOUTHWEST/WEST

Angelo's | *BBQ* — 25
Bailey's | *Steak* — 22
🆕 Blue Sushi | *Japanese* — 23
Bonnell's | *SW* — 27
Brownstone | *Amer.* — 21
Buffet/Kimbell | *Amer.* — 22
Buttons | *Amer.* — 23

Café Modern | *Eclectic* 23
Charleston's | *Amer.* 21
Cousin's | *BBQ* 22
Eddie V's | *Seafood/Steak* 26
El Fenix | *Tex-Mex* 20
Fireside Pies | *Pizza* 23
Fred's | *Burgers* 22
Gloria's | *Salvadoran/Tex-Mex* 22
🔁 Kincaid's | *Burgers* 25
La Familia | *Mex.* 25
Lambert's | *Steak* 24
Lanny's Alta | *Eclectic* 27
Love Shack | *Burgers* 23
Pei Wei | *Asian* 20
Railhead | *BBQ* 25
🔁 Saint-Emilion | *French* 29
Sushi Axiom | *Japanese* 26
Szechuan Chinese | *Chinese* 24
Tillman's | *Amer.* 20

DOWNTOWN/ SUNDANCE SQUARE

🔁 Bob's | *Steak* 25
Cantina Laredo | *Mex.* 21
🔁 Del Frisco's | *Steak* 27
Ferre | *Italian* 18
Grace | *Amer.* 25
Mi Cocina | *Tex-Mex* 21
Pappas Burgers | *Burgers* 24
P.F. Chang's | *Chinese* 21
Piranha | *Japanese* 21
Reata | *SW* 25
Ruth's Chris | *Steak* 26
Taverna | *Italian* 22
Texas/Brazil | *Brazilian/Steak* 24

FAR NORTH

Fred's | *Burgers* 22

FOREST PARK/ HOSPITAL DISTRICT/ SOUTH SIDE/ UNIVERSITY AREA

Blue Mesa | *SW* 23
Café Brazil | *Coffee* 20
Cat City Grill | *Amer.* 21
Cousin's | *BBQ* 22
Dutch's | *Burgers* 22
Ellerbe | *Amer.* 26
Esperanza's | *Mex.* 27
Lili's Bistro | *Eclectic* 26
Nonna Tata | *Italian* 27
Pappadeaux | *Cajun/Seafood* 23
Paris Coffee | *Coffee* 23
🆕 Shinjuku Station | *Japanese* -

Silver Fox | *Steak* 22
Spiral Diner | *Diner/Veg.* 22
Yucatan Taco | *Mex.* 22
Zoë's Kitchen | *Amer.* 19

NORTH SIDE/ STOCKYARDS

Byblos | *Lebanese* 27
Cattlemen's | *Steak* 23
Cooper's BBQ | *BBQ* 25
Esperanza's | *Mex.* 27
Joe T. Garcia's | *Tex-Mex* 20
Lonesome Dove | *SW* 27
Love Shack | *Burgers* 23

Denton County

FLOWER MOUND

Empress/China | *Chinese* 24
Piranha | *Japanese* 21

HIGHLAND VILLAGE

Snuffer's | *Burgers* 19

LEWISVILLE

Cantina Laredo | *Mex.* 21
Jinbeh | *Japanese* 22
Mama's Daughters' | *Diner* 19

ROANOKE

🔁 Babe's Chicken | *Southern* 25
Twisted Root | *Burgers* 23

Mid-Cities

ARLINGTON

🔁 Babe's Chicken | *Southern* 25
🔁 Cacharel | *French* 27
Cheesecake | *Amer.* 20
Chuy's | *Tex-Mex* 21
First Chinese | *Chinese* 24
Gloria's | *Salvadoran/Tex-Mex* 22
🔁 Kincaid's | *Burgers* 25
Olenjack's | *Amer.* 25
Pappadeaux | *Cajun/Seafood* 23
Pei Wei | *Asian* 20
P.F. Chang's | *Chinese* 21
Piccolo Mondo | *Italian* 24
Piranha | *Japanese* 21
Rudy's | *BBQ* 25
Twisted Root | *Burgers* 23

BEDFORD

Pappadeaux | *Cajun/Seafood* 23

HURST

Carrabba's | *Italian* 23

Northeast Tarrant County

ALLIANCE

Cousin's | *BBQ* — 22
Z Kincaid's | *Burgers* — 25
Sonny Bryan's | *BBQ* — 24

COPPELL

Hard Eight BBQ | *BBQ* — 25

GRAPEVINE

Z Bob's | *Steak* — 25
Boi Na Braza | *Brazilian/Steak* — 25
Cantina Laredo | *Mex.* — 21
Carrabba's | *Italian* — 23
Empress/China | *Chinese* — 24
Ferrari's | *Italian* — 23
Fireside Pies | *Pizza* — 23
Main St. Bistro | *French* — 21
P.F. Chang's | *Chinese* — 21
Silver Fox | *Steak* — 22

HALTOM CITY

First Chinese | *Chinese* — 24

SOUTHLAKE

Blue Mesa | *SW* — 23
Brio | *Italian* — 22
Café Express | *Eclectic* — 20
Cheesecake | *Amer.* — 20
Coal Vines | *Italian* — 24
Z Kincaid's | *Burgers* — 25
Kirby's | *Steak* — 24
Mi Cocina | *Tex-Mex* — 21
Pei Wei | *Asian* — 20
Snuffer's | *Burgers* — 19
Taco Diner | *Mex.* — 21
Truluck's | *Seafood* — 24

WATAUGA

Chef Point Café | *Southern* — 24

Rural

BURLESON

Z Babe's Chicken | *Southern* — 25
Sushi Axiom | *Japanese* — 26

CROWLEY

Cousin's | *BBQ* — 22

Special Features

Listings cover the best in each category and include names, locations and Food ratings. Multi-location restaurants' features may vary by branch.

BREAKFAST

(See also Hotel Dining)

Buzzbrews Kitchen	multi.	20
Café Brazil	multi.	20
Deli News	N Dallas	22
Dream Café	multi.	23
Esperanza's	multi.	27
Highland Pk. Soda	Knox-Henderson	20
Kuby's	Park Cities	22
La Duni	Oak Lawn	24
Lucky's Cafe	Oak Lawn	21
Main St. Bistro	multi.	21
Mama's Daughters'	multi.	19
Paris Coffee	Hospital Dist	23

BRUNCH

Blue Mesa	multi.	23
Bolsa	Oak Cliff	25
Café/Green	Las Colinas	24
Cheesecake	NorthPark	20
Esperanza's	multi.	27
🄩 Fearing's	Uptown	27
Grape	Greenville Ave	26
Hattie's	Oak Cliff	27
Kuby's	Park Cities	22
La Duni	multi.	24
Lawry's	N Dallas	26
Lucky's Cafe	Oak Lawn	21
Maguire's	N Dallas	23
🄩 Mansion	Uptown	26
NEW Marquee	Highland Pk Vill	26
Rathbun's Blue	Preston Ctr	22
Reata	Sundance Sq	25
Toulouse	Knox-Henderson	22
Ziziki's	multi.	24

BUSINESS DINING

🄩 Abacus	Knox-Henderson	27
🄩 Al Biernat's	Oak Lawn	27
Bailey's	NorthPark	22
🄩 Bob's	multi.	25
Bonnell's	SW	27
Brio	Southlake	22
Brownstone	Near W	21
🄩 Cacharel	Arlington	27
Cadot	N Dallas	25
Café/Green	Las Colinas	24
Café Pacific	Park Cities	27
Capital Grille	multi.	26

Cat City Grill	Hospital Dist	21
Chamberlain's Steak	Addison	25
Charlie Palmer Steak	Downtown D	25
City Café	W Lovers Ln	21
🄩 Del Frisco's	multi.	27
Eddie V's	Cultural Dist	26
🄩 Fearing's	Uptown	27
Five Sixty	Downtown D	24
Grace	Downtown FW	25
Jasper's	West Plano	24
Kenichi	Victory Pk	21
Kirby's	multi.	24
Lambert's	Near W	24
Lavendou	N Dallas	24
🄩 Mansion	Uptown	26
NEW Marquee	Highland Pk Vill	26
🄩 Mercury	Preston Forest	28
Mi Piaci	Addison	26
Morton's	Uptown	26
🄩 Nana	Market Ctr	27
Nick & Sam's	Uptown	27
Nobu	Uptown	26
Nosh Euro	West Plano	24
Oceanaire	Galleria	23
Ocean Prime	Uptown	21
Olenjack's	Arlington	25
Palm	W End	25
🄩 Pappas Bros.	Love Field	28
Perry's Steak	Uptown	26
Piccolo Mondo	Arlington	24
NEW Private Social	Uptown	-
Pyramid	Arts Dist	29
Reata	Sundance Sq	25
🄩 Saint-Emilion	Cultural Dist	29
Screen Door	Arts Dist	23
Sevy's	Preston Ctr	23
Silver Fox	Frisco	22
🄩 Stephan Pyles	Arts Dist	27
Steve Fields	West Plano	28
Sullivan's	N Dallas	24
III Forks	N Dallas	24
Truluck's	multi.	24

CELEBRITY CHEFS

Nick Badovinus		
Neighborhood Services	W Lovers Ln	25
Anthony Bombaci		
🄩 Nana	Market Ctr	27

Jon Bonnell	
Bonnell's | **SW**	27
Tom Colicchio	
Craft Dallas | **Victory Pk**	24
Tiffany Derry	
NEW Private Social | **Uptown**	–
Dean Fearing	
Z Fearing's | **Uptown**	27
Scott Gottlich	
Z Bijoux | **W Lovers Ln**	28
Lanny Lancarte	
Lanny's Alta | **Cultural Dist**	27
Tim Love	
Lonesome Dove | **Stockyards**	27
Nobu Matsuhisa	
Nobu | **Uptown**	26
Brian Olenjack	
Olenjack's | **Arlington**	25
Charlie Palmer	
Charlie Palmer Steak | **Downtown D**	25
Wolfgang Puck	
Five Sixty | **Downtown D**	24
Stephan Pyles	
Samar | **Arts Dist**	26
Z Stephan Pyles | **Arts Dist**	27
Kent Rathbun	
Z Abacus | **Knox-Henderson**	27
Jasper's | **West Plano**	24
Rathbun's Blue | **Preston Ctr**	22
Teiichi Sakurai	
Tei An | **Arts Dist**	26
Chris Ward	
Z Mercury | **Preston Forest**	28
Tre Wilcox	
NEW Marquee | **Highland Pk Vill**	26

CHILD-FRIENDLY

(Alternatives to the usual fast-food places; * children's menu available)

Z Babe's Chicken* | **multi.**	25
Blue Mesa* | **multi.**	23
Café Brazil* | **multi.**	20
Café Express* | **multi.**	20
Campisi's* | **Greenville Ave**	23
Cat City Grill* | **Hospital Dist**	21
Celebration* | **Love Field**	24
Charleston's* | **SW**	21
Cheesecake* | **multi.**	20
Chuy's* | **multi.**	21
Cooper's BBQ | **Stockyards**	25
Cousin's* | **multi.**	22
Deli News* | **N Dallas**	22
Dream Café* | **multi.**	23
El Fenix | **multi.**	20

Esperanza's | **multi.**	27
Ferrari's* | **multi.**	23
Fireside Pies* | **multi.**	23
Gloria's* | **multi.**	22
Highland Pk. Soda | **Knox-Henderson**	20
Houston's/Hillstone | **Addison**	24
I Fratelli* | **Irving**	23
India Palace* | **Preston Forest**	22
NEW Jack's Chowhound | **Location Varies**	–
Jinbeh* | **multi.**	22
Joe T. Garcia's* | **N Side**	20
Kenny's Burger* | **Frisco**	22
Z Kincaid's | **multi.**	25
La Familia* | **Near W**	25
Maguire's* | **N Dallas**	23
Main St. Bistro* | **multi.**	21
Mama's Daughters'* | **multi.**	19
Mia's* | **Lemmon Ave**	23
Mi Cocina* | **multi.**	21
Olenjack's* | **Arlington**	25
Pei Wei* | **multi.**	20
P.F. Chang's* | **multi.**	21
NEW Platia Greek* | **Frisco**	–
Railhead | **Cultural Dist**	25
Sevy's* | **Preston Ctr**	23
Snuffer's* | **multi.**	19
Sonny Bryan's* | **multi.**	24
Via Reál* | **Las Colinas**	23
Zoë's Kitchen* | **multi.**	19

DESSERT SPECIALISTS

Bonnell's | **SW**	27
Capital Grille | **Uptown**	26
Cheesecake | **multi.**	20
Dream Café | **multi.**	23
Eden | **W Lovers Ln**	–
Hibiscus | **Knox-Henderson**	26
La Duni | **multi.**	24
Main St. Bistro | **multi.**	21
Z Mansion | **Uptown**	26
Z Nana | **Market Ctr**	27
Z Pappas Bros. | **Love Field**	28
Z Saint-Emilion | **Cultural Dist**	29

DINING ALONE

(Other than hotels and places with counter service)

Aboca's | **Richardson**	23
Asian Mint/Mint | **Medical City**	22
Sushi Axiom | **Uptown**	26
NEW Blue Sushi | **Near W**	–
Buffet/Kimbell | **Cultural Dist**	22
Café Brazil | **multi.**	20

Campisi's | **multi.**	23
Cane Rosso | **Deep Ellum**	-
Cat City Grill | **Hospital Dist**	21
NEW Cedars Social | **Downtown D**	20
Cindi's Deli | **Preston Hollow**	21
City Café | **W Lovers Ln**	21
Coal Vines | **multi.**	24
Cosmic Café | **Oak Lawn**	-
Deli News | **N Dallas**	22
Dream Café | **multi.**	23
Eno's Pizza | **Oak Cliff**	25
Ferre | **Sundance Sq**	18
Fireside Pies | **multi.**	23
First Chinese | **Richardson**	24
Fred's | **Far North**	22
Gloria's | **multi.**	22
Holy Grail Pub | **West Plano**	-
I Fratelli | **Irving**	23
Kenny's Burger | **Frisco**	22
Kenny's Wood Fired | **Addison**	26
⊠ Kincaid's | **multi.**	25
La Duni | **multi.**	24
La Familia | **Near W**	25
L'Ancestral | **Knox-Henderson**	25
Lavendou | **N Dallas**	24
Maguire's | **N Dallas**	23
Malai | **W Vill**	-
Mama's Daughters' | **Market Ctr**	19
Mango | **Park Cities**	24
NEW Marquee | **Highland Pk Vill**	26
Meddlesome Moth | **Market Ctr**	22
NEW Meso Maya | **Preston Forest**	-
Mia's | **Lemmon Ave**	23
NEW Oddfellows | **Oak Cliff**	-
Olenjack's | **Arlington**	25
Olivella's | **Park Cities**	24
Railhead | **Cultural Dist**	25
Reata | **Sundance Sq**	25
Rise N° 1 | **W Lovers Ln**	25
Shinsei | **W Lovers Ln**	25
Snuffer's | **multi.**	19
Square Burger | **McKinney**	-
⊠ Stephan Pyles | **Arts Dist**	27
Urban Crust | **East Plano**	23
NEW Whiskey Cake | **West Plano**	20
Yutaka | **Uptown**	28

ENTERTAINMENT

(Call for days and times of performances)

Avanti | live music | **Uptown**	23
Bailey's | live music | **multi.**	22
Bavarian Grill | live music | **East Plano**	26
Buffet/Kimbell | live music | **Cultural Dist**	22
Byblos | belly dancer | **N Side**	27
⊠ Cacharel | guitarist | **Arlington**	27
Café Madrid | classical/ flamenco | **Knox-Henderson**	23
Café/Green | live music | **Las Colinas**	24
Clay Pit | live music | **Addison**	23
Cool River | cover bands | **Las Colinas**	21
Cosmic Café | varies | **Oak Lawn**	-
⊠ Del Frisco's | piano | **N Dallas**	27
Eno's Pizza | jazz/live bands | **Oak Cliff**	25
Fred's | live music | **Near W**	22
⊠ French Rm. | jazz | **Downtown D**	28
Gloria's | DJ/live salsa | **multi.**	22
Joe T. Garcia's | mariachi | **N Side**	20
Kirby's | live music | **Southlake**	24
Kuby's | accordion | **Park Cities**	22
La Calle Doce | varies | **multi.**	25
Maguire's | jazz | **N Dallas**	23
Nick & Sam's | piano | **Uptown**	27
⊠ Pappas Bros. | piano | **Love Field**	28
Piccolo Mondo | piano | **Arlington**	24
Ranch/Las Colinas | live bands | **Las Colinas**	26
Reata | vocalists | **Sundance Sq**	25
Rick's Chophse. | live music | **McKinney**	-
Sambuca | live music | **Uptown**	22
Seasons 52 | live music | **West Plano**	24
Steve Fields | varies | **West Plano**	28
Sullivan's | jazz/live bands | **N Dallas**	24
III Forks | varies | **N Dallas**	24

FOOD TRUCKS

NEW Bacon Wagon | **Location Varies**	-
Cane Rosso Mobile | **Location Varies**	-
Green House | **Location Varies**	-
NEW Jack's Chowhound | **Location Varies**	-
NEW Nammi Truck | **Location Varies**	-
NEW Ruthie's | **Location Varies**	-

HISTORIC PLACES

(Year opened; * building)

1885 | Rick's Chophse.* | **McKinney**	-
1890 | Babe's Chicken* | **Burleson**	25

1891 | S&D Oyster* | **Uptown** — 25

1896 | Urban Crust* | **East Plano** — 23

1906 | Hôtel St. Germain* | **Uptown** — 26

1908 | Local* | **Deep Ellum** — 26

1912 | French Rm.* | **Downtown D** — 28

1912 | Highland Pk. Soda | **Knox-Henderson** — 20

1918 | El Fenix | **multi.** — 20

1920 | Hattie's* | **Oak Cliff** — 27

1920 | Lucia* | **Oak Cliff** — 29

1923 | Bolla* | **Uptown** — ─

1926 | Paris Coffee | **Hospital Dist** — 23

1927 | Bubba's* | **Park Cities** — 23

1929 | Square Burger* | **McKinney** — ─

1932 | Spiral Diner* | **Hospital Dist** — 22

1935 | Joe T. Garcia's | **N Side** — 20

1940 | Hacienda* | **Knox-Henderson** — 23

1946 | Campisi's | **multi.** — 23

1946 | Kincaid's | **West** — 25

1946 | Smoke* | **Oak Cliff** — 24

1947 | Cattlemen's | **Stockyards** — 23

1950 | Al Biernat's* | **Oak Lawn** — 27

1957 | Zodiac | **Downtown D** — 24

1958 | Angelo's | **Near W** — 25

1958 | Mama's Daughters' | **Market Ctr** — 19

1958 | Sonny Bryan's | **Love Field** — 24

1961 | Kuby's | **Park Cities** — 22

HOTEL DINING

Adolphus Hotel
  ⊠ French Rm. | **Downtown D** — 28

Belmont Hotel
  Smoke | **Oak Cliff** — 24

Fairmont Dallas
  Pyramid | **Arts Dist** — 29

Four Seasons Resort & Club
  Café/Green | **Las Colinas** — 24

Grand Hotel
  Rick's Chophse. | **McKinney** — ─

Hilton Anatole Hotel
  ⊠ Nana | **Market Ctr** — 27

Hotel Palomar
  Central 214 | **Park Cities** — 19

Joule Hotel
  Charlie Palmer Steak | **Downtown D** — 25

Omni Dallas Hotel
  ⊠ Bob's | **Downtown D** — 25

Omni Ft. Worth Hotel
  ⊠ Bob's | **Downtown FW** — 25

Ritz-Carlton Hotel
  ⊠ Fearing's | **Uptown** — 27

Rosewood Crescent Hotel
  Nobu | **Uptown** — 26

Rosewood Mansion
  ⊠ Mansion | **Uptown** — 26

St. Germain Hôtel
  Hôtel St. Germain | **Uptown** — 26

Stoneleigh Hotel
  Bolla | **Uptown** — ─

Westin Galleria Hotel
  Oceanaire | **Galleria** — 23

W Hotel
  Craft Dallas | **Victory Pk** — 24

ZaZa Hotel
  Dragonfly | **Uptown** — 19

LATE DINING

(Weekday closing hour)

Buzzbrews Kitchen | varies | **Knox-Henderson** — 20

Byblos | varies | **N Side** — 27

Café Brazil | varies | **multi.** — 20

NEW Cedars Social | varies | **Downtown D** — 20

NEW Company Café | 2 AM | **Uptown** — ─

Dish | varies | **Oak Lawn** — 20

Fred's | 12 AM | **multi.** — 22

Fuel City Tacos | 24 hrs. | **Downtown D** — ─

Holy Grail Pub | 2 AM | **West Plano** — ─

Kenny's Wood Fired | varies | **Addison** — 26

NEW Marquee | varies | **Highland Pk Vill** — 26

Snuffer's | varies | **Greenville Ave** — 19

Twisted Root | varies | **Greenville Ave** — 23

MEET FOR A DRINK

Sushi Axiom | **Uptown** — 26

Bailey's | **multi.** — 22

Blue Fish | **Allen** — 24

NEW Blue Sushi | **Near W** — 23

Bolla | **Uptown** — ─

Brio | **Southlake** — 22

Brownstone | **Near W** — 21

Buttons | **SW** — 23

Café Pacific | **Park Cities** — 27

Capital Grille | **Uptown** — 26

Cat City Grill | **Hospital Dist** — 21

NEW Cedars Social | **Downtown D**	20
Central 214 | **Park Cities**	19
Charlie Palmer Steak | **Downtown D**	25
Cool River | **Las Colinas**	21
Cyclone Anaya's | **multi.**	21
Z Del Frisco's | **multi.**	27
Dish | **Oak Lawn**	20
Dragonfly | **Uptown**	19
Eddie V's | **Cultural Dist**	26
Z Fearing's | **Uptown**	27
Ferre | **Sundance Sq**	18
Fred's | **Near W**	22
Grace | **Downtown FW**	25
Grape | **Greenville Ave**	26
Hard Eight BBQ | **Coppell**	25
Holy Grail Pub | **West Plano**	-
Jasper's | **West Plano**	24
Kenichi | **Victory Pk**	21
Maguire's | **N Dallas**	23
Malai | **W Vill**	-
Z Mansion | **Uptown**	26
NEW Marquee | **Highland Pk Vill**	26
Meddlesome Moth | **Market Ctr**	22
Z Mercury | **Preston Forest**	28
NEW Meso Maya | **Preston Forest**	-
Mi Cocina | **multi.**	21
Z Nana | **Market Ctr**	27
Nick & Sam's | **Uptown**	27
Nick/Sam's Grill | **Uptown**	25
Ocean Prime | **Uptown**	21
Olenjack's | **Arlington**	25
Palm | **W End**	25
Porch | **Knox-Henderson**	22
R+D Kitchen | **Preston Ctr**	24
Ranch/Las Colinas | **Las Colinas**	26
Rathbun's Blue | **Preston Ctr**	22
Reata | **Sundance Sq**	25
Samar | **Arts Dist**	26
Sevy's | **Preston Ctr**	23
NEW Shinjuku Station | **Hospital Dist**	-
Steel | **Oak Lawn**	23
Z Stephan Pyles | **Arts Dist**	27
Sullivan's | **N Dallas**	24
NEW Texas Spice | **Downtown D**	-
Tillman's | **multi.**	20
NEW Wild Salsa | **Downtown D**	-
Yao Fuzi | **West Plano**	26

NEWCOMERS

Bacon Wagon | **Location Varies**	-
Bee Enchiladeria | **Oak Cliff**	22
Blue Sushi | **Near W**	23
Cedars Social | **Downtown D**	20
Company Café | **multi.**	-
Jack's Chowhound | **Location Varies**	-
Komali | **Uptown**	24
Lockhart | **Oak Cliff**	21
Z Lucia | **Oak Cliff**	29
Marquee | **Highland Pk Vill**	26
Mesa | **Oak Cliff**	-
Meso Maya | **Preston Forest**	-
Nammi Truck | **Location Varies**	-
Oddfellows | **Oak Cliff**	-
Platia Greek | **Frisco**	-
Princi Italia | **Preston Royal**	-
Private Social | **Uptown**	-
Ruthie's | **Location Varies**	-
Shinjuku Station | **Hospital Dist**	-
Texas Spice | **Downtown D**	-
Velvet Taco | **Knox-Henderson**	-
Whiskey Cake | **West Plano**	20
Wild Salsa | **Downtown D**	-

OFFBEAT

Angelo's | **Near W**	25
Z Babe's Chicken | **multi.**	25
NEW Bee Enchiladeria | **Oak Cliff**	22
Buzzbrews Kitchen | **multi.**	20
Chef Point Café | **Watauga**	24
Chuy's | **multi.**	21
Cosmic Café | **Oak Lawn**	-
Dream Café | **Uptown**	23
Fred's | **Near W**	22
Fuel City Tacos | **Downtown D**	-
Highland Pk. Soda | **Knox-Henderson**	20
Spiral Diner | **Hospital Dist**	22
Tillman's | **multi.**	20

OUTDOOR DINING

(G=garden; P=patio; R=rooftop; S=sidewalk; T=terrace; W=waterside)

Arcodoro/Pomodoro | P | **Uptown**	21
Bavarian Grill | G | **East Plano**	26
Bolsa | P | **Oak Cliff**	25
Buffet/Kimbell | G | **Cultural Dist**	22
Café Modern | P | **Cultural Dist**	23
Café Nasher | T | **Arts Dist**	25
Celebration | P | **Love Field**	24
Chuy's | P | **Knox-Henderson**	21
Cosmic Café | P | **Oak Lawn**	-
Dragonfly | P, W | **Uptown**	19
Dream Café | P | **multi.**	23
Z Fearing's | P | **Uptown**	27

Ferre | P | **Sundance Sq** | 18
Fireside Pies | P | **Knox-Henderson** | 23
Fred's | P | **multi.** | 22
Gloria's | P | **multi.** | 22
Jasper's | P | **West Plano** | 24
Joe T. Garcia's | G, P, W | **N Side** | 20
La Duni | G, P, S | **NorthPark** | 24
Malai | P | **W Vill** | -
🆉 Mansion | T | **Uptown** | 26
🆕 Marquee | P | **Highland Pk Vill** | 26
Mi Piaci | P, W | **Addison** | 26
Nonna Tata | S | **Hospital Dist** | 27
Ocean Prime | P | **Uptown** | 21
Parigi | P | **Oak Lawn** | 25
🆕 Platia Greek | P | **Frisco** | -
Reata | P | **Sundance Sq** | 25
Rise N° 1 | P | **W Lovers Ln** | 25
Samar | P | **Arts Dist** | 26
Sambuca | P | **Uptown** | 22
🆕 Shinjuku Station | P | **Hospital Dist** | -
Sushi Axiom | P | **multi.** | 26
Taco Diner | P | **multi.** | 21
Taverna | P | **Knox-Henderson** | 22
🆕 Texas Spice | P | **Downtown D** | -
Toulouse | P | **Knox-Henderson** | 22
Urban Crust | R | **East Plano** | 23
🆕 Wild Salsa | P | **Downtown D** | -

PEOPLE-WATCHING

🆉 Abacus | **Knox-Henderson** | 27
🆉 Al Biernat's | **Oak Lawn** | 27
Bolla | **Uptown** | -
Bonnell's | **SW** | 27
Brownstone | **Near W** | 21
Café Pacific | **Park Cities** | 27
Charlie Palmer Steak | **Downtown D** | 25
🆉 Del Frisco's | **multi.** | 27
Dragonfly | **Uptown** | 19
Eddie V's | **Cultural Dist** | 26
🆉 Fearing's | **Uptown** | 27
Five Sixty | **Downtown D** | 24
🆉 French Rm. | **Downtown D** | 28
Grace | **Downtown FW** | 25
Hibiscus | **Knox-Henderson** | 26
Javier's | **Knox-Henderson** | 24
Lonesome Dove | **Stockyards** | 27
🆉 Mansion | **Uptown** | 26
🆕 Marquee | **Highland Pk Vill** | 26
🆉 Mercury | **Preston Forest** | 28
Mi Cocina | **Park Cities** | 21
Nick & Sam's | **Uptown** | 27

Nobu | **Uptown** | 26
Nosh Euro | **Oak Lawn** | 24
Ocean Prime | **Uptown** | 21
Palm | **W End** | 25
🆕 Private Social | **Uptown** | -
🆉 Saint-Emilion | **Cultural Dist** | 29
Salum | **Uptown** | 26
Samar | **Arts Dist** | 26
Shinsei | **W Lovers Ln** | 25
Steel | **Oak Lawn** | 23
🆉 Stephan Pyles | **Arts Dist** | 27
Tillman's | **multi.** | 20

POWER SCENES

🆉 Abacus | **Knox-Henderson** | 27
🆉 Al Biernat's | **Oak Lawn** | 27
🆉 Bijoux | **W Lovers Ln** | 28
🆉 Bob's | **multi.** | 25
Bonnell's | **SW** | 27
Café Pacific | **Park Cities** | 27
Capital Grille | **multi.** | 26
Charlie Palmer Steak | **Downtown D** | 25
Craft Dallas | **Victory Pk** | 24
🆉 Del Frisco's | **multi.** | 27
Eddie V's | **Cultural Dist** | 26
🆉 Fearing's | **Uptown** | 27
🆉 French Rm. | **Downtown D** | 28
Grace | **Downtown FW** | 25
Jasper's | **West Plano** | 24
Kenichi | **Victory Pk** | 21
Lambert's | **Near W** | 24
Lanny's Alta | **Cultural Dist** | 27
Lonesome Dove | **Stockyards** | 27
🆉 Mansion | **Uptown** | 26
🆕 Marquee | **Highland Pk Vill** | 26
🆉 Mercury | **Preston Forest** | 28
Morton's | **Uptown** | 26
🆉 Nana | **Market Ctr** | 27
Nick & Sam's | **Uptown** | 27
Nobu | **Uptown** | 26
Nosh Euro | **Oak Lawn** | 24
Oceanaire | **Galleria** | 23
Ocean Prime | **Uptown** | 21
Palm | **W End** | 25
🆉 Pappas Bros. | **Love Field** | 28
🆕 Private Social | **Uptown** | -
🆉 Saint-Emilion | **Cultural Dist** | 29
Samar | **Arts Dist** | 26
Shinsei | **W Lovers Ln** | 25
🆉 Stephan Pyles | **Arts Dist** | 27

QUIET CONVERSATION

Adelmo's | **Knox-Henderson** | 25
🆉 Bijoux | **W Lovers Ln** | 28

☑ Cacharel | **Arlington**		27
Cadot | **N Dallas**		25
Café/Green | **Las Colinas**		24
City Café | **W Lovers Ln**		21
Ellerbe | **Hospital Dist**		26
☑ French Rm. | **Downtown D**		28
Grape | **Greenville Ave**		26
Hôtel St. Germain | **Uptown**		26
L'Ancestral | **Knox-Henderson**		25
Lavendou | **N Dallas**		24
☑ Mansion | **Uptown**		26
Mi Piaci | **Addison**		26
☑ Nana | **Market Ctr**		27
Rise Nº 1 | **W Lovers Ln**		25
☑ Saint-Emilion | **Cultural Dist**		29
Suze | **Preston Hollow**		27
Zodiac | **Downtown D**		24

ROMANTIC PLACES

Addison Cafe | **Addison**		25
Bailey's | **NorthPark**		22
☑ Bijoux | **W Lovers Ln**		28
☑ Cacharel | **Arlington**		27
Cadot | **N Dallas**		25
Charlie Palmer Steak | **Downtown D**		25
Eddie V's | **Cultural Dist**		26
Five Sixty | **Downtown D**		24
☑ French Rm. | **Downtown D**		28
Grape | **Greenville Ave**		26
Hôtel St. Germain | **Uptown**		26
Lanny's Alta | **Cultural Dist**		27
Lavendou | **N Dallas**		24
Lili's Bistro | **S Side**		26
Local | **Deep Ellum**		26
Lonesome Dove | **Stockyards**		27
☑ NEW Lucia | **Oak Cliff**		29
☑ Mansion | **Uptown**		26
☑ Mercury | **Preston Forest**		28
Mi Piaci | **Addison**		26
☑ Nana | **Market Ctr**		27
Ocean Prime | **Uptown**		21
Rise Nº 1 | **W Lovers Ln**		25
☑ Saint-Emilion | **Cultural Dist**		29
Screen Door | **Arts Dist**		23
Suze | **Preston Hollow**		27

SENIOR APPEAL

Aboca's | **Richardson**		23
Adelmo's | **Knox-Henderson**		25
☑ Babe's Chicken | **multi.**		25
Bubba's | **Park Cities**		23
☑ Cacharel | **Arlington**		27
Café Pacific | **Park Cities**		27
Celebration | **Love Field**		24
Cindi's Deli | **multi.**		21

City Café | **W Lovers Ln**		21
Deli News | **N Dallas**		22
El Fenix | **multi.**		20
Highland Pk. Soda | **Knox-Henderson**		20
Kirby's | **multi.**		24
Kuby's | **Park Cities**		22
L'Ancestral | **Knox-Henderson**		25
Lawry's | **N Dallas**		26
Mama's Daughters' | **multi.**		19
Royal China | **Preston Royal**		26
Zodiac | **Downtown D**		24

SINGLES SCENES

Sushi Axiom | **Uptown**		26
Blue Mesa | **Southlake**		23
NEW Blue Sushi | **Near W**		23
Cane Rosso | **Deep Ellum**		–
NEW Cedars Social | **Downtown D**		20
Chuy's | **multi.**		21
Cool River | **Las Colinas**		21
Cyclone Anaya's | **multi.**		21
Dragonfly | **Uptown**		19
Eddie V's | **Cultural Dist**		26
Fireside Pies | **multi.**		23
Gloria's | **multi.**		22
Grimaldi's | **multi.**		26
Hacienda | **Knox-Henderson**		23
Holy Grail Pub | **West Plano**		–
Kenichi | **Victory Pk**		21
Malai | **W Vill**		–
Mi Cocina | **multi.**		21
Neighborhood Services | **W Lovers Ln**		25
Nick/Sam's Grill | **Uptown**		25
Porch | **Knox-Henderson**		22
R+D Kitchen | **Preston Ctr**		24
Sambuca | **multi.**		22
Sevy's | **Preston Ctr**		23
Steel | **Oak Lawn**		23
Sullivan's | **N Dallas**		24
NEW Whiskey Cake | **West Plano**		20
Yucatan Taco | **Hospital Dist**		22

TRENDY

☑ Abacus | **Knox-Henderson**		27
NEW Blue Sushi | **Near W**		23
Bolla | **Uptown**		–
Bolsa | **Oak Cliff**		25
Bonnell's | **SW**		27
Brownstone | **Near W**		21
NEW Cedars Social | **Downtown D**		20
Central 214 | **Park Cities**		19

Charlie Palmer Steak | **Downtown D**	25
NEW Company Café | **multi.**	-
Craft Dallas | **Victory Pk**	24
Dish | **Oak Lawn**	20
Eddie V's | **Cultural Dist**	26
Ellerbe | **Hospital Dist**	26
Z Fearing's | **Uptown**	27
Fireside Pies | **multi.**	23
Five Sixty | **Downtown D**	24
Fuel City Tacos | **Downtown D**	-
Grace | **Downtown FW**	25
Hattie's | **Oak Cliff**	27
Hibiscus | **Knox-Henderson**	26
Kenichi | **Victory Pk**	21
NEW Komali | **Uptown**	24
Lambert's | **Near W**	24
Lanny's Alta | **Cultural Dist**	27
NEW Lockhart | **Oak Cliff**	21
Love Shack | **Stockyards**	23
Z NEW Lucia | **Oak Cliff**	29
Malai | **W Vill**	-
Maple/Motor | **Love Field**	25
NEW Marquee | **Highland Pk Vill**	26
Meddlesome Moth | **Market Ctr**	22
NEW Mesa | **Oak Cliff**	-
Neighborhood Services | **W Lovers Ln**	25
Nick/Sam's Grill | **Uptown**	25
Nobu | **Uptown**	26
Nonna | **Lemmon Ave**	25
Nonna Tata | **Hospital Dist**	27
Nosh Euro | **multi.**	24
Ocean Prime | **Uptown**	21
Porch | **Knox-Henderson**	22
NEW Princi Italia | **Preston Royal**	-
NEW Private Social | **Uptown**	-
R+D Kitchen | **Preston Ctr**	24
Rathbun's Blue | **Preston Ctr**	22
Salum | **Uptown**	26
Samar | **Arts Dist**	26
Screen Door | **Arts Dist**	23
NEW Shinjuku Station | **Hospital Dist**	-
Shinsei | **W Lovers Ln**	25
Smoke | **Oak Cliff**	24
Z Stephan Pyles | **Arts Dist**	27
Tei An | **Arts Dist**	26
Tillman's | **multi.**	20
Urban Crust | **East Plano**	23
Urban Taco | **multi.**	20
NEW Velvet Taco | **Knox-Henderson**	-
NEW Whiskey Cake | **West Plano**	20
Yucatan Taco | **Hospital Dist**	22
Yutaka | **Uptown**	28

VIEWS

Buffet/Kimbell | **Cultural Dist**	22
Z Cacharel | **Arlington**	27
Café Modern | **Cultural Dist**	23
Café Nasher | **Arts Dist**	25
Café/Green | **Las Colinas**	24
Dragonfly | **Uptown**	19
Five Sixty | **Downtown D**	24
Mi Piaci | **Addison**	26
Z Nana | **Market Ctr**	27
Reata | **Sundance Sq**	25
NEW Texas Spice | **Downtown D**	-

VISITORS ON EXPENSE ACCOUNT

Z Abacus | **Knox-Henderson**	27
Z Al Biernat's | **Oak Lawn**	27
Bailey's | **multi.**	22
Z Bijoux | **W Lovers Ln**	28
Z Bob's | **multi.**	25
Café Pacific | **Park Cities**	27
Capital Grille | **multi.**	26
Chamberlain's Steak | **Addison**	25
Charlie Palmer Steak | **Downtown D**	25
Craft Dallas | **Victory Pk**	24
Z Del Frisco's | **multi.**	27
Eddie V's | **Cultural Dist**	26
Z Fearing's | **Uptown**	27
Five Sixty | **Downtown D**	24
Z French Rm. | **Downtown D**	28
Grace | **Downtown FW**	25
Hôtel St. Germain | **Uptown**	26
Z Mansion | **Uptown**	26
NEW Marquee | **Highland Pk Vill**	26
Z Mercury | **Preston Forest**	28
Morton's | **Uptown**	26
Z Nana | **Market Ctr**	27
Nick & Sam's | **Uptown**	27
Nobu | **Uptown**	26
Oceanaire | **Galleria**	23
Ocean Prime | **Uptown**	21
Z Pappas Bros. | **Love Field**	28
Perry's Steak | **Uptown**	26
Pyramid | **Arts Dist**	29
Z Saint-Emilion | **Cultural Dist**	29
Screen Door | **Arts Dist**	23
Silver Fox | **Frisco**	22
Steel | **Oak Lawn**	23
Z Stephan Pyles | **Arts Dist**	27
Tei An | **Arts Dist**	26
Texas/Brazil | **multi.**	24
III Forks | **N Dallas**	24
Truluck's | **multi.**	24

WINNING WINE LISTS

Z Abacus | **Knox-Henderson** 27
Adelmo's | **Knox-Henderson** 25
Z Al Biernat's | **Oak Lawn** 27
Arcodoro/Pomodoro | **Uptown** 21
Bailey's | **NorthPark** 22
Z Bijoux | **W Lovers Ln** 28
Z Bob's | **multi.** 25
Café/Green | **Las Colinas** 24
Café Pacific | **Park Cities** 27
Capital Grille | **Uptown** 26
Chamberlain's Steak | **Addison** 25
Charlie Palmer Steak | **Downtown D** 25
Craft Dallas | **Victory Pk** 24
Z Del Frisco's | **multi.** 27
Eddie V's | **Cultural Dist** 26
Z Fearing's | **Uptown** 27
Ferre | **Sundance Sq** 18
Five Sixty | **Downtown D** 24
Fogo/Chão | **Addison** 25
Z French Rm. | **Downtown D** 28

Grace | **Downtown FW** 25
I Fratelli | **Irving** 23
Lonesome Dove | **Stockyards** 27
Z Mansion | **Uptown** 26
Z Mercury | **Preston Forest** 28
Mi Piaci | **Addison** 26
Morton's | **Uptown** 26
Z Nana | **Market Ctr** 27
Nick & Sam's | **Uptown** 27
Ocean Prime | **Uptown** 21
Palm | **W End** 25
Z Pappas Bros. | **Love Field** 28
Perry's Steak | **Uptown** 26
Pyramid | **Arts Dist** 29
Ruth's Chris | **N Dallas** 26
Z Saint-Emilion | **Cultural Dist** 29
Steel | **Oak Lawn** 23
Z Stephan Pyles | **Arts Dist** 27
Sullivan's | **N Dallas** 24
III Forks | **N Dallas** 24
Truluck's | **Uptown** 24
Yao Fuzi | **West Plano** 26

HOUSTON

Chez Nous* (Humble)

Original Ninfa's*

Perry's Steakhouse* (Clear Lake)

Niko Niko's

Vic & Anthony's

Ibiza

Reef

Brennan's

Indika

Barnaby's

Backstreet Café

Tony Mandola's

Brasserie 19

Da Marco

Niko Niko's

Hugo's

Mark's

Churrascos

Goode Co. Texas Seafood

Café Rabelais

Americas (The Woodlands)

Brenner's

Americas

Mockingbird Bistro

Chuy's

Eddie V's

Pappadeaux

Haven

Carrabba's

Tony's

Ouisie's Table

Kiran's

Masraff's

Del Frisco's

RDG + Bar Annie

Pappas Bros.

Beck's Prime

Pappasito's Cantina*

Goode Co. Texas BBQ*

Goode Co. Texas Seafood

Fogo de Chão

Churrascos

Taste of Texas

Eddie V's

Brenner's*

Le Mistral

Houston

Memorial Park

Sam Houston Tollway (Toll road)

Westpark Tollway (Toll road)

Katy Fwy

maps.google.com

Map data ©2012 Google, Sanborn

Google

*Check for other locations

Most Popular

1. Da Marco | *Italian*
2. Brennan's | *Creole*
3. Mark's | *American*
4. Carrabba's | *Italian*
5. Pappas Bros. | *Steak*
6. Américas | *S American*
7. Hugo's | *Mexican*
8. Goode Co. TX BBQ | *BBQ*
9. Becks Prime | *Burgers*
10. Reef | *Seafood*
11. Perry's Steakhouse | *Steak*
12. Tony's | *Continental/Italian*
13. Backstreet Café | *American*
14. Pappasito's Cantina | *Tex-Mex*
15. Eddie V's | *Seafood/Steak*
16. Ibiza | *Mediterranean*
17. Pappadeaux | *Cajun/Seafood*
18. Chuy's | *Tex-Mex*
19. Del Frisco's | *Steak*
20. Le Mistral | *French*
21. Mockingbird Bistro | *Amer.*
22. Goode Co. TX Seafood | *Seafood*
23. Haven | *American*
24. Ninfa's/Orig. Ninfa's* | *Tex-Mex*
25. Vic & Anthony's | *Steak*
26. Brenner's | *Steak*
27. Kiran's | *Indian*
28. RDG + Bar Annie* | *Amer./SW*
29. Taste of Texas* | *Steak*
30. Fogo de Chão | *Brazilian/Steak*
31. Churrascos | *S American*
32. Brasserie 19 | *American/French*
33. Indika | *Indian*
34. Niko Niko's* | *Greek*
35. Café Rabelais | *French*
36. Chez Nous* | *French*
37. Masraff's | *Continental*
38. Ouisie's Table* | *Southern*
39. Barnaby's Café* | *American*
40. Tony Mandola's* | *Seafood*

Many of the above restaurants are among the Houston area's most expensive, but if popularity were calibrated to price, a number of other restaurants would surely join their ranks. To illustrate this, we have added two lists comprising Houston's Best Buys on page 161 and 162.

KEY NEWCOMERS

Our editors' picks among this year's arrivals. See full list at p. 231.

Ava Kitchen & Whiskey | *Amer.* | A cocktail-fueled scene in River Oaks

Bird & The Bear | *American* | River Oaks' bistro-like Southerner

Brasserie 19 | *Amer./Fr.* | Chic River Oaks hit with a big bar scene

Coppa | *Italian* | Buzzy nouveau Italian in the Heights

Liberty Kitchen & Oyster | *American* | Seafood and steaks in the Heights

Philippe | *American/French* | Chic Galleria French with Texas influences

Pondicheri | *Indian* | Updated street fare in a stylish River Oaks setting

Triniti | *American* | Seasonal cooking in a modish setting on Lower Shepherd

Uchi | *Japanese* | Austin's heavy-hitting sushi star is heading to Montrose

Underbelly | *Amer.* | Chris Shepherd's upcoming paean to pork in Montrose

---

* Indicates a tie with restaurant above

Top Food

29 | Da Marco | *Italian*

28 | Chez Nous | *French*
Mark's | *American*
Pappas Bros. | *Steak*

27 | Nino's | *Italian*
Brasserie Max & Julie | *Fr.*
Brennan's | *Creole*
Del Frisco's | *Steak*
Kiran's | *Indian*
Brenner's | *Steak*
Tony Mandola's | *Seafood*

26 | Uptown Sushi | *Japanese*
Pesce | *Seafood*
Mockingbird Bistro | *Amer.*
Perry's Steakhouse | *Steak*
Vic & Anthony's | *Steak*
Dolce Vita | *Italian*
Irma's* | *Mexican*
Morton's | *Steak*
Backstreet Café | *American*
Kanomwan | *Thai*

Capital Grille | *Steak*
Tony's | *Continental/Italian*
Rudy & Paco | *Pan-Latin*
Eddie V's | *Seafood/Steak*
Goode Co. TX Seafood | *Seafood*
Le Mistral | *French*
Damian's Cucina | *Italian*
Rainbow Lodge | *American*
Café Rabelais | *French*
Grimaldi's | *Pizza*
Hugo's | *Mexican*
Indika | *Indian*
Quattro* | *Italian*
Ruth's Chris | *Steak*

25 | Ibiza | *Mediterranean*
Reef | *Seafood*
Breakfast Klub | *Soul Food*
Glass Wall | *American*
Lynn's | *Steak*
Mosquito Cafe* | *Eclectic*
Churrascos | *S American*

BY CUISINE

AMERICAN (NEW)

28 | Mark's
26 | Mockingbird Bistro
Backstreet Café
Rainbow Lodge
25 | Glass Wall

AMERICAN (TRAD.)

25 | Breakfast Klub
Lankford Grocery
24 | Houston's/Hillstone
Christian's Tailgate
23 | Barnaby's Café

BARBECUE

24 | Goode Co. TX BBQ
Luling City Market
22 | Beaver's
21 | County Line
Pappas Bar-B-Q

BURGERS

25 | Goode Co. Burgers
Lankford Grocery
24 | Becks Prime

Christian's Tailgate
Pappas Burgers

CAJUN/CREOLE

27 | Brennan's
Tony Mandola's
25 | Treebeards
24 | Danton's Gulf Coast
BB's Cafe

ECLECTIC

25 | Mosquito Cafe
24 | Hobbit Cafe
Tiny Boxwoods
22 | Black Walnut Café
Sambuca

FRENCH

28 | Chez Nous
27 | Brasserie Max & Julie
26 | Le Mistral
Café Rabelais
25 | Bistro Le Cep

Excludes places with low votes

Vote at zagat.com

QUICK BITES

25 Goode Co. Burgers
   Treebeards
   Lankford Grocery
   Niko Niko's
24 Becks Prime

TRENDY

29 Da Marco
28 Mark's
27 Del Frisco's
25 Haven
24 Philippe

WINNING WINE LISTS

29 Da Marco
28 Mark's
   Pappas Bros.
27 Brasserie Max & Julie
   Brennan's

WORTH A TRIP

28 Chez Nous (Humble)
26 Rudy & Paco (Galveston)
25 Mosquito Cafe (Galveston)
24 Américas (The Woodlands)
22 Gaido's (Galveston)

BY LOCATION

DOWNTOWN

26 Vic & Anthony's
   Irma's
   Morton's
   Quattro
25 Treebeards

GALLERIA

28 Pappas Bros.
27 Del Frisco's
   Kiran's
26 Morton's
   Capital Grille

HEIGHTS

26 Rainbow Lodge
25 Glass Wall
   Zelko Bistro
   Branch Water Tavern
   Star Pizza

LOWER SHEPHERD

25 Churrascos
   Divino
   Au Petit Paris
   Star Pizza
24 Hobbit Cafe

MEMORIAL

27 Brenner's
26 Perry's Steakhouse
   Eddie V's
   Goode Co. TX Seafood
25 Taste of Texas

MIDTOWN

27 Brennan's
26 Damian's

25 Ibiza
   Reef
   Breakfast Klub

MONTROSE

29 Da Marco
28 Mark's
27 Nino's
   Brasserie Max & Julie
26 Dolce Vita

RICE VILLAGE

26 Café Rabelais
24 Prego
   El Meson
   Benjy's
23 Bombay Brasserie

RIVER OAKS

27 Brenner's
   Tony Mandola's
26 Mockingbird Bistro
   Backstreet Café
25 Fleming's Prime

SUGAR LAND

26 Perry's Steakhouse
   Grimaldi's
24 Becks Prime
   Pappasito's Cantina
23 Carrabba's

SW HOUSTON

25 Churrascos
   Fung's Kitchen
24 Rudi Lechner's
21 Chuy's
   Pappas Bar-B-Q

THE WOODLANDS

- 26 Perry's Steakhouse
- Grimaldi's
- 25 Fleming's Prime
- 24 Américas
- Jasper's

UPPER KIRBY DISTRICT

- 26 Pesce
- Eddie V's
- 25 Kata Robata
- Haven
- 24 Becks Prime

WEST HOUSTON

- 26 Le Mistral
- 25 Lynn's
- Bistro Le Cep
- Fadi's Mediterranean
- 24 Bistro Provence

WEST U

- 26 Goode Co. TX Seafood
- 25 Goode Co. Burgers
- 24 Café Chino
- Goode Co. TX BBQ
- Amazón Grill

Top Decor

28 Brennan's

27 Rainbow Lodge
Mark's

26 Vic & Anthony's
Philippe
Tony's
Brenner's
Kiran's
Eddie V's
Perry's Steakhouse

25 Gigi's Asian Bistro
Capital Grille
Américas
RDG + Bar Annie
Artista
Pesce
Pappas Bros.
Grove
Masraff's*
Fleming's Prime

24 Haven
Le Mistral
Mockingbird Bistro
Jasper's
Chez Nous
Bistro Alex
Brasserie Max & Julie
Sambuca*
Taste of Texas
*17
Strip House*
Stella Sola
Up
Del Frisco's
Quattro
Smith & Wollensky
Backstreet Café
Tiny Boxwoods
Morton's
Da Marco

OUTDOORS

Artista
Baba Yega
Backstreet Café
Brennan's
Grappino di Nino

Grove
La Griglia
Rainbow Lodge
RDG + Bar Annie
Taco Milagro

ROMANCE

Brennan's
Chez Nous
Chez Roux
Da Marco
Le Mistral

Mark's
Rainbow Lodge
Restaurant CINQ
Tony's
Valentino

ROOMS

Américas (River Oaks)
Bistro Alex
Del Frisco's
Mark's
Masraff's

Philippe
*17
Soma
Tony's
Valentino

VIEWS

Artista
Brenner's
Chez Roux
Del Frisco's
Grove

Rainbow Lodge
Reef
Trevisio
Up
Vargo's

Vote at zagat.com

Top Service

27 Brennan's
Vic & Anthony's
Pappas Bros.
Chez Nous
Da Marco
Mark's
Rudy & Paco*

26 Pesce
Capital Grille
Le Mistral
Tony's
Del Frisco's
Fogo de Chão
Damian's Cucina Italiana

25 Masraff's
Rainbow Lodge
Perry's Steakhouse
Ruth's Chris
Kiran's
Tony Mandola's

Backstreet Café
Morton's
Eddie V's
Brenner's
Brasserie Max & Julie
Nino's*
Crapitto's Cucina Italiana
Mockingbird Bistro*
Frank's Chop House
Taste of Texas
Fleming's Prime

24 Smith & Wollensky
Philippe
Palm
Quattro
Haven
Shade
Branch Water Tavern
Carmelo's
Ciao Bello

Best Buys

In order of Bang for the Buck rating.

1. Bellaire Broiler Burger
2. 100% Taquito
3. Mission Burritos
4. Dessert Gallery
5. Goode Co. Burgers
6. Hobbit Cafe
7. Becks Prime
8. Lankford Grocery
9. Avalon Diner
10. BB's Cafe
11. Teotihuacan
12. Treebeards
13. Christian's Tailgate
14. Breakfast Klub
15. Fadi's Mediterranean
16. 59 Diner
17. Buffalo Grille
18. Cleburne Cafeteria
19. Pronto Cucinino
20. Pei Wei

21. Zoë's Kitchen
22. Pappas Bar-B-Q
23. Goode Co. TX BBQ
24. Café Express
25. Black Walnut Café
26. Mosquito Cafe
27. Jenni's Noodle House
28. Barnaby's Café
29. Luling City Market
30. Grimaldi's
31. Chuy's
32. Niko Niko's
33. Pappas Burgers
34. Berryhill Baja Grill
35. Ruggles Cafe Bakery
36. Collina's
37. Baba Yega
38. Candelari's Pizzeria
39. Paulie's
40. Spanish Flowers

OTHER GOOD VALUES

Amazón Grill
Arpi's Phoenicia Deli
Beaver's
Bernie's Burger Bus
Blue Nile
Bombay Pizza
Cafe Lili
Cafe Piquet
Café Pita+
Cafe Red Onion
Dolce Vita
Dot Coffee Shop
Down House
Eatsie Boys
El Gran Malo
Empire Café
Floyd's
Fung's Kitchen
Hubcap Grill
Huynh
Jax Grill
Jus' Mac
Kanomwan
La Mexicana
Little Bigs
Madras Pavilion
Maria Selma
Melange Creperie
Modular
Ninfa's/Orig. Ninfa's
Ocean Palace
Otilia's
Perbacco
Pizzitola's
Rudi Lechner's
Saldivia's South American Grill
Star Pizza
Sylvia's
Taco Milagro
Tan Tan
Torchy's Tacos
Van Loc

Houston

NEW Alto Pizzeria *Pizza* ▽ 22 | 26 | 20 | $27

River Oaks | West Ave. | 2800 Kirby Dr., 2nd fl. (Westheimer Rd.) | 713-386-6460 | www.avaalto.com
Another from Robert Del Grande and company (Ava, Grove, RDG), this River Oaks pizzeria occupies a spiffy second-story perch that's quickly become the place to "see and be seen"; expect stone-oven pizzas plus pastas and antipasti washed down with a wide-ranging list of beers, spirits and wines.

Amazón Grill *S American* 24 | 18 | 19 | $23

West U | West University | 5114 Kirby Dr. (Bissonnet St.) | 713-522-5888 | www.cordua.com
This West U South American from the folks behind Américas is a casual spot offering solid value in its "tasty" eats (the "complimentary plantain chips with sauces" "are a plus") served "cafeteria-style"; the vibe is truly "family-friendly", so expect "lots of kids."

Z Américas *S American* 24 | 25 | 23 | $47

River Oaks | 2040 W. Gray St. (bet. McDuffe St. & Shepherd Dr.) | 832-200-1492
The Woodlands | 21 Waterway Ave. (Lake Robbins Dr.) | 281-367-1492
www.cordua.com
"Sample the tastes of South America" at this upscale duo in River Oaks and The Woodlands from the Cordúa family (Amazon Grill, Artista, Churrascos) with "wonderful", "top-notch" cooking and "fanciful" decor; service receives mixed reviews, and beware of acoustics that "can be painful at peak times"; P.S. the Galleria original has closed.

Antica Osteria *Italian* 24 | 21 | 23 | $46

West U | 2311 Bissonnet St. (Greenbriar Dr.) | 713-521-1155 | www.anticarestaurant.com
"Forget the menu, the gold is on the specials board" at this "neighborhood gem" near West U, Rice and the Med Center dishing up "homey" Italian fare at "reasonable prices"; "attentive service" and a setting in a "charming" old house cement its status as a "romantic" standby.

Arcodoro *Italian* 22 | 21 | 21 | $49

Galleria | Centre at Post Oak | 5000 Westheimer Rd. (Post Oak Blvd.) | 713-621-6888 | www.arcodoro.com
An "international" crowd convenes at this bustling Italian "hangout" in the Galleria area serving up "consistent" if "pricey" pastas, pizzas and Sardinian plates; the "attractive" strip-mall space is divided into a casual grill and more formal dining area, but come spring, the place to be is on the patio; P.S. there's a Dallas sib called Arcodoro & Pomodoro.

Armandos *Tex-Mex* 20 | 22 | 20 | $40

River Oaks | 2630 Westheimer Rd. (Kirby Dr.) | 713-520-1738 | www.armandosrestaurant.com
"Socialites" and other "loyal", "older" customers make the scene at this "clubby" River Oaks Tex-Mexer set in "flashy" art-adorned digs,

where the "solid", "not-too-adventurous" cooking gains a lift from "wonderful margaritas"; perhaps it's "unnecessarily pricey", but it's "loud", "fun" and most "go for the people-watching" anyway.

Arpi's Phoenicia Deli *Mideastern* ▽ 26 | 18 | 17 | $13

Royal Oaks | 12151 Westheimer Rd. (Houston Ctr.) | 281-558-0416

Phoenicia Deli *Mideastern*

NEW **Downtown** | 1001 Austin St. (McKinney St.) | 832-360-2222
www.phoeniciafoods.com

"Huge lines at lunch" are a regular occurrence at this inexpensive Middle Eastern near Royal Oaks with a new market offshoot Downtown; it moves mounds of meze and shawarma, and though the "cafeteria setting" is not much, "snappy" service makes up for it

NEW Artisans *French* – | – | – | M

Midtown | 3201 Louisiana St. (Elgin St.) | 713-529-9111 |
www.artisansrestaurant.com

Opening in winter 2012, this bistro from the folks at Le Mistral brings the Denis brothers' brand of French cooking to the mini-Restaurant Row along Louisiana Street in Midtown; it's set to serve an accessible, well-priced menu in a comfortable room with lots of dark wood, seating around an open kitchen and a glass-enclosed bar that's sure to be a scene.

Artista 🗷 *American* 24 | 25 | 22 | $48

Downtown | Hobby Center for the Performing Arts | 800 Bagby St. (bet. Rusk & Walker Sts.) | 713-278-4782 | www.cordua.com

"Stunning" views of Downtown are the showpiece at this Cordúa-owned dining room in the Hobby Center featuring a Latin-inflected New American menu that's "tops" "before the theater"; just don't be surprised by "spotty" service, "pricey" bills or valet parking fees that border on "outrageous."

NEW Arturo Boada Cuisine Ⓜ *American* ▽ 28 | 19 | 27 | $44

Briargrove | 6510 Del Monte Dr. (Voss Rd.) | 713-782-3011 |
www.boadacuisine.com

At his eponymous Briargrove New American, longtime local chef Arturo Boada serves a diverse, crowd-pleasing lineup of steaks, pastas and wood-oven pizzas, as well as a handful of dishes exhibiting "Latin flair" like papas bravas with sliced Spanish chorizo; add in moderate pricing, "enthusiastic" service and a vibrant (if "noisy") setting, and early word says it's a "gem."

Arturo's Uptown Italiano 🗷 *Italian* 22 | 22 | 22 | $49

Uptown | Uptown Park | 1180 Uptown Park Blvd. (Post Oak Blvd.) |
713-621-1180 | www.arturosuptown.com

"Pleasant" is the word on this "upscale" Uptown eatery where a wide array of Italian dishes comes served inside the Tuscan-styled space or out on the "shady patio"; despite some charges of "underwhelming" fare, it's usually bustling thanks to lunching "business types" and a "captive audience" from the surrounding condos; P.S. chef Arturo Boada's 2011 departure may not be reflected in the Food score.

Ashiana *Indian*

▽ 25 | 19 | 23 | $27

West Houston | 12610 Briar Forest Dr. (Dairy Ashford Rd.) | 281-679-5555 | www.ashiana.cc

"Get past the strip-mall exterior", because fans say "excellent food awaits" at this West Houston Indian; its "outdated" looks are overcome by modest pricing, "nice" service and a boffo lunchtime buffet.

Au Petit Paris ☒ *French*

25 | 20 | 23 | $49

Lower Shepherd | 2048 Colquitt St. (Shepherd Dr.) | 713-524-7070 | www.aupetitparisrestaurant.com

"*Très charmant*" purr fans of this Lower Shepherd "gem" famed for its "truly French" fare served in a rehabbed bungalow; whether it's "cozy" or just plain "cramped" is up for debate, though all agree it has a "homey", "pleasant" vibe, aided by a "welcoming" staff and prices that are moderate for the area.

Aura ☒Ⓜ *American*

▽ 29 | 20 | 29 | $41

Missouri City | 3340 FM 1092 Rd. (Hwy. 6) | 281-403-2872 | www.aura-restaurant.com

This "gem" "tucked away" in a Missouri City strip mall is a "pleasant surprise" for chef Frédéric Perrier's "fantastic" New American cuisine with French touches and a focus on fresh fish; prices "won't break the bank" either, so consensus is it's "worth the drive from Houston."

❚NEW❚ Ava Kitchen & Whiskey Bar ☒ *American*

19 | 23 | 18 | $47

River Oaks | West Ave. | 2800 Kirby Dr. (Westheimer Rd.) | 713-386-6460 | www.avaalto.com

A downstairs sibling to River Oaks' Alto, this "chic but casual" New American by Robert Del Grande provides midpriced bites, cocktails and ample "people-watching"; the setting's "sophisticated", although early word on the food is "so-so."

Avalon Diner *American*

21 | 15 | 19 | $14

❚NEW❚ **Memorial** | 8823 Katy Frwy. (Brogden Rd.) | 713-590-4377
River Oaks | 2417 Westheimer Rd. (Revere St.) | 713-527-8900
Stafford | The Fountains | 12810 Southwest Frwy. (Fountain Lake Circle) | 281-240-0213
www.avalondiner.com

"A mix of hungover young professionals and chipper families" frequents these "all-American diners" dotted around Houston with "tasty" burgers and other eats with "just enough grease to soak up your sins from last night"; expect low prices, a "snappy" "smart-alec" staff and digs that can be "a madhouse on weekend mornings."

Azuma *Japanese*

23 | 22 | 20 | $33

Downtown | 909 Texas Ave. (Travis St.) | 713-223-0909 ☒
Rice Village | 5600 Kirby Dr. (Nottingham St.) | 713-432-9649

Azuma on the Lake *Japanese*

Sugar Land | 15830 Southwest Frwy. (Hwy. 6) | 281-313-0518
www.azumarestaurant.com

The "full spectrum" of sushi plus solid "supporting dishes" makes this "hopping" Japanese trio the preferred pick for "young" scenesters and locals alike; the atmosphere's "trendy, but not stuck-up" and costs are decent, but given the oft-"crowded" conditions, expect a few "flaws" in service.

Baba Yega *American*

| 21 | 20 | 21 | $20 |

Montrose | 2607 Grant St. (Missouri St.) | 713-522-0042 | www.babayega.com

This "quirky" Montrose stop since 1975 "never fails to satisfy" fans with its "wide"-ranging, "healthy" American menu served in a space "carved out of a rambling old house" with "beautiful" outdoor seating; it's "relaxed" and well priced, although many say Sunday's brunch buffet "is the best reason to go."

Backstreet Café *American*

| 26 | 24 | 25 | $39 |

River Oaks | 1103 S. Shepherd Dr. (Clay St.) | 713-521-2239 | www.backstreetcafe.net

There's "lots of character" at this "quaint old house" in River Oaks, a perpetual "favorite" for "stellar" midpriced American fare "with something for everyone" backed by "great wines" selected by Sean Beck (also "quite the mixologist"); "the backyard patio is lovely in pleasant weather", and "Sunday brunch is a real treat" too.

Barbed Rose ☒ *American*

| - | - | - | M |

Alvin | 113 E. Sealy St. (Gordon St.) | 281-585-2272 | www.barbedrose.com

This ambitious American in Alvin's quaint town center rolls out the requisite pricey chops plus more unusual items like ostrich, wild boar and artisanal cheeses and breads; it's set in a sweet, wood-framed structure with a nicely spruced-up interior and easygoing mood all around; P.S. next door is its more casual Burger Bar.

Barnaby's Café *American*

| 23 | 16 | 21 | $19 |

Briargrove | 5750 Woodway Dr. (Bering Dr.) | 713-266-0046
Montrose | 414 W. Gray St. (bet. Stanford & Taft Sts.) | 713-522-8898
Montrose | 604 Fairview St. (Hopkins St.) | 713-522-0106
River Oaks | 1701 S. Shepherd Dr. (Haddon St.) | 713-520-5131
Baby Barnaby's *American*
Montrose | 602 Fairview St. (Hopkins St.) | 713-522-4229
www.barnabyscafe.com

A sentimental "local favorite", this Houston chainlet is a find for "ample portions" of "tasty" American "comfort food" set down in "kitschy" pooch-themed digs by an "eccentric crew"; some say "a bit overrated and too cute by half", though it's "hard to beat for pure value"; P.S. Baby Barnaby's in Montrose serves breakfast only.

Bayou City Seafood & Pasta *Cajun/Seafood*

| 22 | 17 | 22 | $27 |

Galleria | 4730 Richmond Ave. (Vossdale Rd.) | 713-621-6602 | www.bayoucityseafood.net

"For quick Cajun food", surveyors seek out this "good-value" Galleria spot that "fulfills expectations" with "tasty" seafood selections like gumbo, crawfish and po' boys served in a "casual" full-service setting.

| | FOOD | DECOR | SERVICE | COST |

BB's Cafe *Cajun*

24 | 13 | 20 | $15

Downtown | 509 Louisiana St. (bet. Prairie St. & Texas Ave.) | 713-236-8269

NEW Heights | 2701 White Oak Dr. (Studewood St.) | 713-868-8000 ◐

Montrose | 2710 Montrose Blvd. (Westheimer Rd.) | 713-524-4499 ◐

www.bbscafe.com

Surveyors "hankering for a huge-and-tasty po' boy" head to this bare-bones, budget-friendly Cajun trio that "saves you a trip to New Orleans"; the Heights and Montrose branches are also hailed as "good late-night options."

Beaver's Ⓜ *BBQ*

22 | 17 | 21 | $23

Heights | 2310 Decatur St. (Washington Ave.) | 713-864-2328 | www.beavershouston.com

Showcasing "unconventional" riffs on Texas 'cue, this "laid-back" joint in the lower Heights from Monica Pope (t'afia) features a mid-priced menu that's "more locavore than carnivore", with an emphasis on "organic meats" used for its smoked ribs and brisket; with "inventive" cocktails and microbrewed beers, it's a "fun" place to "go with friends", with a patio that's "inviting enough to move into for the afternoon."

☒ Becks Prime *Burgers*

24 | 16 | 20 | $15

Briargrove | 2615 Augusta Dr. (Westheimer Rd.) | 713-266-9901

Downtown | Downtown Tunnel | 919 Milam St. (Walker St.) | 713-659-6122 ☒

NEW Heights | 115 W. 19th St. (Yale St.) | 713-470-1176

Memorial | Memorial Park Golf Course Clubhse. | 1001 E. Memorial Loop (Westcott St.) | 713-863-8188

Memorial | Memorial City Mall | 514 Memorial City Way (Gessner Dr.) | 713-463-4486

Upper Kirby District | 2902 Kirby Dr. (Kipling St.) | 713-524-7085

West Houston | 11000 Westheimer Rd. (Wilcrest Dr.) | 713-952-2325

West Houston | 1202 Dairy Ashford St. (Katy Frwy.) | 281-493-3806

Sugar Land | 1822 Hwy. 6 S. (Southwest Frwy.) | 281-242-6300

The Woodlands | Grogan's Mill Village Ctr. | 2120 Buckthorne Pl. (Grogans Mill Rd.) | 281-367-3600

www.becksprime.com

Additional locations throughout the Houston area

"Sometimes you just want a burger" and this chainlet delivers with "beefy" patties plus "satisfying" sandwiches and salads served up "fast" in "no-frills" interiors or out on pleasant patios (the Briargrove locale sports some "sprawling" old oak trees); a few quibble with relatively "costly" prices, but it remains a "dependable" bet for a "quick" bite.

☒ Bellaire Broiler Burger ☒ *Burgers*

24 | 9 | 17 | $10

Bellaire | 5216 Bellaire Blvd. (Bissonnet St.) | 713-668-8171

For "melty cheese on a juicy patty", burger aficionados say you "gotta try" this circa-1957 "local legend" in Bellaire – Houston's

No. 1 Bang for the Buck – also plying "greasy-spoon" standards in a "retro" diner setting; the decor "hasn't changed in years" (to put it kindly), though most don't seem to mind.

Benjy's *American* | 24 | 22 | 23 | $35 |

Heights | 5922 Washington Ave. (Knox St.) | 713-868-1131
Rice Village | 2424 Dunstan St. (bet. Kelvin & Morningside Drs.) | 713-522-7602
www.benjys.com

These "see-and-be-seen" spots in Rice Village and on trendy Washington Avenue are "perennial favorites" for a "diverse", "thoughtfully prepared" New American menu; a "friendly, knowledgeable" staff, "delicious brunch" and "great happy hour" are added perks, but the "lively" atmosphere is "way too noisy" for some.

NEW Bernie's Burger Bus M *Hamburgers* | - | - | - | I |

Location varies; see website | 281-386-2447 | www.berniesburgerbus.com

The former personal chef of Houston Rockets star Shane Battier is in the driver's seat of this retooled school bus serving hamburgers that are a far cry from those of cafeteria days; look for freshly ground Black Angus beef, homemade buns and condiments all complemented by hand-cut fries smothered with the likes of blue cheese and truffles.

Berryhill Baja Grill *Mexican* | 20 | 15 | 16 | $16 |

West U | 5110 Buffalo Spdwy. (Westpark Dr.) | 713-667-8226
Champions | Champions Vill. | 5482 FM 1960 W. (Champion Forest Dr.) | 281-444-8844
Galleria | 1717 Post Oak Blvd. (San Felipe St.) | 713-871-8226
Heights | 702 E. 11th St. (Beverly St.) | 713-225-2252
Memorial | Memorial City Mall | 731 Memorial City Way (bet. Gaylord Dr. & Katy Frwy.) | 713-932-8226
Montrose | Hawthorne Sq. | 3407 Montrose Blvd. (Hawthorne St.) | 713-523-8226
River Oaks | 2639 Revere St. (Westheimer Rd.) | 713-526-8080
Sugar Land | Sugar Creek Shopping Ctr. | 13703 Southwest Frwy. (Sugar Creek Center Blvd.) | 281-313-8226
The Woodlands | Market St. | 9595 Six Pines Dr. (Lake Woodlands Dr.) | 281-298-8226
www.berryhillbajagrill.com
Additional locations throughout the Houston area

The "standout" fish tacos are an "addiction" for many at this homegrown Mexican chain favored for its "cheap", "filling" "fresh"-tasting fare; a "casual", kid-friendly vibe prevails at most locales, with the exception of the Montrose branch in Houston, which may be best known for its wild Sunday brunch.

NEW Bird & The Bear *American* | - | - | - | M |

River Oaks | 2810 Westheimer Rd. (Virginia St.) | 713-528-2473 | www.thebirdandthebearbistro.com

This genteel River Oaks American and sibling of Ousie's Table has a similarly upscale vibe and a Southern-inflected menu incorporating flavors from near and far, from the Gulf Coast to North Africa; its

	FOOD	DECOR	SERVICE	COST

contemporary setting features large windows and a palette of red, white and black.

Bistro Alex *Creole*
22 | 24 | 21 | $42

Memorial | Hotel Sorella | 800 Sorella Ct. (I-10 W.) | 713-827-3545 | www.bistroalex.com

This "cousin to Brennan's" in the Hotel Sorella in Memorial serves Texan-inflected Creole cuisine like turtle soup, plus lots of beef and a jazz brunch on Sundays; many find the sophisticated setting with outdoor bar "gorgeous", although reviews on the food are mixed, and some say the service is "almost nonexistent, especially for the price."

Bistro Lancaster *American*
∇ 24 | 22 | 24 | $56

Downtown | Lancaster Hotel | 701 Texas Ave. (Louisiana St.) | 713-228-9500 | www.thelancaster.com

This "old standard" in the Lancaster Hotel is "perfect pre- or post-theater" when attending the Alley and Jones Hall (both across the street), with its "limited but well-chosen" lineup of "simple" New American dishes and handsome "pubby" surroundings; it's not inexpensive, but "they always make sure you make your curtain."

Bistro Le Cep *French*
25 | 21 | 23 | $37

West Houston | 11112 Westheimer Rd. (Wilcrest Dr.) | 713-783-3985 | www.bistrolecep.com

"Real French country cooking without the pretence" is yours at this "true bistro" on the West Side, where a "warm and accommodating" staff makes the "cozy" "faux-rustic setting" "feel like home"; although it's not cheap, the "special Sunday suppers" for $23.95 are a "bargain."

Bistro Provence ⊠ *French*
24 | 21 | 22 | $39

West Houston | 13616 Memorial Dr. (bet. Kirkwood Rd. & Wilcrest Dr.) | 713-827-8008 | www.bistroprovence.us

Set "off the beaten path" "in a quiet strip center" in West Houston, this "cute" little French bistro is worth seeking out for its "reliably delicious", "authentic" fare matched with "worthy wines"; though the closely set dining room can feel "tight", moderate prices and an affable, "quirky" staff keep the mood "relaxed."

Black Walnut Café *Eclectic*
22 | 21 | 18 | $19

Rice Village | Village Arcade | 5510 Morningside Dr. (bet. Rice & University Blvds.) | 713-526-5551

Katy | 23233 Cinco Ranch Blvd. (Grand Pkwy.) | 281-371-2233

Sugar Land | First Colony Mall | 16535 Southwest Frwy. (Hwy. 6) | 281-565-7800

The Woodlands | 2520 Research Forest Dr. (Grogans Mill Rd.) | 281-362-1678

www.blackwalnutcafe.com

Like "a high-end coffee shop", this Eclectic quartet works well for "casual breakfasts" or takeout from a wide-ranging menu that spans from grilled cheese to pasta to pot roast; it's basically "self-service", but the settings are pleasant and prices low too.

Block 7 *Eclectic*
21 | 16 | 20 | $30

Heights | 720 Shepherd Dr. (bet. Floyd & Rose Sts.) | 713-572-2565 |
www.block7wineco.com

A combination wine bar, retailer and Eclectic eatery, this "vibrant"
lower Heights entry is especially known for its signature burger and
"killer" vino list and frequent tastings; though parking can be hard to
come by, inside is "cavernous" and modern, with slick concrete
floors, plenty of tables and a convivial 35-ft. bar.

Blue Nile *Ethiopian*
▽ 25 | 15 | 18 | $22

Southwest Houston | 9400 Richmond Ave. (Westerland Dr.) |
713-782-6882 | www.bluenilerestaurant.com

"One of the city's few" Ethiopians, this Southwest Houstoner offers
"new tastes" in the form of "wonderful" "spicy" stews and traditional injera bread you "eat with your hands"; service and setting
aren't strong suits, but at least prices are pleasing.

Bombay Brasserie *Indian*
23 | 16 | 21 | $27

Rice Village | Rice Village Arcade | 2414 University Blvd. (Morningside Dr.) |
713-355-2000

Narin's Bombay Brasserie *Indian*

Galleria | 3005 W. Loop S. (Oakshire Dr.) | 713-622-2005
www.narinsbombaybrasserie.com

A "dependable" bet for subcontinental cooking, this Indian duo in
Rice Village and the Galleria area features all the "traditional"
dishes available à la carte or in a bountiful lunchtime buffet; a
"pleasant" ambiance and modest prices complete the picture.

Bombay Pizza Co. *Pizza*
▽ 23 | 15 | 22 | $14

Downtown | 914 Main St. (bet. McKinney & Walker Sts.) |
713-654-4444 | www.bombaypizzaco.com

"An adventure", this Downtown pizzeria is a "neat" concept providing a "fun mash-up of flavors" via Indian toppings on thin crusts
(picture pies topped with tandoori chicken or saag paneer, as well as
classic combos like basil and tomato); the setting's strictly functional, with "quick" service and low costs.

Branch Water Tavern ●Ⓜ *American*
25 | 20 | 24 | $36

Heights | 510 Shepherd Dr. (bet. Blossom & Gibson Sts.) |
713-863-7777 | www.branchwatertavern.com

Smitten fans "can't say enough good things" about this Heights New
American putting out "fabulous" fare and small plates backed by "creative" cocktails and "amazing bourbons"; the pubby space is "loud",
but "pleasant" and "well-informed" service completes the picture.

☒ Brasserie Max & Julie *French*
27 | 24 | 25 | $44

Montrose | 4315 Montrose Blvd. (Richmond Ave.) | 713-524-0070 |
www.maxandjulie.net

The "quintessential" French brasserie, this "lovely" Montrose
charmer pairs "fantastic", "authentic" fare with "excellent" Gallic
wines; the "atmosphere will make you believe you're in Paris", and
it's even more pleasant "when someone else is treating."

	FOOD	DECOR	SERVICE	COST

NEW Brasserie 19 *American/French* | 23 | 22 | 22 | $46

River Oaks | River Oaks Ctr. | 1962 W. Gray St. (Driscoll St.) |
713-524-1919 | www.brasserie19.com

"It feels like South Beach" at this "energetic" "see-and-be-seen"
River Oaks brasserie pulling a "beautiful" "Lamborghini"-driving
crowd for "excellent" French–New American cuisine and "well-
priced" wines you peruse on an iPad; it's perpetually "packed"
with a bar that's "standing room only", so the "only complaint
is the acoustics."

BRC Gastropub *American* | 20 | 18 | 19 | $28

Heights | 519 Shepherd Dr. (bet. Blossom & Gibson Sts.) |
713-861-2233 | www.brcgastropub.com

Heights denizens have this "fun", "loud" gastropub dispensing
"delicious craft beer", growlers to go and American bar fare like
mac 'n' cheese in a daily changing array of flavors; the decor is
"clever" (with a large red rooster out front signaling the louche
name) though detractors dis the "chaotic" scene, calling it "a
glorified hamburger joint."

Breakfast Klub *Soul Food* | 25 | 13 | 20 | $16

Midtown | 3711 Travis St. (Alabama St.) | 713-528-8561 |
www.thebreakfastklub.com

"Worth standing in line for", this Midtown soul-food stop is beloved
for its delightfully "heart-stopping" breakfast fare (think "wings and
waffles") and other "fantastic" diner-style American grub; the setting's strictly utilitarian, but you'll find a "friendly, involved" staff
and a "diverse", "very-Houston" crowd.

Ø Brennan's *Creole* | 27 | 28 | 27 | $56

Midtown | 3300 Smith St. (Stuart St.) | 713-522-9711 |
www.brennanshouston.com

A "landmark", this Midtown "grande dame" and sib of the famed
Commander's Palace in New Orleans is "the place to indulge" in
"fabulous" Southwestern-Creole dishes like turtle soup and ba-
nanas Foster; it's ranked No. 1 for Service and Decor in Houston
thanks to "exceptional hospitality" that "makes you feel like royalty"
plus an "absolutely gorgeous" interior cementing its status as a "go-
to" for "birthdays and special occasions" or the "amazing" jazz
brunch on Sundays; P.S. jackets suggested.

Ø Brenner's *Steak* | 27 | 26 | 25 | $59

Memorial | 10911 Katy Frwy. (bet. Brittmoore Rd. & Wycliffe Dr.) |
713-465-2901
River Oaks | 1 Birdsall St. (Memorial Dr.) | 713-868-4444
www.brennerssteakhouse.com

A longtime "tradition" for beef, this steakhouse duo from the
Landry's chain boasts "impressive" cuts and a staff that "waits
on you hand and foot"; "you can't beat the" atmosphere either,
with both the circa-1936 Memorial branch and its River Oaks offshoot featuring "dark", wood-trimmed quarters deemed "perfect
for a special occasion."

Brio Tuscan Grille   *Italian*   22 | 23 | 22 | $33

Memorial | CityCentre | 12808 Queensbury Ln. (Town & Country Blvd.) | 713-973-9610

The Woodlands | Woodlands Mall | 1201 Lake Woodlands Dr. (I-45) | 281-465-8993

www.brioitalian.com

See review in Dallas/Ft. Worth Directory.

Broken Spoke Café   ⊠ Ⓜ *Belgian*   21 | 16 | 17 | $23

Heights | 1809 Washington Ave. (Sabine St.) | 713-863-7029 | www.brokenspokecafe.com

Occupying the space that was once Café Montrose, this lower Heights Belgian specializes in "wonderful" "mussels, frites and beer", with more than a dozen brews on tap in a low-key setting.

Buffalo Grille, The   *American*   21 | 13 | 18 | $15

West U | 4080 Bissonnet St. (Buffalo Spdwy.) | 713-661-3663

Briargrove | 1301 S. Voss Rd. (bet. San Felipe St. & Woodway Dr.) | 713-784-3663

www.thebuffalogrille.com

"Wonderful" "all-day breakfasts" (featuring "enormous" flapjacks and "thick-cut bacon") bring in the crowds at these American sibs in Briargrove and West U also dishing up "comfort-food" classics for lunch and dinner too; counter service and modest tabs keep in step with the cozy folksy settings.

Café Chino   *Chinese*   24 | 19 | 23 | $23

West U | 3285 Southwest Frwy. (Edloe St.) | 713-524-4433 | www.cafechinohouston.com

Comfortable and "convenient", this West U Chinese is touted for its Hunan fare ranked "a notch above"; a "quiet" setting, "accommodating" service and "reasonable prices" keep it tried-and-true.

Café Express   *Eclectic*   20 | 16 | 16 | $16

Briargrove | 6570 Woodway Dr. (Voss Rd.) | 713-935-9222

Champions | Champions Vill. | 5311 FM 1960 W. (bet. Fairlake & Ramsey Lns.) | 832-484-9222

Downtown | 650 Main St. (bet. Capitol St. & Texas Ave.) | 713-237-9222 ⊠

Uptown | Uptown Park | 1101 Uptown Park Blvd. (Post Oak Blvd.) | 713-963-9222

Meyerland | Meyerland Plaza | 210 Meyerland Plaza (I-610) | 713-349-9222

Montrose | Museum of Fine Arts | 5601 S. Main St. (Binz St.) | 713-639-7370

River Oaks | 1422 W. Gray St. (Waugh Dr.) | 713-522-3100

Upper Kirby District | 3200 Kirby Dr. (Main St.) | 713-522-3994

Webster | 19443 Gulf Frwy. (Bay Area Blvd.) | 281-554-6999

Sugar Land | First Colony Mall | 15930 City Walk (Hwy. 6) | 281-980-9222

www.cafe-express.com

Additional locations throughout the Houston area

Loyalists "load up on the freebies" at the condiment bar of this "up-scale fast-food" mini-chain known for its "satisfying", "fresh", "healthy" Eclectic fare; speedy counter service and "value" prices overcome institutional settings some liken "to a bus station."

Cafe Lili 🗷 *Mideastern*   24 | 11 | 23 | $20

Galleria | 5757 Westheimer Rd. (bet. Chimney Rock Rd. & Fountain View Dr.) | 713-952-6969 | www.cafelili.com

Family-run "little jewel" in the Galleria area dishing out "traditional Lebanese" cuisine and other Middle Eastern classics; the setting may be spartan and the lighting "too bright", but low prices and "wonderful" service "make up for it."

Cafe Piquet *Cuban*   ▽ 22 | 18 | 20 | $17

Bellaire | 5757 Bissonnet St. (bet. Chimney Rock Rd. & Renwick Dr.) | 713-664-1031 | www.cafepiquet.net

"Authentic Cuban" in Bellaire catering to a "family"-friendly crowd with well-priced cooking in casual digs.

Café Pita+ *E European*   ▽ 23 | 7 | 16 | $20

West Houston | 10890 Westheimer Rd. (Wilcrest Dr.) | 713-953-7237 | www.cafepita.weebly.com

Enticing Eastern European fare from the cultural crossroads of Bosnia is the draw at this "interesting" BYO in West Houston; though some say "the decor is grim" and "the waiters sometimes surly", there is more than enough charm on the plate.

Café Rabelais 🗷 *French*   26 | 22 | 23 | $39

Rice Village | 2442 Times Blvd. (bet. Kelvin & Morningside Drs.) | 713-520-8841 | www.caferabelais.com

"Super-cute and super-French", this "quaint" "little" Rice Village bistro pleases patrons with "fabulous", midpriced fare and an "incredible" wine list; service varies "from great to vaguely amused", and "you'll be banging chairs with your neighbors", but that's all part of the charm; P.S. no reservations.

Cafe Red Onion *Pan-Latin*   23 | 18 | 20 | $27

Northwest Houston | 12440 Northwest Frwy. (bet. Bingle Rd. & 43rd St.) | 713-957-0957

Upper Kirby District | 3910 Kirby Dr. (bet. Richmond Ave. & Southwest Frwy.) | 713-807-1122 🗷 www.caferedonion.com

Despite the "bland, cookie-cutter" settings, there's plenty of "vibrant" cooking on display at this Pan-Latin duo in Upper Kirby and Northwest Houston featuring a "fantastic variety" of "out-of-the-ordinary" Central and South American dishes "so pretty, you'll want to take a photo"; they're "unpretentious" all the way, from the "friendly" service down to the value pricing.

Candelari's Pizzeria *Pizza*   16 | 15 | 16 | $16

Medical Center | 2617 W. Holcombe Blvd. (Kirby Dr.) | 713-662-2825

Heights | 6002 Washington Ave. (bet. TC Jester Blvd. & Westcott Ave.) | 832-200-1474

NEW West Houston | 14545 Memorial Dr. (bet. Dairy Ashford Rd. & Winter Oaks Dr.) | 281-497-0612

(continued)

(continued)

Candelari's Pizzeria

Cypress | 25680 Hwy. 290 (bet. Hempstead & Spring-Cypress Rds.) | 281-373-0039
Katy | 6825 S. Fry Rd. (Grand Pkwy.) | 281-395-6746
www.candelaris.com

"Family-friendly" chainlet of "neighborhood pizzerias" with a "nice variety" of pies and housemade sausages served in "boisterous" digs; meals offer "great value", and lunchtime boasts an all-you-can-eat buffet.

Canopy *American*   23 | 20 | 22 | $35

Montrose | 3939 Montrose Blvd. (bet. Branard & Sul Ross Sts.) | 713-528-6848 | www.canopyhouston.com

Seasonal fare is the focus of this "good-value" Montrose American from Claire Smith (Shade) providing a "delicious", "varied" menu and "inspired cocktails" in a "comfortable", if "noisy", dining room decked out with murals of trees and other eco-chic touches; early-birds can also pick up coffee, house-baked breads and pastries, or settle in for a full breakfast any day of the week.

Cantina Laredo *Mexican*   21 | 19 | 20 | $26

West Houston | 11129 Westheimer Rd. (Wilcrest Dr.) | 713-952-3287 | www.cantinalaredo.com
See review in Dallas/Ft. Worth Directory.

Capital Grille *Steak*   26 | 25 | 26 | $61

Galleria | 5365 Westheimer Rd. (Yorktown St.) | 713-623-4600 | www.thecapitalgrille.com
See review in Dallas/Ft. Worth Directory.

NEW Capitol at St. Germain ⊠ *American*   - | - | - | E

Downtown | 705 Main St. (Capitol St.) | 713-492-2454 | www.thecapitolhouston.com

An exciting addition to Downtown, this bi-level supper club in a landmarked building presents live music against an opulent backdrop of soaring ceilings, chandeliers, columns and plush furnishings that include oversized booths; on the pricey menu are shareable, internationally inspired American plates and upscale cocktails, some made with the namesake elderflower liqueur.

Carmelo's *Italian*   24 | 23 | 24 | $42

West Houston | 14795 Memorial Dr. (bet. Dairy Ashford Rd. & Eldridge Pkwy.) | 281-531-0696 | www.carmelosrestaurant.com
See review in Austin and the Hill Country Directory.

⊠ Carrabba's Italian Grill *Italian*   23 | 20 | 22 | $29

Briargrove | 1399 S. Voss Rd. (bet. San Felipe St. & Woodway Dr.) | 713-468-0868
Champions | Champions Vill. | 5440 FM 1960 W. (Champion Forest Dr.) | 281-397-8255
Northwest Houston | 7540 Hwy. 6 N. (bet. Longenbaugh & Ridge Park Drs.) | 281-859-9700
Upper Kirby District | 3115 Kirby Dr. (Branard St.) | 713-522-3131

(continued)

Carrabba's Italian Grill

West Houston | 11339 Katy Frwy. (bet. Kirkwood Rd. & Wilcrest Dr.) | 713-464-6595

Webster | 502 W. Bay Area Blvd. (bet. Hwy. 3 & I-45) | 281-338-0574

Kingwood | 750 Kingwood Dr. (Chestnut Ridge Dr.) | 281-358-5580

Sugar Land | 2335 Hwy. 6 S. (bet. Lexington & Town Center Blvds.) | 281-980-4433

The Woodlands | 25665 1-45 N. Hwy. (bet. Briar Rock Rd. & Valley Wood Dr.) | 281-367-9423

www.carrabbas.com

"Mainstream" Italian cooking comes in "plentiful" portions at this "reasonably priced" franchise ranked a solid bet "for a casual night out" with the family; "long waits" prevail at most locales, although seasoned patrons proclaim "you're best off" with the "family-owned originals" in Briargrove and the Upper Kirby District in Houston.

Charivari ☒ *Continental*
24 | 17 | 23 | $48

Midtown | 2521 Bagby St. (McGowen St.) | 713-521-7231 | www.charivarirest.com

"Old-world Europe" comes to Houston via this "refined" Midtown restaurant, a "favorite" for special occasions, thanks to its "exquisite" Continental menu peppered with "ambitious" Transylvanian specialties; "professional" service makes up for the somewhat "stodgy" strip-mall setting.

Cheesecake Factory *American*
20 | 19 | 19 | $28

Galleria | The Galleria | 5015 Westheimer Rd. (Post Oak Blvd.) | 713-840-0600

NEW Memorial | Memorial City Mall | 600 Memorial City Way (Gaylord Dr.) | 713-932-6344

Sugar Land | First Colony Mall | 16535 Southwest Frwy. (Hwy. 6) | 281-313-9500

The Woodlands | Woodlands Mall | 1201 Lake Woodlands Dr. (I-45) | 281-419-3400

www.thecheesecakefactory.com

"The menu is longer than a Thomas Pynchon novel" at this "popular", "over-the-top" national chain moving "massive" helpings of "quality" Americana, including "supremely delicious" cheesecake; critics call it "generic and overpriced" for what it is, but the "Vegas"-style settings remain "loud" and "crowded" nonetheless.

☑ Chez Nous ☒ *French*
28 | 24 | 27 | $64

Humble | 217 S. Ave. G. (bet. Granberry & Staitti Sts.) | 281-446-6717 | www.cheznousfrenchrestaurant.com

A "foodie" "mecca" in the "quiet city of Humble", this "expensive" top-rated French is "worth the drive" thanks to its "outstanding" market-driven cuisine, "excellent" wines and "superior service"; the setting in an old church is "romantic" enough that you may just see someone "pop the question"; P.S. jackets suggested.

	FOOD	DECOR	SERVICE	COST

Chez Roux ⊠Ⓜ *French*

-	-	-	VE

Montgomery | La Torretta Del Lago | 600 La Torretta Blvd. (Del Lago Blvd.) | 936-448-4400 | www.latorrettalakeresort.com

"Superlative in every category (including price)" sums up this French in the ritzy La Torretta Del Lago Resort & Spa from legendary London-based chef Albert Roux; it features a "world-class" seasonal menu in a modern, waterside setting whose centerpiece is a glass-enclosed wine cellar showcasing a stellar collection of bottles.

Christian's Tailgate Bar & Grill *Burgers*

24	13	16	$14

NEW Heights | 2820 White Oak Dr. (bet. Oxford & Studewood Sts.) | 713-863-1207 ◗
Memorial | 7340 Washington Ave. (Katy Frwy.) | 713-864-9744 ⊠
Midtown | 2000 Bagby St. (Pierce St.) | 713-527-0261 ◗
www.christianstailgate.com

"A staple in the burger community", this "sports-bar" trio turns out thick, "old-fashioned" patties and other American eats in "crowded" "frat-house" settings fueled by plenty of beer; "service needs work", but the prices make up for it.

Churrascos *S American*

25	22	24	$39

Lower Shepherd | 2055 Westheimer Rd. (Shepherd Dr.) | 713-527-8300
Southwest Houston | 9705 Westheimer Rd. (Gessner Rd.) | 713-952-1988
NEW Sugar Land | 1520 Lake Pointe Pkwy. (Southwest Frwy.) | 832-532-5300
www.cordua.com

"Heaven on earth for carnivores", this meaty trio from the Cordúa family on Lower Shepherd and in Southwest Houston and Sugar Land provides "flavorful", "melt-in-your-mouth" steaks with a South American twist, plus pisco sours and a "fabulous" tres leches cake for dessert; add in an "inviting" setting and "gracious" service and though it's not cheap, most maintain it "never lets you down."

Chuy's *Tex-Mex*

21	20	20	$19

Northwest Houston | 19827 Northwest Frwy. (Hwy. 6) | 281-970-0341
River Oaks | 2706 Westheimer Rd. (Kirby Dr.) | 713-524-1700
Southwest Houston | 9350 Westheimer Rd. (bet. Gessner & Piney Point Rds.) | 713-278-2489
Webster | 20975 Gulf Frwy. Frontage Rd. (Texas Ave.) | 281-554-2489
Humble | 20502 Hwy. 59 N. (Cantertrot Dr.) | 281-540-7778
NEW Katy | 21300 Katy Frwy. (bet. Ernstes Rd. & New Hope Ln.) | 832-772-1277
Shenandoah | 18035 I-45 S. (bet. Research Forest Dr. & Hwy. 242) | 936-321-4440
www.chuys.com
See review in Austin and the Hill Country Directory.

Ciao Bello *Italian*

20	22	24	$44

Galleria | Houston Galleria | 5161 San Felipe St. (Sage Rd.) | 713-960-0333 | www.ciaobellohouston.com

"Stylish" "New York"-style Italian in the Galleria area from Tony Vallone (Tony's); expect pizzas, pastas and "gracious service", alhough more than a few find the execution "uneven" given the pedigree and the "pricey" tabs.

Ciro's *Italian*   23 | 19 | 23 | $28

Memorial | 9755 Katy Frwy. (Bunker Hill Rd.) | 713-467-9336 |
www.ciros.com

Long "a solid choice for basic Italian" in Memorial where regulars report "delicious" fare "like nonna makes" matched with warm service; most find the setting just off the freeway accessible, if not exciting.

Cleburne Cafeteria ⊄ *American*   23 | 14 | 20 | $16

West U | 3606 Bissonnet St. (Mercer St.) | 713-667-2386 |
www.cleburnecafeteria.com

"Step into a bygone era" at this longtime West U cafeteria doling out "Texas-sized" helpings of "homestyle" American cooking to a "senior" crowd; though it offers "great value" for the money, the setting is sparse, and cynics quip you'll want to "bring your own seasoning."

Collina's *Pizza*   22 | 13 | 20 | $18

Greenway Plaza Area | 3835 Richmond Ave. (bet. Timmons Ln. & Weslayan St.) | 713-621-8844
Heights | 502 W. 19th St. (Nicholson St.) | 713-869-0492
Memorial | 8800 Katy Frwy. (bet. Campbell & Voss Rds.) | 713-365-9497
www.collinas.com

An area "standby", this "bustling", "kid-friendly" pizzeria chain works for both "casual" eat-in meals and delivery; service is "efficient" and the settings are "comfy" enough, while BYO keeps the cost down.

NEW Convivio *Spanish*   - | - | - | M

Heights | 700 S. Durham Dr. (Floyd St.) | 832-360-1750 |
www.conviviohouston.com

Amid the buzz of the lower Heights, this newcomer provides pre- and post-carousing sustenance via tapas with flavors from all over Spain; the warm digs and moderate tabs make it a destination in itself.

NEW Coppa *Italian*   ∇ 25 | 23 | 23 | $39

Heights | 5555 Washington Ave. (TC Jester Blvd.) | 713-426-4260 |
www.copparistorante.com

A "pleasant surprise" in the Heights, this moderately priced Italian (and sibling of Brasserie 19 and Ibiza) has been hot since day one thanks to its "new takes on traditional dishes" like tuna crudo, goat ravioli and pizzas topped with ham and eggs; "knowledgeable" service and an "energetic" yet "comfortable" ambiance seal the deal.

County Line, The *BBQ*   21 | 20 | 21 | $26

North Houston | 13850 Cutten Rd. (Richardson Rd.) | 281-537-2454 |
www.countyline.com

See review in San Antonio Directory.

Crapitto's Cucina Italiana ⊠ *Italian*   22 | 20 | 25 | $37

Galleria | 2400 Mid Ln. (Westheimer Rd.) | 713-961-1161 |
www.crapittos.com

"Don't let the name keep you away" from this Galleria Italian, a "neighborhood" spot for "consistently good" "old-world" fare served by an "attentive" crew; easygoing prices match the comfy setting, and there's also a "fabulous deck" for balmy evenings.

Cullen's Upscale American Grille M *American*

▽ 17 | 26 | 23 | $38

Clear Lake | 11500 Space Center Blvd. (Genoa Red Bluff Rd.) | 281-991-2000 | www.cullenshouston.com

This "humongous" multiconcept American in Clear Lake features a flashy "Vegas-like" interior with private eating areas, a lounge, ballroom and weekend music; "the menu ranges from burgers to steak", although many say the food's "not up to par" for the setting or prices.

Cyclone Anaya's *Tex-Mex*

21 | 20 | 20 | $26

Briargrove | 5761 Woodway Dr. (Augusta Dr.) | 713-339-4552
Heights | 1710 Durham Dr. (Inker St.) | 713-862-3209
Memorial | City Ctr. | 800 Town & Country Blvd. (Queensbury Ln.) | 713-461-1300
Midtown | 309 Gray St. (Bagby St.) | 713-520-6969
www.cycloneanaya.com

"Popular neighborhood watering holes" for "deadly margaritas" and midpriced Tex-Mex cooking that's "not too adventurous but always appealing"; service and settings vary by locale, although most boast outdoor seating and a well-attended happy hour.

Daily Grill *American*

21 | 18 | 20 | $30

Galleria | Houston Galleria | 5085 Westheimer Rd. (bet. McCue Rd. & Post Oak Blvd.) | 713-960-5997 | www.dailygrill.com
See review in Austin and the Hill Country Directory.

Z Da Marco ⊠M *Italian*

29 | 24 | 27 | $61

Montrose | 1520 Westheimer Rd. (bet. Ridgewood & Windsor Sts.) | 713-807-8857 | www.damarcohouston.com

"Tuscany" comes to Texas via this Montrose Italian – voted No. 1 for Food and Most Popular in Houston – whipping up "memorable" meals with "sublime", "homemade pastas" and "amazing things with truffles" in an "intimate" setting tended by a "knowledgeable" staff; yes, it's "crowded" and "you'll take a hit in the pocketbook, but you won't mind"; P.S. beer and wine only.

Damian's Cucina Italiana ⊠ *Italian*

26 | 22 | 26 | $44

Midtown | 3011 Smith St. (bet. Anita & Rosalie Sts.) | 713-522-0439 | www.damians.com

This Midtown "classic" is a "steady performer" for "old-fashioned" Italian-Americana proffered by an "outstanding" staff that "makes you feel like family"; a few find the "upscale" setting "a little tired", but it's "comfortable" enough, and "you get a lot for your money."

D'Amico's Italian Market Café *Italian*

23 | 19 | 20 | $29

NEW **Heights** | 2802 White Oak Dr. (Studewood St.) | 713-868-3400
Rice Village | Village Arcade | 5510 Morningside Dr. (bet. Rice & University Blvds.) | 713-526-3400
www.damico-cafe.com

After nearly 15 years in the Rice Village, this "casual Italian" restaurant and grocery has added a second spot in the Heights; both

	FOOD	DECOR	SERVICE	COST

boast inexpensive menus of homemade pastas served in "intimate" ("crowded") digs with tables against the shelves and a suitably "family atmosphere."

Danton's Gulf Coast
Seafood Kitchen *Cajun/Seafood*

| 24 | 21 | 23 | $34 |

Montrose | 4611 Montrose Blvd. (Hwy. 59) | 713-807-8883 | www.dantonsseafood.com

"Some of the best seafood in town" is the catch at this Montrose fish house favored for its "high-quality" Gulf Coast–centric menu featuring loads of fresh oysters and Cajun classics like slow-cooked gumbo; although the ambiance with a fishing motif and obligatory service suggests an "upscale Red Lobster", it also features "nice" touches like a pleasant patio and a blues brunch on Sundays.

☒ Del Frisco's
Double Eagle Steak House *Steak*

| 27 | 24 | 26 | $67 |

Galleria | 5061 Westheimer Rd. (bet. McCue Rd. & Post Oak Blvd.) | 713-355-2600 | www.delfriscos.com
See review in Dallas/Ft. Worth Directory.

Dessert Gallery
Bakery & Café *American/Dessert*

| 23 | 16 | 20 | $14 |

Galleria | 1616 Post Oak Blvd. (San Felipe St.) | 713-622-0007
Upper Kirby District | 3600 Kirby Dr. (Richmond Ave.) | 713-522-9999
www.dessertgallery.com

Devotees "devour the cakes with abandon" at these bakeries in the Galleria and Upper Kirby District also offering "to-die-for" cookies and savories like moderately priced boxed lunches, salads and other American items; some find the confections on the "dry" side, though it remains a lunchtime "go-to" for many.

Dimassi's Mediterranean
Buffet *Mideastern*

| 19 | 12 | 16 | $16 |

Medical Center | 8236 Kirby Dr. (La Concha Ln.) | 713-526-5111
Galleria | 5064 Richmond Ave. (Sage Rd.) | 713-439-7481
West Houston | 10811 Westheimer Rd. (Walnut Bend Ln.) | 713-780-0125
Stafford | 12350 Southwest Frwy. (Airport Blvd.) | 281-565-2480
The Woodlands | 1640 Lake Woodlands Dr. (Pinecroft Dr.) | 281-363-0200
www.dimassisbuffet.com

"Basic, basic, basic", these Middle Eastern buffets offer a "pretty good" selection of "fresh" items like kebabs and lamb shanks in spare settings; "quick" service and "low" pricing make it an "everyday spot" for many.

Divino ☒ *Italian*

| 25 | 18 | 23 | $40 |

Lower Shepherd | 1830 W. Alabama St. (bet. Hazard & Woodhead Sts.) | 713-807-1123 | www.divinohouston.com

"It looks like a hole-in-the-wall, but the food is amazing" swoon supporters of this Lower Shepherd trattoria whose "simply delicious" Italian menu is inspired by the rich cuisine of Emilia-Romagna; "excellent wines", "friendly service" and relatively "cheap" pricing make it "great for a date."

	FOOD	DECOR	SERVICE	COST

Dolce Vita Pizzeria Enoteca *Italian*   26 | 17 | 21 | $32

Montrose | 500 Westheimer Rd. (Whitney St.) | 713-520-8222 |
www.dolcevitahouston.com

"Fabulous pizzas" with "beautiful blistered crusts" are the main attraction at this Montrose Italian from Marco Wiles (Da Marco) also putting out "innovative" antipasti and well-chosen wines; it's bustling most nights with a "noisy" crowd, so "go early", or prepare to wait.

Dot Coffee Shop ◐ *Diner*   - | - | - | I

Hobby | 7006 Gulf Frwy. (Woodridge Dr.) | 713-644-7669
"Nostalgic diner food" is available 24/7 at this Hobby stop that's been around since 1967.

NEW Down House ◐ *American*   - | - | - | M

Heights | 1801 Yale St. (18th St.) | 713-864-3696 |
www.downhousehouston.com

With proudly advertised local-ingredient sourcing, an appealingly eclectic list of draft beers and long hours (7–2 AM daily), this moderately priced American is a worthy addition to the Heights' ever-blossoming dining scene; set in a modest structure, the laid-back setting features sofas and booths and appropriately easygoing service.

NEW Eatsie Boys *Eclectic*   - | - | - | I

Montrose | Location varies; see website | 845-430-8479 |
www.eatsieboys.com

Born from the late-night cravings of its owners, this Eclectic truck offers outrageous sandwiches on Slow Dough and Grateful Bread pretzel buns and baguettes plus handcrafted ice cream and gelato in unusual flavors like sweet corn and red curry; it rolls all over town, but after the daily grind, the truck can also be hired for catering events.

Eddie V's Prime Seafood *Seafood/Steak*   26 | 26 | 25 | $55

Memorial | CityCentre | 12848 Queensbury Ln. (Town & Country Blvd.) |
832-200-2380
Upper Kirby District | West Ave. | 2800 Kirby Dr. (Westheimer Rd.) |
713-874-1800
www.eddiev.com

See review in Austin and the Hill Country Directory.

NEW El Gran Malo ◐ *Mexican*   - | - | - | I

Heights | 2307 Ella Blvd. (23rd St.) | 832-767-3405 |
www.elgranmalo.com

Located west of the Heights, this self-billed 'gastrocantina' presents contemporary takes on Mexican finger foods, which are modestly priced and paired with infused tequilas and inventive, locally attuned cocktails; though the setting is somewhat sparse, it's pepped up with quirky adornments like a whimsical mural.

El Meson *Pan-Latin*   24 | 17 | 23 | $30

Rice Village | 2425 University Blvd. (Morningside Dr.) |
713-522-9306 | www.elmeson.com

Family-run Rice Village eatery with an "excellent" array of tapas and Pan-Latin dishes, including "good Cuban, which is rare to ind in town"; modest prices, "incredible wines" and live guitar boost the appeal.

NEW El Real Tex-Mex

19 | 18 | 19 | $24

Montrose | Tower Theater | 1201 Westheimer Rd. (Yoakum Blvd.) | 713-524-1201 | www.elrealtexmex.com

Bryan Caswell (Reef, Stella Sola, *Next Iron Chef*) is behind this much-anticipated Montrose Tex-Mex putting out "classic", "old-school" eats in a "fun", "cleverly renovated" old theater with vintage films playing in the background; although the posole and margaritas earn raves, critics claim the food's "so overhyped it could not help but disappoint", and it's not cheap either.

El Tiempo Tex-Mex

23 | 18 | 22 | $29

Montrose | 1308 Montrose Blvd. (Clay St.) | 713-807-8996

El Tiempo Cantina Tex-Mex

Greenway Plaza Area | 3130 Richmond Ave. (Eastside St.) | 713-807-1600

Heights | 5602 Washington Ave. (Asbury St.) | 713-681-3645 www.eltiempocantina.com

"It's all about the fajitas" at this Inner Loop Tex-Mex trio also favored by singles who mingle at the bar "getting sloshed" on "killer margaritas"; "noisy" acoustics come with the territory, but some are surprised to find it "a bit pricey" too.

Empire Café American

20 | 15 | 16 | $18

Montrose | 1732 Westheimer Rd. (bet. Dunlavy & Woodhead Sts.) | 713-528-5282 | www.empirecafe.com

"On weekends the line goes down Westheimer" at this "popular" Montrose American in a former gas station best known for its "great breakfasts", coffee and "massive, rich desserts" served counter-style.

Escalante's Tex-Mex

21 | 20 | 21 | $24

Briargrove | 6582 Woodway Dr. (Voss Rd.) | 713-461-5400

Galleria | Highland Vill. | 4053 Westheimer Rd. (Suffolk Dr.) | 713-623-4200

Memorial | 12821 Kimberly Ln. (bet. Bough Ln. & Memorial Dr.) | 713-467-5577

Meyerland | 590 Meyerland Plaza (Beechnut St.) | 713-663-7080

Sugar Land | 15933 City Walk (Hwy. 6) | 281-242-1100 www.escalantes.net

"Upscale" Tex-Mex chainlet attracting a mix of families and a "see-and-be-seen" crowd for "fajitas and 'ritas", "guacamole made fresh at the table" and other "solid" eats; the "cheery, bustling" digs feature patio seating at most locales.

Fadi's Mediterranean Mideastern

25 | 16 | 18 | $16

Briargrove | 8383 Westheimer Rd. (Dunvale Rd.) | 713-532-0666

Meyerland | 4738 Beechnut St. (Loop Frwy.) | 713-666-4644

West Houston | 12360 Westheimer Rd. (bet. Dairy Ashford Rd. & Kirkwood Dr.) | 281-556-8390 www.fadiscuisine.com

Much more than meze is on the menu at these cafeteria-style outposts specializing in "fresh", "authentic" Med and Middle Eastern specialties including skewers, meat pies and "healthy" items too; the "casual" tile-clad surroundings are "pleasant" enough, but it's the "value" prices that "can't be beat."

Feast *British* | 24 | 18 | 23 | $43

Montrose | 219 Westheimer Rd. (Bagby St.) | 713-529-7788 | www.feasthouston.com

"A must for any self-respecting foodie", this "homage to offal" in Montrose serves a "ballsy" British menu featuring "bold, adventurous and seriously delicious" "snout-to-tail" dishes; prices are "reasonable", while a "down-to-earth" staff and a "cute and cozy" Arts and Crafts setting complete the package.

NEW Felix 55 *American* | – | – | – | M

Rice Village | 5510 Morningside Dr. (bet. Rice & University Blvds.) | 713-590-0610 | www.felix55.com

This stylish entry in Rice Village puts out seasonal New American cuisine and classic cocktails; early word says the food is solid, but the "service needs to catch up."

59 Diner *Diner* | 18 | 17 | 18 | $15

Lower Shepherd | 3801 Farnham St. (Sandman St.) | 713-523-2333 ●
Memorial | 10407 Katy Frwy. (bet. Gessner Rd. & Sam Houston Tollway) | 713-984-2500 ●
Northwest Houston | 17695 Tomball Pkwy. (Gessner Rd.) | 832-237-7559 ●
Katy | 20210 Katy Frwy. (Fry Rd.) | 281-599-8500 ●
Missouri City | 6302 Hwy. 6 (Glenn Lakes Ln.) | 281-208-4900
Stafford | 12550 Southwest Frwy. (Kirkwood Rd.) | 281-242-5900 ●
www.59diner.com

"A greasy spoon that does it right", this "popular" "retro" chain slings "basic" American "comfort food" 24-7 (except at Missouri City); it works for a "quick", "cheap" stop, and it's "good for kids" too.

5115 Restaurant & Lounge *American* | 23 | 22 | 22 | $46
(fka Ruggles Grille 5115)

Galleria | Saks Fifth Ave. | 5115 Westheimer Rd. (McCue Rd.) | 713-963-8067 | www.51fifteen.com

Regulars rely on this "dependable" Galleria "sleeper" in Saks for a "versatile" menu of New American cuisine elevated by elaborate "special" desserts; though the "quiet", "not-too-crowded" ambiance is a plus, some patrons find prices "on the expensive side."

Fleming's Prime Steakhouse & | 25 | 25 | 25 | $56
Wine Bar *Steak*

Memorial | Town & Country Vill. | 788 W. Sam Houston Pkwy. (Queensbury Ln.) | 713-827-1120
River Oaks | River Oaks Ctr. | 2405 W. Alabama St. (Revere St.) | 713-520-5959
The Woodlands | Woodlands Mall | 1201 Lake Woodlands Dr. (I-45) | 281-362-0103
www.flemingssteakhouse.com

"They know their meat" at this chop shop chain where "well-aged" steaks and 100 "fabulous" wines by the glass are ferried by a "proessional" staff in "clubby" "dark-wood" surroundings so packed "it begs the question – is there really a recession going on?"; "high" prices aside, it "always hits the spot", though the unconvinced note there's "nothing here you can't find anywhere else in Texas."

Floyd's Cajun Kitchen *Cajun/Seafood*   ▽ 27 | 20 | 24 | $21
Pearland | 1300 E. Broadway St. (Shauntel St.) | 281-993-8385
Floyd's Cajun Seafood House *Cajun/Seafood*
Webster | 20760 Gulf Frwy. (Nasa Rd. 1) | 281-332-7474
www.floydscajun.com

"Outstanding" seafood, "great gumbos" and cold beer keep customers sated at these inexpensive Cajun pit stops in Pearland and Webster; the setting's "like a bar" with occasional live music and a "fun, casual" vibe.

Fogo de Chão *Brazilian/Steak*   25 | 23 | 26 | $55
Briargrove | 8250 Westheimer Rd. (bet. Dunvale & Old Farm Rds.) | 713-978-6500 | www.fogodechao.com

"Indulge in pure gluttony" at this Brazilian steakhouse chain, a "celebration of meats" where an endless array of "luscious cuts" "keep on coming" in a "constant stream of skewers" and the "well-stocked salad bar" even makes it "great for vegetarians"; settings are "attractive and comfortable", but "expect to spend a lot."

Frank's Chop House *Steak*   23 | 22 | 25 | $44
Greenway Plaza Area | 3736 Westheimer Rd. (bet. Timmons Ln. & Weslayan St.) | 713-572-8600 | www.frankschophouse.com

"Consistent" all around, this Greenway Plaza Area American is a "neighborhood" go-to for steaks, chops and other comfort fare served in "casual" digs; look for happy-hour specials and Sunday night deals.

Fratelli's ☒ *Italian*   ▽ 19 | 14 | 20 | $22
Northwest Houston | 10989 Northwest Frwy. (34th St.) | 713-957-1150 | www.fratellishouston.com

Family-run Italian in a Northwest Houston strip center putting out "homestyle" cooking in an area otherwise overrun with chains; expect "good" service and modest bills.

Fung's Kitchen *Chinese/Seafood*   25 | 16 | 20 | $30
Southwest Houston | 7320 Southwest Frwy. (Fondren Rd.) | 713-779-2288 | www.eatatfungs.com

"A madhouse during dim sum hours", this sprawling Southwest Houston stalwart earns a faithful following for its "authentic" morsels and "excellent" banquet-style seafood straight from the tanks; "true fans" leave feeling gratified, although given the "crowds" and the "waits", it's certainly "not relaxing."

Fusion Taco ●☒Ⓜ *Eclectic*   - | - | - | I
Location varies; see website | 713-422-2882 | www.fusiontacotruck.com

There is plenty of fusion, but more than just tacos, at this mobile Eclectic turning out Mexican-style finger foods with Asian, Indian and even Jamaican fillings (think jerk chicken quesadillas, tikka ma sala tacos and the like); it's a spicy favorite when it decamps at th lunchtime famer's market Downtown each week.

Gaido's *Seafood*
22 | 19 | 22 | $40

Galveston | 3800 Seawall Blvd. (37th St.) | 409-762-9625 | www.gaidos.com

"The grande dame of the Texas coast" since 1911, this "old-tim seafood house" in Galveston charms guests with "fresh", familia preparations ranked a "cut above" the competition; both the "expe rienced staff" and the nautical looks done up in "grand old fade style" "with a nice view of the Gulf" "haven't changed in decades" but then prices are refreshingly retro too.

Giacomo's Ⓜ *Italian*
23 | 17 | 22 | $26

Upper Kirby District | 3215 Westheimer Rd. (Bammel Ln.) | 713-522-1934 | www.giacomosciboevino.com

Lynette Hawkins (ex La Mora) is at the stoves at this Upper Kirby District "gem", a fast-casual concept specializing in Venetian-inspire small plates (*cicchetti*), "homemade pastas" and eclectic, inexpensiv wines from all over Italy; it has a "quirky", retro feel, with turquois tabletops, dark-brown accents and bold graphics dominating th space; service is "charming" and prices a downright "bargain."

Gigi's Asian Bistro & Dumpling Bar *Asian*
24 | 25 | 21 | $40

Galleria | 5085 Westheimer Rd. (McCue Rd.) | 713-629-8889 | www.gigisasianbistro.com

Twentysomethings thrill to this Asian bistro in the Galleria set i "chic" digs outfitted with 15,000 "beautiful" silk cherry blos soms; despite some service quirks, most marvel at the "mouth watering" array of regional dishes and "inspiring" cocktails, an the all-you-can-eat dim sum special (on Saturdays and Sundays) i "a great deal" too.

Glass Wall Ⓜ *American*
25 | 21 | 23 | $47

Heights | 933 Studewood St. (10th St.) | 713-868-7930 | www.glasswalltherestaurant.com

A "stunning mix" of "fresh", local ingredients turns up in the "so phisticated" New American dishes (think "higher-end comfor food") at this Heights "favorite" where the fare is bolstered by "dar ing", "spot-on" wine pairings from sommelier/co-owner Shepar Ross; add in "a simple, yet elegant" modern setting with an ope kitchen, and "the only negative is the noise level."

Goode Co. Hamburgers & Taqueria *Burgers*
25 | 16 | 19 | $15

West U | 4902 Kirby Dr. (Westpark Dr.) | 713-520-9153 | www.goodecompany.com

"Honest-to-goodness mesquite-grilled burgers" and other "tasty Tex-Mex "soul food" standards hit the spot at this West U counter service joint where "prices won't bust the bank"; it's jammed wit "families" most nights, and also "fills up fast" for breakfast ("one o the best in town").

	FOOD	DECOR	SERVICE	COST

◪ Goode Co. Texas BBQ *BBQ*

| 24 | 18 | 18 | $18 |

West U | 5109 Kirby Dr. (bet. Bissonnet St. & Westpark Dr.) | 713-522-2530

Memorial | 8911 Katy Frwy. (Brogden Rd.) | 713-464-1901

Northwest Houston | 20102 Northwest Frwy. (FM 1960) | 832-678-3562

www.goodecompany.com

BBQ buffs find it "hard not to like" this "cheap and cheerful" cafeteria-style chainlet that "sets the standard" with its "delicious", "smoky" meats, "excellent sides" and signature jalapeño-cheese bread; the decor "screams Texas" with memorabilia and saddles cluttering up the interior, and though the crowded Kirby branch has limited indoor seating, there's plenty of picnic tables outside.

Goode Co. Texas Seafood *Seafood*

| 26 | 20 | 23 | $28 |

West U | 2621 Westpark Dr. (Kirby Dr.) | 713-523-7154

Memorial | 10211 Katy Frwy. (Frostwood Dr.) | 713-464-7933

www.goodecompany.com

"You can get your fish just how you want it" at these midpriced "local favorites" in Memorial and West U, where "a ton of fresh Gulf seafood" is gussied up with "Mexican or Creole" finishes, or prepared "skillfully and simply" with their signature "mesquite touch"; neither branch is particularly "fancy", although the West U original is full of "old-time" atmosphere with seating in a railway car, while the Memorial branch is pleasant and spacious; P.S. "get the Campechana" (it's a Mexican seafood cocktail).

Grappino di Nino ⊠ *Italian*

| 25 | 23 | 22 | $33 |

Montrose | 2817 W. Dallas St. (La Rue St.) | 713-528-7002 | www.ninos-vincents.com

"The patio is just the thing for a spring or autumn evening" at this very "social" Vincent Mandola–owned Montrose Italian that's "usually wall-to-wall with beautiful Houstonians" tucking into "satisfying" small plates, pizzas and pastas; moderate prices, top-"quality" service and live music most nights are other reasons it's so "popular."

Grimaldi's *Pizza*

| 26 | 20 | 21 | $21 |

Sugar Land | First Colony Mall | 16535 Southwest Frwy. (Hwy. 6) | 281-265-2280

The Woodlands | 20 Waterway Ct. (bet. Lake Robbins Dr. & Timberloch Pl.) | 281-465-3500

www.grimaldispizzeria.com

See review in Dallas/Ft. Worth Directory.

Grotto *Italian*

| 22 | 23 | 22 | $36 |

Galleria | 4715 Westheimer Rd. (Loop Frwy.) | 713-622-3663

The Woodlands | 9595 Six Pines Dr. (Lake Woodlands Dr.) | 281-419-4252

www.grottohouston.com

This "solid" Galleria Italian in the Landry's empire "always delivers" for "movers and shakers" who count on "dependable", midpriced Neopolitan cooking set down in a "see-and-be-seen" setting; yet despite the "vibrant" atmosphere, it's too "loud" for many, and others insist it "lost its appeal" when sold by the Vallone family a few years back; P.S. The Woodlands branch is more sedate.

Grove, The *American* 19 | 25 | 21 | $39

Downtown | Discovery Green | 1611 Lamar St. (Crawford St.) |
713-337-7321 | www.thegrovehouston.com

"The view is hard to beat" at this "hip" Downtown American
"overlooking Discovery Green" and boasting an "airy, modern
look plus a "fabulous" rooftop deck and bar; yet despite an "intrigu-
ing" locavore-leaning menu and an impressive culinary pedigree
(with Robert Del Grande as an owner), several surveyors dub the
food "nothing special."

Guadalajara *Tex-Mex* 21 | 17 | 20 | $23

Downtown | 1201 San Jacinto St. (Dallas St.) | 713-650-0101
Memorial | 9799 Katy Frwy. (bet. Bunker Hill Rd. & Memorial City Way) |
713-461-5300
Upper Kirby District | 2925 Southwest Frwy. (Wakefurest Ave.) |
713-942-0772
The Woodlands | 27885 North Frwy. (bet. Lake Front Circle &
Lake Woodlands Dr.) | 281-362-0774
www.guad.com

Pretty "standard", this chain of haciendas turns out "good", if "run-
of-the-mill", Tex-Mex cooking in margarita-fueled settings that are
pleasant for the genre; efficient service and decent prices keep them
"tried-and-true."

Haven ☒ *American* 25 | 24 | 24 | $43

Upper Kirby District | 2502 Algerian Way (Kirby Dr.) | 713-581-6101
www.havenhouston.com

A "pioneer in the eat-local movement", this "cool" Upper Kirby
American from Randy Evans features "marvelous", midpriced small
and large plates spotlighting artisanal and organic ingredients "in
delicious new ways"; service is "attentive" and the setting has a
"Texas-gone-green-and-sustainable vibe" with "sleek", "beautiful"
decor designed from reclaimed materials.

Hearsay ◗ *American* - | - | - | M

Downtown | W.L. Foley Bldg. | 218 Travis St. (Congress St.) |
713-225-8079 | www.hearsayhouston.com

Surveyors "love the cool vibe" of this Downtown New American set
in a "beautiful", uniquely retooled 1880s brick building with high
ceilings, striking chandeliers and an ample bar; perhaps the eats
take a backseat to the "inspired drinks", but the appetizers are
"great" and well priced, and a "terrific staff" adds to the drinking
and dining pleasure.

Hillstone *American* 24 | 22 | 24 | $37
(fka Houston's)

Upper Kirby District | 4848 Kirby Dr. (Westpark Dr.) | 713-529-2386
Houston's *American*
Galleria | 5888 Westheimer Rd. (Fountain View Dr.) | 713-975-1947
www.hillstone.com

A "chain worth going out of your way for", this crowd-pleasing franchise churns out "solid" if "not spectacular" American standards in

"upscale-casual" quarters (complete with bustling "bar scenes"); "spot-on" service and prices "to fit any budget" are added perks, even if more than a few are "puzzled" by the constant "lines."

Hobbit Cafe *Eclectic*

24 | 19 | 22 | $16

Lower Shepherd | 2243 Richmond Ave. (Greenbriar Dr.) | 713-526-5460 | www.myhobbitcafe.com

"Dear to the heart" of many, this "quirky" Lower Shepherd cafe – "established pre-'*Lord of the Rings*' movies" – has been dishing out "tasty", "vegetarian-friendly" Eclectic fare for almost four decades; it's "not much on looks", but that suits the affordable tabs and "relaxed" vibe.

Hubcap Grill ☒ ⊅ *American*

∇ 27 | 13 | 21 | $13

Downtown | 1111 Prairie (bet. Fannin & San Jacinto Sts.) | 713-223-5885

NEW Heights | 1133 W. 19th St. (Beall St.) | 713-862-0555 www.hubcapgrill.com

Some of "the best burgers in Houston" turn up at this diminutive, no-frills counter-service American Downtown offering a variety of toppings, from kalamata olives to Cheetos, with cheeky names like the Quadruple Heart Clogger (with hot dogs, bacon, chili and cheese); some say "overrated", although the Heights branch pleases with lots of microbrews, two patios, a jukebox and flat-screen TVs.

☑ Hugo's *Mexican*

26 | 23 | 23 | $41

Montrose | 1600 Westheimer Rd. (Mandell St.) | 713-524-7744 | www.hugosrestaurant.net

This upscale Montrose Mexican is known for its "brilliantly executed", "modern" dishes "with a twist" and "kick-butt" margaritas "shaken at your table"; service is "excellent" and the attractive setting is always "humming with patrons", so "the only drawback is the noise level"; P.S. be sure to reserve ahead for Sunday's "fabulous brunch."

Hungry's Café & Bistro *Eclectic*

22 | 17 | 19 | $20

Rice Village | 2356 Rice Blvd. (bet. Greenbriar & Morningside Drs.) | 713-523-8652

West Houston | 14714 Memorial Dr. (Dairy Ashford Rd.) | 281-493-1520 www.hungryscafe.com

There's "something to please everyone" at this long-standing duo in Rice Village and West Houston with an Eclectic-American menu that leans toward "healthy" items like wraps, kebabs and salads; it's "cheap, reliable" and the "casual" settings are well-suited to kids.

Huynh ☒ *Vietnamese*

∇ 26 | 16 | 21 | $20

Downtown | 912 St. Emanuel St. (McKinney St.) | 713-224-8964 | www.huynhrestauranthouston.com

"A great find tucked away" in the old Chinatown part of Downtown, this Vietnamese whips up "fantastic" fare at a great price; though the space is fairly bare-bones, the mood is "warm and inviting" thanks to some of the "friendliest" staff around; P.S. you "can BYO" for a pittance.

	FOOD	DECOR	SERVICE	COST

Ibiza ⓂMediterranean 25 | 21 | 24 | $43

Midtown | 2450 Louisiana St. (McGowen St.) | 713-524-0004 | www.ibizafoodandwinebar.com

"The small plates steal the show" at chef Charles Clark's "stylish" Midtowner where "clean-flavored" modern Med dishes gain a lift from a "superb" 500-bottle wine list (highlighted on an eye-popping display wall); the "high-energy" setting is perpetually overflowing with "beautiful people", but an "experienced" staff keeps the mood "pleasant", no matter how "jammed and noisy" it gets.

Indika Ⓜ Indian 26 | 22 | 23 | $42

Montrose | 516 Westheimer Rd. (Whitney St.) | 713-524-2170 | www.indikausa.com

"The flavors are fantastic" at this "modern" Montrose Indian attracting "adventurous" eaters with "fabulously inventive" cuisine that's "not your typical tandoori"; an "upscale" contemporary setting, "knowledgeable" service and an "inspired" cocktail list are clues that it's "not cheap", but certainly "worth it" for an "exciting" meal.

Irma's Ⓩ Mexican 26 | 20 | 23 | $23

Downtown | 22 N. Chenevert St. (Ruiz St.) | 713-222-0767 | www.irmashouston.com

"Menus? we don't need no stinkin' menus" is the m.o. at this funky Downtown Mexican where "Irma herself" "tells you what they've got each day" and customers choose from an array of "wonderfully authentic" dishes (don't miss the rightly famous lemonade); it's a "fun" place and a local "institution", though a few find fault with bills that feel a touch "overpriced"; P.S. dinner served Thursday-Saturday and often on game days.

Jasper's American 24 | 24 | 23 | $43

The Woodlands | Market St. | 9595 Six Pines Dr. (Lake Woodlands Dr.) | 281-298-6600 | www.jaspers-restaurant.com
See review in Austin and the Hill Country Directory.

Jax Grill American 21 | 14 | 18 | $19

Bellaire | 6510 S. Rice Ave. (Bissonnet St.) | 713-668-3606 Ⓩ
Heights | 1613 Shepherd Dr. (Eigel St.) | 713-861-5529
www.jaxgrillhouston.com

"Exactly what you want your neighborhood place to be", these "easy" twins prove "reliable" for "better-than-average" American "comfort food" at wallet-friendly prices; both thrive in casual, "bar"-like digs with counter service, though the lower Heights address kicks things up on weekends with "rockin'" live zydeco bands.

Jeannine's Bistro Ⓩ Belgian - | - | - | M

Montrose | 106 Westheimer Rd. (Bagby St.) | 713-874-0220 | www.jeanninesbistro.com

Montrose Belgian serving up "hearty" eats like mussels and frites and beef stew all washed down with a number of idiosyncratic beers; it's not fancy, but it's inviting, and moderate bills complete the picture.

	FOOD	DECOR	SERVICE	COST

Jenni's Noodle House *Vietnamese* | 19 | 13 | 19 | $16 |

Galleria | 2027 Post Oak Blvd. (Lynn Ln.) | 713-621-4200
Heights | 602 E. 20th St. (Oxford St.) | 713-862-3344
Lower Shepherd | 3111 S. Shepherd Dr. (Alabama St.) | 713-523-7600
www.noodlesrule.com

Regulars rely on these BYO Vietnamese sibs in the Galleria, Heights and Lower Shepherd for "quick", "light" meals of "tasty" phos and curries offered alongside dumplings, edamame and other Asian items; "friendly" staffers work the hip, bare-bones settings, though a few find the bills "rather pricey for noodles and broth."

NEW Jus' Mac ⓜ *American* | - | - | - | I |

Heights | 2617 Yale St. (bet. 26th & 27th Sts.) | 713-622-8646
Sugar Land | 16525 Lexington Blvd. (Austin Pkwy.) | 832-886-4757
www.jusmac.com

"A novel concept" now in two locations in the Heights and Sugar Land, this nostalgic American serves mostly mac 'n' cheese dressed up in a number of ways well outside of the box; it's casual, kid-friendly and easy on the wallet, if tough on the arteries.

Kanomwan ⓩ *Thai* | 26 | 6 | 13 | $21 |

Neartown | 736½ Telephone Rd. (Lockwood St.) | 713-923-4230

Gastronomes gush over this Neartown BYO Thai (aka 'Telephone Thai') whipping up "fabulous" food at "unbeatable" prices; the service and setting are no frills, but it remains an "institution" nonetheless.

Kata Robata *Japanese* | 25 | 21 | 22 | $41 |

Upper Kirby District | 3600 Kirby Dr. (Richmond Ave.) |
713-526-8858 | www.katarobata.com

"Fantastic sushi" with "modern twists" keeps crowds coming to this Upper Kirby Japanese also sending out "wonderful" small plates from the kitchen (like Kobe beef skewers) "for those who don't like the raw stuff"; though the "beautifully designed" space hosts a 'chic' crowd, the bills "leave a surprisingly small dent in the wallet."

Katz's Deli ◑ *Deli* | 20 | 15 | 18 | $19 |

Montrose | 616 Westheimer Rd. (Montrose Blvd.) | 713-521-3838
Katz's Express *Deli*
The Woodlands | Portofino Ctr. | 19075 I-45 N. (bet. Research Forest Dr. & Wellman Rd.) | 936-321-1880
www.ilovekatzs.com

"Huge sandwiches" lead the lineup at this New York–style deli in Montrose (with an abbreviated outpost in The Woodlands) whose interior and menu is a paean to the Big Apple; it's open 24/7 and a "preferred all-night nosh pit" for many, even if critics say it's only "so-so" and "overpriced" to boot.

Kenny & Ziggy's New York Delicatessen *Deli* | 24 | 18 | 21 | $21 |

Galleria | 2327 Post Oak Blvd. (Westheimer Rd.) | 713-871-8883 |
www.kennyandziggys.com

"Houston's answer to the Carnegie Deli" is this "classic Jewish" spot in the Galleria, where "you pay top dollar" for "fabulous smoked

	FOOD	DECOR	SERVICE	COST

fish" and piles of pastrami so big, some are "amazed that the table don't tip over"; appropriately "abrupt" service and a spiffy loo make it a haven for homesick New Yorkers.

Killen's Steakhouse ⊠ *Steak* — | — | — | E

Pearland | 2804 S. Main St. (Walnut St.) | 281-485-0844 | www.killenssteakhouse.com

Meat lovers call this Pearland chophouse a "hidden gem" fo "melt-in-your-mouth" steaks, "fantastic sides" and "excellen desserts" ("the crème brûlée is a must"); it's not cheap, but "ex ceptional" service and handsome surroundings make it "worth th trip south of town."

⊠ Kiran's *Indian* 27 | 26 | 25 | $51

Galleria | 4100 Westheimer Rd. (Mid Ln.) | 713-960-8472 | www.kiranshouston.com

"The kitchen shows a lot of flair" at this Galleria-area venue spe cializing in "wonderful" Indian fusion cuisine like you might find a "Bombay's top restaurant"; "elegant" surroundings and an "at tentive", "well-trained" staff help justify the "expensive" tab and make it a "lovely place to dine."

Kirby's Steakhouse *Steak* 24 | 22 | 23 | $52

The Woodlands | 1111 Timberloch Pl. (I-45) | 281-362-1121 | www.kirbyssteakhouse.com

See review in Dallas/Ft. Worth Directory.

NEW Kris Bistro & Wine Lounge ⊠Ⓜ *French* — | — | — | M

North Houston | 7070 Allensby St. (I-45 N.) | 713-358-5079 | www.krisbistro.com

Students at North Houston's Culinary Institute LeNôtre ge hands-on professional experience at this adjoining French bistro the preparations based on locally sourced ingredients are mean to comfort, just like the relaxed, art-filled setting and, best of all the moderate prices.

La Griglia *Italian* 22 | 24 | 23 | $39

River Oaks | River Oaks Ctr. | 2002 W. Gray St. (bet. McDuffie St. & Shepherd Dr.) | 713-526-4700 | www.lagrigliarestaurant.com

After two decades on the scene, this River Oaks Italian remains "loud and crowded" with a "power-lunch" clientele cramming in fo solid cooking (with loads of "off-the-menu options") served in up scale environs by a "terrific" crew; some say it's "not the same since it was taken over by Landry's", although late hours and happy-hou deals are pleasing to many.

La Mexicana *Mexican* ∇ 18 | 18 | 20 | $16

Montrose | 1018 Fairview St. (Montrose Blvd.) | 713-521-0963 | www.lamexicanarestaurant.com

"There's a simple, homey feel" at this "longtime" "neighborhood fa vorite" in Montrose for basic Mexican grub; cheap prices are a plus as is a "nice patio" to complement that margarita.

Lankford Grocery & Market 🗷🍴 *Burgers*

`25` `8` `17` `$13`

Midtown | 88 Dennis St. (Genesee St.) | 713-522-9555 |
www.lankfordgrocery.com

This Midtown "dive" has long been a destination for "old-fashioned" burgers and other budget-friendly Americana offered from breakfast till afternoon; "nonexistent service" and an unintentionally "kitschy setting" in a "creaky old building with a slanted floor" only "add to the quirky charm."

Laurenzo's *Steak*

`21` `20` `23` `$39`

Heights | 4412 Washington Ave. (Patterson St.) | 713-880-5111 |
www.laurenzos.net

Bearing the family name that is instantly recognizable to Houston diners (from Ninfa's and El Tiempo), this Heights steakhouse specializes in robust American fare like "excellent" prime rib in "ample" portions; prices are moderate and the dining room is dark wood-paneled and sports viewing-friendly, but the kitchen is far more ambitious than other game-watching joints on Washington Avenue.

Le Mistral *French*

`26` `24` `26` `$55`

West Houston | 1400 Eldridge Pkwy. (bet. Brimhurst & Westerloch Drs.) |
832-379-8322 | www.lemistralhouston.com

"Paris meets Houston" at this "fantastic" upscale French in West Houston where the Denis brothers roll out "exceptional", "traditional" cuisine with especially "beautiful desserts" (the chocolate soufflé is a highlight); "attentive" service and a "warm, cozy" setting evoke "quiet luxury" make it "one of the best" in town.

🆕 Liberty Kitchen & Oyster Bar *American/Seafood*

`-` `-` `-` `M`

Heights | 1050 Studewood St. (11th St.) | 713-802-0533 |
www.libertykitchenoyster.com

Lance Fegen (ex BRC Gastropub, Glass Wall) heads the kitchen at this Heights entry that specializes in bivalves and other seafood while also grilling up Traditional American landlubber grub like burgers and steaks; moderate prices are matched by casual, diner-esque decor that mixes rustic and modern elements.

🆕 Line & Lariat *American*

`-` `-` `-` `E`

Downtown | Hotel Icon | 220 Main St. (Congress St.) |
832-667-4470 | www.hotelicon.com

Refined versions of the region's most popular dishes are the highlights of this somewhat pricey Modern Texan, the latest dining addition to Downtown's Hotel Icon; soaring ceilings, marble columns and luxe furnishings – some with a 'cowboy cool' feel, as a nod to the venue's name – make for quite the dramatic interior.

Little Bigs *Burgers*

`17` `10` `15` `$14`

Montrose | 2703 Montrose Blvd. (Westheimer Rd.) | 713-521-2447 |
www.littlebigshouston.com

"Lots of fun", this "slider emporium" in Montrose from Bryan Caswell and his crew (Reef, Stella Sola and *Next Iron Chef*) boasts an array of "original" burgers and "good wines with very little markup"; critics call it "overrated", especially given the owners' pedigree, although the "casual" digs are frequently bustling, especially late at night.

Little Miss Cupcake Ⓜ⊅ *Dessert*

_ | _ | _ | I

Galveston | Location varies | 281-546-0834
Operating in Galveston, this sweets source trades solely in cupcakes crafted from traditional recipes plus an additional special creation each week; despite the limited lineup, this vintage pink-hued truck has loads of fans who follow it daily via Twitter.

Luigi's *Italian*

▽ 26 | 25 | 25 | $32

Galveston | 2328 Strand St. (bet. Tremont & 24th Sts.) |
409-763-6500 | www.luigisrestaurantgalveston.com
"*Grazie,* Luigi" gush grateful fans of the "authentic" Sicilian-tempered fare at this "not-to-be-missed" eatery nicely sited "in an old bank building" on Galveston's historic Strand; the "fresh ingredients" and "simpler-is-better" cooking are true to the classic Italian experience, as is the "outstanding service."

Luling City Market *BBQ*

24 | 14 | 16 | $17

Galleria | 4726 Richmond Ave. (I-610) | 713-871-1903 |
www.lulingcitymarket.com
"Tender smoked brisket" is served up with a "wonderful, vinegar-based sauce" "on traditional butcher paper" at this Galleria-area BBQ "hole-in-the-wall" that's been going strong for three decades; "ice-cold beer", cheap tabs and a "rustic", "old-school vibe" complete the package; P.S. it's unrelated to City Market in Luling, Texas.

Lupe Tortilla *Tex-Mex*

22 | 18 | 19 | $24

Heights | 1511 Shepherd Dr. (Eigel St.) | 713-231-9040
North Houston | 15315 North Frwy. (Richey Rd.) | 281-873-6220
Northwest Houston | 22465 Tomball Pkwy. (Lakewood Crossing Dr.) | 832-843-0004
Upper Kirby District | 2414 Southwest Frwy. (bet. Greenbriar St. & Kirby Dr.) | 713-522-4420
West Houston | 318 Stafford St. (I-10) | 281-496-7580
Webster | 891 W. Bay Area Blvd. (I-45) | 281-338-2711
Katy | 703 W. Grand Pkwy. S. (Kingsland Blvd.) | 281-392-2322
Sugar Land | 15801 Southwest Frwy. (Hwy. 6) | 281-265-7500
Pearland | 2728 Smith Ranch Rd. (bet. Broadway St. & Hughes Ranch Rd.) | 281-888-8200
The Woodlands | 19437 I-45 S. (Lake Woodlands Dr.) | 281-298-5274
Additional locations throughout the Houston area
These "hectic" Tex-Mexers pull in lots of "families" with "mouthwatering" beef fajitas wrapped with homemade tortillas plus play areas for the little 'uns; perhaps the other items are only "fair", but prices are decent and "you can't go wrong with one of their margaritas."

Lynn's Steakhouse ⊠ *Steak*

25 | 24 | 24 | $51

West Houston | 955½ Dairy Ashford St. (bet. I-10 & Memorial Dr.) |
281-870-0807 | www.lynnssteakhouse.com
A "regular stop" on the expense-account circuit, this longtime West Houston steakhouse wins over guests with "satisfying" cuts, "su-

	FOOD	DECOR	SERVICE	COST

perb" service and a "wine list the size of the Yellow Pages"; the digs are certainly "not flashy", though they're "pleasant" enough, although antis allege this old-timer may be a touch "past its prime."

Madras Pavilion *Indian*

| 20 | 15 | 18 | $21 |

Upper Kirby District | 3910 Kirby Dr. (bet. Richmond Ave. & Southwest Frwy.) | 713-521-2617
Sugar Land | 16260 Kensington Dr. (Hwy. 6) | 281-491-3672 | www.themadraspavilion.com

Southern Indian "home cooking" that's vegetarian and kosher to boot is the deal at this "bargain" mini-chain; the settings are beyond simple, but a bountiful lunch buffet adds some color; P.S. the Houston outlet offers some meat dishes.

Mai's Restaurant ●🗷 *Vietnamese*

| ▽ 20 | 17 | 23 | $22 |

Midtown | 3403 Milam St. (Francis St.) | 713-520-5300 | www.maishouston.com

Reopened after a fire that closed it for a year, this beloved Midtown Vietnamese is back serving its wide-ranging, classic menu at affordable rates; while the menu is much the same as before, the setting has gained a lift with a contemporary, bamboo-trimmed look and a full bar.

Mardi Gras Grill *Cajun/Seafood*

| ▽ 25 | 17 | 21 | $24 |

Heights | 1200 Durham Dr. (Nett St.) | 713-864-5600 | www.mardigrasgrill.net

"Drink a lot of beer and eat a lot of crawfish" at this Cajun seafooder in the Heights with a "relaxed atmosphere" and equally relaxed tabs; live music brings in the crowds on weekends.

Maria Selma *Mexican*

| - | - | - | I |

Montrose | 1617 Richmond Ave. (Midelle St.) | 713-528-4920 | www.mariaselma.com

For a decade this Montrose mainstay has been serving moderately priced Mexican fare that is more authentic than most; a relaxed atmosphere with a palapa-covered patio and a lengthy list of tequilas are a few other attractions.

🗷 Mark's American Cuisine *American*

| 28 | 27 | 27 | $75 |

Montrose | 1658 Westheimer Rd. (bet. Dunlavy & Ralph Sts.) | 713-523-3800 | www.marks1658.com

"Magnificent" meals are had at this "delightful", "eccentric" converted church in Montrose where chef Mark Cox crafts "fabulous" New American dishes from "exceptional ingredients"; add in "impeccable" service, and it's "everything you could want in a restaurant", not counting the "expensive" bills.

Masraff's 🗷 *Continental*

| 25 | 25 | 25 | $54 |

Galleria | 1753 Post Oak Blvd. (San Felipe St.) | 713-355-1975 | www.masraffs.com

"You're always made to feel as though you're the only customer that matters" at this Galleria-area Continental that "appeals to the country-club" set; "fantastic" food and a "beautiful", "modern" setting make it a "power-lunch" and "special-occasion" standby.

	FOOD	DECOR	SERVICE	COST

Max's Wine Dive ● *Eclectic*   20 | 16 | 19 | $31

Heights | 4720 Washington Ave. (bet. Parker St. & Shepherd Dr.) | 713-880-8737 | www.maxswinedive.com

This "cool" trio matches "unique", "tasty" Eclectic small plates with "affordable wines", yielding "fun" combos like fried chicken and champagne; all agree that prices are pleasing, but the "cramped" setting and downright "deafening" acoustics make it best for the "under-30" set.

Melange Creperie   *Crêpes*   - | - | - | I

Location varies | 713-291-9933 | www.melangecreperie.wordpress.com

Since this petite cart began operation in March 2010 in a parking lot at the corner of Westheimer and Taft in the heart of Montrose, it has satisfied a niche with its affordable French-style crêpes filled with sweet and savory ingredients far beyond its Parisian inspirations (from ham and cheese and banana-Nutella to palak paneer); a second unit usually plying its wares in the Heights has been added to the mix.

Mission Burritos   *Tex-Mex*   21 | 15 | 19 | $13

Heights | 1609 Durham Dr. (bet. Eigel & Inker Sts.) | 713-426-6634
Lower Shepherd | 2245 W. Alabama St. (bet. Greenbriar Dr. & Revere St.) | 713-529-0535
West Houston | 6168 Hwy. 6 N. (Little York Rd.) | 281-856-0344
Humble | 7025 FM 1960 (Lake Houston Pkwy.) | 281-852-5603
Katy | LaCenterra at Cinco Ranch | 23501 Cinco Ranch Blvd. (Grand Pkwy.) | 281-371-7150
Sugar Land | Lake Pointe Town Ctr. | 15810 Southwest Frwy. (Lake Point Pkwy.) | 281-325-0033
www.missionburritos.com

"Build your own burrito" at this Houston-area Tex-Mex chain where they "aren't shy about heaping on the toppings"; though the settings are certainly nothing fancy (although some branches boast patio seating), devotees declare it "great for a quick lunch" and "one of the best bangs for the buck in town."

Mockingbird Bistro Wine Bar   *American*   26 | 24 | 25 | $50

River Oaks | 1985 Welch St. (McDuffie St.) | 713-533-0200 | www.mockingbirdbistro.com

A "gem" "tucked away in a residential neighborhood" near River Oaks, this New American spotlights "wonderful, creative" seasonal cuisine from chef-owner John Sheely plus a wine menu that "shines"; it's a tad "expensive", but a "warm" staff and a "quaint" setting with an "old European feel" create an overall "inviting" mood.

NEW Modular, The   *Eclectic*   - | - | - | I

Location varies | 713-550-3823 | www.themodularfoodtruck.com

More ambitious than the typical food truck, and many restaurants for that matter, this mobile Eclectic is earning quite the following with its offbeat creations highlighting Japanese and Southern ingredients like sous-vide pork belly and duck confit wings; tiny and shiny, it makes appearances throughout the inner Loop.

	FOOD	DECOR	SERVICE	COST

Monarch *American*
▽ 21 | 23 | 22 | $76

Medical Center | Hotel ZaZa | 5701 Main St. (Ewing St.) | 713-527-1800 | www.hotelzazahouston.com

The chic Hotel ZaZa near the Medical Center is home to this ritzy New American, which is best known for its "see-and-be-seen" scene; the menu features items like lamb-chop lollipops and a full lineup of steaks, though jaded critics call it "expensive for what it is."

Morton's The Steakhouse *Steak*
26 | 24 | 25 | $67

Downtown | 1001 McKinney St. (bet. Fannin & Main Sts.) | 713-659-3700
Galleria | Centre at Post Oak | 5000 Westheimer Rd. (Post Oak Blvd.) | 713-629-1946
www.mortons.com

"Corporate types" clamor for the "massive" steaks and "wonderful" sides and wines at these "manly" outposts of the nationwide chophouse chain; they're "consistent", from the "top-notch" service to the "dark", "noisy" settings and premium prices, and if some find them "nothing special", they're "rarely disappointing" either.

Mo's . . . A Place for Steaks *Steak*
▽ 21 | 21 | 19 | $62

Galleria | 1801 Post Oak Blvd. (bet. San Felipe St. & Westheimer Rd.) | 713-877-0720 | www.mosaplaceforsteaks.com

An outpost of a Milwaukee-based chain, this handsome Galleria-area steakhouse traffics in "first-class" filets and chops with digs and service deemed "typical" of the genre; it boasts a bustling streetside patio, while late nights and weekends, this meatery becomes a real "meat market" with "cougars" on the prowl.

Mosquito Cafe *Eclectic*
25 | 19 | 21 | $20

Galveston | 628 14th St. (Winnie St.) | 409-763-1010 | www.mosquitocafe.com

"One of the few places in Galveston that doesn't have a fryer", this Eclectic counter-service spot is known for its "creative" savories, baked goods and "wonderful weekend breakfasts"; it's set in an 1870s edifice in the Historical District with a "nice patio" for sunny days.

Niko Niko's *Greek*
25 | 14 | 18 | $18

Downtown | Market Sq. | 301 Milam St. (Congress St.) | 713-224-4976
Montrose | 2520 Montrose Blvd. (Missouri St.) | 713-528-4976
www.nikonikos.com

"Damn good" is the consensus on this budget Montrose Hellenic dispensing "classic Greek cooking" in "generous" portions like kebabs that "rock" and potatoes full of "buttery bliss"; there's "always a line", but the "self-serve" setup moves fast, and it's all "worth it" for the "tasty" bites; P.S. the Downtown branch on Market Square Park is quaint, with outdoor seating and lunch options for office dwellers.

Ninfa's *Tex-Mex*
24 | 18 | 21 | $24

Hobby | 8553 Gulf Frwy. (Monroe Rd.) | 713-943-3183
Bellaire | 5423 Bellaire Blvd. (Chimney Rock Rd.) | 713-432-0003
Downtown | Shops at Houston Ctr. | 1200 McKinney St. (San Jacinto St.) | 713-655-8206 ⑤

(continued)

(continued)

Ninfa's

Uptown | 1650 Post Oak Blvd. (San Felipe St.) | 713-623-6060
Upper Kirby District | 3601 Kirby Dr. (Richmond Ave.) | 713-520-0203
West Houston | 14737 Memorial Dr. (Thicket Ln.) | 281-497-5100
Missouri City | 5730 Hwy. 6 (bet. Riverstone & University Blvds.) |
281-499-5070

Original Ninfa's on Navigation *Tex-Mex*

Neartown | 2704 Navigation Blvd. (bet. Delano & Nagle Sts.) |
713-228-1175
www.ninfas.com

The circa-1973 original on Navigation is "still the best" of this Tex-Mex chain beloved for its "can't-be-beat" fajitas wrapped in tortillas "so fresh that it seems like a Mexican grandmother made them" all washed down with "terrific margaritas"; the servers have "been around" since the old days too, so devotees "don't even bother" with the newer locales, though they certainly have their fans.

☑ Nino's 🅢 *Italian*   27 | 22 | 25 | $39

Montrose | 2817 W. Dallas St. (La Rue St.) | 713-522-5120 |
www.ninos-vincents.com

Perhaps the menu's "not wildly creative", but this family-owned, mid-priced '70s-era Montrose mainstay is "always a pleasure" thanks to its "dependably *delizioso*" red-sauce dishes; there's a "real Italian feel" to the setting – an old house decorated with plants and pottery – and an ever-present owner who "greets guests warmly" adds to the charm. P.S. it shares a courtyard with sibs Grappino and Vincent's.

Nit Noi *Thai*   19 | 16 | 18 | $21

Bellaire | 4703 Richmond Ave. (Loop Frwy.) | 713-621-6088
Champions | Red Oak Shopping Ctr. | 850 FM 1960 W. (Red Oak Dr.) |
281-444-7650 🅢
Memorial | Woodway Sq. 2 | 6395 Woodway Dr. (Voss Rd.) |
713-789-1711
West Houston | Royal Oaks Vill. | 11807 Westheimer Rd.
(bet. Crescent Park & Kirkwood Drs.) | 281-597-8200
The Woodlands | 6700 Woodlands Pkwy. (Kuykendahl Rd.) |
281-367-3355

Nit Noi Cafe *Thai*

Downtown | 2020 Louisiana St. (St. Joseph Pkwy.) | 713-652-5855
Downtown | 301 Main St. (Congress St.) | 713-225-1069
West Houston | 1005 Dairy Ashford St. (I-10) | 281-496-9200 🅢
www.nitnoithai.com

"Fresh-flavored" Thai cuisine comes in "ample" helpings at this Houston chain of casual cafes; though diehards are "disappointed" by less-than-"authentic" fare, modest prices and "fast" service mean it's an area fixture for "takeout."

Oceanaire Seafood Room *Seafood*   23 | 23 | 23 | $59

Galleria | Houston Galleria | 5061 Westheimer Rd. (bet. McCue Rd. &
Post Oak Blvd.) | 832-487-8862 | www.theoceanaire.com

"Don Draper would fit right in" at this "elegant" duo in Dallas and Houston, where vintage "ocean-liner" decor sets the tone for "de-

"pendable" seafood, "fresh" oysters and stiff drinks; an "attentive", "well-trained" staff and a "relaxed atmosphere" are part of the "classy" package, though some still find it "overpriced."

Ocean Palace *Chinese*

| 24 | 18 | 20 | $24 |

Alief | Hong Kong City Mall | 11215 Bellaire Blvd. (Boone Rd.) | 281-988-8898

A "first choice for dim sum", this Alief Chinese pulls in the "church crowds" on Sunday with its "authentic" morsels and seafood dinners; prices are fair and service and decor are "pretty good" for the genre, making it a "favorite" of many.

Oh My Pocket Pies *Eclectic*

| - | - | - | I |

Location varies; see website | no phone | www.ohmypocketpies.com

Portable pies are the gimmick at this cute red truck turning out flaky pastries stuffed with Salisbury steak, chicken relleno and such plus burgers and fries; an expanded menu and greater coverage of the Houston area are currently in the works.

Olivette *American*

| ▽ 21 | 20 | 22 | $42 |

Uptown | The Houstonian | 111 N. Post Oak Ln. (bet. Memorial & Woodway Drs.) | 713-685-6713 | www.houstonian.com

Catering to a "captive" business crowd, this dining room in the Houstonian Hotel, Club and Spa near Uptown features "very good" New American cuisine (crab cakes, strip steak) at expense-account prices; the woody setting is "intimate" to some, "drab" to others, although most appreciate the low-key mood and well-spaced tables that encourage conversation.

100% Taquito *Mexican*

| 23 | 16 | 18 | $12 |

West U | 3245 Southwest Frwy. (Buffalo Spdwy.) | 713-665-2900 | www.100taquito.com

"Easier than finding" a "real" taco truck, this West U strip-mall taqueria dispenses "authentic" "Mex-Mex" street fare in a "funky" "air-conditioned space"; the vibe is "laid-back", with prices and service that are equally "down-to-earth."

Otilia's *Mexican*

| - | - | - | I |

Spring Branch | 7710 Long Point Rd. (Wirt Rd.) | 713-681-7203

Champions cheer the "excellent", "authentic" homestyle Mexican cooking at this "family-run" Spring Branch standby; "don't expect much in terms of atmosphere" or service, but vibrant flavors and accompanying value make it "worth driving for."

Ouisie's Table *Southern*

| 24 | 23 | 24 | $42 |

River Oaks | 3939 San Felipe St. (bet. Drexel Dr. & Willowick Rd.) | 713-528-2264 | www.ouisiestable.com

A "tony" crowd favors this "been-around-forever" River Oaks belle serving "modern", "elegant" takes on Southern cuisine in a setting that's "quietly sophisticated without being stuffy"; service is "attentive" and as for the food, many find it "generally excellent", if a touch "pricey" "for what you get."

	FOOD	DECOR	SERVICE	COST

Palm, The *Steak*

25 | 20 | 24 | $64

Galleria | Briar Grove Plaza | 6100 Westheimer Rd. (Greenridge Dr.) |
713-977-2544 | www.thepalm.com
See review in San Antonio Directory.

Pappadeaux *Cajun/Seafood*

23 | 20 | 21 | $32

Hobby | Hobby Airport | 7800 Airport Blvd. (Broadway St.) |
713-847-7622
Medical Center | 2525 S. Loop W. (bet. Buffalo Spdwy. & Kirby Dr.) |
713-665-3155
Champions | 7110 FM 1960 W. (Cutten Rd.) | 281-580-5245
Galleria | 6015 Westheimer Rd. (Greenridge Dr.) | 713-782-6310
Memorial | 10499 Katy Frwy. (bet. Attingham Dr. & Town & Country Blvd.) |
713-722-0221
Northwest Houston | 13080 Hwy. 290 (bet. Hollister St. &
NW Central Dr.) | 713-460-1203
Upper Kirby District | 2410 Richmond Ave. (Kirby Dr.) |
713-527-9137
West Houston | 12109 Westheimer Rd. (Houston Center Blvd.) |
281-497-1110
Stafford | 12711 Southwest Frwy. (bet. Hwy. 90A & Kirkwood Rd.) |
281-240-5533
The Woodlands | 18165 I-45 S. (Shenandoah Park Dr.) | 936-321-4200
www.pappadeaux.com
Additional locations throughout the Houston area
"If you leave hungry, it's your fault" at these "Texas-sized crab
shacks" cranking out "insanely gargantuan" helpings of Cajun seafood
offering "tremendous value for the money"; the mood's "cheerful", although "service can be spotty" and many find it "too noisy" to boot.

Pappas Bar-B-Q *BBQ*

21 | 16 | 19 | $17

Downtown | 1100 Smith St. (Franklin St.) | 713-759-0018 🏢
Downtown | 3814 Little York Rd. (Hwy. 59) | 713-697-4417
Downtown | 4430 I-45 N. (Crosstimbers St.) | 713-697-9533
Northwest Houston | 12917 Northwest Frwy. (Rte. 290) | 713-462-2550
Northwest Houston | 7007 Hwy. 59 S. (Bellaire Blvd.) | 713-772-4557
Southwest Houston | 9797 Westheimer Rd. (Gessner Rd.) |
713-780-0081
Southwest Houston | 9815 Bissonnet St. (Centre Pkwy.) | 713-777-1661
Webster | 20794 Gulf Frwy. (FM 528) | 281-332-1285
Humble | 19713 Eastex Frwy./Hwy. 59 (FM 1960) | 281-446-0441
The Woodlands | 27752 I-45 N. (Wild Forest Rd.) | 281-363-2647
www.pappas.com
Additional locations throughout the Houston area
These BBQ chain links deliver "tender", "well-smoked" meats and
"all the trimmings" with "minimal" fanfare in spiffy environs; perhaps
they're "nothing to write home about", but regulars rate them "good
for what they are" – "fast", cheap and well suited for "takeout."

🏢 Pappas Bros. Steakhouse 🏢 *Steak*

28 | 25 | 27 | $71

Galleria | 5839 Westheimer Rd. (bet. Augusta & Bering Drs.) |
713-780-7352 | www.pappasbros.com
The "melt-in-your-mouth" steaks "blow the competition away" at
this "classy" chophouse pair in Dallas and Houston where the

"excellent" cuts are matched with an "unbelievable" wine list ("a sommelier's dream"); yes, they're "pricey", but "impeccable" service and "elegant, masculine" settings make them a "favorite for special occasions."

Pappas Burgers *Burgers*

| 24 | 17 | 18 | $19 |

Hobby | Hobby Airport | 7800 Airport Blvd. (Broadway St.) | 281-657-6168
Galleria | 5815 Westheimer Rd. (bet. Chimney Rock Rd. & Fountain View Dr.) | 713-975-6082
www.pappasburger.com

"The burgers, fries and shakes all are winners" at this popular chainlet offering solid bang for the buck; the sports-bar settings are especially "lively" on game days, and if service is uneven, at least "they try hard."

Pappasito's Cantina *Tex-Mex*

| 24 | 19 | 20 | $26 |

Medical Center | 2515 S. Loop W. (bet. Buffalo Spdwy. & Kirby Dr.) | 713-668-5756
Briargrove | 6445 Richmond Ave. (Hillcroft Ave.) | 713-784-5253
FM 1960 | 7050 FM 1960 W. (Cutten Rd.) | 281-893-5030
Memorial | 10409 Katy Frwy. (bet. Gessner Rd. & Sam Houston Tollway) | 713-468-1913
North Houston | 15280 I-45 N. (Lockhaven Dr.) | 281-821-4505
Northwest Houston | 13070 Hwy. 290 (Langfield Rd.) | 713-462-0245
Upper Kirby District | 2536 Richmond Ave. (Kirby Dr.) | 713-520-5066
Webster | 20099 I-45 S. (Nasa Rd. 1) | 281-338-2885
Humble | 10005 FM 1960 Bypass W. (Hwy. 59) | 281-540-8664
Sugar Land | 13750 Southwest Frwy. (Dairy Ashford Rd.) | 281-565-9797
www.pappasitos.com
Additional locations throughout the Houston area

The "awesome" beef fajitas are the standouts on the otherwise "solid, but not out-of-this-world" Tex-Mex menu at these "rambunctious" chain cantinas set in expansive "Disney-esque" digs and staffed by a "pleasant, but harried" crew; those who carp about "long waits" and "too-high" prices for the genre are often won over after a few of their signature margaritas.

Pappas Seafood *Seafood*

| 24 | 20 | 21 | $33 |

Almeda | 6945 I-45 S. (Rustic St.) | 713-641-0318
Lower Shepherd | 3001 S. Shepherd Dr. (Marshall St.) | 713-522-4595
North Houston | 11301 I-45 N. (Aldine Bender Rd.) | 281-999-9928
Webster | 19991 I-45 S. (Medical Center Blvd.) | 281-332-7546
Humble | 20410 Hwy. 59 N. (bet. FM 1960 & Townsen Blvd.) | 281-446-7707
Galena Park | 12010 I-10 E. (Federal Rd.) | 713-453-3265
www.pappasseafood.com

Customers who "have been coming for over 20 years" commend this crowd-pleasing chainlet for "big plates" of "traditional", "Gulf-style" seafood served up in "family-friendly" environs; though it certainly delivers "good" service and "value for your money", it's all a bit "predictable" to some.

Paulie's ☒ *Italian* 24 | 17 | 17 | $19

Montrose | 1834 Westheimer Rd. (bet. Driscoll & Morse Sts.) |
713-807-7271 | www.pauliesrestaurant.com

"A little more upscale" than your usual Italian cafe, this Montrose
entry offers "wonderfully prepared" panini, salads and pizza plus
fine espresso, wine and sweets; "prompt" service and a pleasant
vibe make it a "great neighborhood spot."

Pei Wei Asian Diner *Asian* 20 | 16 | 18 | $16

West U | Plaza in the Park | 5110 Buffalo Spdwy. (Westpark Dr.) |
713-661-0900

Champions | Champions Vill. | 5203 FM 1960 W.
(off Champion Forest Dr.) | 281-885-5430

Memorial | 1413 S. Voss Rd. (bet. San Felipe St. & Woodway Dr.) |
713-785-1620

Montrose | 1005 Waugh Dr. (bet. Clay & Dallas Sts.) | 713-353-7366

Northwest Houston | 12020 FM 1960 W. (bet. Eldridge Pkwy. &
Fallbrook Dr.) | 281-571-4990

West Houston | 14008 Memorial Dr. (Kirkwood Rd.) | 281-506-3500

Webster | 19411 Gulf Frwy. (Bay Area Blvd.) | 281-554-9876

Kingwood | Kingwood Commons | 702 Kingwood Dr.
(Chestnut Ridge Dr.) | 281-318-2877

Katy | Highland Town Ctr. | 1590 S. Mason Rd. (Highland Knolls Dr.) |
281-392-1410

Sugar Land | Town Center at Lakeside | 16101 Kensington Dr. (Hwy. 6) |
281-240-1931
www.peiwei.com
Additional locations throughout the Houston area
See review in Dallas/Ft. Worth Directory.

Peli Peli *S African* - | - | - | M

Northwest Houston | Vintage Park | 110 Vintage Park Blvd. (Louetta Rd.) |
281-257-9500 | www.pelipeli.com

"Innovative" South African cuisine is the hook at this lively Northwest
Houston restaurant set in "romantic", low-lit digs with an artistically
rendered 30-ft.-tall Acacia tree inside; service can be uneven and it
flies somewhat under the radar, but those in the know say it's "worth
the drive"; P.S. live music on weekends.

Perbacco ☒ *Italian* - | - | - | M

Downtown | 700 Milam St. (Capitol St.) | 713-224-2422 |
www.perbaccohouston.blogspot.com

"Convenient" for business lunches or the theater, this Downtown
Italian is an "oasis" for a "quick" midpriced bite; the word on the
food is "decent, but nothing exceptional."

Perry's Steakhouse & Grille *Steak* 26 | 26 | 25 | $55

Champions | 9730 Cypresswood Dr. (Cutten Rd.) | 281-970-5999

Memorial | 9827 Katy Frwy. (bet. Bunker Hill & Gessner Rds.) |
832-358-9000

Clear Lake | 487 Bay Area Blvd. (bet. Sea Liner & Seawolf Drs.) |
281-286-8800

Katy | LaCenterra at Cinco Ranch | 23501 Cinco Ranch Blvd.
(Grand Pkwy.) | 281-347-3600

(continued)

Perry's Steakhouse & Grille

Sugar Land | Sugar Land Town Sq. | 2115 Town Square Pl.
Southwest Frwy.) | 281-565-2727
The Woodlands | 6700 Woodlands Pkwy. (Kuykendahl Rd.) |
281-362-0569
www.perryssteakhouse.com

An "elegant place for business or special occasions", this chophouse
chain is the place to "impress" with "wonderful" steaks, "outstanding"
wines and a signature pork chop that's "not to be missed" ("everything
pales next to the pork"); "top-notch" service and "attractive" settings
are added perks, but it's "pretty damn expensive" "unless you're on
an expense account"; P.S. live jazz and piano at most locales.

Pesce ⊠ *Seafood*

26 | 25 | 26 | $52

Upper Kirby District | Upper Kirby Shopping Ctr. | 3029 Kirby Dr.
(Alabama St.) | 713-522-4858 | www.pescehouston.com

A "polished" example in the Landry's empire, this "popular" Upper
Kirby seafooder helmed by chef Mark Holley presents a "well-thought-
out" menu spanning from raw bar selections to sushi and crab cakes;
it earns kudos for its "spot-on" service and "elegant" setting with or-
nate aquatic details, though a few feel stung by "sky-high" tabs.

P.F. Chang's China Bistro *Chinese*

21 | 21 | 21 | $29

Galleria | Highland Vill. | 4094 Westheimer Rd. (Drexler Dr.) |
713-627-7220
Northwest Houston | Willowbrook Mall | 18250 Tomball Pkwy.
(Willow Chase Blvd.) | 281-571-4050
West Houston | 11685 Westheimer Rd. (Crescent Park Dr.) |
281-920-3553
Sugar Land | 2120 Lone Star Dr. (Town Center Blvd.) | 281-313-8650
The Woodlands | Woodlands Mall | 1201 Lake Woodlands Dr. (I-45) |
281-203-6350
www.pfchangs.com
See review in Dallas/Ft. Worth Directory.

⊠NEW Philippe Restaurant +

24 | 26 | 24 | $54

Lounge ⊠ *American/French*

Galleria | 1800 Post Oak Blvd. (Ambassador Way) | 713-439-1000 |
www.philippehouston.com

Very "chic", this Galleria-area entry from "tremendously talented"
Philippe Schmit spotlights "top-line" French-American cooking with
playful "Texas twists" (e.g. duck-confit tamales, burgundy beef
cheeks); the "sexy" space features a first-floor zinc bar with its own
menu plus a stylish industrial-contemporary upstairs dining room
with near-"flawless" service and moderate-to-pricey bills.

Piatto *Italian*

22 | 21 | 23 | $35

Galleria | 4925 W. Alabama St. (Post Oak Blvd.) | 713-871-9722
Royal Oaks | 11693 Westheimer Rd. (Crescent Park Dr.) | 281-759-7500
www.piattoristorante.com

"Wonderful!" rave regulars who "always feel welcome" at these
Italian sibs near the Galleria and Royal Oaks turning out "tasty"

from-The-Boot specialties, including a "five-star" fried asparagus appetizer that's become their signature; the mood's "relaxed" despite "crowded" conditions, and prices offer solid "value" too.

Pico's Mex-Mex *Mexican*　　24 | 17 | 22 | $28

Bellaire | 5941 Bellaire Blvd. (Renwick Dr.) | 713-662-8383 | www.picos.net

Truly "authentic" Mexican fare and some of the "best margaritas in the city" (made with "freshly squeezed lime juice") are the hallmarks of this "long-standing family favorite" just west of Bellaire; a "super-nice" staff and modest pricing overcome any quibbles about the beyond-"casual" digs.

Pizzitola's Bar-B-Que 🖾 *BBQ*　　∇ 22 | 12 | 24 | $19

Heights | 1703 Shepherd Dr. (Inker St.) | 713-227-2283 | www.pizzitolas.com

With a "long history of producing fabulous BBQ", this well-worn pit in the Heights from 1935 still keeps 'em coming with "consistent" ribs, links and banana pudding "like grandma makes"; it's not fancy but there are plenty of tables and speedy service for takeout.

🆕 Pondicheri *Indian*　　∇ 20 | 20 | 20 | $25

River Oaks | West Ave. | 2800 Kirby Dr. (Westheimer Rd.) | 713-522-2022 | www.pondichericafe.com

"Mumbai street food" makes up much of the menu at this "new, different" Indian ensconced in the West Ave shopping-condo development near River Oaks; look for modernized dishes like Frankie rolls, lamb burgers and thali plates served up all day in an industrial-chic setting.

Poscol 🅜 *Italian*　　∇ 26 | 19 | 24 | $28

Montrose | 1609 Westheimer Rd. (Mandell St.) | 713-529-2797

At this Montrose eatery – the third Italian in the area from Marco Wiles (Da Marco and Dolce Vita) – "tasty", "traditional dishes" from "the old country" meet up with a plethora of "excellent" small plates, house-cured salumi plus "gems" from an all-Italia wine list; on the downside are a stark strip-center setting and a mix-and-match menu that some customers call "confusing."

Prego *Italian*　　24 | 20 | 23 | $36

Rice Village | 2520 Amherst St. (Kirby Dr.) | 713-529-2420 | www.prego-houston.com

"Lots of repeat customers" laud this "cozy" "neighborhood" trattoria, a "real sleeper" at the edge of Rice Village featuring "generous" helpings of "satisfying" Italian cuisine; a "friendly" staff "that knows your name" increases the appeal, as does the moderate cost.

Pronto Cucinino *Italian*　　21 | 15 | 17 | $15

Medical Center | 3191 W. Holcombe Blvd. (Buffalo Spdwy.) | 713-592-8646
Memorial | 791 Town & Country Blvd. (Queensbury Ln.) | 713-467-8646
Montrose | 1401 Montrose Blvd. (bet. Clay & Gray Sts.) | 713-528-8646
www.pronto-2-go.com

"Consistency" is key at this trio of "fast-casual" Italians providing chopped salads, pastas and "moist" rotisserie chicken "when you're in a hurry"; expect order-at-the-counter service and nicely functional dining rooms.

Quattro *Italian*

26 | 24 | 24 | $54

Downtown | Four Seasons Hotel | 1300 Lamar St. (Austin St.) | 713-276-4700 | www.quattrorestauranthouston.com

"Not your father's hotel food" nod knowing guests of this smartly dressed Italian tucked into the Four Seasons Downtown; "inventive" enoteca-inspired fare, boutique wines and a staff that's as "fabulous" as the ultracontempo setting help distract from tabs that can feel a tad "overpriced" to some; P.S. it gets kudos for its "superb" Sunday buffet brunch.

Ragin' Cajun *Cajun*

21 | 16 | 17 | $18

Downtown | McKinney Place Tunnel | 930 Main St. (bet. McKinney & Travis Sts.) | 713-571-2422 🖾

Galleria | 4302 Richmond Ave. (bet. Drexel Dr. & Mid Ln.) | 713-623-6321

Southwest Houston | Woodlake Sq. | 9600 Westheimer Rd. (Gessner Rd.) | 832-251-7171

Sugar Land | 16100 Kensington Dr. (Hwy. 6) | 281-277-0704 | www.ragin-cajun.com

It "feels like small-town Louisiana" at this "lively", "no-frills" Cajun chainlet famed for "mudbugs", gumbo and "a lot of fried food" washed down with beer in a "shorts and flip-flop" setting; even if some say the food "falls short", "every so often you just gotta go."

☒ Rainbow Lodge Ⓜ *American*

26 | 27 | 25 | $54

Heights | 2011 Ella Blvd. (TC Jester Blvd.) | 713-861-8666 | www.rainbow-lodge.com

Quite "possibly the most romantic setting in Houston" purr patrons of this "delightful" little log cabin perched on the banks of a bayou in the Heights; a "welcoming" staff and a mostly "very good" game-centered American menu make it a mainstay for "special occasions", while the bar is a place "one could go to eat more casually"; brunch and lunch are also less expensive.

RDG + Bar Annie *American/Southwestern*

24 | 25 | 22 | $59

Galleria | 1800 Post Oak Blvd. (Ambassador Way) | 713-840-1111 | www.rdgbarannie.com

"Old-guard Houston meets Robert Del Grande" at this "swanky" three-in-one concept in the Galleria with a cushy lounge, "noisy" bar and "excellent, creative" American-Southwestern menu presented in a "lavish" dining room; it's certainly a "place to be seen", although some are irked by "pricey" tabs and service "with an attitude."

Red Lion Pub, The *Pub Food*

▽ 24 | 17 | 21 | $27

Lower Shepherd | 2316 S. Shepherd Dr. (Fairview St.) | 713-782-3030 | www.redlionhouston.com

Expats extol this "dark" Lower Shepherd tavern for its proper pints and whiskies and classic pub menu augmented by Indian specialties; the warm, wood-paneled interior may be "a little worn" around the edges, but most don't mind given the modest checks.

⚡ Reef 🅢 *Seafood* | 25 | 21 | 22 | $47 |

Midtown | 2600 Travis St. (McGowen St.) | 713-526-8282 |
www.reefhouston.com

"Hottie chef" Bryan Caswell "knows his seafood" gush fans of this
midpriced Midtown "hot spot" known for its "fantastic", "creative"
fare, "fabulous wines" and infamous deep-fried mac 'n' cheese
("don't miss it"); service can be "mixed" and the "modern" setting is
plenty "noisy", but the "superb food makes it all bearable."

Restaurant CINQ 🅢 *Continental/French* | ▽ 27 | 25 | 25 | $72 |

Montrose | La Colombe d'Or | 3410 Montrose Blvd. (bet. Harold &
Hawthorne Sts.) | 713-524-7999 | www.lacolombedorhouston.com
This "elegant" dining room in the boutique La Colombe d'Or hotel in Montrose presents "wonderful" French-Continental cuisine
in a "handsome" renovated dining room aided by "knowledgeable", "attentive" service; prices are up there, but the ambiance
is appropriately "deluxe."

Ristorante Cavour *Italian* | ▽ 24 | 26 | 25 | $62 |

Uptown | Hotel Granduca | 1080 Uptown Park Blvd. (Post Oak Blvd.) |
713-418-1000 | www.granducahouston.com
Hidden inside the ritzy Hotel Granduca Uptown, this dining room
rolls out "excellent" (if "not the most creative") Italian cuisine in a
"quiet", "elegant" setting; a few find the prices and the "white-glove
service" "a bit precious", but it works for a "special occasion."

🆕 Rolling Hunger *Eclectic* | - | - | - | I |

Location varies; see website | 713-992-9670 |
www.therollinghunger.com
This bold-orange truck dishes out an equally bold mash-up of
Korean, Vietnamese and Mexican cuisines crafted in easy-to-
consume forms like bulgogi tacos and banh mi; it often rolls to
Montrose for service during the day, but check its web site or
Twitter for details.

🆕 Roost 🅢 *American* | - | - | - | M |

Lower Shepherd | 1972 Fairview St. (Hazard St.) | 713-523-7667
A young chef whose résumé includes a number of respected area
kitchens preps a diverse array of American dishes, most featuring
local foodstuffs, at this midpriced Lower Shepherd newcomer; set in
a small old house, the environs are comfortably outfitted in light colors, soft woods and white tablecloths.

Rudi Lechner's 🅢 *German* | 24 | 19 | 23 | $31 |

Southwest Houston | Woodlake Sq. | 2503 S. Gessner Rd.
(Westheimer Rd.) | 713-782-1180 | www.rudilechners.com
"It tastes like grandma's in the kitchen" at this Southwest
Houston "standby" dishing out "strudel, sausages, sauerbraten"
and other hearty German specialties; given the affable owner and
"inexpensive" prices, the somewhat "kitschy", "long-in-the-tooth"
looks hardly register with its loyal clientele; P.S. there's polka
Wednesday–Saturday nights.

	FOOD	DECOR	SERVICE	COST

Rudy & Paco ⌧ Pan-Latin
26 | 23 | 27 | $41

Galveston | 2028 Post Office St. (21st St.) | 409-762-3696

This Galveston steak and seafood specialist is "among the best" on the island with well-priced Pan-Latin–inflected meals that kick off with fried plantain chips and chimichurri dipping sauce; the contemporary setting is dressier than its neighborhood brethren (no shorts, please), and is enhanced by "attentive" service.

Ruggles Cafe Bakery American
22 | 17 | 18 | $19

Rice Village | 2365 Rice Blvd. (Morningside Dr.) | 713-520-6662 | www.rugglescafebakery.com

"It's hard to resist getting at least one" of the "fabulous desserts" at this chichi Rice Village cafe, also championed for its "quick, casual" American meals; "parking" hassles are often a problem, but its "comfy-like-an-old-blanket" vibe compensates.

Ruggles Green American
23 | 18 | 16 | $21

Memorial | CityCentre | 801 Town & Country Blvd. (Queensbury Ln.) | 713-464-5557

Upper Kirby District | 2311 W. Alabama St. (bet. Greenbriar & Revere Sts.) | 713-533-0777

www.rugglesgreen.com

A certified-green eatery, this "great, healthy" Upper Kirby option and its CityCentre offshoot dish out a wide-ranging responsible American menu with vegetarian and gluten-free offerings plus hormone-free meats; low-key settings and prices make them equally well suited for a quick bite, dinner with the kids or one of their decadent desserts paired with fair-trade coffee.

Ruggles Grill Ⓜ American
25 | 20 | 21 | $53

Montrose | 903 Westheimer Rd. (Montrose Blvd.) | 713-527-9400 | www.rugglesgrill.com

A mainstay in the heart of Montrose for decades, this New American may no longer be a hot spot, but it continues to lure a loyal following with fairly priced cooking and "exquisite desserts"; it's set in a 1920s house with stained-glass windows and ceiling murals, although a few longtimers lament service with an "attitude", while others find the fare "disappointing" compared to the old days.

Ruth's Chris Steak House Steak
26 | 22 | 25 | $63

Galleria | 6213 Richmond Ave. (Greenridge Dr.) | 713-789-2333 | www.ruthschris.com

See review in San Antonio Directory.

Saldivia's South American Grill Argentinean
- | - | - | M

Southwest Houston | 10234 Westheimer Rd. (Seagler St.) | 713-782-9494 | www.saldivias.com

This family-run restaurant brings the cooking of Argentina and Uruguay to Westheimer with a value-minded menu spotlighting traditional grilled meats and fish (entraña, aka skirt steak, is a signature); the digs are warm, if unassuming, and attract both expats and neighborhood families, with well-priced bottles of Malbec fueling the congenial atmosphere.

	FOOD	DECOR	SERVICE	COST

Sambuca *Eclectic*   22 | 24 | 21 | $38

Downtown | 909 Texas Ave. (Travis St.) | 713-224-5299 |
www.sambucarestaurant.com
See review in Dallas/Ft. Worth Directory.

*17 *American*   24 | 24 | 21 | $51

Downtown | Alden Houston Hotel | 1117 Prairie St. (bet. Fannin &
San Jacinto Sts.) | 832-200-8888 | www.aldenhotels.com
This "chic" New American in the boutique Alden Downtown features
a "creative seasonal menu" in an "intimate" setting; though it works for
a "quiet" meal, some say "service should be better for the price."

Shade *American*   23 | 22 | 24 | $36

Heights | 250 W. 19th St. (bet. Rutland & Yale Sts.) | 713-863-7500 |
www.shadeheights.com
A pioneer in bringing "sophistication to the Heights", this "casually
elegant" spot draws a "fab-looking" crowd for "fresh, flavorful",
"not-overly-complicated" New American cooking "at a good price";
with an "efficient staff" and an "inviting" modern setting done up in
neutral hues, it's also "wonderful for brunch"; P.S. beer and wine only.

Smith & Wollensky *Steak*   24 | 24 | 24 | $72

Galleria | Highland Vill. | 4007 Westheimer Rd. (Drexler Dr.) |
713-621-7555 | www.smithandwollensky.com
This brash Galleria-area outpost of the New York–born chophouse
chain is known for its "excellent" steaks, seafood and "decadent"
desserts served in handsome "see-and-be-seen" surroundings; if
it's "great for a business dinner", those not on an expense account
sometimes find it "not worth the cost"; P.S. late hours are a plus
(open till 1 AM on weekends).

Soma *Japanese*   ▽ 25 | 22 | 25 | $36

Heights | 4820 Washington Ave. (bet. Durham & Shepherd Drs.) |
713-861-2726 | www.somasushi.com
One of the "hippest sushi bars in Houston", this glammed-up Japanese
in the lower Heights caters to foodies and "noisy twentysomethings"
alike with "high-end" raw fare and "fine" Franco-fusion plates from
the kitchen; just know, you'll "pay a premium" for the experience.

NEW Sorrel Urban Bistro *American*   ▽ 16 | 19 | 14 | $38

Lower Shepherd | 2202 W. Alabama St. (Shepherd Dr.) |
713-677-0391 | www.sorrelhouston.com
This new farm-to-table bistro near Lower Shepherd features "innovative" twists on approachable American cooking, with dishes like
Gulf shrimp with Havarti grits and braised brisket with bourbon-
spiked jus; perhaps it's "too soon to tell" about the food, but the
clean-lined space and moderate bills are certainly pleasing.

Sorrento *Italian*   24 | 22 | 22 | $51

Montrose | 415 Westheimer Rd. (bet. Taft & Whitney Sts.) |
713-527-0609 | www.sorrentohouston.com
At this "quiet gem" in Montrose, near-"impeccable" Italian dishes
and a "lovely" villa-style setting with live piano in the background

set the stage "for a romantic dinner"; appropriately "smooth" service and "high prices" complete the package; P.S. Sunday brunch – with free-flowing champagne and mimosas – "is a treat."

Spanish Flowers ● *Mexican*

19 | 17 | 21 | $19

Heights | 4701 N. Main St. (Airline Dr.) | 713-869-1706

Surveyors seeking "Mexican at 3 AM" get their "fix" at this "old-school" "landmark" just north of the Heights known for an expansive menu of "straightforward" favorites bolstered by freshly made tortillas delivered regularly to your table; it's open 24/7 except for Tuesdays, but no matter what the hour, it's "always family-friendly" with "welcoming" service and budget-friendly tabs.

Star Pizza *Pizza*

25 | 13 | 18 | $19

Heights | 77 Harvard St. (Washington Ave.) | 713-869-1241
Lower Shepherd | 2111 Norfolk St. (Shepherd Dr.) | 713-523-0800
www.starpizza.net

"Excellent" "thick"-crusted pies (sort of like "a cross between Chicago and Sicilian") keep crowds coming to this longtime pizza duo in Lower Shepherd and the Heights deemed among the "best" in town; both branches thrive in "funky, laid-back" digs with patio seating, while an "efficient" staff does its best to make the inevitable "waits" a little more bearable.

Stella Sola Ⓜ *Italian*

23 | 24 | 23 | $42

Heights | 1001 Studewood St. (10th St.) | 713-880-1001 |
www.stellasolahouston.com

Occupying a grand brick edifice in the Heights, this energetic Italian from the folks behind Reef showcases "wonderful" Tuscan-inspired fare heavy on the *carne* like wild boar ragu and Wagyu steaks enhanced by "superb wines at fair prices"; service can be uneven, but on the whole, it's a "real find."

Strip House *Steak*

24 | 24 | 22 | $61

Downtown | Shops at Houston Ctr. | 1200 McKinney St. (San Jacinto St.) |
713-659-6000 | www.striphouse.com

A stylish "twist on the classic steakhouse", this burlesque-themed NYC import Downtown offers "mouthwatering" meats and "sinful" sides (think goose-fat potatoes and truffle-creamed spinach) in a "posh", red room with "tasteful" "nudie pics" adorning the walls; "if price isn't an issue", it's a "great choice" for an "adult" evening.

Sullivan's Steakhouse *Steak*

24 | 22 | 24 | $57

Galleria | 4608 Westheimer Rd. (Westcreek Ln.) | 713-961-0333 |
www.sullivanssteakhouse.com

See review in Austin and the Hill Country Directory.

Swinging Door, The Ⓜ *BBQ*

∇ 27 | 14 | 21 | $20

Richmond | 3714 FM 359 (McCrary Rd.) | 281-342-4758 |
www.swingingdoor.com

"It's a shame it's so far out in the boonies" because this long-standing Richmond BBQ joint boasts "great" pecan-smoked meats in a homey setting; in sum, it's a true "rarity" in the Houston area.

	FOOD	DECOR	SERVICE	COST

Sylvia's Enchilada Kitchen *Tex-Mex*   22 | 18 | 20 | $24

Briargrove | 6401 Woodway Dr. (Voss Rd.) | 713-334-7295
West Houston | 12637 Westheimer Rd. (Dairy Ashford Rd.) |
281-679-8300
www.sylviasenchiladakitchen.com

'So many enchiladas, so little time' could be the motto of this West Houston Tex-Mexer and its Briargrove offshoot where "charming chef-owner Sylvia Casares earns a "well-deserved" following for her signature eats; a "homey" atmosphere and "no-pretensions" service fit the bill; P.S. "Sylvia does not kid around with her cabrito."

Taco Milagro *Mexican*   18 | 16 | 16 | $17

Upper Kirby District | 2555 Kirby Dr. (Westheimer Rd.) |
713-522-1999 | www.taco-milagro.com

"Always popular" – "with families during the week and singles on weekends" – this Upper Kirby Mex packs 'em in with slightly "sophisticated" "fast" eats like "unusual" tamales and tacos plus "pitchers of margaritas" for cheap; it's counter service only, although outdoor seating is a perk, as is the tequila bar under a palapa.

Tacos Tierra Caliente *Mexican*   - | - | - | I

Location varies; see website | no phone

This mobile Mexican next to the West Alabama Ice House serves straight-up street-food staples like tacos and tortas stuffed with lengua (tongue), brisket and the like; it's set in an un-ironically retro trailer that harkens back to the recent past when this type of vendor made up the vast majority of mobile kitchens.

T'afia ⓈⓂ *American*   24 | 17 | 22 | $41

Midtown | 3701 Travis St. (bet. Alabama & Winbern Sts.) |
713-524-6922 | www.tafia.com

An "ever-changing" lineup of "innovative" "local and organic foods" is "cooked with love" at chef-owner Monica Pope's "memorable" Midtown New American that "shines"; given the relatively reasonable prices, the only complaint is that many "wish" the clean, modern space "were more welcoming"; P.S. there's also a Saturday farmer's market in the parking lot.

Tan Tan *Chinese/Vietnamese*   ∇ 24 | 10 | 15 | $17

Alief | 6816 Ranchester Dr. (Bellaire Blvd.) | 713-771-1268 ◗
Southwest Houston | 8066 Westheimer Rd. (Dunvale Rd.) | 713-977-6682
www.tantanrestaurant.com

A "late-night staple", this Alief eatery with a Southwest Houston offshoot is "perfect for post-party cravings" with its expansive array of "authentic", "yummy" Chinese-Vietnamese dishes and hot pot that's good for groups; it may be "noisy and crowded", but it's always "cheap", so you really "can't go wrong."

Taste of Texas *Steak*   25 | 24 | 25 | $50

Memorial | 10505 Katy Frwy. (bet. Attingham Dr. & Town & Country Blvd.) | 713-932-6901 | www.tasteoftexas.com

"Expect a wait" at this long-running Memorial steakhouse thanks to its "Texas-sized" filets from an on-site butcher shop, fully "loaded"

FOOD | DECOR | SERVICE | COST

salad bar and overall family-friendly vibe; a nexus for "special-occasion" celebrants, it gains a lift from "great service" and a rustic, Western setting that's "beautifully decorated" come Christmas, though more than a few take issue with the "high prices."

Tasting Room *American*

22 | 23 | 20 | $31

Galleria | Uptown Park | 1101-18 Uptown Park Blvd. (Loop Frwy.) | 713-993-9800 ●
NEW Memorial | CityCentre | 818 Town & Country Blvd. (Queensbury Ln.) | 281-822-1500
Upper Kirby District | 2409 W. Alabama St. (bet. Greenbriar & Kirby Sts.) | 713-526-2242
www.tastingroomwines.com
This vino bar trio in the Galleria, Memorial and Upper Kirby District dispenses deftly prepared New American "finger food" like truffle pizza, panini and cheese plates and sips at moderate cost; with industrial-contemporary looks, loads of space and outdoor seating, it works for "a glass of wine, or several"; P.S. each branch boasts a retail shop.

Teotihuacan *Tex-Mex*

24 | 14 | 23 | $16

Sharpstown | 6579 W. Bellfort St. (Fondren Rd.) | 713-726-9858
Heights | 1511 Airline Dr. (Patton St.) | 713-426-4420
Neartown | 4624 Irvington Blvd. (Cavalcade St.) | 713-695-8757
www.teotihuacanmexicancafe.com
A "favorite" for Tex-Mex in a city full of contenders, this trio earns raves for its "exceptional" home cooking encompassing "heavenly" enchiladas and equally acclaimed breakfasts; despite their modest addresses, they feature "friendly" service and "small-town atmosphere", while prices constitute a "great value" too.

Thai Bistro *Thai*

∇ 22 | 18 | 24 | $21

West U | 3241 Southwest Frwy. (Buffalo Spdwy.) | 713-669-9375
Royal Oaks | Royal Oaks Plaza | 11660 Westheimer Rd. (Crescent Park Dr.) | 281-496-5559 🗷
www.txthaibistro.com
An "everyday favorite" for Thai, this duo in Royal Oaks and West U doles out "reasonably priced" standards in a "quiet, relaxing atmosphere"; it's a "good bet for lunch" too.

Thai Gourmet 🗷 *Thai*

∇ 27 | 14 | 18 | $23

Galleria | 6324 Richmond Ave. (Hillcroft Ave.) | 713-780-7955 | www.thaigourmethouston.com
"Beware the heat" at this "undiscovered" Thai "gem" near the Galleria where "hot really means hot", and the "delicious, authentic" cooking "does not disappoint"; you'll need to get past patchy service and a "seedy, strip-mall exterior", but diehards still declare it among "the best" in town.

III Forks 🗷 *Steak*

24 | 22 | 23 | $63

Downtown | Houston Pavilions | 1201 San Jacinto St. (Dallas St.) | 713-658-9457 | www.3forks.com
See review in Austin and the Hill Country Directory.

Tiny Boxwoods Ⓜ *Eclectic*

24 | 24 | 21 | $27

Greenway Plaza Area | 3614 W. Alabama St. (Saint St.) |
713-622-4224 | www.thompsonhanson.com

"An oasis in the city", this "lovely", "little" Greenway Plaza cafe
set on the grounds of the Thompson + Hanson nursery lures "la-
dies who lunch" and other well-heeled types for "light" meals of salads, pizzettes and sandwiches among other "well-prepared"
Eclectic items; though dining "alfresco" overlooking the "lush"
greenery is truly "delightful", "crowds", counter service and "parking" issues occasionally detract.

Tony Mandola's *Seafood*

27 | 23 | 25 | $39

River Oaks | 1212 Waugh Dr. (Clay St.) | 713-528-3474 |
www.tonymandolas.com

A "home run" for the Mandola family, this River Oaks seafooder attracts "everyone in Houston" thanks to its "diverse" array of
"fabulous" Gulf Coast–style dishes with Creole touches plus a handful of Italian favorites; it's a "bit fancy" with "professional" service
and an attractive if "corporate" setting, though the consensus is it's
"worth every dime."

Tony's Ⓩ *Continental/Italian*

26 | 26 | 26 | $74

Greenway Plaza Area | 3755 Richmond Ave. (Timmons Ln.) |
713-622-6778 | www.tonyshouston.com

"One of Houston's oldest and most elegant", this Greenway Plaza
"legend" from Tony Vallone provides "true white-tablecloth" dining
via "top-notch" Italian-Continental cuisine and "refined" service in a
"date"-worthy setting adorned with world-class art; on the downside are "astronomical" prices and service that can be "a little
stuffy" "unless they know you"; P.S. jackets suggested.

NEW Torchy's Tacos *Mexican*

24 | 14 | 19 | $11

Lower Shepherd | 2411 S. Shepherd Dr. (Fairview St.) |
713-595-8226 | www.torchystacos.com

See review in Austin and the Hill Country Directory.

NEW TQLA *Southwestern/Tex-Mex*

- | - | - | M

Heights | 4601 Washington Ave. (bet. Fowler & Parker Sts.) |
281-501-3237 | www.tqlahouston.com

On festive Washington Avenue near the Heights, this "noisy" newcomer puts the emphasis on its namesake libation with tequilas on
tap, infused and mixed into an array of cocktails; the Tex-Mex menu
includes burgers and some Southwestern classics using green chiles
served up in sleek, barlike digs.

Treebeards Ⓩ *Cajun/Southern*

25 | 15 | 18 | $15

Downtown | 1100 Louisiana St. (Lamar St.) | 713-752-2601
Downtown | The Cloister | 1117 Texas Ave. (bet. Fannin & San Jacinto Sts.) |
713-229-8248
NEW Downtown | Shops at Houston Ctr. | 1200 McKinney St.
(San Jacinto St.) | 713-400-9595
Downtown | Market Sq. | 315 Travis St. (bet. Congress & Preston Sts.) |
713-228-2622

(continued)

Treebeards

Downtown | Downtown Tunnel | 801 Louisiana St. (Rusk St.) |
713-224-6677
www.treebeards.com

Nine-to-fivers rely on this Downtown chainlet for "hearty", "satisfying" plates of Southern-Cajun cooking (think "awesome red beans and rice" and gumbos) capped with slices of "rich" butter cake; everyone agrees the "value" pricing makes up for the cafeteria-style service and rather "informal" setting; P.S. open for weekday lunch only.

Trevisio ⓩ *Italian*   ▽ 22 | 25 | 24 | $38

Medical Center | Texas Medical Ctr. | 6550 Bertner Ave. (Moursund St.) |
713-749-0400 | www.trevisiorestaurant.com

"Indispensable for professional lunches", this Italian "gem" "In the middle of the Texas Medical Center" provides "good, not to-die-for" cooking in a "lovely", convenient setting with a "nice view" from every table; midrange tabs keep it bustling most days.

NEW Triniti *American*   — | — | — | E

Lower Shepherd | 2815 S. Shepherd Dr. (Kipling St.) |
713-527-9090 | www.trinitirestaurant.com

Boasting plenty of local experience, chef Ryan Hildebrand and his team are behind this expensive New American in Lower Shepherd, which groups its artistically ambitious offerings into three categories: savory, sweet and spirits; modern chandeliers, artwork and other design touches are softened by warm woods for an ultimately inviting atmosphere, which includes an open kitchen with surrounding seats.

Truluck's *Seafood*   24 | 23 | 23 | $52

Galleria | 5350 Westheimer Rd. (bet. Sage Rd. & Yorktown St.) |
713-783-7270 | www.trulucks.com

See review in Dallas/Ft. Worth Directory.

ⓩ**NEW** Uchi *Japanese*   29 | 25 | 27 | $56

Montrose | 904 Westheimer Rd. (Grant St.) | 713-522-4808 |
www.uchirestaurants.com

Coming soon; see review in Austin and the Hill Country Directory.

NEW Underbelly *American*   — | — | — | E

Montrose | 1100 Westheimer Rd. (Yoakum Blvd.) | 713-523-1622 |
www.underbellyhouston.com

Scheduled to open in winter 2012, this much-anticipated first solo effort from Chris Shepherd, who wowed foodies at the now-closed Catalan, promises an ambitious New American menu dedicated to all things porcine; the Montrose storefront is set in the middle of a newly bustling restaurant row and boasts an on-site butcher shop.

NEW Up *American*   17 | 24 | 15 | $54

Galleria | Highland Vill. | 3995 Westheimer Rd. (Drexler Dr.) |
713-640-5416 | www.uprestaurant.com

A "beautiful" contemporary space with tremendous "views of Galleria and Downtown" sets the tone at this relatively recent arrival serving a New American menu with Mediterranean accents; though some customers call it "promising", cynics suggest it's been "over-hyped" with high prices "for mediocre food."

Uptown Sushi *Japanese*   26 | 22 | 22 | $45

Uptown | Uptown Park | 1131-14 Uptown Park Blvd. (Post Oak Blvd.) | 713-871-1200 | www.uptown-sushi.com

"Trendy" Uptown Japanese matching "outstanding" fusion rolls and sushi with creative cocktails; decor could be a little "less *Miami Vice*" and some find prices on the high side, but it's a "hot spot" nonetheless.

Valentino *Italian*   ∇ 23 | 23 | 25 | $46

Galleria | Hotel Derek | 2525 W. Loop S. (Westheimer Rd.) | 713-850-9200 | www.valentinohouston.com

Los Angeles restaurateur Piero Selvaggio is behind this spin-off of his venerable Santa Monica–born Italian in the Galleria-area's sleek Hotel Derek; extravagant multicourse meals are rolled out by a "terrific" staff in a "beautiful", cushy setting done up in dark tones and crimson, while the adjacent less-formal space is home to the Vin Bar spotlighting small plates, wines and some stellar people-watching.

Van Loc *Vietnamese*   ∇ 25 | 8 | 17 | $16

Midtown | 3010 Milam St. (Elgin St.) | 713-528-6441 | www.vanlocrestaurant.com

For nearly a quarter century, this no-frills Midtown Vietnamese has been offering "authentic", flavorful dishes from a lengthy menu for a pittance; "fast but minimal" service and bare-bones digs make it best-suited to takeout.

Vargo's *Continental*   ∇ 16 | 28 | 19 | $36

Memorial | 2401 Fondren Rd. (Westheimer Rd.) | 713-782-3888 | www.vargosonline.com

Surveyors "stroll the gardens" and "watch the peacocks" at this decades-old Continental restaurant in Memorial that's long been a standby for weddings and other occasions; as for the food and service, many find it's "seen better days", and insist it's a touch "overpriced" to boot.

⚡ Vic & Anthony's *Steak*   26 | 26 | 27 | $64

Downtown | 1510 Texas Ave. (La Branch St.) | 713-228-1111 | www.vicandanthonys.com

This "classy" Downtown steakhouse near Minute Maid Park "gets it right" with "amazing" meats and "winning" wines deemed "damn expensive" but "worth" it; "top-notch" service and a dark, "romantic" setting with piano nightly cement its status as a "special-occasion" standby.

Vietnam Restaurant, The Ⓢ⒵ *Vietnamese*   ∇ 29 | 21 | 26 | $20

Heights | 605 W. 19th St. (Lawrence St.) | 832-618-1668 | www.thevietnamrestaurant.com

Regulars report this BYO Vietnamese in the Heights is a "must-try" with "fantastic" fare in "good portions" for "fair prices"; "attentive" service and spare, modern digs increase the neighborhood appeal.

	FOOD	DECOR	SERVICE	COST

Vietopia *Vietnamese* | 21 | 20 | 22 | $21 |

West U | 5176 Buffalo Spdwy. (Westpark Dr.) | 713-664-7303 |
www.vietopiarestaurant.com

The "lovely", soaring interior is one of the best things going for this "reliable" pick for "fresh-tasting" Vietnamese fare in West U; the prices are "decent" too.

Vincent's *Italian* | 25 | 21 | 22 | $33 |

Montrose | 2701 W. Dallas St. (Eberhard St.) | 713-528-4313 |
www.ninos-vincents.com

"Wonderful rotisserie chicken" is the star of this contemporary Montrose Italian (and sib of Nino's and Grappino di Nino) that's a "dependable" bet for "good food at good prices" in an easy atmosphere.

NEW Yucatan Taco Stand *Mexican* | 22 | 16 | 14 | $18 |

The Woodlands | 24 Water Way (Waterway Square Pl.) |
281-419-6300 | www.yucatantacostand1.com

See review in Dallas/Ft. Worth Directory.

Zelko Bistro Ⓜ *American* | 25 | 19 | 21 | $30 |

Heights | 705 E. 11th St. (Studewood St.) | 713-880-8691 |
www.zelkobistro.com

Jamie Zelko is the guiding force at this Heights "comfort-food" eatery offering "incredible", "innovative" New American fare from "fresh, quality ingredients" at wallet-friendly prices; the "lovely" bungalow setting is artfully adorned with leather banquettes, mason jar lighting and a recycled wood-paneled bar, all spot-on for the neighborhood.

Zoë's Kitchen *American* | 19 | 14 | 16 | $14 |

Galleria | 5779 San Felipe St. (Bering Dr.) | 713-787-9637
Heights | Integrity Bank Plaza | 4000 Washington Ave. (Center St.) |
713-861-9637
NEW **Memorial** | 12850 Memorial Dr. (Texas 8 Beltway) |
713-984-8804
Upper Kirby District | 3701 S. Shepherd Dr. (Richmond Ave.) |
713-522-7447
www.zoeskitchen.com

See review in Dallas/Ft. Worth Directory.

HOUSTON
INDEXES

Cuisines

Includes names, locations and Food ratings.

AMERICAN

Artista | **Downtown**	24
NEW Arturo Boada | **Briargrove**	28
Aura | **Missouri City**	29
NEW Ava Kitchen | **River Oaks**	19
Avalon Diner | **multi.**	21
Baba Yega | **Montrose**	21
Barnaby's | **multi.**	23
Backstreet Café | **River Oaks**	26
Barbed Rose | **Alvin**	-
Benjy's | **multi.**	24
NEW Bird & The Bear | **River Oaks**	-
Bistro Lancaster | **Downtown**	24
Branch Water | **Heights**	25
NEW Brasserie 19 | **River Oaks**	23
BRC | **Heights**	20
Breakfast Klub | **Midtown**	25
Buffalo Grille | **multi.**	21
Canopy | **Montrose**	23
NEW Capitol/St. Germain | **Downtown**	-
Cheesecake | **multi.**	20
Christian's | **multi.**	24
Cleburne | **West U**	23
Cullen's | **Clear Lake**	17
Daily Grill | **Galleria**	21
Dessert Gallery | **multi.**	23
NEW Down House | **Heights**	-
Empire Café | **Montrose**	20
NEW Felix 55 | **Rice Vill**	-
59 Diner | **multi.**	18
5115 R&L | **Galleria**	23
Frank's | **Greenway Plaza**	23
Glass Wall | **Heights**	25
Grove | **Downtown**	19
Haven | **Upper Kirby**	25
Hearsay | **Downtown**	-
Houston's/Hillstone | **multi.**	24
Hubcap Grill | **multi.**	27
Hungry's | **multi.**	22
Jasper's | **Woodlands**	24
Jax Grill | **multi.**	21
NEW Jus' Mac | **multi.**	-
Lankford Grocery | **Midtown**	25
NEW Liberty Kitchen | **Heights**	-
NEW Line & Lariat | **Downtown**	-
Z Mark's | **Montrose**	28
Mockingbird Bistro | **River Oaks**	26
Monarch | **Medical Ctr**	21
Olivette | **Uptown**	21
Z NEW Philippe | **Galleria**	24
Z Rainbow Lodge | **Heights**	26
RDG/Bar Annie | **Galleria**	24
NEW Roost | **Lower Shepherd**	-
Ruggles Green | **multi.**	23
Ruggles Grill | **Montrose**	25
Ruggles Cafe | **Rice Vill**	22
*17 | **Downtown**	24
Shade | **Heights**	23
NEW Sorrel Urban | **Lower Shepherd**	16
T'afia | **Midtown**	24
Tasting Rm. | **multi.**	22
NEW Triniti | **Lower Shepherd**	-
NEW Underbelly | **Montrose**	-
NEW Up | **Galleria**	17
Zelko Bistro | **Heights**	25
Zoë's Kitchen | **multi.**	19

ARGENTINEAN

Saldivia's | **SW Houston**	-

ASIAN

Gigi's | **Galleria**	24
Pei Wei | **multi.**	20

BARBECUE

Beaver's | **Heights**	22
County Line | **N Houston**	21
Z Goode Co. TX BBQ | **multi.**	24
Luling City Mkt. | **Galleria**	24
Pappas BBQ | **multi.**	21
Pizzitola's | **Heights**	22
Swinging Door | **Richmond**	27

BELGIAN

Broken Spoke | **Heights**	21
Jeannine's Bistro | **Montrose**	-

BRAZILIAN

Fogo/Chão | **Briargrove**	25

BRITISH

Feast | **Montrose**	24
Red Lion | **Lower Shepherd**	24

BURGERS

Avalon Diner	**multi.**	21
☑ Becks Prime	**multi.**	24
☑ Bellaire Burger	**Bellaire**	24
NEW Bernie's Burger	**Location Varies**	–
Christian's	**multi.**	24
Goode Co. Burgers	**West U**	25
Hubcap Grill	**Downtown**	27
Lankford Grocery	**Midtown**	25
Little Bigs	**Montrose**	17
Pappas Burgers	**multi.**	24

CAJUN

Bayou City	**Galleria**	22
BB's Cafe	**multi.**	24
Danton's	**Montrose**	24
Floyd's Cajun	**multi.**	27
Mardi Gras	**Heights**	25
Pappadeaux	**multi.**	23
Ragin' Cajun	**multi.**	21
Tony Mandola's	**River Oaks**	27
Treebeards	**Downtown**	25

CHINESE

(* dim sum specialist)

Café Chino	**West U**	24
Fung's*	**SW Houston**	25
Ocean Palace*	**Alief**	24
P.F. Chang's	**multi.**	21
Tan Tan	**multi.**	24

COFFEE SHOPS/ DINERS

Avalon Diner	**multi.**	21
Buffalo Grille	**multi.**	21
Dot Coffee	**Hobby**	–
59 Diner	**multi.**	18

CONTINENTAL

Charivari	**Midtown**	24
Masraff's	**Galleria**	25
Rest. CINQ	**Montrose**	27
Tony's	**Greenway Plaza**	26
Vargo's	**Memorial**	16

CREOLE

Bistro Alex	**Memorial**	22
☑ Brennan's	**Midtown**	27

CRÊPES

Melange Creperie	**Location Varies**	–

CUBAN

Cafe Piquet	**Bellaire**	22

DELIS

Katz's	**multi.**	20
Kenny/Ziggy's	**Galleria**	24

DESSERT

Cheesecake	**multi.**	20
Dessert Gallery	**multi.**	23
Empire Café	**Montrose**	20
Little Miss Cupcake	**Galveston**	–

EASTERN EUROPEAN

Café Pita+	**W Houston**	23

ECLECTIC

Black Walnut	**multi.**	22
Block 7	**Heights**	21
Café Express	**multi.**	20
NEW Eatsie Boys	**Montrose**	–
Fusion Taco	**Location Varies**	–
Hobbit Cafe	**Lower Shepherd**	24
Hungry's	**multi.**	22
Max's	**Heights**	20
NEW Modular	**Location Varies**	–
Mosquito Cafe	**Galveston**	25
Oh My Pocket	**Location Varies**	–
NEW Rolling Hunger	**Location Varies**	–
Sambuca	**Downtown**	22
Tiny Boxwoods	**Greenway Plaza**	24

ETHIOPIAN

Blue Nile	**SW Houston**	25

FRENCH

NEW Artisans	**Midtown**	–
Au Petit Paris	**Lower Shepherd**	25
Bistro Le Cep	**W Houston**	25
Bistro Provence	**W Houston**	24
☑ Brass. Max/Julie	**Montrose**	27
NEW Brasserie 19	**River Oaks**	23
Café Rabelais	**Rice Vill**	26
☑ Chez Nous	**Humble**	28
Chez Roux	**Montgomery**	–
NEW Kris Bistro	**N Houston**	–
Le Mistral	**W Houston**	26
☑**NEW** Philippe	**Galleria**	24
Rest. CINQ	**Montrose**	27

GERMAN

Rudi Lechner's	**SW Houston**	24

GREEK

Niko Niko's | **multi.** 25

INDIAN

Ashiana | **W Houston** 25
Bombay/Narin's Brass. | **multi.** 23
Bombay Pizza | **Downtown** 23
Indika | **Montrose** 26
Z Kiran's | **Galleria** 27
Madras Pavilion | **multi.** 20
NEW Pondicheri | **River Oaks** 20
Red Lion | **Lower Shepherd** 24

ITALIAN

(N=Northern; S=Southern)
Antica Osteria | **West U** 24
Arcodoro | S | **Galleria** 22
Arturo's | **Uptown** 22
Brio | **multi.** 22
Carmelo's | S | **W Houston** 24
Z Carrabba's | **multi.** 23
Ciao Bello | **Galleria** 20
Ciro's | **Memorial** 23
Collina's | **multi.** 22
NEW Coppa | **Heights** 25
Crapitto's | **Galleria** 22
Z Da Marco | N | **Montrose** 29
Damian's | **Midtown** 26
D'Amico's | **multi.** 23
Divino | N | **Lower Shepherd** 25
Dolce Vita | **Montrose** 26
Fratelli's | **NW Houston** 19
Giacomo's | **Upper Kirby** 23
Grappino di Nino | **Montrose** 25
Grotto | S | **multi.** 22
La Griglia | **River Oaks** 22
Luigi's | **Galveston** 26
Z Nino's | **Montrose** 27
Paulie's | **Montrose** 24
Perbacco | S | **Downtown** –
Piatto | **multi.** 22
Poscol | N | **Montrose** 26
Prego | **Rice Vill** 24
Pronto Cucinino | **multi.** 21
Quattro | **Downtown** 26
Rist. Cavour | N | **Uptown** 24
Sorrento | **Montrose** 24
Stella Sola | **Heights** 23
Tony's | **Greenway Plaza** 26
Trevisio | **Medical Ctr** 22
Valentino | **Galleria** 23
Vincent's | **Montrose** 25

JAPANESE

(* sushi specialist)
Azuma/Azumi* | **multi.** 23
Kata Robata* | **Upper Kirby** 25
Soma* | **Heights** 25
Z NEW Uchi | **Montrose** 29
Uptown Sushi* | **Uptown** 26

JEWISH

Katz's | **multi.** 20
Kenny/Ziggy's | **Galleria** 24

KOSHER/ KOSHER-STYLE

Madras Pavilion | **multi.** 20

MEDITERRANEAN

Ibiza | **Midtown** 25

MEXICAN

Berryhill Baja | **multi.** 20
Cantina Laredo | **W Houston** 21
NEW El Gran Malo | **Heights** –
Z Hugo's | **Montrose** 26
Irma's | **Downtown** 26
La Mexicana | **Montrose** 18
Maria Selma | **Montrose** –
100% Taquito | **West U** 23
Otilia's | **Spring Branch** –
Pico's | **Bellaire** 24
Spanish Flowers | **Heights** 19
Taco Milagro | **Upper Kirby** 18
Tacos Tierra | **Location Varies** –
Teotihuacan | **multi.** 24
Torchy's Tacos | **Lower Shepherd** 24
Yucatan Taco | **Woodlands** 22

MIDDLE EASTERN

Arpi's Phoenicia | **multi.** 26
Cafe Lili | **Galleria** 24
Dimassi's Med. | **multi.** 19
Fadi's | **multi.** 25

PAN-LATIN

Cafe Red Onion | **multi.** 23
El Meson | **Rice Vill** 24
Rudy & Paco | **Galveston** 26

PIZZA

NEW Alto Pizzeria | **River Oaks** 22
Bombay Pizza | **Downtown** 23
Candelari's Pizzeria | **multi.** 16
Collina's | **multi.** 22

Dolce Vita | **Montrose** <u>26</u>
Grimaldi's | **multi.** <u>26</u>
Star Pizza | **multi.** <u>25</u>

PUB FOOD

BRC | **Heights** <u>20</u>
Red Lion | **Lower Shepherd** <u>24</u>

SEAFOOD

Bayou City | **Galleria** <u>22</u>
Danton's | **Montrose** <u>24</u>
Eddie V's | **multi.** <u>26</u>
Floyd's Cajun | **multi.** <u>27</u>
Fung's | **SW Houston** <u>25</u>
Gaido's | **Galveston** <u>22</u>
Goode Co. TX Seafood | **multi.** <u>26</u>
NEW Liberty Kitchen | **Heights** <u>-</u>
Mardi Gras | **Heights** <u>25</u>
Oceanaire | **Galleria** <u>23</u>
Ocean Palace | **Alief** <u>24</u>
Pappadeaux | **multi.** <u>23</u>
Pappas Seafood | **multi.** <u>24</u>
Pesce | **Upper Kirby** <u>26</u>
Z Reef | **Midtown** <u>25</u>
Tony Mandola's | **River Oaks** <u>27</u>
Truluck's | **Galleria** <u>24</u>

SMALL PLATES

(See also Spanish tapas specialist)
Branch Water | Amer. | **Heights** <u>25</u>
Divino | Italian | **Lower Shepherd** <u>25</u>
Dolce Vita | Italian | **Montrose** <u>26</u>
Feast | British | **Montrose** <u>24</u>
Giacomo's | Italian | <u>23</u>
  Upper Kirby
Grappino di Nino | Italian | <u>25</u>
  Montrose
Haven | Amer. | **Upper Kirby** <u>25</u>
Hearsay | Amer. | **Downtown** <u>-</u>
Ibiza | Med. | **Midtown** <u>25</u>
Kata Robata | Japanese | <u>25</u>
  Upper Kirby
Max's | Eclectic | **Heights** <u>20</u>
Poscol | Italian | **Montrose** <u>26</u>
RDG/Bar Annie | Amer. | <u>24</u>
  Galleria
Sambuca | Eclectic | **Downtown** <u>22</u>
Tasting Rm. | Amer. | <u>22</u>
  Memorial
Valentino | Italian | **Galleria** <u>23</u>

SOUL FOOD

Breakfast Klub | **Midtown** <u>25</u>

SOUTH AFRICAN

Peli Peli | **NW Houston** <u>-</u>

SOUTH AMERICAN

Amazón Grill | **West U** <u>24</u>
Z Américas | **multi.** <u>24</u>
Churrascos | **multi.** <u>25</u>

SOUTHERN

Cleburne | **West U** <u>23</u>
Ouisie's | **River Oaks** <u>24</u>
Treebeards | **Downtown** <u>25</u>

SOUTHWESTERN

RDG/Bar Annie | **Galleria** <u>24</u>
NEW TQLA | **Heights** <u>-</u>

SPANISH

(* tapas specialist)
NEW Convivio* | **Heights** <u>-</u>

STEAKHOUSES

Barbed Rose | **Alvin** <u>-</u>
Z Brenner's | **multi.** <u>27</u>
Capital Grille | **Galleria** <u>26</u>
Churrascos | **multi.** <u>25</u>
Z Del Frisco's | **Galleria** <u>27</u>
Eddie V's | **multi.** <u>26</u>
Fleming's Prime | **multi.** <u>25</u>
Fogo/Chão | **Briargrove** <u>25</u>
Frank's | **Greenway Plaza** <u>23</u>
Killen's | **Pearland** <u>-</u>
Kirby's | **Woodlands** <u>24</u>
Laurenzo's | **Heights** <u>21</u>
Lynn's | **W Houston** <u>25</u>
Morton's | **multi.** <u>26</u>
Mo's | **Galleria** <u>21</u>
Palm | **Galleria** <u>25</u>
Z Pappas Bros. | **Galleria** <u>28</u>
Perry's Steak | **multi.** <u>26</u>
Ruth's Chris | **Galleria** <u>26</u>
Smith/Wollensky | **Galleria** <u>24</u>
Strip Hse. | **Downtown** <u>24</u>
Sullivan's | **Galleria** <u>24</u>
Taste/TX | **Memorial** <u>25</u>
III Forks | **Downtown** <u>24</u>
Z Vic & Antony's | **Downtown** <u>26</u>

TEX-MEX

Armandos | **River Oaks** <u>20</u>
Chuy's | **multi.** <u>21</u>
Cyclone Anaya's | **multi.** <u>21</u>
NEW El Real | **Montrose** <u>19</u>

El Tiempo | **multi.** _23_
Escalante's | **multi.** _21_
Goode Co. Burgers | **West U** _25_
Guadalajara | **multi.** _21_
Lupe Tortilla | **multi.** _22_
Mission Burritos | **multi.** _21_
Ninfa's | **multi.** _24_
Pappasito's | **multi.** _24_
Sylvia's | **multi.** _22_
Teotihuacan | **multi.** _24_
NEW TQLA | **Heights** _-_

THAI

Kanomwan | **Neartown** _26_
Nit Noi | **multi.** _19_
Thai Bistro | **multi.** _22_
Thai Gourmet | **Galleria** _27_

URUGUAYAN

Saldivia's | **SW Houston** _-_

VEGETARIAN

Hobbit Cafe | **Lower Shepherd** _24_
Madras Pavilion | **multi.** _20_
Ruggles Green | **multi.** _23_

VIETNAMESE

Huynh | **Downtown** _26_
Jenni's Noodle | **multi.** _19_
Mai's | **Midtown** _20_
Tan Tan | **multi.** _24_
Van Loc | **Midtown** _25_
Vietnam | **Heights** _29_
Vietopia | **West U** _21_

Locations

Includes names, cuisines and Food ratings.

Houston

ALIEF/SHARPSTOWN

Ocean Palace	*Chinese*	24
Tan Tan	*Chinese/Viet.*	24
Teotihuacan	*Tex-Mex*	24

ALMEDA/HOBBY/ PASADENA

Dot Coffee	*Diner*	-
Ninfa's	*Tex-Mex*	24
Pappadeaux	*Cajun/Seafood*	23
Pappas Burgers	*Burgers*	24
Pappas Seafood	*Seafood*	24

BELLAIRE/ MEDICAL CENTER/ WEST U

Amazón Grill	*S Amer.*	24
Antica Osteria	*Italian*	24
☑ Bellaire Burger	*Burgers*	24
Berryhill Baja	*Mex.*	20
Buffalo Grille	*Amer.*	21
Café Chino	*Chinese*	24
Cafe Piquet	*Cuban*	22
Candelari's Pizzeria	*Pizza*	16
Cleburne	*Amer.*	23
Dimassi's Med.	*Mideast.*	19
Goode Co. Burgers	*Burgers*	25
☑ Goode Co. TX BBQ	*BBQ*	24
Goode Co. TX Seafood	*Seafood*	26
Tax Grill	*Amer.*	21
Monarch	*Amer.*	21
Ninfa's	*Tex-Mex*	24
Nit Noi	*Thai*	19
100% Taquito	*Mex.*	23
Pappadeaux	*Cajun/Seafood*	23
Pappasito's	*Tex-Mex*	24
Pei Wei	*Asian*	20
Pico's	*Mex.*	24
Pronto Cucinino	*Italian*	21
Thai Bistro	*Thai*	22
Trevisio	*Italian*	22
Vietopia	*Viet.*	21

BRIARGROVE

NEW Arturo Boada	*Amer.*	28
Barnaby's	*Amer.*	23

☑ Becks Prime	*Burgers*	24
Buffalo Grille	*Amer.*	21
Café Express	*Eclectic*	20
☑ Carrabba's	*Italian*	23
Cyclone Anaya's	*Tex-Mex*	21
Escalante's	*Tex-Mex*	21
Fadi's	*Mideast.*	25
Fogo/Chão	*Brazilian/Steak*	25
Pappasito's	*Tex-Mex*	24
Sylvia's	*Tex-Mex*	22

CHAMPIONS

Berryhill Baja	*Mex.*	20
Café Express	*Eclectic*	20
☑ Carrabba's	*Italian*	23
Nit Noi	*Thai*	19
Pappadeaux	*Cajun/Seafood*	23
Pei Wei	*Asian*	20
Perry's Steak	*Steak*	26

DOWNTOWN

Artista	*Amer.*	24
Azuma/Azumi	*Japanese*	23
BB's Cafe	*Cajun*	24
☑ Becks Prime	*Burgers*	24
Bistro Lancaster	*Amer.*	24
Bombay Pizza	*Pizza*	23
Café Express	*Eclectic*	20
NEW Capitol/St. Germain	*Amer.*	-
Grove	*Amer.*	19
Guadalajara	*Tex-Mex*	21
Hearsay	*Amer.*	-
Hubcap Grill	*Amer.*	27
Huynh	*Viet.*	26
Irma's	*Mex.*	26
NEW Line & Lariat	*Amer.*	-
Morton's	*Steak*	26
Niko Niko's	*Greek*	25
Ninfa's	*Tex-Mex*	24
Nit Noi	*Thai*	19
Pappas BBQ	*BBQ*	21
Perbacco	*Italian*	-
Arpi's Phoenicia	*Mideast.*	26
Quattro	*Italian*	26
Ragin' Cajun	*Cajun*	21
Sambuca	*Eclectic*	22
*17	*Amer.*	24

Strip Hse.	*Steak*	24
Ill Forks	*Steak*	24
Treebeards	*Cajun/Southern*	25
Z Vic & Antony's	*Steak*	26

FM 1960/KLEIN

Pappasito's	*Tex-Mex*	24

GALLERIA/UPTOWN

Arcodoro	*Italian*	22
Arturo's	*Italian*	22
Bayou City	*Cajun/Seafood*	22
Berryhill Baja	*Mex.*	20
Café Express	*Eclectic*	20
Cafe Lili	*Mideast.*	24
Capital Grille	*Steak*	26
Cheesecake	*Amer.*	20
Ciao Bello	*Italian*	20
Crapitto's	*Italian*	22
Daily Grill	*Amer.*	21
Z Del Frisco's	*Steak*	27
Dessert Gallery	*Amer./Dessert*	23
Dimassi's Med.	*Mideast.*	19
Escalante's	*Tex-Mex*	21
5115 R&L	*Amer.*	23
Gigi's	*Asian*	24
Grotto	*Italian*	22
Houston's/Hillstone	*Amer.*	24
Jenni's Noodle	*Viet.*	19
Kenny/Ziggy's	*Deli*	24
Z Kiran's	*Indian*	27
Luling City Mkt.	*BBQ*	24
Masraff's	*Continental*	25
Morton's	*Steak*	26
Mo's	*Steak*	21
Bombay/Narin's Brass.	*Indian*	23
Ninfa's	*Tex-Mex*	24
Oceanaire	*Seafood*	23
Olivette	*Amer.*	21
Palm	*Steak*	25
Pappadeaux	*Cajun/Seafood*	23
Z Pappas Bros.	*Steak*	28
Pappas Burgers	*Burgers*	24
P.F. Chang's	*Chinese*	21
Z NEW Philippe	*Amer./French*	24
Piatto	*Italian*	22
Ragin' Cajun	*Cajun*	21
RDG/Bar Annie	*Amer./SW*	24
Rist. Cavour	*Italian*	24
Ruth's Chris	*Steak*	26
Smith/Wollensky	*Steak*	24

Sullivan's	*Steak*	24
Tasting Rm.	*Amer.*	22
Thai Gourmet	*Thai*	27
Truluck's	*Seafood*	24
NEW Up	*Amer.*	17
Uptown Sushi	*Japanese*	26
Valentino	*Italian*	23
Zoë's Kitchen	*Amer.*	19

GREENWAY PLAZA AREA

Collina's	*Pizza*	22
El Tiempo	*Tex-Mex*	23
Frank's	*Steak*	23
Tiny Boxwoods	*Eclectic*	24
Tony's	*Continental/Italian*	26

HEIGHTS

BB's Cafe	*Cajun*	24
Beaver's	*BBQ*	22
Z Becks Prime	*Burgers*	24
Benjy's	*Amer.*	24
Berryhill Baja	*Mex.*	20
Block 7	*Eclectic*	21
Branch Water	*Amer.*	25
BRC	*Amer.*	20
Broken Spoke	*Belgian*	21
Candelari's Pizzeria	*Pizza*	16
Christian's	*Burgers*	24
Collina's	*Pizza*	22
NEW Convivio	*Spanish*	-
NEW Coppa	*Italian*	25
Cyclone Anaya's	*Tex-Mex*	21
D'Amico's	*Italian*	23
NEW Down House	*Amer.*	-
NEW El Gran Malo	*Mex.*	-
El Tiempo	*Tex-Mex*	23
Glass Wall	*Amer.*	25
Hubcap Grill	*Amer.*	27
Jax Grill	*Amer.*	21
Jenni's Noodle	*Viet.*	19
NEW Jus' Mac	*Amer.*	-
Laurenzo's	*Steak*	21
NEW Liberty Kitchen	*Amer./Seafood*	-
Lupe Tortilla	*Tex-Mex*	22
Mardi Gras	*Cajun/Seafood*	25
Max's	*Eclectic*	20
Mission Burritos	*Tex-Mex*	21
Pizzitola's	*BBQ*	22
Z Rainbow Lodge	*Amer.*	26
Shade	*Amer.*	23

Soma	*Japanese*	25
Spanish Flowers	*Mex.*	19
Star Pizza	*Pizza*	25
Stella Sola	*Italian*	23
Teotihuacan	*Tex-Mex*	24
NEW TQLA	*SW/Tex-Mex*	-
Vietnam	*Viet.*	29
Zelko Bistro	*Amer.*	25
Zoë's Kitchen	*Amer.*	19

LOWER SHEPHERD

Au Petit Paris	*French*	25
Churrascos	*S Amer.*	25
Divino	*Italian*	25
59 Diner	*Diner*	18
Hobbit Cafe	*Eclectic*	24
Jenni's Noodle	*Viet.*	19
Mission Burritos	*Tex-Mex*	21
Pappas Seafood	*Seafood*	24
Red Lion	*Pub*	24
NEW Roost	*Amer.*	-
NEW Sorrel Urban	*Amer.*	16
Star Pizza	*Pizza*	25
Torchy's Tacos	*Mex.*	24
NEW Triniti	*Amer.*	-

MEMORIAL/
SPRING BRANCH

Avalon Diner	*Amer.*	21
Z Becks Prime	*Burgers*	24
Berryhill Baja	*Mex.*	20
Bistro Alex	*Creole*	22
Z Brenner's	*Steak*	27
Brio	*Italian*	22
Cheesecake	*Amer.*	20
Christian's	*Burgers*	24
Ciro's	*Italian*	23
Collina's	*Pizza*	22
Cyclone Anaya's	*Tex-Mex*	21
Eddie V's	*Seafood/Steak*	26
Escalante's	*Tex-Mex*	21
59 Diner	*Diner*	18
Fleming's Prime	*Steak*	25
Z Goode Co. TX BBQ	*BBQ*	24
Goode Co. TX Seafood	*Seafood*	26
Guadalajara	*Tex-Mex*	21
Nit Noi	*Thai*	19
Otilia's	*Mex.*	-
Pappadeaux	*Cajun/Seafood*	23
Pappasito's	*Tex-Mex*	24
Pei Wei	*Asian*	20
Perry's Steak	*Steak*	26

Pronto Cucinino	*Italian*	21
Ruggles Green	*Amer.*	23
Taste/TX	*Steak*	25
Tasting Rm.	*Amer.*	22
Vargo's	*Continental*	16
Zoë's Kitchen	*Amer.*	19

MEYERLAND/
WESTBURY

Café Express	*Eclectic*	20
Escalante's	*Tex-Mex*	21
Fadi's	*Mideast.*	25

MIDTOWN

NEW Artisans	*French*	-
Breakfast Klub	*Soul*	25
Z Brennan's	*Creole*	27
Charivari	*Continental*	24
Christian's	*Burgers*	24
Cyclone Anaya's	*Tex-Mex*	21
Damian's	*Italian*	26
Ibiza	*Med.*	25
Lankford Grocery	*Burgers*	25
Mai's	*Viet.*	20
Z Reef	*Seafood*	25
T'afia	*Amer.*	24
Van Loc	*Viet.*	25

MONTROSE

Baba Yega	*Amer.*	21
Barnaby's	*Amer.*	23
BB's Cafe	*Cajun*	24
Berryhill Baja	*Mex.*	20
Z Brass. Max/Julie	*French*	27
Café Express	*Eclectic*	20
Canopy	*Amer.*	23
Z Da Marco	*Italian*	29
Danton's	*Cajun/Seafood*	24
Dolce Vita	*Italian*	26
NEW Eatsie Boys	*Eclectic*	-
NEW El Real	*Tex-Mex*	19
El Tiempo	*Tex-Mex*	23
Empire Café	*Amer.*	20
Feast	*British*	24
Grappino di Nino	*Italian*	25
Z Hugo's	*Mex.*	26
Indika	*Indian*	26
Jeannine's Bistro	*Belgian*	-
Katz's	*Deli*	20
La Mexicana	*Mex.*	18
Little Bigs	*Burgers*	17
Maria Selma	*Mex.*	-

Restaurant	Cuisine	Rating
Z Mark's	*Amer.*	28
Niko Niko's	*Greek*	25
Z Nino's	*Italian*	27
Paulie's	*Italian*	24
Pei Wei	*Asian*	20
Poscol	*Italian*	26
Pronto Cucinino	*Italian*	21
Rest. CINQ	*Continental/French*	27
Ruggles Grill	*Amer.*	25
Sorrento	*Italian*	24
Z NEW Uchi	*Japanese*	29
NEW Underbelly	*Amer.*	-
Vincent's	*Italian*	25

NEARTOWN

Restaurant	Cuisine	Rating
Kanomwan	*Thai*	26
Ninfa's	*Tex-Mex*	24
Teotihuacan	*Tex-Mex*	24

NORTH HOUSTON

Restaurant	Cuisine	Rating
County Line	*BBQ*	21
NEW Kris Bistro	*French*	-
Lupe Tortilla	*Tex-Mex*	22
Pappasito's	*Tex-Mex*	24
Pappas Seafood	*Seafood*	24

NORTHWEST HOUSTON

Restaurant	Cuisine	Rating
Cafe Red Onion	*Pan-Latin*	23
Z Carrabba's	*Italian*	23
Chuy's	*Tex-Mex*	21
59 Diner	*Diner*	18
Fratelli's	*Italian*	19
Z Goode Co. TX BBQ	*BBQ*	24
Lupe Tortilla	*Tex-Mex*	22
Pappadeaux	*Cajun/Seafood*	23
Pappas BBQ	*BBQ*	21
Pappasito's	*Tex-Mex*	24
Pei Wei	*Asian*	20
Peli Peli	*S African*	-
P.F. Chang's	*Chinese*	21

RICE VILLAGE

Restaurant	Cuisine	Rating
Azuma/Azumi	*Japanese*	23
Benjy's	*Amer.*	24
Black Walnut	*Eclectic*	22
Bombay/Narin's Brass.	*Indian*	23
Café Rabelais	*French*	26
D'Amico's	*Italian*	23
El Meson	*Pan-Latin*	24
NEW Felix 55	*Amer.*	-
Hungry's	*Eclectic*	22

Restaurant	Cuisine	Rating
Prego	*Italian*	24
Ruggles Cafe	*Amer.*	22

RIVER OAKS

Restaurant	Cuisine	Rating
NEW Alto Pizzeria	*Pizza*	22
Z Américas	*S Amer.*	24
Armandos	*Tex-Mex*	20
NEW Ava Kitchen	*Amer.*	19
Avalon Diner	*Amer.*	21
Backstreet Café	*Amer.*	26
Barnaby's	*Amer.*	23
Berryhill Baja	*Mex.*	20
NEW Bird & The Bear	*Amer.*	-
NEW Brasserie 19 | *Amer./French*		23
Z Brenner's	*Steak*	27
Café Express	*Eclectic*	20
Chuy's	*Tex-Mex*	21
Fleming's Prime	*Steak*	25
La Griglia	*Italian*	22
Mockingbird Bistro	*Amer.*	26
Ouisie's	*Southern*	24
NEW Pondicheri	*Indian*	20
Tony Mandola's	*Seafood*	27

ROYAL OAKS

Restaurant	Cuisine	Rating
Arpi's Phoenicia	*Mideast.*	26
Piatto	*Italian*	22
Thai Bistro	*Thai*	22

SOUTHWEST HOUSTON

Restaurant	Cuisine	Rating
Blue Nile	*Ethiopian*	25
Churrascos	*S Amer.*	25
Chuy's	*Tex-Mex*	21
Fung's	*Chinese/Seafood*	25
Pappas BBQ	*BBQ*	21
Ragin' Cajun	*Cajun*	21
Rudi Lechner's	*German*	24
Saldivia's	*Argent.*	-
Tan Tan	*Chinese/Viet.*	24

UPPER KIRBY DISTRICT

Restaurant	Cuisine	Rating
Z Becks Prime	*Burgers*	24
Café Express	*Eclectic*	20
Cafe Red Onion	*Pan-Latin*	23
Z Carrabba's	*Italian*	23
Dessert Gallery	*Amer./Dessert*	23
Eddie V's	*Seafood/Steak*	26
Giacomo's	*Italian*	23
Guadalajara	*Tex-Mex*	21

Haven | *Amer.* 25
Houston's/Hillstone | *Amer.* 24
Kata Robata | *Japanese* 25
Lupe Tortilla | *Tex-Mex* 22
Madras Pavilion | *Indian* 20
Ninfa's | *Tex-Mex* 24
Pappadeaux | *Cajun/Seafood* 23
Pappasito's | *Tex-Mex* 24
Pesce | *Seafood* 26
Ruggles Green | *Amer.* 23
Taco Milagro | *Mex.* 18
Tasting Rm. | *Amer.* 22
Zoë's Kitchen | *Amer.* 19

WEST HOUSTON

Ashiana | *Indian* 25
🅉 Becks Prime | *Burgers* 24
Bistro Le Cep | *French* 25
Bistro Provence | *French* 24
Café Pita+ | *E Euro.* 23
Candelari's Pizzeria | *Pizza* 16
Cantina Laredo | *Mex.* 21
Carmelo's | *Italian* 24
🅉 Carrabba's | *Italian* 23
Dimassi's Med. | *Mideast.* 19
Fadi's | *Mideast.* 25
Hungry's | *Eclectic* 22
Le Mistral | *French* 26
Lupe Tortilla | *Tex-Mex* 22
Lynn's | *Steak* 25
Mission Burritos | *Tex-Mex* 21
Ninfa's | *Tex-Mex* 24
Nit Noi | *Thai* 19
Pappadeaux | *Cajun/Seafood* 23
Pei Wei | *Asian* 20
P.F. Chang's | *Chinese* 21
Sylvia's | *Tex-Mex* 22

Bay Area

CLEAR LAKE/ LEAGUE CITY/ WEBSTER

Café Express | *Eclectic* 20
🅉 Carrabba's | *Italian* 23
Chuy's | *Tex-Mex* 21
Cullen's | *Amer.* 17
Floyd's Cajun | *Cajun/Seafood* 27
Lupe Tortilla | *Tex-Mex* 22
Pappas BBQ | *BBQ* 21
Pappasito's | *Tex-Mex* 24
Pappas Seafood | *Seafood* 24

Pei Wei | *Asian* 20
Perry's Steak | *Steak* 26

Outlying Areas

ALVIN

Barbed Rose | *Amer.* -

ATASCOCITA/ HUMBLE/KINGWOOD

🅉 Carrabba's | *Italian* 23
🅉 Chez Nous | *French* 28
Chuy's | *Tex-Mex* 21
Mission Burritos | *Tex-Mex* 21
Pappas BBQ | *BBQ* 21
Pappasito's | *Tex-Mex* 24
Pappas Seafood | *Seafood* 24
Pei Wei | *Asian* 20

CYPRESS

Candelari's Pizzeria | *Pizza* 16

GALENA PARK

Pappas Seafood | *Seafood* 24

GALVESTON

Gaido's | *Seafood* 22
Little Miss Cupcake | *Dessert* -
Luigi's | *Italian* 26
Mosquito Cafe | *Eclectic* 25
Rudy & Paco | *Pan-Latin* 26

KATY/BROOKSHIRE

Black Walnut | *Eclectic* 22
Candelari's Pizzeria | *Pizza* 16
Chuy's | *Tex-Mex* 21
59 Diner | *Diner* 18
Lupe Tortilla | *Tex-Mex* 22
Mission Burritos | *Tex-Mex* 21
Pei Wei | *Asian* 20
Perry's Steak | *Steak* 26

MISSOURI CITY/ RICHMOND/ STAFFORD/ SUGAR LAND

Aura | *Amer.* 29
Avalon Diner | *Amer.* 21
Azuma/Azumi | *Japanese* 23
🅉 Becks Prime | *Burgers* 24
Berryhill Baja | *Mex.* 20
Black Walnut | *Eclectic* 22
Café Express | *Eclectic* 20

Ƶ Carrabba's | *Italian*	23
Cheesecake | *Amer.*	20
Churrascos | *S Amer.*	25
Dimassi's Med. | *Mideast.*	19
Escalante's | *Tex-Mex*	21
59 Diner | *Diner*	18
Grimaldi's | *Pizza*	26
NEW Jus' Mac | *Amer.*	-
Lupe Tortilla | *Tex-Mex*	22
Madras Pavilion | *Indian*	20
Mission Burritos | *Tex-Mex*	21
Ninfa's | *Tex-Mex*	24
Pappadeaux | *Cajun/Seafood*	23
Pappasito's | *Tex-Mex*	24
Pei Wei | *Asian*	20
Perry's Steak | *Steak*	26
P.F. Chang's | *Chinese*	21
Ragin' Cajun | *Cajun*	21
Swinging Door | *BBQ*	27

MONTGOMERY

Chez Roux | *French*	-

PEARLAND

Floyd's Cajun | *Cajun/Seafood*	27
Killen's | *Steak*	-
Lupe Tortilla | *Tex-Mex*	22

SHENANDOAH

Chuy's | *Tex-Mex*	21

SPRING/ WASHINGTON/ THE WOODLANDS

Ƶ Américas | *S Amer.*	24
Ƶ Becks Prime | *Burgers*	24
Berryhill Baja | *Mex.*	20
Black Walnut | *Eclectic*	22
Brio | *Italian*	22
Ƶ Carrabba's | *Italian*	23
Cheesecake | *Amer.*	20
Dimassi's Med. | *Mideast.*	19
Fleming's Prime | *Steak*	25
Grimaldi's | *Pizza*	26
Grotto | *Italian*	22
Guadalajara | *Tex-Mex*	21
Jasper's | *Amer.*	24
Katz's | *Deli*	20
Kirby's | *Steak*	24
Lupe Tortilla | *Tex-Mex*	22
Nit Noi | *Thai*	19
Pappadeaux | *Cajun/Seafood*	23
Pappas BBQ | *BBQ*	21
Perry's Steak | *Steak*	26
P.F. Chang's | *Chinese*	21
Yucatan Taco | *Mex.*	22

Special Features

Listings cover the best in each category and include names, locations and Food ratings. Multi-location restaurants' features may vary by branch.

BREAKFAST

(See also Hotel Dining)

Avalon Diner	**multi.**	21
Barnaby's	**multi.**	23
☑ Becks Prime	**Memorial**	24
Berryhill Baja	**multi.**	20
Black Walnut	**multi.**	22
Breakfast Klub	**Midtown**	25
Buffalo Grille	**multi.**	21
Cheesecake	**Galleria**	20
El Tiempo	**multi.**	23
Empire Café	**Montrose**	20
59 Diner	**multi.**	18
Goode Co. Burgers	**West U**	25
Irma's	**Downtown**	26
Katz's	**multi.**	20
Kenny/Ziggy's	**Galleria**	24
La Mexicana	**Montrose**	18
Lankford Grocery	**Midtown**	25
Pico's	**Bellaire**	24
Tiny Boxwoods	**Greenway Plaza**	24

BRUNCH

Arcodoro	**Galleria**	22
Ashiana	**W Houston**	25
Baba Yega	**Montrose**	21
Backstreet Café	**River Oaks**	26
Beaver's	**Heights**	22
Benjy's	**Rice Vill**	24
🆕 Bird & The Bear	**River Oaks**	-
Bistro Alex	**Memorial**	22
Bistro Lancaster	**Downtown**	24
🆕 Brasserie 19	**River Oaks**	23
BRC	**Heights**	20
☑ Brennan's	**Midtown**	27
☑ Brenner's	**multi.**	27
Canopy	**Montrose**	23
Cheesecake	**Galleria**	20
Ciao Bello	**Galleria**	20
Danton's	**Montrose**	24
🆕 El Real	**Montrose**	19
El Tiempo	**multi.**	23
Gigi's	**Galleria**	24
Grove	**Downtown**	19

Guadalajara	**multi.**	21
Haven	**Upper Kirby**	25
Hearsay	**Downtown**	-
Hobbit Cafe	**Lower Shepherd**	24
☑ Hugo's	**Montrose**	26
Hungry's	**multi.**	22
Indika	**Montrose**	26
Le Mistral	**W Houston**	26
Masraff's	**Galleria**	25
Max's	**Heights**	20
Mockingbird Bistro	**River Oaks**	26
Monarch	**Medical Ctr**	21
Ninfa's	**multi.**	24
Ouisie's	**River Oaks**	24
Prego	**Rice Vill**	24
Quattro	**Downtown**	26
☑ Rainbow Lodge	**Heights**	26
RDG/Bar Annie	**Galleria**	24
Ruggles Grill	**Montrose**	25
Shade	**Heights**	23
🆕 Sorrel Urban	**Lower Shepherd**	16
Sorrento	**Montrose**	24
Stella Sola	**Heights**	23
Tiny Boxwoods	**Greenway Plaza**	24
Vargo's	**Memorial**	16
Zelko Bistro	**Heights**	25

BUSINESS DINING

☑ Américas	**River Oaks**	24
Artista	**Downtown**	24
🆕 Arturo Boada	**Briargrove**	28
🆕 Ava Kitchen	**River Oaks**	19
🆕 Bird & The Bear	**River Oaks**	-
Bistro Alex	**Memorial**	22
🆕 Brasserie 19	**River Oaks**	23
☑ Brennan's	**Midtown**	27
☑ Brenner's	**multi.**	27
Canopy	**Montrose**	23
Capital Grille	**Galleria**	26
Carmelo's	**W Houston**	24
Chez Roux	**Montgomery**	-
Churrascos	**multi.**	25

Ø Da Marco | **Montrose**	29
Damian's | **Midtown**	26
Ø Del Frisco's | **Galleria**	27
Eddie V's | **Upper Kirby**	26
NEW Felix 55 | **Rice Vill**	–
5115 R&L | **Galleria**	23
Fleming's Prime | **River Oaks**	25
Frank's | **Greenway Plaza**	23
Grove | **Downtown**	19
Haven | **Upper Kirby**	25
Ø Hugo's | **Montrose**	26
Ibiza | **Midtown**	25
Jasper's | **Woodlands**	24
Kirby's | **Woodlands**	24
NEW Line & Lariat | **Downtown**	–
Lynn's | **W Houston**	25
Ø Mark's | **Montrose**	28
Masraff's | **Galleria**	25
Mockingbird Bistro | **River Oaks**	26
Monarch | **Medical Ctr**	21
Morton's | **multi.**	26
Mo's | **Galleria**	21
Ø Nino's | **Montrose**	27
Oceanaire | **Galleria**	23
Olivette | **Uptown**	21
Palm | **Galleria**	25
Ø Pappas Bros. | **Galleria**	28
Perbacco | **Downtown**	–
Perry's Steak | **multi.**	26
Ø NEW Philippe | **Galleria**	24
Quattro | **Downtown**	26
RDG/Bar Annie | **Galleria**	24
Ø Reef | **Midtown**	25
Rest. CINQ | **Montrose**	27
Rist. Cavour | **Uptown**	24
Ruth's Chris | **Galleria**	26
*17 | **Downtown**	24
Smith/Wollensky | **Galleria**	24
Stella Sola | **Heights**	23
Strip Hse. | **Downtown**	24
Sullivan's | **Galleria**	24
III Forks | **Downtown**	24
Tony Mandola's | **River Oaks**	27
Tony's | **Greenway Plaza**	26
Trevisio | **Medical Ctr**	22
Truluck's | **Galleria**	24
NEW Up | **Galleria**	17
Valentino | **Galleria**	23
Ø Vic & Antony's | **Downtown**	26

CELEBRITY CHEFS

Arturo Boada	
NEW Arturo Boada | **Briargrove**	28
Bryan Caswell	
NEW El Real | **Montrose**	19
Little Bigs | **Montrose**	17
Ø Reef | **Midtown**	25
Stella Sola | **Heights**	23
Charles Clark	
Ibiza | **Midtown**	25
Tyson Cole	
Ø NEW Uchi | **Montrose**	29
Michael Cordua	
Ø Américas | **River Oaks**	24
Mark Cox	
Ø Mark's | **Montrose**	28
David Denis	
Le Mistral | **W Houston**	26
Randy Evans	
Haven | **Upper Kirby**	25
Lance Fegen	
NEW Liberty Kitchen | **Heights**	–
Irma Galvan	
Irma's | **Downtown**	26
Robert Del Grande	
NEW Alto Pizzeria | **River Oaks**	22
NEW Ava Kitchen | **River Oaks**	19
Grove | **Downtown**	19
RDG/Bar Annie | **Galleria**	24
Lynette Hawkins	
Giacomo's | **Upper Kirby**	23
Ryan Hildebrand	
NEW Triniti | **Lower Shepherd**	–
Mark Holley	
Pesce | **Upper Kirby**	26
Ronnie Killen	
Killen's | **Pearland**	–
Monica Pope	
Beaver's | **Heights**	22
T'afia | **Midtown**	24
Kent Rathbun	
Jasper's | **Woodlands**	24
Albert Roux	
Chez Roux | **Montgomery**	–
Philippe Schmit	
Ø NEW Philippe | **Galleria**	24
John Sheely	
Mockingbird Bistro | **River Oaks**	26

Chris Shepherd
  NEW Underbelly | **Montrose** -

Claire Smith
  Canopy | **Montrose** 23
  Shade | **Heights** 23

Marco Wiles
  Z Da Marco | **Montrose** 29

Jamie Zelko
  Zelko Bistro | **Heights** 25

CHILD-FRIENDLY

(Alternatives to the usual fast-food places; * children's menu available)

Amazón Grill* | **West U**	24
Avalon Diner* | **Stafford**	21
Baba Yega | **Montrose**	21
Barnaby's | **multi.**	23
Z Becks Prime* | **multi.**	24
NEW Bernie's Burger | **Location Varies**	-
Berryhill Baja* | **River Oaks**	20
Black Walnut* | **multi.**	22
Breakfast Klub | **Midtown**	25
Buffalo Grille* | **multi.**	21
Café Express* | **multi.**	20
Cafe Red Onion* | **multi.**	23
Candelari's Pizzeria* | **multi.**	16
Z Carrabba's* | **multi.**	23
Cheesecake* | **Galleria**	20
Chuy's* | **multi.**	21
Ciro's* | **Memorial**	23
Cleburne* | **West U**	23
Collina's | **multi.**	22
D'Amico's | **Rice Vill**	23
Dessert Gallery* | **multi.**	23
El Meson | **Rice Vill**	24
59 Diner* | **multi.**	18
Gaido's* | **Galveston**	22
Goode Co. Burgers* | **West U**	25
Z Goode Co. TX BBQ | **West U**	24
Hobbit Cafe* | **Lower Shepherd**	24
Hungry's* | **multi.**	22
NEW Jus' Mac | **multi.**	-
La Mexicana* | **Montrose**	18
Lupe Tortilla* | **multi.**	22
Niko Niko's* | **multi.**	25
Ninfa's* | **multi.**	24
Nit Noi* | **multi.**	19
Ocean Palace | **Alief**	24
100% Taquito | **West U**	23
Otilia's* | **Spring Branch**	-
Pappasito's* | **Upper Kirby**	24

Pappas Seafood* | **multi.**	24
Paulie's | **Montrose**	24
Pei Wei* | **multi.**	20
P.F. Chang's* | **multi.**	21
Pico's* | **Bellaire**	24
Ragin' Cajun* | **multi.**	21
Rudi Lechner's* | **SW Houston**	24
Star Pizza* | **multi.**	25
Swinging Door | **Richmond**	27
Sylvia's* | **multi.**	22
Taco Milagro* | **Upper Kirby**	18
Taste/TX* | **Memorial**	25
Teotihuacan* | **multi.**	24
Zoë's Kitchen* | **multi.**	19

DESSERT SPECIALISTS

Benjy's | **Rice Vill**	24
Z Brennan's | **Midtown**	27
Cheesecake | **multi.**	20
Chez Roux | **Montgomery**	-
Churrascos | **multi.**	25
Z Da Marco | **Montrose**	29
Dessert Gallery | **multi.**	23
Empire Café | **Montrose**	20
Z Mark's | **Montrose**	28
Z NEW Philippe | **Galleria**	24
Quattro | **Downtown**	26
Ruggles Grill | **Montrose**	25
Ruggles Cafe | **Rice Vill**	22
Tony's | **Greenway Plaza**	26

DINING ALONE

(Other than hotels and places with counter service)

Avalon Diner | **multi.**	21
Barnaby's | **multi.**	23
Z Becks Prime | **Heights**	24
Z Bellaire Burger | **Bellaire**	24
Black Walnut | **Sugar Land**	22
Café Rabelais | **Rice Vill**	26
Christian's | **multi.**	24
Churrascos | **multi.**	25
Dimassi's Med. | **multi.**	19
Dot Coffee | **Hobby**	-
El Meson | **Rice Vill**	24
59 Diner | **multi.**	18
Giacomo's | **Upper Kirby**	23
Goode Co. Burgers | **West U**	25
Z Goode Co. TX BBQ | **multi.**	24
Goode Co. TX Seafood | **multi.**	26
Hearsay | **Downtown**	-

Hobbit Cafe	**Lower Shepherd**	24
🅴 Hugo's	**Montrose**	26
Hungry's	**multi.**	22
Indika	**Montrose**	26
Kata Robata	**Upper Kirby**	25
Katz's	**multi.**	20
Kenny/Ziggy's	**Galleria**	24
Mission Burritos	**multi.**	21
Mockingbird Bistro	**River Oaks**	26
Otilia's	**Spring Branch**	-
Pappas BBQ	**multi.**	21
Pappas Burgers	**Hobby**	24
Pei Wei	**multi.**	20
Perbacco	**Downtown**	-
Poscol	**Montrose**	26
Pronto Cucinino	**multi.**	21
RDG/Bar Annie	**Galleria**	24
🅴 Reef	**Midtown**	25
Tony Mandola's	**River Oaks**	27
Vietopia	**West U**	21

ENTERTAINMENT

(Call for days and times of performances)

Artista	live music	**Downtown**	24
Backstreet Café	jazz	**River Oaks**	26
Breakfast Klub	live music	**Midtown**	25
🅴 Brennan's	jazz	**Midtown**	27
Carmelo's	accordion	**W Houston**	24
Churrascos	live music	**multi.**	25
Cullen's	varies	**Clear Lake**	17
🆕 El Real	varies	**Montrose**	19
5115 R&L	varies	**Galleria**	23
Grappino di Nino	jazz	**Montrose**	25
🅴 Hugo's	Mexican folk	**Montrose**	26
Jax Grill	zydeco	**Heights**	21
Masraff's	guitar	**Galleria**	25
Ouisie's	jazz	**River Oaks**	24
🅴 Pappas Bros.	piano	**Galleria**	28
Pico's	harp/guitar	**Bellaire**	24
Rudi Lechner's	polka	**SW Houston**	24
Ruggles Grill	jazz	**Montrose**	25
Sambuca	live music	**Downtown**	22
Sullivan's	jazz/live bands	**Galleria**	24

Taco Milagro	DJs/live bands	**Upper Kirby**	18
Tony's	piano	**Greenway Plaza**	26
Trevisio	jazz	**Medical Ctr**	22
🅴 Vic & Antony's	piano	**Downtown**	26

FOOD TRUCKS

🆕 Bernie's Burger	**Location Varies**	-
🆕 Eatsie Boys	**Montrose**	-
Fusion Taco	**Location Varies**	-
Little Miss Cupcake	**Galveston**	-
Melange Creperie	**Location Varies**	-
🆕 Modular	**Location Varies**	-
Oh My Pocket	**Location Varies**	-
🆕 Rolling Hunger	**Location Varies**	-
Tacos Tierra	**Location Varies**	-

HISTORIC PLACES

(Year opened; * building)

1870	Treebeards*	**Downtown**	25
1889	Hearsay*	**Downtown**	-
1895	Luigi's*	**Galveston**	26
1900	T'afia*	**Midtown**	24
1906	Rainbow Lodge*	**Heights**	26
1911	Gaido's	**Galveston**	22
1912	Capitol/St. Germain*	**Downtown**	
1915	Crapitto's*	**Galleria**	22
1924	*17*	**Downtown**	24
1926	Bistro Lancaster*	**Downtown**	24
1930	Shade*	**Heights**	23
1935	Pizzitola's	**Heights**	22
1936	Brenner's	**Memorial**	27
1937	Christian's	**multi.**	24
1938	Avalon Diner	**River Oaks**	21
1939	Lankford Grocery	**Midtown**	25
1948	Roost*	**Lower Shepherd**	-
1957	Bellaire Burger	**Bellaire**	24
1960	Beaver's*	**Heights**	22
1960	Benjy's*	**Rice Vill**	24

HOTEL DINING

Alden Houston Hotel		
*17	**Downtown**	24
Four Seasons Hotel		
Quattro	**Downtown**	26

LATE DINING

MEET FOR A DRINK

NEWCOMERS

Bird & The Bear | **River Oaks**	–
Brasserie 19 | **River Oaks**	23
Capitol/St. Germain | **Downtown**	–
Convivio | **Heights**	–
Coppa | **Heights**	25
Down House | **Heights**	–
Eatsie Boys | **Montrose**	–
El Gran Malo | **Heights**	–
El Real | **Montrose**	19
Felix 55 | **Rice Vill**	–
Jus' Mac | **multi.**	–
Kris Bistro | **N Houston**	–
Liberty Kitchen | **Heights**	–
Line & Lariat | **Downtown**	–
Modular | **Location Varies**	–
🆕 Philippe | **Galleria**	24
Pondicheri | **River Oaks**	20
Rolling Hunger | **Location Varies**	–
Roost | **Lower Shepherd**	–
Sorrel Urban | **Lower Shepherd**	16
TQLA | **Heights**	–
Triniti | **Lower Shepherd**	–
🆕 Uchi | **Montrose**	29
Underbelly | **Montrose**	–
Up | **Galleria**	17

OFFBEAT

Beaver's | **Heights**	22
Breakfast Klub | **Midtown**	25
Broken Spoke | **Heights**	21
Café Pita+ | **W Houston**	23
Chuy's | **multi.**	21
🆕 Eatsie Boys | **Montrose**	–
Feast | **Montrose**	24
Goode Co. TX Seafood | **West U**	26
Hearsay | **Downtown**	–
Hobbit Cafe | **Lower Shepherd**	24
Irma's | **Downtown**	26
Jenni's Noodle | **multi.**	19
🆕 Jus' Mac | **Heights**	–
Lankford Grocery | **Midtown**	25
🆕 Modular | **Location Varies**	–
Niko Niko's | **Montrose**	25
100% Taquito | **West U**	23
🆕 Pondicheri | **River Oaks**	20
Ragin' Cajun | **Galleria**	21
Star Pizza | **Lower Shepherd**	25
Swinging Door | **Richmond**	27
🆕 Up | **Galleria**	17

OUTDOOR DINING

(G=garden; P=patio; S=sidewalk; T=terrace; W=waterside)

Amazón Grill | P | **West U**	24
Arcodoro | P | **Galleria**	22
Artista | T | **Downtown**	24
Ashiana | P | **W Houston**	25
Baba Yega | P | **Montrose**	21
Barnaby's | P | **multi.**	23
Backstreet Café | G, P | **River Oaks**	26
Beaver's | P | **Heights**	22
🆕 Becks Prime | P | **multi.**	24
Berryhill Baja | P | **multi.**	20
Black Walnut | P | **multi.**	22
🆕 Brennan's | P | **Midtown**	27
Café Express | P | **multi.**	20
Chuy's | P | **River Oaks**	21
Crapitto's | P | **Galleria**	22
D'Amico's | P | **Rice Vill**	23
Dolce Vita | P | **Montrose**	26
El Tiempo | P | **multi.**	23
Empire Café | P | **Montrose**	20
Goode Co. Burgers | P | **West U**	25
🆕 Goode Co. TX BBQ | P | **West U**	24
Grappino di Nino | P | **Montrose**	25
Grotto | P | **Woodlands**	22
Grove | P | **Downtown**	19
Hobbit Cafe | P | **Lower Shepherd**	24
🆕 Hugo's | P | **Montrose**	26
Ibiza | P | **Midtown**	25
Indika | P | **Montrose**	26
Jasper's | P | **Woodlands**	24
La Griglia | P | **River Oaks**	22
La Mexicana | P | **Montrose**	18
Lankford Grocery | P | **Midtown**	25
Le Mistral | P | **W Houston**	26
Masraff's | P | **Galleria**	25
Niko Niko's | P | **Montrose**	25
Ninfa's | P | **Neartown**	24
🆕 Nino's | P | **Montrose**	27
Otilia's | P | **Spring Branch**	–
Ouisie's | G, P | **River Oaks**	24
P.F. Chang's | P | **multi.**	21
Pico's | P | **Bellaire**	24
🆕 Rainbow Lodge | G, P, T, W | **Heights**	26
RDG/Bar Annie | P | **Galleria**	24
Red Lion | P | **Lower Shepherd**	24
Sambuca | P | **Downtown**	22
Star Pizza | P | **multi.**	25

Vote at zagat.com

Sylvia's | P | **multi.**	22
Taco Milagro | P | **Upper Kirby**	18
T'afia | P | **Midtown**	24
Tony Mandola's | P | **River Oaks**	27
Treebeards | P | **Downtown**	25
Trevisio | P | **Medical Ctr**	22
Vincent's | P | **Montrose**	25

PEOPLE-WATCHING

🆕 Alto Pizzeria | **River Oaks**	22
Amazón Grill | **West U**	24
Armandos | **River Oaks**	20
Artista | **Downtown**	24
🆕 Ava Kitchen | **River Oaks**	19
Avalon Diner | **River Oaks**	21
Baba Yega | **Montrose**	21
Benjy's | **multi.**	24
Berryhill Baja | **Montrose**	20
Block 7 | **Heights**	21
Branch Water | **Heights**	25
🆕 Brasserie 19 | **River Oaks**	23
Chuy's | **River Oaks**	21
Ciao Bello | **Galleria**	20
🆕 Coppa | **Heights**	25
❷ Del Frisco's | **Galleria**	27
Dolce Vita | **Montrose**	26
Eddie V's | **Upper Kirby**	26
El Tiempo | **multi.**	23
Empire Café | **Montrose**	20
Escalante's | **Galleria**	21
5115 R&L | **Galleria**	23
Grotto | **Galleria**	22
Ibiza | **Midtown**	25
Irma's | **Downtown**	26
La Griglia | **River Oaks**	22
❷ Mark's | **Montrose**	28
Max's | **Heights**	20
Mo's | **Galleria**	21
Palm | **Galleria**	25
Pesce | **Upper Kirby**	26
P.F. Chang's | **Galleria**	21
❷🆕 Philippe | **Galleria**	24
RDG/Bar Annie | **Galleria**	24
❷ Reef | **Midtown**	25
Sambuca | **Downtown**	22
*17 | **Downtown**	24
Smith/Wollensky | **Galleria**	24
Sorrento | **Montrose**	24
Stella Sola | **Heights**	23
Sullivan's | **Galleria**	24
Taco Milagro | **Upper Kirby**	18

Tasting Rm. | **Galleria**	22
Tony's | **Greenway Plaza**	26
🆕 TQLA | **Heights**	-
🆕 Up | **Galleria**	17
Uptown Sushi | **Uptown**	26
Valentino | **Galleria**	23
❷ Vic & Antony's | **Downtown**	26

POWER SCENES

❷ Américas | **River Oaks**	24
Bistro Alex | **Memorial**	22
🆕 Brasserie 19 | **River Oaks**	23
❷ Brennan's | **Midtown**	27
❷ Brenner's | **multi.**	27
Capital Grille | **Galleria**	26
Carmelo's | **W Houston**	24
Ciao Bello | **Galleria**	20
❷ Da Marco | **Montrose**	29
❷ Del Frisco's | **Galleria**	27
Eddie V's | **Upper Kirby**	26
Fleming's Prime | **Memorial**	25
Grove | **Downtown**	19
Ibiza | **Midtown**	25
Irma's | **Downtown**	26
Jasper's | **Woodlands**	24
La Griglia | **River Oaks**	22
❷ Mark's | **Montrose**	28
Monarch | **Medical Ctr**	21
Morton's | **multi.**	26
Mo's | **Galleria**	21
Palm | **Galleria**	25
❷ Pappas Bros. | **Galleria**	28
❷🆕 Philippe | **Galleria**	24
Quattro | **Downtown**	26
RDG/Bar Annie | **Galleria**	24
Rest. CINQ | **Montrose**	27
Rist. Cavour | **Uptown**	24
Ruth's Chris | **Galleria**	26
*17 | **Downtown**	24
Strip Hse. | **Downtown**	24
Sullivan's | **Galleria**	24
III Forks | **Downtown**	24
Tony's | **Greenway Plaza**	26
Trevisio | **Medical Ctr**	22
Valentino | **Galleria**	23
❷ Vic & Antony's | **Downtown**	26

QUIET CONVERSATION

Au Petit Paris | **Lower Shepherd**	25
Carmelo's | **W Houston**	24
Charivari | **Midtown**	24

Z Chez Nous | **Humble**	28
Chez Roux | **Montgomery**	-
Crapitto's | **Galleria**	22
Damian's | **Midtown**	26
5115 R&L | **Galleria**	23
Le Mistral | **W Houston**	26
NEW Line & Lariat | **Downtown**	-
Lynn's | **W Houston**	25
Ouisie's | **River Oaks**	24
Quattro | **Downtown**	26
Rest. CINQ | **Montrose**	27
Rist. Cavour | **Uptown**	24
Ruth's Chris | **Galleria**	26
*17 | **Downtown**	24
Thai Bistro | **West U**	22
Trevisio | **Medical Ctr**	22
Valentino | **Galleria**	23
Vargo's | **Memorial**	16

ROMANTIC PLACES

Antica Osteria | **West U**	24
Artista | **Downtown**	24
Au Petit Paris | **Lower Shepherd**	25
Z Brennan's | **Midtown**	27
Carmelo's | **W Houston**	24
Z Chez Nous | **Humble**	28
Chez Roux | **Montgomery**	-
Crapitto's | **Galleria**	22
Cullen's | **Clear Lake**	17
Z Da Marco | **Montrose**	29
Damian's | **Midtown**	26
5115 R&L | **Galleria**	23
Kirby's | **Woodlands**	24
Le Mistral | **W Houston**	26
Luigi's | **Galveston**	26
Lynn's | **W Houston**	25
Z Mark's | **Montrose**	28
Masraff's | **Galleria**	25
Z Rainbow Lodge | **Heights**	26
Rest. CINQ | **Montrose**	27
Rist. Cavour | **Uptown**	24
*17 | **Downtown**	24
Tony's | **Greenway Plaza**	26
Valentino | **Galleria**	23
Vargo's | **Memorial**	16

SENIOR APPEAL

Avalon Diner | **Memorial**	21
Bistro Lancaster | **Downtown**	24
Brio | **Memorial**	22
Carmelo's | **W Houston**	24

Cleburne | **West U**	23
Crapitto's | **Galleria**	22
Dot Coffee | **Hobby**	-
59 Diner | **multi.**	18
Gaido's | **Galveston**	22
Kirby's | **Woodlands**	24
Masraff's | **Galleria**	25
Ouisie's | **River Oaks**	24
Rudi Lechner's | **SW Houston**	24
Tony's | **Greenway Plaza**	26
Vargo's | **Memorial**	16

SINGLES SCENES

NEW Alto Pizzeria | **River Oaks**	22
Armandos | **River Oaks**	20
Arturo's | **Uptown**	22
Benjy's | **Heights**	24
Berryhill Baja | **Montrose**	20
Branch Water | **Heights**	25
NEW Brasserie 19 | **River Oaks**	23
NEW Coppa | **Heights**	25
Cyclone Anaya's | **multi.**	21
Dolce Vita | **Montrose**	26
Eddie V's | **Upper Kirby**	26
NEW El Gran Malo | **Heights**	-
El Tiempo | **multi.**	23
Empire Café | **Montrose**	20
Fleming's Prime | **multi.**	25
La Griglia | **River Oaks**	22
Laurenzo's | **Heights**	21
Max's | **Heights**	20
Pesce | **Upper Kirby**	26
Z NEW Philippe | **Galleria**	24
RDG/Bar Annie | **Galleria**	24
Z Reef | **Midtown**	25
Sambuca | **Downtown**	22
Smith/Wollensky | **Galleria**	24
NEW Sorrel Urban | **Lower Shepherd**	16
Stella Sola | **Heights**	23
Sullivan's | **Galleria**	24
Taco Milagro | **Upper Kirby**	18
Tasting Rm. | **Galleria**	22
NEW TQLA | **Heights**	-
Uptown Sushi | **Uptown**	26
Yucatan Taco | **Woodlands**	22

TRENDY

NEW Alto Pizzeria | **River Oaks**	22
Z Américas | **River Oaks**	24
Armandos | **River Oaks**	20
Arturo's | **Uptown**	22

Quattro | **Downtown** 26

RDG/Bar Annie | **Galleria** 24

Z Reef | **Midtown** 25

Rest. CINQ | **Montrose** 27

Rist. Cavour | **Uptown** 24

Ruth's Chris | **Galleria** 26

*17 | **Downtown** 24

Smith/Wollensky | **Galleria** 24

Strip Hse. | **Downtown** 24

Ill Forks | **Downtown** 24

Tony's | **Greenway Plaza** 26

NEW Trinity | **Lower Shepherd** -

Truluck's | **Galleria** 24

Z NEW Uchi | **Montrose** 29

NEW Underbelly | **Montrose** -

Valentino | **Galleria** 23

Z Vic & Antony's | **Downtown** 26

WINE BARS

Block 7 | **Heights** 21

Divino | **Lower Shepherd** 25

Dolce Vita | **Montrose** 26

Fleming's Prime | **multi.** 25

Giacomo's | **Upper Kirby** 23

Ibiza | **Midtown** 25

Max's | **Heights** 20

Mockingbird Bistro | **River Oaks** 26

Arpi's Phoenicia | **Downtown** 26

Poscol | **Montrose** 26

Quattro | **Downtown** 26

RDG/Bar Annie | **Galleria** 24

Tasting Rm. | **multi.** 22

WINNING WINE LISTS

NEW Alto Pizzeria | **River Oaks** 22

Arcodoro | **Galleria** 22

NEW Ava Kitchen | **River Oaks** 19

Backstreet Café | **River Oaks** 26

Benjy's | **Rice Vill** 24

Branch Water | **Heights** 25

Z Brass. Max/Julie | **Montrose** 27

NEW Brasserie 19 | **River Oaks** 23

Z Brennan's | **Midtown** 27

Z Brenner's | **multi.** 27

Café Rabelais | **Rice Vill** 26

Capital Grille | **Galleria** 26

Carmelo's | **W Houston** 24

Chez Roux | **Montgomery** -

Churrascos | **multi.** 25

Ciao Bello | **Galleria** 20

NEW Coppa | **Heights** 25

Z Da Marco | **Montrose** 29

Z Del Frisco's | **Galleria** 27

El Meson | **Rice Vill** 24

Fogo/Chão | **Briargrove** 25

Giacomo's | **Upper Kirby** 23

Glass Wall | **Heights** 25

Ibiza | **Midtown** 25

Z Kiran's | **Galleria** 27

Lynn's | **W Houston** 25

Z Mark's | **Montrose** 28

Mockingbird Bistro | **River Oaks** 26

Morton's | **multi.** 26

Z Pappas Bros. | **Galleria** 28

Pesce | **Upper Kirby** 26

Z NEW Philippe | **Galleria** 24

Poscol | **Montrose** 26

Prego | **Rice Vill** 24

RDG/Bar Annie | **Galleria** 24

Z Reef | **Midtown** 25

T'afia | **Midtown** 24

Tasting Rm. | **Galleria** 22

Tony's | **Greenway Plaza** 26

Valentino | **Galleria** 23

Z Vic & Antony's | **Downtown** 26

Zelko Bistro | **Heights** 25

WORTH A TRIP

Galveston

Gaido's 22

Luigi's 26

Mosquito Cafe 25

Rudy & Paco 26

Humble

Z Chez Nous 28

Montgomery

Chez Roux -

The Woodlands

Z Américas 24

SAN ANTONIO

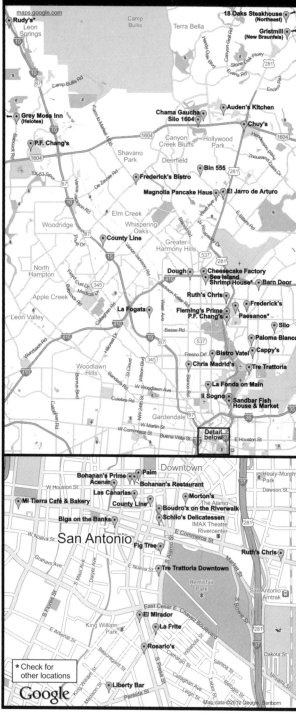

Most Popular

1. Biga on the Banks | *American*
2. Boudro's | *Steak*
3. Bohanan's | *Steak*
4. Dough | *Pizza*
5. Rudy's | *BBQ*
6. Il Sogno | *Italian*
7. Paesanos | *Italian*
8. Silo | *American*
9. Bistro Vatel | *French*
10. Frederick's | *Asian/French*
11. Ácenar | *Tex-Mex*
12. La Frite | *Belgian*
13. Morton's* | *Steak*
14. Rosario's | *Mexican*
15. Tre Trattoria* | *Amer./Italian*
16. Las Canarias | *American*
17. Cappy's | *American/Eclectic*
18. Sandbar Fish* | *Seafood*
19. El Mirador | *Mexican*
20. Ruth's Chris* | *Steak*
21. Chuy's | *Tex-Mex*
22. Chris Madrid's | *Burgers*
23. El Jarro de Arturo* | *Mexican*
24. Fleming's Prime* | *Steak*
25. Mi Tierra* | *Tex-Mex*
26. County Line | *BBQ*
27. Gristmill | *American*
28. Auden's Kitchen | *American*
29. La Fogata* | *Mexican*
30. Paloma Blanca* | *Mexican*
31. Schilo's Deli* | *Deli*
32. Liberty Bar | *Eclectic*
33. P.F. Chang's* | *Chinese*
34. Cheesecake Factory | *American*
35. Palm* | *Steak*
36. Chama Gaucha | *Brazilian/Steak*
37. La Fonda on Main* | *Mexican*
38. 18 Oaks | *Steak*
39. Barn Door* | *Steak*
40. Bin 555* | *American*
41. Fig Tree* | *Continental*
42. Grey Moss Inn* | *American*
43. Magnolia Pancake* | *Amer.*
44. Sea Island Shrimp | *Seafood*

Many of the above restaurants are among the San Antonio area's most expensive, but if popularity were calibrated to price, a number of other restaurants would surely join their ranks. To illustrate this, we have added two lists comprising San Antonio's Best Buys on page 244.

KEY NEWCOMERS

Our editors' picks among this year's arrivals. See full list at p. 280.

Drew's | *American* | Comfort food and cocktails in Stone Oak

Esquire Tavern | *Pub Food* | River Walker gets a revamped seasonal menu

Feast | *American* | Small plates and cocktails in a stylish Southtown setting

Ocho | *Pan-Latin* | Pan-Latin plates and a view of the River Walk

Q on the Riverwalk | *BBQ* | Global BBQ in Downtown's Hyatt Regency

Restaurant Gwendolyn | *American* | River Walk entry stresses sustainability

Tejas Steakhouse | *Steak* | Campfire cooking in rural Bulverde

Vegeria | *Vegan* | Vegan cooking with Mexican twists in Alamo Heights

* Indicates a tie with restaurant above

Top Food

28 Bistro Vatel | *French*

27 Sorrento | *Italian*
Bohanan's | *Steak*
Dough | *Pizza*
Silo | *American*
Il Sogno | *Italian*
Gourmet Burger Grill | *Burgers*
Sandbar Fish | *Seafood*
Grey Moss Inn | *American*

26 Biga on the Banks | *American*
Morton's | *Steak*
Las Canarias | *American*
Sea Island Shrimp | *Seafood*
La Frite | *Belgian*
Grimaldi's | *Pizza*
Cappy's | *American/Eclectic*
Ruth's Chris | *Steak*
Frederick's | *Asian/French*

25 Wildfish | *American/Seafood*
Fogo de Chão | *Brazilian/Steak*

Magnolia Pancake | *Amer.*
Fleming's Prime | *Steak*
Grill/Leon Springs | *Eclectic*
Paloma Blanca* | *Mexican*
Rudy's | *BBQ*
Cooper's | *BBQ*
Josephine St. Cafe | *American*
Palm* | *Steak*
Cappyccino's | *American*
Chama Gaucha* | *Brazil./Steak*
Taco Taco | *Tex-Mex*

24 Rosario's | *Mexican*
Piatti | *Italian*
Schilo's Deli* | *Deli*
Texas de Brazil | *Brazilian*
Bistro Bakery/Café Artistes |
Bakery/Fr.
Tre Trattoria | *Italian*
Roaring Fork | *Southwestern*
Chris Madrid's | *Burgers*
Fig Tree* | *Continental*

BY CUISINE

AMERICAN (NEW)

27 Silo
26 Biga on the Banks
Las Canarias
Cappy's
25 Wildfish

AMERICAN (TRAD.)

27 Grey Moss Inn
25 Magnolia Pancake
Josephine St. Cafe
24 Chesters Hamburger Co.
Tip Top Cafe

FRENCH

28 Bistro Vatel
26 Frederick's
24 Bistro Bakery/Café Artistes
23 Coco Chocolate Lounge
22 Lüke

ITALIAN

27 Sorrento
Dough
Il Sogno
24 Piatti
Tre Trattoria

MEXICAN

25 Paloma Blanca
24 Rosario's
23 El Jarro de Arturo
La Gloria
22 El Mirador

SEAFOOD

27 Sandbar Fish
26 Sea Island Shrimp
25 Wildfish
24 Boudro's
23 Pappadeux

STEAKHOUSES

27 Bohanan's
26 Morton's
Ruth's Chris
25 Fogo de Chão
Fleming's Prime

TEX-MEX

25 Taco Taco
24 Pappasito's Cantina
La Margarita
23 Scenic Loop Café
22 La Hacienda/Los Barrios

Excludes places with low votes

BY SPECIAL FEATURE

BREAKFAST

26 Las Canarias
25 Magnolia Pancake
   Taco Taco
24 Schilo's Deli
22 El Mirador

BRUNCH

26 Las Canarias
   Cappy's
25 Paloma Blanca
22 Madhatters
21 Aldino at the Vineyard

BUSINESS DINING

28 Bistro Vatel
27 Bohanan's
   Silo
   Il Sogno
26 Biga on the Banks

CHILD-FRIENDLY

26 Cappy's
24 Rosario's
23 Big'z Burger
20 Aldaco's-Stone Oak
19 Two Bros. BBQ

DINING ALONE

28 Bistro Vatel
27 Il Sogno
   Gourmet Burger Grill
   Sandbar Fish
26 Las Canarias

MEET FOR A DRINK

27 Bohanan's
   Silo
26 Biga on the Banks
   Morton's
25 Paloma Blanca

PEOPLE-WATCHING

24 Bistro Bakery/Café Artistes
23 Liberty Bar

POWER SCENES

   La Gloria
22 Lüke
   Ácenar

27 Il Sogno
   Sandbar Fish
26 Biga on the Banks
25 Grill/Leon Springs
   Palm

QUICK BITES

27 Dough
   Gourmet Burger Grill
25 Rudy's
24 Tre Trattoria
22 Madhatters

QUIET CONVERSATION

28 Bistro Vatel
27 Grey Moss Inn
26 Biga on the Banks
   Las Canarias
   Frederick's

SINGLES SCENES

25 Wildfish
   Fleming's Prime
   Grill/Leon Springs
23 Coco Chocolate Lounge
22 Azúca

TRENDY

27 Dough
   Il Sogno
23 Liberty Bar
   Auden's Kitchen
   La Gloria

WINNING WINE LISTS

27 Bohanan's
   Silo
   Il Sogno
   Sandbar Fish
   Grey Moss Inn

ALAMO HEIGHTS

27 Sorrento
Silo
26 Cappy's
Frederick's
25 Paloma Blanca

DOWNTOWN

27 Bohanan's
26 Morton's
Ruth's Chris
25 Fogo de Chão
Palm

NORTH

27 Gourmet Burger Grill
24 Chesters Hamburger Co.
23 El Jarro de Arturo
22 La Fogata
La Hacienda/Los Barrios

NORTH CENTRAL

27 Dough
Gourmet Burger Grill

26 Ruth's Chris
25 Magnolia Pancake
24 India Oven

QUARRY

25 Fleming's Prime
24 Piatti
23 20nine Restaurant
22 Five Guys
Paesanos

RIVER WALK

26 Biga on the Banks
Las Canarias
24 Fig Tree
Boudro's
22 Paesanos

SOUTHTOWN

26 La Frite
24 Rosario's
23 Liberty Bar
22 El Mirador
Guenther House

Top Decor

27 Las Canarias	Chama Gaucha
Chart House	Guenther House
26 Biga on the Banks	Fleming's Prime
Grey Moss Inn	**24** Tre Trattoria
25 Gristmill	Fig Tree
Paloma Blanca	Barbaresco
Aldaco's Stone Oak	Josephine St. Cafe
Silo	Morton's*
Coco Chocolate Lounge	Cappy's
Roaring Fork	**23** Bohanan's

OUTDOORS

Aldaco's-Stone Oak	Monterey
Bin 555	Paesanos
La Hacienda/Los Barrios	Roaring Fork
La Gloria	Tre Trattoria
Lüke	Welfare Café

ROMANCE

Biga on the Banks	Olmos Park Bistro
Bistro Vatel	Ounce
Bohanan's	Restaurant Gwendolyn
Citrus	Silo
Fig Tree	Welfare Café

ROOMS

Barbaresco	Francesca's
Biga on the Banks	Grill/Leon Springs
Bohanan's	Lüke
Citrus	Silo
18 Oaks	Welfare Café

VIEWS

Biga on the Banks	Gristmill
Boudro's	La Gloria
Chart House	Las Canarias
18 Oaks	Little Rhein
Francesca's	Welfare Café

Top Service

26 Chama Gaucha
Silo
Bohanan's
Grey Moss Inn*
Fogo de Chão
Las Canarias

Morton's
Cappy's
La Frite
Frederick's
Fleming's Prime
Il Sogno
Formosa Garden

25 Ruth's Chris
Josephine St. Cafe
Biga on the Banks
Bistro Vatel

24 18 Oaks
Palm
Dough

Best Buys

In order of Bang for the Buck rating.

1. Five Guys
2. Chesters Hamburger Co.
3. Taco Taco
4. Chris Madrid's
5. Gourmet Burger Grill
6. Big'z Burger Joint
7. Josephine St. Cafe
8. Magnolia Pancake
9. Asia Kitchen
10. Guenther House
11. Rudy's
12. Schilo's Deli
13. Sea Island Shrimp
14. Alamo Café
15. Tip Top Cafe
16. Pei Wei
17. Cove
18. Madhatters
19. Mi Tierra
20. Formosa Garden

OTHER GOOD VALUES

Beto's Comida
Boehler's
Cappyccino's
County Line
Dodging Duck
El Bucanero
Green Vegetarian
Huisache Grille
Jerusalem Grill
La Hacienda/Los Barrios

La Tuna Grill
Mediterranean Turkish Grill
Picnikins Patio
Rolling Pig
Stonewerks
Teka Molino
Tiago's Cabo Grill
Torres Taco
Two Bros. BBQ
Vegeria

San Antonio

Ácenar *Tex-Mex* 22 | 23 | 20 | $29

River Walk | 146 E. Houston St. (bet. Soledad & St. Mary's Sts.) |
210-222-2362 | www.acenar.com
A local "favorite", this "hipster" Mexican beyond the "touristy" part
of the River Walk boasts a spacious patio that's lots of "fun"; expect
a "modern" setting and an "inventive Nuevo-Tex" menu (with tableside guacamole) washed down with "amazing" cocktails.

Alamo Café *Tex-Mex* 21 | 18 | 21 | $16

North | 14250 Hwy. 281 N. (Bitters Rd.) | 210-495-2233
Northwest | 10060 I-10 W. (Wurzbach Rd.) | 210-691-8827
www.alamocafe.com
Where "the police eat, so it must be good", this "reliable" duo on the
Northside puts out "better-than-average" Tex-Mex eats and "melt-in-
your-mouth" tortillas; while the "inexpensive" tabs, "friendly" service
and "low-key" setting get kudos, long weekend waits are a downside.

Aldaco's Mexican Cuisine *Mexican* – | – | – | I

Downtown | 100 Hoefgen Ave. (bet. Center & Commerce Sts.) |
210-222-0561 | www.aldacos.net
"Longtime favorite" Downtown Mexican for "solid" low-cost cooking and margaritas off the River Walk and near the Alamodome.

Aldaco's-Stone Oak *Mexican* 20 | 25 | 22 | $26

Stone Oak | 20079 Stone Oak Pkwy. (Hardy Oak Blvd.) | 210-494-0561 |
www.aldacos-stoneoak.com
"Gorgeous" patio views from the highest point in the city, plus a dramatic tile interior makes for a refined setting at this Mexican in Stone
Oak; "authentic" fare and powerful margaritas keep it hopping.

Aldino at the Vineyard *Italian* 21 | 22 | 22 | $31

Loop 1604 | Vineyard Ctr. | 1203 Loop 1604 NW (Blanco Rd.) |
210-340-0000 | www.aldinos.com
An "older crowd" favors this midpriced Loop 1604 Italian inspiring
"positive feelings" with "good, not great" cooking, "personable" service and a "quaint, out-of-the-way" location.

Aldo's Ristorante Italiano *Italian* 24 | 22 | 23 | $43

Medical Center | 8539 Fredericksburg Rd. (Wurzbach Rd.) |
210-696-2536 | www.aldos.us
"You'd never guess you're still in the city" at this Med Center Italian
"gem" in a "lovely old home" where Aldo himself oversees "good, if not
imaginative" fare and "excellent" service; a piano player on weekends
cements its "first-date" status; it's also popular for business lunches.

Antlers Lodge ⚠Ⓜ *Southwestern* ▽ 24 | 24 | 19 | $49

San Antonio West | Hyatt Regency Hill Country Resort & Spa |
9800 Hyatt Resort Dr. (Rogers Rd.) | 210-520-4001 |
www.hillcountry.hyatt.com
All the little "extras" – like expansive Hill Country views and fine
wines – are what make the difference at this elegant Southwestern din-

ing room in the far West Hyatt Resort favored by hotel guests and day trippers alike; the "expensive" meals of rib-eye and game are "up to the mark", even if service is sometimes "below par for the cost."

Asia Kitchen ☑ *Thai*   <u>24</u> | <u>16</u> | <u>22</u> | $16

San Antonio West | 1739 SW Loop 410 (Marbach Rd.) | 210-673-0662 | www.asia-kitchen.com

A "lunchtime salvation" on the Westside; expect "good", "fast" Thai cooking (including veggie options) for not too much dough in a purely functional setting.

Auden's Kitchen *American*   <u>23</u> | <u>21</u> | <u>22</u> | $30

Stone Oak | Plaza at Concord Park | 700 E. Sonterra Blvd. (Sigma Rd.) | 210-494-0070 | www.audenskitchen.com

A "much-needed" alternative to the area's "chain-dining" options, this Stone Oak New American from Bruce Auden (Biga on the Banks) features a "delicious" "comfort-food" menu starring some "delectable" fried chicken; "casual" digs, moderate tabs and a "friendly" vibe make it "pleasant all around."

Azúca Nuevo Latino *Nuevo Latino*   <u>22</u> | <u>22</u> | <u>19</u> | $31

Southtown | 713 S. Alamo St. (bet. Durango Blvd. & Presa St.) | 210-225-5550 | www.azuca.net

"Live salsa" on weekends and a "caliente happy hour" are the main draws at this festive Southtowner plying a "well-executed" menu washed down with "authentic" mojitos; it's "loud, crowded" and service can be uneven, but most insist it's a "good" time nonetheless.

Barbaresco ☑ *Italian*   <u>19</u> | <u>24</u> | <u>18</u> | $36

North Central | 9715 San Pedro Ave. (McCarty Rd.) | 210-231-0989 | www.barbaresco.net

A "gorgeous" interior is the main selling point of this North Central expanse filled with dramatic artwork and exotic woods; service is "pleasant", but many find the Italian fare "not memorable", although live music during the extended happy hour turns the central bar into a party.

Barn Door, The *Steak*   <u>22</u> | <u>19</u> | <u>22</u> | $29

Alamo Heights | 8400 N. New Braunfels Ave. (bet. Crownhill Blvd. & Edgehill Dr.) | 210-824-0116 | www.barndoorrestaurant.com

"One of the oldest steakhouses in town", this circa-1953 meatery in Alamo Heights puts out "solid dinners" in a "cute, barnlike" space that "hasn't changed" in years, "including the clientele"; some say it's "not as good as it used to be", but at least it won't cost you much.

Beto's Comida Latina *S American*   <u>21</u> | <u>10</u> | <u>16</u> | $15

North | 8142 Broadway St. (Flamingo Dr.) | 210-930-9393 | www.betoscomidalatina.com

This "roadside joint" on the Northside is a "go-to" for "tasty empanadas" and other Latin items served alongside traditional Mex inside or on the patio; cheap tabs, "casual" digs and "slow", but "friendly" service complete the package.

	FOOD	DECOR	SERVICE	COST

☑ Biga on the Banks *American* | 26 | 26 | 25 | $50 |

River Walk | 203 S. St. Mary's St. (Market St.) | 210-225-0722 | www.biga.com

"First-rate all the way" – and San Antonio's Most Popular restaurant – this "sophisticated" River Walk respite puts out an "excellent", "innovative" mix of New American and Southwest fare from chef-owner Bruce Auden in "industrial-chic" surroundings; add an "accommodating", "knowledgeable" staff and it's worth the "splurge"; P.S. look for pre- and post-theater prix fixe dinners as well as half-price options on entrees on weekends.

Big'z Burger Joint Ⓜ *Burgers* | 23 | 16 | 18 | $14 |

Loop 1604 | 2303 N. Loop 1604 W. (Huebner Rd.) | 210-408-2029 | www.bigz-burgerjoint.com

"Terrific burgers" prepared with "gourmet" touches await at this Loop 1604 "joint" from chef Andrew Weissman (Il Sogno, Sandbar) also offering "quality fries", thick shakes plus beer and wine "to wash it all down"; the setting's "about as casual as you can get", but includes a play area "with plenty of room for the kids to run around."

Bin 555 ⓩ *American* | 23 | 21 | 21 | $34 |

North Central | Shops at Artisans Alley | 555 W. Bitters Rd. (bet. Blanco Rd. & West Ave.) | 210-496-0555 | www.bin555.com

A "plethora of petite plates" packed with "big flavors" are on offer at this chic North Central wine bar with New American nibbles from chef-owner Jason Dady (The Lodge, Tre Trattoria); a few find it "a bit overpriced" given such "small portions" and its strip-mall setting, but a "knowledgeable" staff and an inviting patio encourage most to "drink and nibble" all night.

Bistro Bakery *Bakery* | 24 | 20 | 21 | $21 |

Olmos Park | 4300 McCullough Ave. (Olmos Dr.) | 210-824-3884 | www.bistrobakery.net

Café des Artistes Ⓜ *French*

Downtown | San Antonio Museum of Art | 200 W. Jones Ave. (Ave. B) | 210-978-8155 | www.sacafedesartistes.com

"Close your eyes, open your mouth and you're in Paris" at this bakery and bistro in upscale Olmos Park purveying "delightful" "light" bites and pastries ("the best croissants!") all served "cheerfully" in a modest space; the ovens also supply goods for siblings Café des Artistes at the San Antonio Museum of Art and neighboring Bistro Vatel.

☑ Bistro Vatel Ⓜ *French* | 28 | 20 | 25 | $46 |

Olmos Park | 218 E. Olmos Dr. (McCullough Ave.) | 210-828-3141 | www.bistrovatel.com

It may be a "low-key" bistro in an Olmos Park strip mall but its "lovely" fish, hanger steaks and other "super", "high-quality" French fare from Damien Watel earn it San Antonio's No. 1 Food rating; a "cozy atmosphere" and "good-value" pricing further inspire repeat visits; P.S. the $45 prix fixe menu is "a deal."

	FOOD	DECOR	SERVICE	COST

Boardwalk Bistro ⊠ *Mediterranean* — 23 | 18 | 20 | $26

Near North | The Boardwalk | 4011 Broadway St. (Thorman Pl.) | 210-824-0100 | www.boardwalkbistro.net

Patrons praise this "charming" Near North bistro purveying "well-prepared" Med dishes in a Tuscan–style setting with yellow walls and copper pots hanging throughout; its locale close to museums and shopping keeps it "packed at lunch", while "personal" service, a "stepped-up" dinner menu and live jazz make it "romantic" at night.

NEW Boehler's Bar & Grille *American* — ▽ 19 | 20 | 18 | $26

Near North | 328 E. Josephine St. (Ave. A) | 210-227-1890 | www.boehlersbarandgrille.com

Near North bar and grill set in a "historic" 1890 edifice with "so much character" (formerly housing the Liberty Bar); compared with the setting, some find the New American fare "disappointing", although the overall mood is "enjoyable", and happy hour is a plus.

☑ Bohanan's — 27 | 23 | 26 | $72
Prime Steaks & Seafood *Steak*

Downtown | 219 E. Houston St., 2nd fl. (bet. Navarro & St. Mary's Sts.) | 210-472-2600 | www.bohanans.com

☑ Bohanan's Bar *American*

Downtown | 221 E. Houston St. (bet. Navarro & St. Mary's Sts.) | 210-472-2202 | www.bohanansbar.com

A "classic steakhouse done right", this "much-loved" Downtown entry "exceeds expectations" with "outstanding" beef, a "stellar bar with well-made cocktails" and an "old-school" vibe; "expensive" tabs hardly faze the "expense-account" clientele; P.S. the bar is on the ground floor and stays open later with a light menu.

☑ Boudro's on the Riverwalk *Seafood/Steak* — 24 | 22 | 22 | $40

River Walk | 421 E. Commerce St. (bet. Losoya & Presa Sts.) | 210-224-8484 | www.boudros.com

It's always a "party" at this River Walk spot where "tourists and locals" angle for an outside seat for "mouthwatering" seafood and steaks with Texas touches, "famous" tableside guac and "strong drinks" that "will have you down for the count"; "exceptional people-watching" and "attentive service" seal the deal; P.S. "make reservations."

Canyon Café *Southwestern* — 20 | 22 | 20 | $22

Quarry | Alamo Quarry Mkt. | 255 E. Basse Rd. (bet. Hwy. 281 & Jones Maltsberger Rd.) | 210-821-3738 | www.canyoncafe.com

A "rustic" converted Quarry factory building sets the scene at this "cozy" Southwestern attracting a "yuppie" clientele with "designer" margaritas ("you only need one") and "Mexican fare with a California twist" that's "about right for the price."

Cappyccino's ⊠ *American* — 25 | 21 | 23 | $22

Alamo Heights | 5003 Broadway St. (Mary D. Ave.) | 210-828-6860 | www.cappyccinos.com

"Fun for after-work cocktails or a late-night nosh", this "friendly" "neighborhood bar" in Alamo Heights offers a "no-surprises" New

	FOOD	DECOR	SERVICE	COST

American menu of "top-notch" burgers and such backed by an "exhaustive" cocktail list; the atmosphere's "relaxing", and it shares a shaded patio with sibling Cappy's.

Cappy's Restaurant *American/Eclectic*
26 | 24 | 25 | $38

Alamo Heights | 5011 Broadway St. (Mary D. Ave.) | 210-828-9669 | www.cappysrestaurant.com

"An Alamo Heights institution", this New American–Eclectic offers "upscale dining without the stuffy atmosphere" with "something for every taste and budget"; it's "often crowded", but maintains a "charming, comfortable" vibe thanks to an owner who "cares" and a "wonderful" staff; it's also "one of the few 'adult' restaurants in town where you can carry a conversation."

Carrabba's Italian Grill *Italian*
23 | 20 | 22 | $29

Northwest | 12507 I-10 W. (bet. De Zavala Rd. & Woodstone Dr.) | 210-694-4191 | www.carrabbas.com

See review in Houston Directory.

☑ Chama Gaucha *Brazilian/Steak*
25 | 25 | 26 | $45

Stone Oak | Sonterra Pl. | 18318 Sonterra Pl. (Loop 1604) | 210-564-9400 | www.chamagaucha.com

"They don't skimp on the meat" at this upscale Stone Oak Brazilian steakhouse where "super-fast" servers ferry "succulent" cuts ("more food than you can imagine") and "fulfill any request", earning them the No. 1 Service score in San Antonio; it's "expensive", although the cost covers all you can eat and the "beautiful" setting includes a "mind-blowing" salad bar.

☑ Chart House *Seafood*
15 | 27 | 18 | $47

Downtown | Tower of the Americas | 600 Hemisfair Plaza Way (Alamo St.) | 210-223-3101 | www.chart-house.com

The "spectacular" panoramic view of Downtown is the main attraction for "tourists" at this revolving restaurant chain outpost atop the Tower of the Americas; however, many find the "less-than-stellar" seafood "not up to Chart House standards", and "overpriced" to boot.

Cheesecake Factory *American*
20 | 19 | 19 | $28

NEW La Cantera | The Shops at La Cantera | 15900 La Cantera Pkwy. (Loop 164) | 210-558-1900

Loop 410 | North Star Mall | 7400 San Pedro Ave. (I-410) | 210-798-2222 | www.thecheesecakefactory.com

See review in Houston Directory.

Chesters Hamburger Company *Burgers*
24 | 16 | 18 | $13

Loop 410 | 1006 Loop 410 NE (New Braunfels Ave.) | 210-805-8600

North | 16609 San Pedro Ave. (Thousand Oaks Dr.) | 210-494-3333

Northwest | 9980 I-10 W. (Wurzbach Rd.) | 210-699-1222

There are "no frills and none needed" at this affordable American mini-chain beloved for its "great, juicy" "old-fashioned" burgers and "cold" brews; the picnic-style setting is especially "popular for lunch"; it's a rollicking game-night venue too.

Chris Madrid's 🅂 *Burgers*

| 24 | 15 | 18 | $14 |

Near North | 1900 Blanco Rd. (Hollywood Ave.) | 210-735-3552 | www.chrismadrids.com

"*Puro* San Antonio", this Near North "classic" is famous for its "delicious" "megaburgers" "full of cheesy, beefy goodness" (get the Macho nacho-topped patty "if you have something to prove"); it "isn't highbrow", but the mood's "celebratory", and it's a "funky" experience

Chuy's *Tex-Mex*

| 21 | 20 | 20 | $19 |

North | 18008 San Pedro Ave. (Loop 1604) | 210-545-0300 | www.chuys.com

See review in Austin and the Hill Country Directory.

CIA Bakery Café Ⓜ *Bakery*

| ▽ 25 | 18 | 19 | $18 |

Near North | CIA Campus, Bldg. 2 | 312 Pearl Pkwy. (Karnes St.) | 210-554-6464 | www.ciachef.edu

"The pastries will take your breath away" at this Culinary Institute of America campus cafe set in the fashionable Pearl Brewery complex and vending goodies like pearl-sugar brioche and chocolate-caramel tarts; look for "pricey" sandwiches and other light fare, but space is "limited", so you'll need to "fight the crowds" to score a table

Ciao Lavanderia 🅂 *Italian*

| 24 | 18 | 22 | $30 |

Olmos Park | 226 E. Olmos Dr. (El Prado Dr.) | 210-822-3990 | www.ciaofoodandwine.com

A "satisfying" Italian menu with "a surprise or two", plus "efficient" service and a reasonable bill mark this "warm neighborhood place" in Olmos Park.

Cibolo Moon *American*

| – | – | – | M |

Northeast | JW Marriott San Antonio Hill Country | 23808 Resort Pkwy. (Marriott Pkwy.) | 210-403-3434 | www.jwsanantonio.com

Casual all-day American in the JW Marriott San Antonio Hill Country resort with Texas-inspired dishes like bison meatloaf and chicken-fried steak; the "atmospheric" setting includes an ample bar stocked with specialty tequilas and wines on tap.

Citrus *American/Eclectic*

| ▽ 26 | 24 | 24 | $45 |

Downtown | Hotel Valencia | 150 E. Houston St. (St. Mary's St.) | 210-230-8412 | www.hotelvalencia.com

"More than a hotel restaurant", this "chic" entry in Downtown's Valencia proves a "wonderful choice" for business or a date thanks to its "excellent" Eclectic–New American menu that changes with the seasons; the "upscale" setting also boasts River Walk views from the upper deck; P.S. breakfast and paella lunches are also popular.

Coco Chocolate Lounge & Bistro ●🅂Ⓜ *Dessert/French*

| 23 | 25 | 21 | $34 |

North Central | 18402 Hwy. 281 N. (Loop 1604) | 210-491-4480 | www.sa-coco.com

"Brace yourself for something not very Texan" at this "luxurious" "Moulin Rouge–inspired" French in North Central done up in "bordello

	FOOD	DECOR	SERVICE	COST

"eds" with a glitzy chandelier and velvet lounging pillows strewn throughout; the "well-thought-out" bistro menu weaves chocolate into many of the dishes, from the savories to the decadent desserts, and even the martinis; P.S. look for DJs, live salsa and jazz on weekends.

Cooper's Old Time Pit Bar-B-Que *BBQ*

| 25 | 14 | 17 | $20 |

New Braunfels | 1125 N. Loop 337 (Rivercrest Dr.) | 830-627-0627 | www.coopersbbq.com

See review in Austin and the Hill Country Directory.

County Line, The *BBQ*

| 21 | 20 | 21 | $26 |

River Walk | 111 W. Crockett St. (Presa St.) | 210-229-1941
Northwest | 10101 I-10 (Wurzbach Rd.) | 210-641-1998
www.countyline.com

"Beefy portions" of Texas barbecue mean you get "lots of bang for your buck" at this regional chain featuring "full sit-down service" – a step up from down-home joints following the "no silverware, no plates" formula; all thrive in "friendly", "rowdy" digs, with "tourists" taking over the River Walk locale, while locals swing into the Northwest San Antonio branch for "free, live music" on weekends.

Cove, The Ⓜ *American*

| 23 | 17 | 17 | $16 |

Near North | 606 W. Cypress St. (Fredericksburg Rd.) | 210-227-2683 | www.thecove.us

"Listen to local cover bands while your kids are romping in the playground" at this "quirky" combo restaurant/Laundromat/car wash serving "local, organic" American eats (think lamb burgers and fish tacos) with craft beers; the sprawling Near North venue setting also features a patio that fills up on weekends with a "youngish" college crowd lured in part by the "cheap" tabs.

Cypress Grille Ⓜ *American*

| ▽ 24 | 21 | 23 | $27 |

Boerne | 170 S. Main St. (Blanco Rd.) | 830-248-1353 | www.cypressgrilleboerne.com

"A pleasant surprise" tucked in an unassuming building in Boerne, this ambitious New American puts out "creative" dishes like pecan-smoked quail alongside a full lineup of steaks; an "attractive" woody setting and affable service help make it "worth the trip."

Dodging Duck Brewhaus & Restaurant *Eclectic*

| - | - | - | I |

Boerne | 402 River Rd. (Mesquite St.) | 830-248-3825 | www.dodgingduck.com

House-brewed beers and a mill pond stocked with ducks are the main draws at this casual Eclectic in Boerne; the affordable, wide-ranging menu features burgers, wraps and salads delivered in a rustic interior or out on the scenic patio.

ⓩ Dough *Pizza*

| 27 | 21 | 24 | $26 |

North Central | Blanco Junction Shopping Ctr. | 6989 Blanco Rd. (Loop 410) | 210-979-6565 | www.doughpizzeria.com

"Mama mia!", there are "lines out the door every night" at this otherwise unassuming North Central pizzeria (with a new Dallas offshoot) plying "superlative", "thin-crust" Neapolitan pies and other "fab" Italian items "done with panache" including a "not-to-be-missed" housemade burrata; a "knowledgeable" staff rewards patient diners with "terrific" service, "generous wine pours" and modest bills, making it a "definite must-go."

NEW Drew's American Grill American — — — M

Stone Oak | 18740 Stone Oak Pkwy. (N. Loop 1604) | 210-483-7600 | www.drewsamericangrill.com

Meaty American grill fare and a stylish setting come together at this Stone Oak newcomer providing upscale-casual dining at moderate rates; look for sliders, pizza, short ribs and strip steaks capped with top-notch desserts and cocktails like a spiked egg cream.

DUK (Dady Underground Kitchen) ●☒ American — — — I

Location varies | no phone

It's "Jason Dady on wheels" at this bright-yellow truck dispensing New American cooking from the brains and brawn behind Bin 555 and Tre Trattoria, among others; prices for plates top out at $12, and the night-time moveable feasts feature self-described 'jacked-up' creations from his imaginative whims; check Twitter for locations.

18 Oaks Steakhouse Steak 23 21 24 $56

Northeast | JW Marriott San Antonio Hill Country | 23808 Resort Pkwy. (Marriott Pkwy.) | 210-403-3434 | www.jwsanantonio.com

Upscale steakhouse in the JW Marriott San Antonio Hill Country resort with "incredible" cuts and a refined setting overlooking the golf course; Sunday brunch is a popular option.

El Bucanero Mexican/Seafood — — — I

Eastside | 2818 S. WW White Rd. (Alma Dr.) | 210-333-0909 | www.elbucanero-sa.com

Off the beaten track but on foodies' radar, this Eastside family-owned Mexican seafood pearl shines with super-fresh Sinaloa-style specialties like ceviche; the digs are humble and it's BYO only, in keeping with the bargain prices; P.S. a Northside branch is in the works.

El Jarro de Arturo Mexican 23 20 20 $24

North | 13421 San Pedro Ave. (Bitters Rd.) | 210-494-5084 | www.eljarro.com

"Packed with locals", this 35-year-old Northside "legend" is known for its "high-octane" margaritas, "huge menu" of Mexican standards and busy Sunday brunch buffet; moderate prices "triumph" over "iffy" service, and the ambiance gains a lift from live bands that turn the patio into a fiesta on Friday and Saturday nights.

El Mirador Mexican 22 19 21 $22

Southtown | 722 S. St. Mary's St. (Durango Blvd.) | 210-225-9444 | www.elmiradorsatx.com

This "family-owned" Southtown eatery has been dishing up "authentic" Mexican "home cooking" for more than 40 years, including

	FOOD	DECOR	SERVICE	COST

special Saturday soups along with some "fairly healthy" Tex-Mex and interior dishes as well; "amazingly low" prices are part of the appeal, as is the "lovely" hacienda setting with a shaded patio – it's worth it for "the charm" alone.

El Mirasol *Mexican*

| | - | - | - | M |

Churchill Estates | Churchill Pl. | 13489 Blanco Rd. (bet. Cadillac Dr. & Churchill Estates Blvd.) | 210-479-8765 | www.sasmexicanfood.com

Soluna *Mexican*

Alamo Heights | 7959 Broadway St. (Sunset Rd.) | 210-930-8070

The vivid decor matches the colorful plates of creative Mexican cuisine at this longtime Churchill Estates bistro and sister restaurant Soluna in Alamo Heights; both deliver well-honed flavors, strong margaritas and rightly famous flame-roasted salsa, all at moderate cost.

⛿ Esquire Tavern *Pub Food*

| | - | - | - | M |

Downtown | 155 E. Commerce St. (St. Mary's St.) | 210-222-2521 | www.esquiretavern-sa.com

Recently rebooted by new owners with a "fantastic" face-lift and a "memorable" menu of midpriced pub plates, this circa-1933 River Walk bar is once again a happening Downtown hangout; a "young", "friendly" staff works the bi-level space, which includes a 100-ft. wooden bar and a wrought-iron balcony overlooking the water.

⛿ Feast *American*

| | - | - | - | M |

Southtown | 1024 S. Alamo St. (bet. Cedar & Mission Sts.) | 210-354-1024 | www.feastsa.com

Tongues are wagging about Southtown's latest player in the small-plates dining scene, this hip New American delivering fanciful dishes (categorized as hot/chilled/grilled/crispy/melted) and inspired takes on classic cocktails; it has a cool, ethereal look with crystal chandeliers and acrylic furniture set against white walls; pricing, however, is decidedly down-to-earth.

Fig Tree Restaurant, The ⓩ *Continental*

| | 24 | 24 | 23 | $61 |

River Walk | 515 Villita St. (bet. Alamo & Presa Sts.) | 210-224-1976 | www.figtreerestaurant.com

One of "the most elegant" entries along the River Walk, this "romantic" (and costly) Continental resides in a 19th-century residence in historic La Villita, providing "wonderful" atmosphere along with "fine" classic cuisine; "attentive but not overbearing" service adds to the allure.

⛿ Five Guys *Burgers*

| | 22 | 14 | 19 | $11 |

Selma | Woodlake Mkt. | 6531 FM 78 (Foster Rd.) | 210-661-5238

Quarry | Quarry Vill. | 260 E. Basse Rd. (Tuxedo Ave.) | 210-822-6200

Westside | Westpointe Ctr. | 8603 State Hwy. 151 (Ingram Rd.) | 210-543-2700

www.fiveguys.com

This crowd-pleasing fast-fooder – San Antonio's No. 1 Bang for the Buck – trades in "gut-busting burgers", "yummy fries" and all-you-can-eat peanuts while you wait; ok, some nonfans call it "overrated" and "slow", but the "terrific value" trumps all.

Fleming's Prime Steakhouse & Wine Bar *Steak*

25 | 25 | 25 | $56

Quarry | Alamo Quarry Mkt. | 255 E. Basse Rd. (bet. Hwy. 281 & Jones Maltsberger Rd.) | 210-824-9463 | www.flemingssteakhouse.com
See review in Houston Directory.

☑ Fogo de Chão *Brazilian/Steak*

25 | 23 | 26 | $55

Downtown | Rivercenter Mall | 849 E. Commerce St. (bet. Alamo Plaza & Bowie St.) | 210-227-1700 | www.fogodechao.com
See review in Houston Directory.

Formosa Garden *Chinese*

23 | 20 | 25 | $21

North Central | 1011 Loop 410 NE (New Braunfels Ave.) | 210-828-9988 | www.formosagarden.com
"Texas-sized" sushi rolls and "fresh" Chinese fare keep locals coming to this North Central Asian also cooking up meat and veggies on hibachi tables; affordable rates and contemporary digs keep it busy at lunch, and it's a "go-to" for weeknight takeout.

Francesca's at Sunset *Southwestern*

▽ 26 | 26 | 25 | $49

La Cantera | Westin La Cantera Resort | 16441 La Cantera Pkwy. (Fiesta Texas Dr.) | 210-558-2442 | www.westinlacantera.com
Surveyors swear the sunset views aren't the only thing that's "spectacular" at this ritzy, recently refurbished dining room in the "beautiful" Westin La Cantera Resort; "perfectly presented" seasonal Southwestern cuisine, fine wines and "top-notch" service all come together for a "memorable", if "expensive", meal

Frederick's ☑ *Asian/French*

26 | 20 | 25 | $44

Alamo Heights | 7701 Broadway St. (Nottingham Pl.) | 210-828-9050 | www.frederickssa.com

Frederick's Bistro *Asian/French*

Churchill Estates | 14439 Military Hwy. NW (Huebner Rd.) | 210-888-1500 | www.fredericksbistro.com
"Gentlemanly" owner Frederick Costa makes you "feel welcome" at these white-linen bistros in Alamo Heights and Churchill Estates rolling out "exquisite" French-Asian fare; it "rarely gets better" elsewhere but note that prices are "expensive" and style mavens find that the strip-center locales detract from an otherwise "elegant" experience

Godai Sushi Bar & Restaurant ☑ *Japanese*

▽ 28 | 19 | 22 | $30

North Central | 11203 West Ave. (Blanco Rd.) | 210-348-6781 | www.godaisushi.com
A "vast selection" of "ultrafresh" fish lures a faithful following to this midpriced North Central Japanese helmed by "personable" chef owner Goro; whether you choose to sit at the bar or snag a seat in the "rustic" dining room, "come early" because it gets "packed" especially on weekends.

	FOOD	DECOR	SERVICE	COST

Golden Wok *Chinese*

| 20 | 16 | 19 | $18 |

Medical Center | 8822 Wurzbach Rd. (bet. Fredericksburg Rd. & IH 10 W.) | 210-615-8282
San Antonio West | 8230 Marbach Rd. (Loop 410) | 210-674-2577
www.golden-wok.com

"Excellent" dim sum rolled out on carts on weekends is the driving force behind these Austin and San Antonio Sino sibs, also favored for "fast" weekday lunches; decor varies by locale, but "bargain" prices are constants.

Gourmet Burger Grill *Burgers*

| 27 | 17 | 21 | $15 |

North | CityView | 11224 Huebner Rd. (McDermott Frwy.) | 210-558-9200
North Central | The Legacy | 18414 Hwy. 281 N. (Loop 1604) | 210-545-3800
www.gourmetburgergrill.com

"Perfectly seasoned" lamb, bison, tuna and veggie patties add zest to the usual burger grind at these "gourmet" grills in San Antonio, also slinging more "traditional" varieties; prices are pleasing, but the looks are strictly "strip-mall chic" with a spare, functional design.

Green Vegetarian Cuisine *Vegetarian*

| - | - | - | I |

Downtown | 1017 N. Flores St. (Euclid Ave.) | 210-320-5865
NEW **Churchill Estates** | Alon Towne Shopping Ctr. | 10003 NW Military Hwy. (Wurzbach Pkwy.) | 210-233-1249
www.greensanantonio.com

A "welcome oasis in the carnivore-happy state of Texas", this Downtown cafe – and San Antonio's only strictly vegetarian and ko-sher restaurant – proffers "playful" items like 'neatloaf' and Buffalo tofu wings; factor in a funky feel and low prices, and fans only wonder why it isn't more "crowded"; P.S. the Churchill Estates branch is new.

⊠ Grey Moss Inn *American*

| 27 | 26 | 26 | $45 |

Helotes | 19010 Scenic Loop Rd. (Blue Hill Dr.) | 210-695-8301 | www.grey-moss-inn.com

With "all the charm of a country inn a short distance from San Antonio", this "delightful hideaway" in Helotes hosts "romantic din-ners" galore in its "rustic" interior or its "beautiful" courtyard; the "unique" Texas-accented American menu features "delicious" steaks cooked on an outdoor grill, although some find the bills a touch costly.

Grill at Leon Springs *Eclectic*

| 25 | 23 | 23 | $40 |

Leon Springs | 24116 I-10 W. (Boerne Stage Rd.) | 210-698-8797 | www.leonspringsgrill.com

"Casually dressed Texans" sup on seasonal Eclectic fare at this well-priced grill in Leon Springs; although the "creative" menu earns ku-dos, it's the "lovely" "old stone building" and "lively" outdoor scene (with music Thursdays–Saturdays) that make it truly "worth the drive"; P.S. weekend brunch is a find for foodies, and a bargain.

Grimaldi's *Pizza*

| 26 | 20 | 21 | $21 |

La Cantera | Shops at La Cantera | 15900 La Cantera Pkwy. (Loop 1604) | 210-690-4949

(continued)

(continued)

Grimaldi's

NEW **Quarry** | The Quarry Vill. | 330 E. Basse Rd.
(Jones Maltsberger Rd.) | 210-832-8288 |
www.grimaldispizzeria.com
See review in Dallas/Ft. Worth Directory.

🛛 Gristmill, The *American*

21 | 25 | 22 | $23

New Braunfels | Historic Gruene | 1287 Gruene Rd. (Hunter Rd.) |
830-625-0684 | www.gristmillrestaurant.com
Once the boiler room of an 1878 cotton gin, this rambling building
overlooking the river in New Braunfels' historic Gruene district provides a "lovely setting" for Americana like chicken-fried steak and
burgers in "plentiful" portions; if some find the food only "ok", at
least "you can't beat the view", and the prices aren't bad either;
P.S. long lines on sunny days are the norm.

Guenther House *American*

22 | 25 | 22 | $18

Southtown | 205 E. Guenther St. (King William St.) | 210-227-1061 |
www.guentherhouse.com
Groupies never mind the "million calories" and just "go for it" at this
Southtown cafe on the Pioneer Flour Mills estate whipping up "superb" baked goods ("huge cinnamon rolls", "wonderful waffles",
"fresh biscuits") plus well-priced American breakfast and lunchtime
fare; the "sunlit" space is in a "quaint" historic building, though most
"eat outside under the arbor"; P.S. there's also a museum and gift
shop on-site.

Huisache Grille & Wine Bar *American*

▽ 28 | 28 | 28 | $25

New Braunfels | 303 W. San Antonio St. (bet. Academy & Hill Aves.) |
830-620-9001 | www.huisache.com
A "fabulous", frequently changing American menu that features Hill
Country standards is supported by "excellent" service, delivering a
"recommend-to-all" experience at this New Braunfels "favorite";
the airy, timbered setting, housed in a 1920s-era building, is "relaxing", and friendly prices leave enough in folks' wallets to shop the
vendors at the on-site 'grassmarket.'

Il Sogno 🅼 *Italian*

27 | 23 | 25 | $48

Near North | Pearl Brewery | 200 E. Grayson St. (Karnes St.) |
210-223-3900 | www.pearlbrewery.com
A "don't-miss" antipasti table "tempts" on arrival and leads to "expertly prepared", "innovative" Italian plates from chef Andrew
Weissman (Sandbar) at this Near Northerner in the Pearl Brewery
complex; it's "pricey", but service is "impeccable", making entree into
the "always" a-"buzz" industrial dining room "worth waiting" for.

India Oven *Indian*

24 | 14 | 19 | $22

North Central | 1031 Patricia Dr. (West Ave.) | 210-366-1033 |
www.indiaoven.biz
"Tucked away in a nondescript strip mall, but nicely decorated inside", this North Central Indian offers "tasty" fare and one of the

"best lunch buffets in town"; pricing is gentle, and when "cravings hit, it delivers a solid performance."

Jerusalem Grill ●Ⓜ *Mideastern*   ▽ 24 | 11 | 16 | $20

Westside | 3259 Wurzbach Rd. (bet. Ingram Rd. & Van Cleave) | 210-680-8400 | www.jerusalemgrill.net

"Great hummus" is a staple at this Middle Eastern hideaway tucked in a corner of a busy Westside strip center; make affordable selections from the ample hot/cold case or rely on friendly table service for suggestions; Friday afternoon's roast lamb special sells out fast.

Josephine St. Cafe Ⓩ *American*   25 | 24 | 25 | $19

Near North | 400 E. Josephine St. (Ave. A) | 210-224-6169 | www.josephinestcafe.com

"Kick back" and enjoy the "warm, hospitable" atmosphere (and odd tree growing through the ceiling) at this "unusual of unusuals" American steak-and-whiskey joint; a Near North meeting spot for 30-plus years, it's "full of life and noise" – and while the dining area is cramped, the "reasonable prices" for the "consistently" "solid food" make it "worth the wait."

Kirby's Steakhouse *Steak*   24 | 22 | 23 | $52

Loop 1604 | 123 Loop 1604 NE (Stone Oak Pkwy.) | 210-404-2221 | www.kirbyssteakhouse.com

See review in Dallas/Ft. Worth Directory.

La Fogata *Mexican*   22 | 23 | 22 | $25

North | 2427 Vance Jackson Rd. (bet. Addax & Nassau Drs.) | 210-340-1337 | www.lafogata.com

A "lush" courtyard filled with "fountains and greenery" creates a "fabulous atmosphere" for sipping "potent" margaritas at this longtime Northside hacienda nestled in the 'burbs; aside from the "high-octane" tipples, there's also "wonderful", "authentic" Mexican *comida* that's priced well too.

La Fonda on Main *Mexican*   21 | 22 | 22 | $24

Near North | 2415 N. Main Ave. (Woodlawn Ave.) | 210-733-0621 | www.lafondaonmain.com

Set in a converted "old house" along the streets of historic Near Northside, this "landmark" cantina (purportedly the oldest Mexican eatery in town) dishes up "classic" interior dishes as well as "solid Tex-Mex" standards at moderate cost; perhaps the food's "nothing special", but the "lovely patio" strung with Christmas lights certainly is.

La Frite Ⓩ Ⓜ *Belgian*   26 | 20 | 25 | $40

Southtown | 728 S. Alamo St. (Presa St.) | 210-224-7555 | www.lafritesa.com

"Terrific", "real-deal" Belgian bistro plats (like moules frites), a "convivial" ambiance and a "fantastic selection" of beer and wine put this simple Southtown cafe on le map du affordable favorites; P.S. the adjacent wine bar often buzzes during the weeknight happy hour.

La Gloria *Mexican*

23 | 21 | 16 | $20

Near North | Pearl Brewery | 100 E. Grayson St. (Elmira St.) | 210-267-9040 | www.lagloriaicehouse.com

"Funky" and "informal", this Near North cantina in the Pearl Brewery from Johnny Hernandez specializes in "wonderful" "fantastically spiced" Mexican street food in small plates that are "fun to share"; fans overlook uneven service and "not cheap" à la carte pricing and focus on the "picturesque" views from the quieter end of the River Walk.

La Hacienda de Los Barrios *Tex-Mex*

22 | 19 | 21 | $19

North | 18747 Redland Rd. (Gold Canyon Rd.) | 210-497-8000

Los Barrios *Tex-Mex*

North | 4223 Blanco Rd. (Basse Rd.) | 210-732-6017 | www.lhdlb.com

The "family traditions" run deep at this longtime Blanco Road "gem" and its north-of-1604 offshoot dispensing "real-deal" renditions of "genuine" Tex-Mex recipes; they're "not fancy" but they're a "favorite for any occasion", thanks to solid service, "reasonable prices" and a "fun" atmosphere with patio seating and roving mariachis.

La Margarita Mexican Restaurant & Oyster Bar *Tex-Mex*

24 | 20 | 22 | $26

Market Square | El Mercado | 120 Produce Row (Santa Rosa St.) | 210-227-7140 | www.lamargarita.com

"Touristy but tasty" sums up this Tex-Mex standby located in the historic El Mercado shopping district in Downtown San Antonio plying standards like fajitas and margaritas; service is "consistently good", just know it gets "crowded" during the lunch and dinner rush.

☒ Las Canarias *American*

26 | 27 | 26 | $50

River Walk | Omni La Mansión del Rio Hotel | 112 College St. (bet. Navarro & St. Mary's Sts.) | 210-518-1063 | www.lamansion.com

"Excellent scenery" from the tables overlooking the River Walk earn this romantic New American in the Omni the city's top Decor score, making it a locals' choice for "date nights" or "special occasions"; add in an "innovative" menu and "exemplary" service, and it really "stands out on its own", even as a hotel restaurant.

La Tuna Grill ☒ *Eclectic*

∇ 23 | 19 | 19 | $17

Southtown | 100 Probandt St. (Cevallos St.) | 210-212-5727 | www.latunagrill.com

A "deliciously other-side-of-the-trackish" locale (on the tracks that run through Southtown) is a selling point for this "fun", "laid-back" spot where diners snag a seat "under the pecan trees" with "one of the best burgers in the civilized world"; cheap Eclectic grub like fish tacos and chicken-fried steak plus ample cold beer round out the offerings.

Liberty Bar *Eclectic*

23 | 19 | 22 | $31

Southtown | 1111 S. Alamo St. (Sheridan St.) | 210-227-1187 | www.liberty-bar.com

Still "a San Antonio landmark" even after its move from a "lopsided barnlike house" to a converted Southtown convent, this "old favorite" provides loads of "fun" with a "creative" Eclectic menu, "warm" hospitality and a lively bar scene.

Little Rhein Steak House *Steak*

| 21 | 21 | 22 | $53 |

River Walk | La Villita | 231 S. Alamo St. (Market St.) | 210-225-2111 | www.littlerheinsteakhouse.com

"One of the oldest and grandest in San Antonio", this River Walk charmer inhabits a "delightful" "historic building" with "crowded little rooms" and terrace seating; it boats a "classic" steakhouse menu, "relaxed but extremely attentive" service and prices on the "high" side.

Luce Ristorante e Enoteca ☒ *Italian*

| 23 | 23 | 23 | $36 |

Northwest | The Strand | 11255 Huebner Rd. (McDermott Frwy.) | 210-561-9700 | www.lucesanantonio.com

"Forget it's in a Northwest strip center" and focus on the "homemade everything" at this "lovely" Italian fine diner with moderate prices to suit its low-key setting.

Lüke *French/German*

| 22 | 20 | 19 | $39 |

Downtown | Embassy Suites | 129 E. Houston St. (Soledad Ave.) | 210-227-5853 | www.lukesanantonio.com

This "delicious respite" Downtown comes from New Orleans chef John Besh (August, La Provence) and is set in a somewhat "odd location" inside a new Embassy Suites (though it's not the hotel restaurant); it serves a mostly "excellent" French-German brasserie menu that's "not just the same old, same old" backed by "fantastic local and Belgian beers"; despite "inconsistent" service, its reasonable bills, "old-style bar" and quiet River Walk patio make it a popular pre- or post-theater treat.

Madhatters Tea *Sandwiches/Tearoom*

| 22 | 21 | 17 | $17 |

Southtown | 320 Beauregard St. (Alamo St.) | 210-212-4832 | www.madhatterstea.com

"Out-of-the-ordinary compositions" of the sandwiches-and-salads variety match the "quirky", "creative" *Alice's Adventures in Wonderland* theme at this midpriced spot for "tasty breakfasts and lunches" in Southtown; high tea and pastries can make for a particularly "sweet afternoon", especially if you take a table on the "deck scented by pecan trees."

Magnolia Pancake Haus *American*

| 25 | 17 | 22 | $17 |

North Central | Embassy Oaks Shopping Ctr. | 606 Embassy Oaks (West Ave.) | 210-496-0828 | www.magnoliapancakehaus.com

"You're truly missing out" if you don't hit this country-casual North Central American specializing in "excellent" pancakes and other affordable "home cookin'"-style breakfast plates (plus some salads and sandwiches for lunch); just "go early" or "be prepared to wait", especially on weekends when it's "jam-packed"; P.S. open until 2 PM daily.

Max's Wine Dive ● *Eclectic*

| 20 | 16 | 19 | $31 |

Quarry | Quarry Vill. | 340 E. Basse Rd. (Jones Maltsberger Rd.) | 210-444-9547 | www.maxswinedive.com

See review in Houston Directory.

	FOOD	DECOR	SERVICE	COST

NEW Mediterranean Turkish Grill *Turkish* ▽ 20 | 12 | 18 | $30

North Central | North Star Sq. | 8507 McCullough Ave. (Rector Dr.) | 210-399-1645 | www.kmturkishgrill.com

Folks who've tried this Turk in North Central "absolutely love" its meze, kebabs and other specialties; like its nondescript strip-center setting, the decor is far from upscale, but on the plus side, the portions are ample and the prices moderate thanks in part to the no-fee BYO policy.

Mi Tierra Café & Bakery ● *Tex-Mex* 22 | 23 | 21 | $20

Market Square | El Mercado | 218 Produce Row (bet. San Saba & Santa Rosa Sts.) | 210-225-1262 | www.mitierracafe.com

The "fiesta never stops" at this 24/7 Market Square "landmark" decked out in "kitsch" galore with "year-round" Christmas lights, streamers and mariachi guitarists making the rounds; even if some say the Tex-Mex fare's only "ok" and the vibe's "kind of corny", the "strong drinks" redeem, and it's hard to leave here in a "bad mood."

Monterey, The ● *American* - | - | - | I

Southtown | 1127 S. St. Mary's (bet. Pereida & Stieren Sts.) | 210-745-2581 | www.themontereysa.com

"Incredibly inventive" American snacks grab the spotlight at this Southtown spot, a renovated gas station with "limited inside seating" and three times the space on the "great" patio; like the food menu, the considerable wine and beer selection is "affordably priced", just as you would expect from such an "eclectic, casual" environment.

Morton's The Steakhouse *Steak* 26 | 24 | 25 | $67

Downtown | Rivercenter Mall | 300 E. Crockett St. (Bonham St.) | 210-228-0700 | www.mortons.com

See review in Houston Directory.

Myron's Prime Steakhouse *Steak* ▽ 28 | 24 | 25 | $44

NEW **Churchill Estates** | Alon Towne Shopping Ctr. | 10003 NW Military Hwy. (Wurzbach Pkwy.) | 210-493-3031
New Braunfels | 136 N. Castell Ave. (San Antonio St.) | 830-624-1024
www.myronsprime.com

"Tender, juicy" steaks in "great portions" are "worth the price" at this elegant New Braunfels chophouse set in a vintage movie house; the recently opened Churchill Estates sequel brings the same menu, complete with "traditional side dishes and a nice wine list", vibe and "good service" to a San Antonio audience.

NEW Ocho *Pan-Latin* - | - | - | M

Downtown | Hotel Havana | 1015 Navarro St. (St. Mary's St.) | 210-222-2008 | www.havanasanantonio.com

Old-school cocktails are reinvented and paired with creative Pan-Latin small plates and desserts at this new lounge in Downtown's boutique Hotel Havana; of the two distinct seating areas, the bright indoor/outdoor setting upstairs is the more modern, with glass, steel and views of the River Walk, while the candlelit cave downstairs oozes old-world charm.

	FOOD	DECOR	SERVICE	COST

Olmos Park Bistro *French*
▽ 28 | 26 | 29 | $51

Olmos Park | 4331 McCullough Ave. (Earl St.) | 210-826-0222 |
www.bistroatolmospark.com

"Incredible" French savories and "showstopping" desserts come
in "beautiful presentations" and "generous" portions at this
"wonderful neighborhood place" in Olmos Park; the interior is
"casual" enough for a meal with the family, but for a bit of romance,
try the patio.

Oma's Haus *German*
- | - | - | I

New Braunfels | 541 Hwy. 46 S. (Freiheit Rd.) | 830-625-3280 |
www.omashaus.com

This schnitzel *und* strudel house in New Braunfels underscores the
town's German roots with a menu chock-full of Teutonic favorites
(sausage, potato pancakes), while an on-site gift shop and slightly
elevated prices also have a tourist-town bent; regulars know to take
home bakery treats like Black Forest cake and fudge for later.

Ounce Prime Steakhouse *Steak*
▽ 22 | 23 | 18 | $74

Loop 1604 | Vineyard Ctr. | 1401 Loop 1604 NW (Blanco Rd.) |
210-493-6200 | www.ounceprimesteakhouse.com

Quite "a few seating options, from open to private" areas with curtains, mean this sophisticated steakhouse in a Loop 1604 strip center works for everything from "romantic" "special occasions" to
dressy nights out with friends; the menu includes a selection of "unbelievable Akaushi beef", but if you don't "have the budget" for such
"high-priced" wares, consider the "great" centerpiece bar for apps
and "after-work drinks."

Paesanos *Italian*
22 | 23 | 23 | $38

Quarry | Lincoln Heights | 555 E. Basse Rd. (Treeline Park) | 210-828-5191
Paesanos Riverwalk *Italian*
River Walk | 111 W. Crockett St. (Presa St.) | 210-227-2782
Paesanos 1604 *Italian*
Loop 1604 | 3622 Paesanos Pkwy. (Loop 1604) | 210-493-1604
www.joesfood.com

"The shrimp Paesano is legendary" at this "popular", decades-old
Quarry Italian pumping out "dependable" dishes in "comfy" if
"noisy" quarters that "work well with big parties"; despite the same
"wonderful" menu and "accommodating" service at both the 1604
and River Walk spin-offs, loyalists sniff they're "not nearly as good"
as the original.

Palm, The *Steak*
25 | 20 | 24 | $64

Downtown | 233 E. Houston St. (bet. Navarro & St. Mary's Sts.) |
210-226-7256 | www.thepalm.com

Romantics take their "best girl" to this "old-school" chophouse
chain for "fabulous" steaks and seafood set down by an "excellent" staff in "classy" quarters adorned with celebrity carica-
tures; it's also a mainstay for "business" events and pre-game
meals – just "allow an extra notch" in your belt since "everything's
huge", including the tab.

Paloma Blanca *Mexican*

25 | 25 | 23 | $27

Alamo Heights | Cambridge Shopping Ctr. | 5800 Broadway St. (Circle St.) | 210-822-6151 | www.palomablanca.net

"Not your run-of-the-mill" Tex-Mex, this Alamo Heights fixture features "fabulous", "high-end" interior Mexican cooking (the "freshly made salsa's so good you'll eat two baskets of chips without realizing it") and "sublime", "strong" margaritas; a "lovely" space with an inviting patio makes it easy to overlook sometimes "snooty" service.

Pappadeaux *Cajun/Seafood*

23 | 20 | 21 | $32

Loop 410 | 76 NE Loop 410 (bet. Jones Maltsberger Rd. & McCullough Ave.) | 210-340-7143 | www.pappadeaux.com
See review in Houston Directory.

Pappasito's Cantina *Tex-Mex*

24 | 19 | 20 | $26

Northwest | 10501 I-10 W. (bet. Huebner & Wurzbach Rds.) | 210-691-8974 | www.pappasitos.com
See review in Houston Directory.

Pei Wei Asian Diner *Asian*

20 | 16 | 18 | $16

Loop 1604 | Northwoods Shopping Ctr. | 1802 Loop 1604 NE (Rte. 281) | 210-507-9160
Northwest | The Strand | 11267 Huebner Rd. (bet. Expo Blvd. & McDermott Frwy.) | 210-561-5600
Northwest | 11398 Bandera Rd. (Brae Ridge Dr.) | 210-523-0040
Quarry | Shops at Lincoln Heights | 999 E. Basse Rd. (Broadway St.) | 210-507-3600
San Antonio West | 430 Loop 1604 NW (Potranco Rd.) | 210-507-5520
www.peiwei.com
See review in Dallas/Ft. Worth Directory.

NEW Perry's Steakhouse & Grille *Steak*

26 | 26 | 25 | $55

La Cantera | The Shops at La Cantera | 15900 La Cantera Pkwy. (Loop 1604) | 210-558-6161 | www.perryssteakhouse.com
See review in Houston Directory.

P.F. Chang's China Bistro *Chinese*

21 | 21 | 21 | $29

La Cantera | The Shops at La Cantera | 15900 La Cantera Pkwy. (Loop 1604) | 210-507-6500
Quarry | Alamo Quarry Mkt. | 255 E. Basse Rd. (bet. Hwy. 281 & Jones Maltsberger Rd.) | 210-507-1000
www.pfchangs.com
See review in Dallas/Ft. Worth Directory.

Piatti *Italian*

24 | 21 | 21 | $33

Quarry | Alamo Quarry Mkt. | 255 E. Basse Rd. (bet. Hwy. 281 & Jones Maltsberger Rd.) | 210-832-0300 | www.piatti.com

Quarry diners are "pleasantly surprised" that the fare at this Italian chain link is "prepared to high standards", served via such "attentive" staffers and priced so reasonably, especially the "great prix fixe dinner" including three courses and a glass of wine; a "high noise level" is the norm in the "busy", airy setting with fireplace and bar, so for intimate conversation, the patio may be "a better choice."

Picnikins Patio Café 🅱 African/American ▽ 24 | 15 | 22 | $22

North Central | Blanco Junction Shopping Ctr. | 6901 Blanco Rd.
(Loop 410) | 210-616-0954 | www.picnikinspatiocafe.com

By day, this bright, bustling, "simple" North Central storefront
serves "yummy", value-priced American soups, salads and sandwiches; by night, it transforms into an inviting bistro offering "excellent" dinners, some of which feature "interesting" South African
inspiration, all ferried by "nice people."

NEW Q on the Riverwalk BBQ ▽ 24 | 21 | 22 | $44

River Walk | Hyatt Regency San Antonio | 123 Losoya St. (bet. College &
Crockett Sts.) | 210-222-1234 | www.sanantonioregency.hyatt.com

"Not the usual hotel restaurant", this venue in the River Walk's
Hyatt Regency smokes and grills a global array of barbecue, from
Texas brisket to Brazilian churrasco to Korean kalbi; though it's located in the lobby, the modern setting with a view into the kitchen is
a bright spot, as is the "solicitous service"; P.S. breakfast is also offered and, like lunch, it's a buffet.

NEW Restaurant ▽ 27 | 24 | 25 | $65
Gwendolyn 🅱🅼 American

Downtown | 152 E. Pecan St. (St. Mary's St.) | 210-222-1849 |
www.restaurantgwendolyn.com

Food is cooked like it was before the Industrial Revolution (no mix-
ers, deep fryers or anything with a motor), and "if the vegetables
and meat don't come from the local area, you won't find them" on
the menu – that's the unique "culinary credo" of this "wonderful"
Downtown American where the preparations are as "superb" tasting as they are "strong on healthy options"; though the fare, offered
only in three- and five-course prix fixe dinners, "seems a bit pricey"
to some, the experience comes complete with "personalized service" and a quaint (read: "quite small") setting that reflects the
rustic Victorian concept.

Roaring Fork Southwestern 24 | 25 | 24 | $36

Loop 1604 | Plaza Las Campanas | 1806 Loop 1604 NW (bet. Blanco &
Huebner Rds.) | 210-479-9700 | www.roaringfork.com

See review in Austin and the Hill Country Directory.

NEW Rolling Pig 🅼 BBQ - | - | - | I

Location Varies; see website | 210-667-5246 | www.rollingpigsatx.com

The wide world of pork – from bacon pancakes to Boudin balls, boar
burgers and schnitzel – stars daily at this well-priced mobile swine
station focusing on local, seasonal ingredients; look for it at the corner of Nacogdoches and 410 during lunch or the Quarry Farmers
Market on selected Sundays.

Rosario's Mexican 24 | 19 | 21 | $26

Southtown | 910 S. Alamo St. (St. Mary's St.) | 210-223-1806 |
www.rosariossa.com

The "crowds don't lie" – the affordable Mex whipped up at this
"friendly" Southtown "hot spot" is "amazing", not to mention "au-

thentic" "right down to the tripe and sweetbreads"; with vibrant colors and local art to add visual interest, it's the sort of place that locals "take visitors to – but "don't bring your grandparents", because the vast space with a "great bar", weekend live music and general *fiesta* feel means it gets "stunningly loud" in here.

☑ Rudy's *BBQ*   25 | 16 | 20 | $16

Selma | 15560 I-35 N. (Evans Rd.) | 210-653-7839
Westside | 10623 Westover Hills Blvd. (Hwy. 151) | 210-520-5552
Leon Springs | 24152 I-10 W. (Boerne Stage Rd.) | 210-698-2141
www.rudys.com

You can smell the smoke from "a mile away" at these "solid-as-a-rock" chain pit stops doling out "tender" BBQ brisket ("go for the extra moist") and "mouthwatering ribs" sided with "amazing" "signature creamed corn"; most are set in refurbished gas stations, so you can line up "cafeteria-style", "order by the pound" and fill up your tank on the way out – talk about "true fast food."

Ruth's Chris Steak House *Steak*   26 | 22 | 25 | $63

Downtown | St. Paul Sq. | 1170 E. Commerce St. (I-37) | 210-227-8847
North Central | Concord Plaza | 7720 Jones Maltsberger Rd.
(McAllister Frwy.) | 210-821-5051
www.ruthschris.com

"Always a hit with the expense-account crowd", this "steadfast" chain "pampers" patrons with "thick", "buttery" steaks and "top-notch" service in "clubby" surroundings; it all adds up to a "quality" experience, though one with "few surprises, positive or negative."

Sandbar Fish House & Market ☒Ⓜ *Seafood*   27 | 23 | 23 | $41

Near North | Pearl Brewery | 200 E. Grayson St. (Karnes St.) |
210-212-2221 | www.sandbarsa.com

"Every single dish is crafted with total precision" and tastes "superb" at this Near North seafooder overseen by Andrew Weissman (Il Sogno); its steel-and-white-tile locale in the Pearl Brewery complex is "a little stark" and the tabs are a bit "pricey", but don't let that deter you – it's unquestionably "worth it."

Scenic Loop Café *American/Tex-Mex*   23 | 19 | 21 | $35

Leon Springs | 25615 Boerne Stage Rd. (Scenic Loop Rd.) |
210-687-1818 | www.scenicloopcafe.com

Day-trippers trot out to this "off-the-beaten-track" Hill Country cafe adjacent to the Rose Palace in Leon Springs (and its occasional wafting "horse fragrance") for "good" renditions of moderately priced American and Tex-Mex fare; on weekends, the patio bar gets a lift from live music while kids jump around in the spacious outdoor play area.

Schilo's Delicatessen ☒ *Deli*   24 | 18 | 20 | $17

Downtown | 424 E. Commerce St. (Presa St.) | 210-223-6692 |
www.schilos.com

On the San Antonio scene since 1917, this Downtown deli "landmark" is "the place to go" for "overstuffed sandwiches", soups, strudels and other "hearty", "German-style" delicacies washed down with "old-time" homemade root beer; well-worn tables and brew signs help maintain the original feel, while the "bargain" prices are refreshingly retro to boot; P.S. closes at 8:30 PM.

Sea Island Shrimp House *Seafood*   26 | 17 | 19 | $17

Selma | The Forum | 8223 Agora Pkwy. (bet. Forum Pkwy. & Phoenix Ave.) | 210-658-1100
Loop 410 | 322 W. Rector St. (San Pedro Ave.) | 210-342-7771
Northwest | 10303 IH 10 W. (McDermott Frwy.) | 210-558-8989
Northwest | Bandera Pointe Shopping Ctr. | 11715 Bandera Rd. (Loop 1604) | 210-681-7000
Northwest | 5959 NW Loop 410 (Roxbury Dr.) | 210-520-3033
Southside | 2119 SW Military Dr. (I-35) | 210-921-9700
www.shrimphouse.com

The Loop 410 locale has "been packing them in for over 40 years", but all branches of this "famous San Antonio chain" are "crowded" with folks "waiting to order" its "great shrimp" and other "wonderful seafood"; devotees opine that "if they put white tablecloths on the table, they could triple the price", but as it stands now, the nautically themed digs are casual and the rates are "reasonable" – no wonder it's a "favorite family destination."

☑ Silo *American*   27 | 25 | 26 | $41

Alamo Heights | 1133 Austin Hwy. (Mt. Calvary Dr.) | 210-824-8686

☑ Silo 1604 *American*

Loop 1604 | Ventura Plaza | 434 N. Loop 1604 NW (off Access Rd. 1604) | 210-483-8989
www.siloelevatedcuisine.com

Admirers attest it's "impossible to go wrong" at this Alamo Heights bistro or its Loop 1604 spin-off serving up "surprising" New American fare in "chic" digs blessed with "cool" bar scenes; tabs are "pricey, but not outrageous" – no wonder both are so "popular."

☑ Sorrento ☒ *Italian*   27 | 17 | 23 | $29

Alamo Heights | 5146 Broadway St. (Grove Pl.) | 210-824-0055 | www.sorrentopizzeria.com

"Great" pizza is the highlight of this Alamo Heights Italian with a ristorante component preparing antipasti, pastas and entrees; wallet-friendly prices match the "homey, comfortable" environment, with red-checkered tablecloths and "families" galore.

Stonewerks Big Rock Grill *American*   20 | 21 | 20 | $23

La Cantera | The Rim | 5807 Worth Pkwy. (Talavera Ridge) | 210-558-9898
Loop 1604 | Vineyard Ctr. | 1201 Loop 1604 NW (Blanco Rd.) | 210-764-0400

Stonewerks Caffe *American*

Quarry | 999 E. Basse Rd. (Broadway St.) | 210-828-3508
www.stonewerks.com

There's "something for everyone" at this "fun" American grill trio turning out "pretty good" eats ("sandwiches as big as my head") that go down well with beer; the sports-bar ambiance is "perfect for happy hour or to watch a game", although with cover bands on weekends, it's certainly not the place for a "quiet dinner"; P.S. the patio seating at some locales is slightly tamer.

Sushihana *Japanese*

▽ 28 | 21 | 25 | $30

Castle Hills | 1810 Military Hwy. NW (Moss Dr.) | 210-340-7808 | www.sushihanasan.com

Sushi purists praise this "best-kept secret" in quiet Castle Hills where "delicious", "fresh" fin fare, "delicate" tempura and "amazing" Japanese fusion items are pumped out of an open kitchen; the "cozy" atmosphere is enhanced by "fabulous" service, making it a "favorite" for many.

Sushi Zushi *Japanese*

23 | 20 | 20 | $30

Downtown | 203 S. St. Mary's St. (Market St.) | 210-472-2900
Alamo Heights | Shops at Lincoln Heights | 999 E. Basse Rd. (Broadway St.) | 210-826-8500
Northwest | The Colonnade | 9867 I-10 W. (Wurzbach Rd.) | 210-691-3332
Stone Oak | Stone Oak Plaza | 18720 Stone Oak Pkwy. (Loop 1604) | 210-545-6100
www.sushizushi.com

Despite the "funny name" there's some "serious sushi" at this "sleek" Japanese chainlet delivering an "immense" (almost "overwhelming") array of "tasty", "imaginative" raw fare at prices that won't "bust your wallet"; service can be "spotty" depending on the locale, but delivery redeems, as do the relatively "late" hours.

Taco Taco *Tex-Mex*

25 | 7 | 18 | $11

Olmos Park | 145 E. Hildebrand Ave. (bet. McCullough & San Pedro Aves.) | 210-822-9533 | www.tacotacosa.com

"Awesome" Tex-Mex at bargain prices and a compact space add up to "long lines to get in" the door of this family-owned Olmos Park eatery; it may not be much to look at, but that doesn't deter devotees who tout it as "maybe the best bargain in America"; P.S. it's open for breakfast and lunch only (until 2 PM).

NEW Tejas Steakhouse & Saloon Ⓜ *Steak*

– | – | – | M

Northeast | 401 Obst Rd. (Specht Rd.) | 830-980-2205 | www.tejassteakhouse.com

This arrival in far Northeast rural Bulverde delivers a full-on cowboy experience without kitsch, complete with a pro rodeo competition out back and antique Western decor; the kitchen confidently handles campfire fare, weaving family recipes and formal training into a relatively affordable meal; cowboys mosey in after the rodeo, so stick around for a few beers; P.S. open Thursdays–Sundays only.

Teka Molino Ⓢ *Tex-Mex*

– | – | – | I

Near North | 7231 San Pedro Ave. (bet. Langton Dr. & Southbridge St.) | 210-344-7281 | www.tekamolino.com

This is one of the city's oldest (since 1937) and most popular bargain Tex-Mex haunts, famous for its house-milled corn masa, big breakfast tacos and heaping combo plates; the interior is utilitarian and the convenient Near North locale with fast drive-thru makes it easy to get hooked.

Texas de Brazil *Brazilian*   24 | 22 | 22 | $50

Downtown | Kress Bldg. | 313 E. Houston St. (bet. Navarro & Presa Sts.) | no phone | www.texasdebrazil.com

See review in Dallas/Ft. Worth Directory.

Tiago's Cabo Grill *Mexican/Tex-Mex*   ∇ 20 | 19 | 22 | $20

La Cantera | The Rim | 17711 I-10 W. (La Cantera Pkwy.) | 210-881-2700
Northwest | Shops at Westpointe | 8403 Hwy. 151 (I-410) | 210-647-3600
www.tiagoscabogrille.com

While fans praise Tex-Mex offerings such as the "flavorful" mahi mahi taco at this duo in La Cantera and the Northwest, some "go just for the Mexican chocolate cake", so "outrageously enticing" it'll "transport you to a happy planet"; the "upscale environment" and moderate prices make it "good for a date night."

Timbo's ⊠ *Burgers*   – | – | – | I

Near North | 1639 Broadway St. (Pearl Pkwy.) | 210-223-1028 | www.timbosburgers.com

Midpriced burger and beer joint in a tucked-away Near North strip adjacent to the busy Pearl complex; the space is all done up in Texas memorabilia and features compact booths with jukeboxes plus picnic tables outside.

Tip Top Cafe Ⓜ🍴 *American*   24 | 12 | 22 | $16

Northwest | 2814 Fredericksburg Rd. (Santa Anna St.) | 210-732-0191 | www.tiptopcafe.com

Sentimentalists swoon over this Northwest "roadhouse", a San Antonio "tradition" since 1938 for "classic" American "comfort food" like pot roast, chicken-fried steak and banana-cream pie dished out by a staff "as old as the building"; given the low prices, "you can't go wrong", unless you're counting "calories."

Torres Taco Haven *Mexican*   – | – | – | I

Southtown | 3119 S. Gevers St. (Greer St.) | 210-532-3049
Southside | 1032 S. Presa St. (bet. Labor & St. Mary's Sts.) | 210-533-2171
www.tacohaven.info

Those in the know say these family-friendly Southside and Southtown Mexican twins are "worth driving across town" for fresh tortillas and "breakfasts all day" at prices that are easy on the wallet; the Southtown outlet is open until 10 PM.

Tre Trattoria ⊠ *Italian*   24 | 24 | 23 | $35

Near North | The Boardwalk | 4003 Broadway St. (bet. Allensworth St. & Thorman Pl.) | 210-805-0333

Tre Trattoria Downtown *American*

Downtown | Fairmount Hotel | 401 S. Alamo St. (Nueva St.) | 210-223-0401
www.tretrattoria.com

These midpriced "Tuscan-inspired" twins in Downtown and Near North from chef-owner Jason Dady (Bin 555, Two Brothers) dish out

	FOOD	DECOR	SERVICE	COST

"satisfying" "family-style" meals, backed by "generous" wine pours and "well-crafted" cocktails; a trendy setting with a "comfortable" bar and outdoor seating plus "outstanding" service prompt many to declare "you can't go wrong here."

20nine Restaurant & Wine Bar *Californian*   23 | 23 | 22 | $39

Quarry | Alamo Quarry Mkt. | 255 E. Basse Rd. (bet. Hwy. 281 & Jones Maltsberger Rd.) | 210-798-9463 | www.20ninewine.com

"Cozy" Quarry wine bar putting out Californian snacks like flatbread pizzas and housemade charcuterie in a "cool, low-lit" setting; it boasts a "wonderful wine list that offers options at all price ranges", and the overall vibe's "not pretentious" either.

Two Bros. BBQ Market *BBQ*   19 | 14 | 21 | $20

North Central | 12656 West Ave. (North Loop Rd.) | 210-496-0222 | www.twobrosbbqmarket.com

"Updated" BBQ is served up in a "kid-friendly" setting with a porch, a playground and frequent live music at this North Central San Antonio 'cue shop from Jason Dady (Lodge, Bin 555) and his brother, Jake; prices are low, though some find the fare ultimately "unsatisfying."

Urban Taco *Mexican*   20 | 18 | 17 | $20

Quarry | Quarry Vill. | 290 E. Basse Rd. (Jones Maltsberger Rd.) | 210-332-5149 | www.urban-taco.com

See review in Dallas/Ft. Worth Directory.

NEW Vegeria ⓢ *Vegan*   - | - | - | I

Alamo Heights | Viva Book Complex | 8407 Broadway St. (Loop 410) | 210-826-4223 | www.myvegeria.com

Vegan to the core, this sunny Alamo Heights Mex-American is earning a devoted following with its green-chile lentil burgers, mushroom tacos and smattering of raw items; both the setting and the prices transport to 1970s Berkeley; P.S. there's also a bakery counter with vegan sweets to go.

Welfare Café Ⓜ *Eclectic*   - | - | - | M

Boerne | 223 Waring-Welfare Rd. (Little Joshua Creek Rd.) | 830-537-3700 | www.welfaretexas.com

"Way out" on a country road outside of small-town Boerne, this "rustic" hideaway set in a former post office now delivers an Eclectic lineup of "big-city food", from steaks to spring rolls to schnitzel; alas, it's "far from home" for many, but a garden patio, live music and family-style Sunday dinners make it a fair-weather weekend destination; it's also becoming a popular spot for weddings.

Wildfish Seafood Grille *American/Seafood*   25 | 23 | 22 | $42

Loop 1604 | Plaza Las Campanas | 1834 Loop 1604 NW (Huebner Rd.) | 210-493-1600 | www.wildfishseafoodgrille.com

A "well-heeled clientele" fills up this "wildly popular" Loop 1604 New American chain link spotlighting "fresh" seafood prepared "with a light touch", as well as extensive raw bar selections; the bar boasts a "major singles scene" – "daunting" acoustics included – so those in the know seek solace on the patio "in nice weather."

Zinc Bistro + Wine Bar ◑ *American*   _ | _ | _ | M

Downtown | 207 N. Presa St. (bet. Commerce & Market Sts.) | 210-224-2900 | www.zincwine.com

A "hidden treasure" for drinks and nibbles Downtown, this reasonably priced bistro and bar offers an edited but interesting New American menu of shared and big plates, plus a deep collection of wines, champagnes, vintage ports and specialty cocktails; the casual yet sophisticated setting in a cozy, historic off-river building is augmented by a large, breezy patio.

Z'Tejas *Southwestern*   22 | 22 | 21 | $28

La Cantera | The Shops at La Cantera | 15900 La Cantera Pkwy. (Loop 1604) | 210-690-3334 | www.ztejas.com
See review in Austin and the Hill Country Directory.

SAN ANTONIO
INDEXES

Cuisines

Includes names, locations and Food ratings.

AMERICAN

Auden's Kitchen | **Stone Oak**	23
Z Biga/Banks | **River Walk**	26
Bin 555 | **N Central**	23
NEW Boehler's | **Near North**	19
Z Bohanan's | **Downtown**	27
Cappyccino's | **Alamo Hts**	25
Cappy's | **Alamo Hts**	26
Cheesecake | **multi.**	20
Chesters | **multi.**	24
Cibolo Moon | **NE**	-
Citrus | **Downtown**	26
Cove | **Near North**	23
Cypress Grille | **Boerne**	24
NEW Drew's | **Stone Oak**	-
DUK | **Location Varies**	-
NEW Feast | **Southtown**	-
Z Grey Moss Inn | **Helotes**	27
Z Gristmill | **New Braunfels**	21
Guenther Hse. | **Southtown**	22
Huisache | **New Braunfels**	28
Josephine St. | **Near North**	25
Z Las Canarias | **River Walk**	26
Magnolia Pancake | **N Central**	25
Monterey | **Southtown**	-
Picnikins Patio | **N Central**	24
NEW Rest. Gwendolyn | **Downtown**	27
Scenic Loop | **Leon Springs**	23
Z Silo | **multi.**	27
Stonewerks | **multi.**	20
Tip Top Cafe | **NW**	24
Wildfish | **Loop 1604**	25
Zinc Bistro | **Downtown**	-

ASIAN

Frederick's | **multi.**	26
Pei Wei | **multi.**	20

BAKERIES

Bistro Bakery/Café Artistes | **Olmos Pk**	24
CIA Bakery | **Near North**	25

BARBECUE

Cooper's BBQ | **New Braunfels**	25
County Line | **multi.**	21
NEW Q/Riverwalk | **River Walk**	24
NEW Rolling Pig | **Location Varies**	-
Z Rudy's | **multi.**	25
Two Bros. BBQ | **N Central**	19

BELGIAN

La Frite | **Southtown**	26

BRAZILIAN

Z Chama Gaucha | **Stone Oak**	25
Z Fogo/Chão | **Downtown**	25
Texas/Brazil | **Downtown**	24

BURGERS

Big'z Burger | **Loop 1604**	23
Chesters | **multi.**	24
Chris Madrid's | **Near North**	24
Cove | **Near North**	23
Z Five Guys | **multi.**	22
Gourmet Burger | **multi.**	27
Timbo's | **Near North**	-

CAJUN

Pappadeaux | **Loop 410**	23

CALIFORNIAN

20nine | **Quarry**	23

CHINESE

(* dim sum specialist)

Formosa Gdn. | **N Central**	23
Golden Wok* | **multi.**	20
P.F. Chang's | **multi.**	21

CONTINENTAL

Fig Tree | **River Walk**	24

DELIS

Schilo's Deli | **Downtown**	24

DESSERT

Cheesecake | **multi.**	20
Coco Chocolate | **N Central**	23

ECLECTIC

Cappy's | **Alamo Hts**	26
Citrus | **Downtown**	26
Dodging Duck | **Boerne**	-
Grill/Leon Springs | **Leon Springs**	25
La Tuna Grill | **Southtown**	23
Liberty Bar | **Southtown**	23
Max's | **Quarry**	20
NEW Rolling Pig | **Location Varies**	-
Welfare Café | **Boerne**	-

FRENCH

Bistro Bakery/Café Artistes | **Downtown**	24
🔲 Bistro Vatel | **Olmos Pk**	28
Coco Chocolate | **N Central**	23
Frederick's | **multi.**	26
Lüke | **Downtown**	22
Olmos Park | **Olmos Pk**	28

GERMAN

Lüke | **Downtown**	22
Oma's Haus | **New Braunfels**	-

INDIAN

India Oven | **N Central**	24

ITALIAN

(N=Northern)

Aldino | **Loop 1604**	21
Aldo's | N | **Medical Ctr**	24
Barbaresco | **N Central**	19
Carrabba's | **NW**	23
Ciao | **Olmos Pk**	24
🔲 Dough | **N Central**	27
Il Sogno | **Near North**	27
Luce Rist. | **NW**	23
Paesanos | **multi.**	22
Piatti | **Quarry**	24
🔲 Sorrento | **Alamo Hts**	27
Tre Trattoria | N | **multi.**	24

JAPANESE

(* sushi specialist)

Godai* | **N Central**	28
Sushihana* | **Castle Hills**	28
Sushi Zushi* | **multi.**	23

MEDITERRANEAN

Boardwalk Bistro | **Near North**	23
🆕 Med. Turkish Grill | **N Central**	20

MEXICAN

Aldaco's | **Downtown**	-
Aldaco's-Stone Oak | **Stone Oak**	20
El Bucanero | **East Side**	-
El Jarro/Arturo | **North**	23
El Mirador | **Southtown**	22
El Mirasol/Soluna | **multi.**	-
La Fogata | **North**	22
La Fonda | **Near North**	21
La Gloria | **Near North**	23
Paloma Blanca | **Alamo Hts**	25
Rosario's | **Southtown**	24
Tiago's | **multi.**	20
Torres Taco | **multi.**	-
Urban Taco | **Quarry**	20

NUEVO LATINO

Azúca | **Southtown**	22

PAN-LATIN

🆕 Ocho | **Downtown**	-

PERSIAN

Jerusalem Grill | **West Side**	24

PIZZA

🔲 Dough | **N Central**	27
Grimaldi's | **multi.**	26

PUB FOOD

🆕 Esquire Tav. | **Downtown**	-

SANDWICHES

(See also Delis)

Madhatters | **Southtown**	22
Picnikins Patio | **N Central**	24

SEAFOOD

🔲 Boudro's | **River Walk**	24
🔲 Chart Hse. | **Downtown**	15
El Bucanero | **East Side**	-
Pappadeaux | **Loop 410**	23
Sandbar | **Near North**	27
Sea Island | **multi.**	26
Wildfish | **Loop 1604**	25

SMALL PLATES

Bin 555 | Amer. | **N Central**	23
🔲 Bohanan's | Amer. | **Downtown**	27
🆕 Esquire Tav. | Eclectic | **Downtown**	-
🆕 Feast | British | **Southtown**	-
Jerusalem Grill | Mideast. | **West Side**	24
La Gloria | Mex. | **Near North**	23
Max's | Eclectic | **Quarry**	20
🆕 Med. Turkish Grill | Turkish | **N Central**	20
Monterey | Amer. | **Southtown**	-
🆕 Ocho | Pan-Latin | **Downtown**	-
Zinc Bistro | Amer. | **Downtown**	-

SOUTH AFRICAN

Picnikins Patio | **N Central**	24

SOUTH AMERICAN

Beto's Comida | **North**	21

SOUTHWESTERN

Antlers Lodge | **West Side**	24
Canyon Café | **Quarry**	20
Francesca's | **La Cantera**	26

Roaring Fork | **Loop 1604** 24

Z'Tejas | **La Cantera** 22

STEAKHOUSES

Barn Door	**Alamo Hts**	22
☑ Bohanan's	**Downtown**	27
☑ Boudro's	**River Walk**	24
☑ Chama Gaucha	**Stone Oak**	25
18 Oaks Stkhse.	**NE**	23
Fleming's Prime	**Quarry**	25
☑ Fogo/Chão	**Downtown**	25
Kirby's	**Loop 1604**	24
Little Rhein	**River Walk**	21
Morton's	**Downtown**	26
Myron's Prime	**multi.**	28
Ounce	**Loop 1604**	22
Palm	**Downtown**	25
Perry's Steak	**La Cantera**	26
Ruth's Chris	**multi.**	26
NEW Tejas Steak	**NE**	-
Texas/Brazil	**Downtown**	24

TEAROOMS

Madhatters | **Southtown** 22

TEX-MEX

Ácenar	**River Walk**	22
Alamo Café	**multi.**	21
Chuy's	**North**	21
La Hacienda/Los Barrios	**North**	22
La Margarita	**Market Sq**	24
Mi Tierra	**Market Sq**	22
Pappasito's	**NW**	24
Scenic Loop	**Leon Springs**	23
Taco Taco	**Olmos Pk**	25
Teka Molino	**Near North**	-
Tiago's	**multi.**	20

THAI

Asia Kitchen | **West Side** 24

TURKISH

Jerusalem Grill | **West Side** 24

NEW Med. Turkish Grill | 20
N Central

VEGETARIAN

(* vegan)

Green Veg. | **multi.** -

NEW Vegeria* | **Alamo Hts** -

Locations

includes names, cuisines and Food ratings.

San Antonio Central

DOWNTOWN

Aldaco's	*Mex.*	-_
Bistro Bakery/Café Artistes	*French*	24
☑ Bohanan's	*Amer./Steak*	27
☑ Chart Hse.	*Seafood*	15
Citrus	*Amer./Eclectic*	26
NEW Esquire Tav.	*Pub*	-_
☑ Fogo/Chão	*Brazilian/Steak*	25
Green Veg.	*Veg.*	-_
Lüke	*French/German*	22
Morton's	*Steak*	26
NEW Ocho	*Pan-Latin*	-_
Palm	*Steak*	25
NEW Rest. Gwendolyn	*Amer.*	27
Ruth's Chris	*Steak*	26
Schilo's Deli	*Deli*	24
Sushi Zushi	*Japanese*	23
Texas/Brazil	*Brazilian*	24
Tre Trattoria	*Amer.*	24
Zinc Bistro	*Amer.*	-_

MARKET SQUARE

La Margarita	*Tex-Mex*	24
Mi Tierra	*Tex-Mex*	22

RIVER WALK

Ácenar	*Tex-Mex*	22
☑ Biga/Banks	*Amer.*	26
☑ Boudro's	*Seafood/Steak*	24
County Line	*BBQ*	21
Fig Tree	*Continental*	24
☑ Las Canarias	*Amer.*	26
Little Rhein	*Steak*	21
Paesanos	*Italian*	22
NEW Q/Riverwalk	*BBQ*	24

SOUTHTOWN

Azúca	*Nuevo Latino*	22
El Mirador	*Mex.*	22
NEW Feast	*Amer.*	-_
Guenther Hse.	*Amer.*	22
La Frite	*Belgian*	26
La Tuna Grill	*Eclectic*	23
Liberty Bar	*Eclectic*	23
Madhatters	*Sandwiches/Tea*	22
Monterey	*Amer.*	-_
Rosario's	*Mex.*	24
Torres Taco	*Mex.*	-_

San Antonio East

EASTSIDE

El Bucanero	*Mex./Seafood*	-_

SELMA

☑ Five Guys	*Burgers*	22
☑ Rudy's	*BBQ*	25
Sea Island	*Seafood*	26

San Antonio North

ALAMO HEIGHTS

Barn Door	*Steak*	22
Cappyccino's	*Amer.*	25
Cappy's	*Amer./Eclectic*	26
Frederick's	*Asian/French*	26
Paloma Blanca	*Mex.*	25
☑ Silo	*Amer.*	27
El Mirasol/Soluna	*Mex.*	-_
☑ Sorrento	*Italian*	27
Sushi Zushi	*Japanese*	23
NEW Vegeria	*Vegan*	-_

BOERNE

Cypress Grille	*Amer.*	24
Dodging Duck	*Eclectic*	-_
Welfare Café	*Eclectic*	-_

CASTLE HILLS

Sushihana	*Japanese*	28

CHURCHILL ESTATES

El Mirasol/Soluna	*Mex.*	-_
Frederick's	*Asian/French*	26
Green Veg.	*Veg.*	-_
Myron's Prime	*Steak*	28

HELOTES

☑ Grey Moss Inn	*Amer.*	27

LA CANTERA

Cheesecake	*Amer.*	20
Francesca's	*SW*	26
Grimaldi's	*Pizza*	26
Perry's Steak	*Steak*	26
P.F. Chang's	*Chinese*	21
Stonewerks	*Amer.*	20
Tiago's	*Mex./Tex-Mex*	20
Z'Tejas	*SW*	22

LOOP 1604

Aldino | *Italian* — 21
Big'z Burger | *Burgers* — 23
Kirby's | *Steak* — 24
Ounce | *Steak* — 22
Paesanos | *Italian* — 22
Pei Wei | *Asian* — 20
Roaring Fork | *SW* — 24
Ƶ Silo | *Amer.* — 27
Stonewerks | *Amer.* — 20
Wildfish | *Amer./Seafood* — 25

LOOP 410

Cheesecake | *Amer.* — 20
Chesters | *Burgers* — 24
Pappadeaux | *Cajun/Seafood* — 23
Sea Island | *Seafood* — 26

MEDICAL CENTER

Aldo's | *Italian* — 24
Golden Wok | *Chinese* — 20

NEAR NORTH

Boardwalk Bistro | *Med.* — 23
NEW Boehler's | *Amer.* — 19
Chris Madrid's | *Burgers* — 24
CIA Bakery | *Bakery* — 25
Cove | *Amer.* — 23
Il Sogno | *Italian* — 27
Josephine St. | *Amer.* — 25
La Fonda | *Mex.* — 21
La Gloria | *Mex.* — 23
Sandbar | *Seafood* — 27
Teka Molino | *Tex-Mex* — ‒
Timbo's | *Burgers* — ‒
Tre Trattoria | *Italian* — 24

NEW BRAUNFELS

Cooper's BBQ | *BBQ* — 25
Ƶ Gristmill | *Amer.* — 21
Huisache | *Amer.* — 28
Myron's Prime | *Steak* — 28
Oma's Haus | *German* — ‒

NORTH

Alamo Café | *Tex-Mex* — 21
Beto's Comida | *S Amer.* — 21
Chesters | *Burgers* — 24
Chuy's | *Tex-Mex* — 21
El Jarro/Arturo | *Mex.* — 23
Gourmet Burger | *Burgers* — 27
La Fogata | *Mex.* — 22
La Hacienda/Los Barrios | *Tex-Mex* — 22

NORTH CENTRAL

Barbaresco | *Italian* — 19
Bin 555 | *Amer.* — 23
Coco Chocolate | *Dessert/French* — 23
Ƶ Dough | *Pizza* — 27
Formosa Gdn. | *Chinese* — 23
Godai | *Japanese* — 28
Gourmet Burger | *Burgers* — 27
India Oven | *Indian* — 24
Magnolia Pancake | *Amer.* — 25
NEW Med. Turkish Grill | *Turkish* — 20
Picnikins Patio | *African/Amer.* — 24
Ruth's Chris | *Steak* — 26
Two Bros. BBQ | *BBQ* — 19

NORTHEAST

Cibolo Moon | *Amer.* — ‒
18 Oaks Stkhse. | *Steak* — 23
NEW Tejas Steak | *Steak* — ‒

NORTHWEST

Alamo Café | *Tex-Mex* — 21
Carrabba's | *Italian* — 23
Chesters | *Burgers* — 24
County Line | *BBQ* — 21
Luce Rist. | *Italian* — 23
Pappasito's | *Tex-Mex* — 24
Pei Wei | *Asian* — 20
Sea Island | *Seafood* — 26
Sushi Zushi | *Japanese* — 23
Tiago's | *Mex./Tex-Mex* — 20
Tip Top Cafe | *Amer.* — 24

OLMOS PARK

Bistro Bakery/Café Artistes | *Bakery* — 24
Ƶ Bistro Vatel | *French* — 28
Ciao | *Italian* — 24
Olmos Park | *French* — 28
Taco Taco | *Tex-Mex* — 25

QUARRY

Canyon Café | *SW* — 20
Ƶ Five Guys | *Burgers* — 22
Fleming's Prime | *Steak* — 25
Grimaldi's | *Pizza* — 26
Max's | *Eclectic* — 20
Paesanos | *Italian* — 22
Pei Wei | *Asian* — 20
P.F. Chang's | *Chinese* — 21
Piatti | *Italian* — 24
Stonewerks | *Amer.* — 20
20nine | *Calif.* — 23
Urban Taco | *Mex.* — 20

STONE OAK

Aldaco's-Stone Oak	*Mex.*	20
Auden's Kitchen	*Amer.*	23
Z Chama Gaucha	*Brazilian/Steak*	25
NEW Drew's	*Amer.*	-
Sushi Zushi	*Japanese*	23

San Antonio South

SOUTHSIDE

Sea Island	*Seafood*	26
Torres Taco	*Mex.*	-

San Antonio West

LEON SPRINGS

Grill/Leon Springs	*Eclectic*	25
Z Rudy's	*BBQ*	25
Scenic Loop	*Amer./Tex-Mex*	23

WESTSIDE

Antlers Lodge	*SW*	24
Asia Kitchen	*Thai*	24
Z Five Guys	*Burgers*	22
Golden Wok	*Chinese*	20
Jerusalem Grill	*Mideast.*	24
Pei Wei	*Asian*	20
Z Rudy's	*BBQ*	25

SAN ANTONIO

LOCATIONS

Special Features

Listings cover the best in each category and include names, locations and Food ratings. Multi-location restaurants' features may vary by branch.

BREAKFAST

(See also Hotel Dining)

El Mirador | **Southtown**	22
Guenther Hse. | **Southtown**	22
La Hacienda/Los Barrios | **North**	22
Magnolia Pancake | **N Central**	25
Mi Tierra | **Market Sq**	22
Schilo's Deli | **Downtown**	24
Taco Taco | **Olmos Pk**	25
Torres Taco | **multi.**	-

BRUNCH

Aldino | **Loop 1604**	21
Cappy's | **Alamo Hts**	26
NEW Drew's | **Stone Oak**	-
NEW Feast | **Southtown**	-
Z Las Canarias | **River Walk**	26
Madhatters | **Southtown**	22
Monterey | **Southtown**	-
Paloma Blanca | **Alamo Hts**	25

BUSINESS DINING

Aldo's | **Medical Ctr**	24
Auden's Kitchen | **Stone Oak**	23
Z Biga/Banks | **River Walk**	26
Z Bistro Vatel | **Olmos Pk**	28
Z Bohanan's | **Downtown**	27
Cappy's | **Alamo Hts**	26
Z Chama Gaucha | **Stone Oak**	25
Citrus | **Downtown**	26
NEW Drew's | **Stone Oak**	-
18 Oaks Stkhse. | **NE**	23
NEW Feast | **Southtown**	-
Fig Tree | **River Walk**	24
Francesca's | **La Cantera**	26
Frederick's | **multi.**	26
Il Sogno | **Near North**	27
Kirby's | **Loop 1604**	24
La Fogata | **North**	22
La Fonda | **Near North**	21
Z Las Canarias | **River Walk**	26
Little Rhein | **River Walk**	21
Luce Rist. | **NW**	23
Lüke | **Downtown**	22
Morton's | **Downtown**	26
Myron's Prime | **Churchill Estates**	28
Ounce | **Loop 1604**	22
Paesanos | **Quarry**	22
Palm | **Downtown**	25

Pappasito's | **NW**	24
Perry's Steak | **La Cantera**	26
NEW Q/Riverwalk | **River Walk**	24
Roaring Fork | **Loop 1604**	24
Ruth's Chris | **multi.**	26
Z Silo | **Alamo Hts**	27
Stonewerks | **multi.**	20
Sushihana | **Castle Hills**	28
Texas/Brazil | **Downtown**	24
Tre Trattoria | **multi.**	24
Wildfish | **Loop 1604**	25

CELEBRITY CHEFS

Bruce Auden
Auden's Kitchen | **Stone Oak**	23
Z Biga/Banks | **River Walk**	26

Jeffery Balfour
Citrus | **Downtown**	26

John Besh
Lüke | **Downtown**	22

Jason Dady
Bin 555 | **N Central**	23
DUK | **Location Varies**	-
Tre Trattoria | **multi.**	24

Johnny Hernandez
La Gloria | **Near North**	23

Damien Watel
Bistro Bakery/Café Artistes | **multi.**	24

Andrew Weissman
Il Sogno | **Near North**	27
Sandbar | **Near North**	27

CHILD-FRIENDLY

(Alternatives to the usual fast-food places; * children's menu available)

Ácenar* | **River Walk**	22
Aldaco's-Stone Oak* | **Stone Oak**	20
Antlers Lodge* | **West Side**	24
Azúca* | **Southtown**	22
Barn Door* | **Alamo Hts**	22
Beto's Comida* | **North**	21
Big'z Burger* | **Loop 1604**	23
Bin 555 | **N Central**	23
Boardwalk Bistro* | **Near North**	23
Z Boudro's* | **River Walk**	24
Cappy's* | **Alamo Hts**	26
Chris Madrid's | **Near North**	24
Chuy's* | **North**	21
Ciao | **Olmos Pk**	24

Cooper's BBQ | **New Braunfels** 25
County Line* | **multi.** 21
Cove* | **Near North** 23
El Jarro/Arturo* | **North** 23
El Mirador | **Southtown** 22
🄔 Five Guys* | **multi.** 22
🄔 Grey Moss Inn* | **Helotes** 27
Josephine St.* | **Near North** 25
La Hacienda/Los Barrios* | **North** 22
La Margarita* | **Market Sq** 24
Madhatters | **Southtown** 22
Mi Tierra* | **Market Sq** 22
Paesanos* | **Loop 1604** 22
Paloma Blanca* | **Alamo Hts** 25
Pei Wei* | **multi.** 20
Piatti* | **Quarry** 24
Rosario's* | **Southtown** 24
Schilo's Deli* | **Downtown** 24
Tip Top Cafe* | **NW** 24
Torres Taco | **multi.** -
Two Bros. BBQ* | **N Central** 19

DESSERT SPECIALISTS

🄔 Biga/Banks | **River Walk** 26
🄔 Bohanan's | **Downtown** 27
Cheesecake | **multi.** 20
Coco Chocolate | **N Central** 23
🆕 Esquire Tav. | **Downtown** -
🄔 Grey Moss Inn | **Helotes** 27
🄔 Las Canarias | **River Walk** 26
Madhatters | **Southtown** 22
Tip Top Cafe | **NW** 24
Zinc Bistro | **Downtown** -

DINING ALONE

(Other than hotels and places with counter service)
Beto's Comida | **North** 21
🄔 Bistro Vatel | **Olmos Pk** 28
🆕 Boehler's | **Near North** 19
Canyon Café | **Quarry** 20
Cappyccino's | **Alamo Hts** 25
Cappy's | **Alamo Hts** 26
Chesters | **multi.** 24
Ciao | **Olmos Pk** 24
El Bucanero | **East Side** -
El Jarro/Arturo | **North** 23
El Mirador | **Southtown** 22
🆕 Esquire Tav. | **Downtown** -
🄔 Five Guys | **multi.** 22
🄔 Fogo/Chão | **Downtown** 25
Gourmet Burger | **multi.** 27
Il Sogno | **Near North** 27
Jerusalem Grill | **West Side** 24

Liberty Bar | **Southtown** 23
Madhatters | **Southtown** 22
🆕 Med. Turkish Grill | **N Central** 20
Pei Wei | **multi.** 20
🄔 Rudy's | **multi.** 25
Sandbar | **Near North** 27
Sushi Zushi | **multi.** 23
Tre Trattoria | **Near North** 24
Zinc Bistro | **Downtown** -

ENTERTAINMENT

(Call for days and times of performances)
Azúca | live music | **Southtown** 22
Beto's Comida | live music | **North** 21
Boardwalk Bistro | jazz/piano | **Near North** 23
County Line | acoustic | **NW** 21
El Jarro/Arturo | live bands | **North** 23
Grill/Leon Springs | live bands | **Leon Springs** 25
India Oven | belly dancers | **N Central** 24
La Hacienda/Los Barrios | varies | **North** 22
La Margarita | mariachi | **Market Sq** 24
🄔 Las Canarias | Spanish guitar | **River Walk** 26
Madhatters | varies | **Southtown** 22
Mi Tierra | mariachi | **Market Sq** 22
Paloma Blanca | guitar/vocals | **Alamo Hts** 25
Rosario's | jazz/Latin band | **Southtown** 24
🄔 Silo | live bands | **Alamo Hts** 27
Welfare Café | live music | **Boerne** -

FOOD TRUCKS

DUK | **Location Varies** -
🆕 Rolling Pig | **Location Varies** -

HISTORIC PLACES

(Year opened; * building)
1847 | Little Rhein* | **River Walk** 21
1853 | Fig Tree* | **River Walk** 24
1878 | Gristmill* | **New Braunfels** 21
1890 | Liberty Bar* | **Southtown** 23
1902 | Bohanan's* | **Downtown** 27
1907 | Canyon Café* | **Quarry** 20
1910 | Josephine St.* | **Near North** 25
1914 | Ocho* | **Downtown** -

1916 | Welfare Café* | **Boerne** ‒

1917 | Schilo's Deli | **Downtown** 24

1920 | Huisache* | **New Braunfels** 28

1929 | Grey Moss Inn | **Helotes** 27

1931 | Aldo's* | **Medical Ctr** 24

1932 | La Fonda | **Near North** 21

1937 | Teka Molino | **Near North** 24

1938 | Tip Top Cafe | **NW** 24

1941 | Mi Tierra | **Market Sq** 22

1953 | Barn Door | **Alamo Hts** 22

1960 | Biga/Banks* | **River Walk** 26

HOTEL DINING

Embassy Suites
  Lüke | **Downtown** 22

Fairmount Hotel
  Tre Trattoria | **Downtown** 24

Hotel Havana
  NEW Ocho | **Downtown** ‒

Hyatt Regency Hill Country
  Antlers Lodge | **West Side** 24

Hyatt Regency San Antonio
  NEW Q/Riverwalk | 24
  River Walk

JW Marriott San Antonio Hill Country
  Cibolo Moon | **NE** ‒
  18 Oaks Stkhse. | **NE** 23

Omni La Mansión del Rio Hotel
  Z Las Canarias | **River Walk** 26

Valencia Hotel
  Citrus | **Downtown** 26

Westin La Cantera Resort
  Francesca's | **La Cantera** 26

LATE DINING

(Weekday closing hour)

Coco Chocolate | varies | 23
  N Central

DUK | 3 AM | **Location Varies** ‒

Jerusalem Grill | 12 AM | 24
  West Side

Max's | varies | **Quarry** 20

Mi Tierra | 24 hrs. | **Market Sq** 22

Monterey | 12 AM | **Southtown** ‒

Zinc Bistro | 12 AM | **Downtown** ‒

MEET FOR A DRINK

Ácenar | **River Walk** 22

Alamo Café | **multi.** 21

Auden's Kitchen | **Stone Oak** 23

Azúca | **Southtown** 22

Barbaresco | **N Central** 19

Z Biga/Banks | **River Walk** 26

NEW Boehler's | **Near North** 19

Z Bohanan's | **Downtown** 27

Cappyccino's | **Alamo Hts** 25

Citrus | **Downtown** 26

Coco Chocolate | **N Central** 23

NEW Drew's | **Stone Oak** ‒

NEW Esquire Tav. | **Downtown** ‒

NEW Feast | **Southtown** ‒

Grill/Leon Springs | **Leon Springs** 25

La Fogata | **North** 22

La Fonda | **Near North** 21

La Gloria | **Near North** 23

Liberty Bar | **Southtown** 23

Lüke | **Downtown** 22

Monterey | **Southtown** ‒

Morton's | **Downtown** 26

Myron's Prime | 28
  Churchill Estates

Palm | **Downtown** 25

Paloma Blanca | **Alamo Hts** 25

Perry's Steak | **La Cantera** 26

NEW Q/Riverwalk | **River Walk** 24

Roaring Fork | **Loop 1604** 24

Z Silo | **Alamo Hts** 27

Tre Trattoria | **multi.** 24

20nine | **Quarry** 23

Zinc Bistro | **Downtown** ‒

Z'Tejas | **La Cantera** 22

NEWCOMERS

Boehler's | **Near North** 19

Drew's | **Stone Oak** ‒

Esquire Tav. | **Downtown** ‒

Feast | **Southtown** ‒

Med. Turkish Grill | **N Central** 20

Ocho | **Downtown** ‒

Q/Riverwalk | **River Walk** 24

Rest. Gwendolyn | **Downtown** 27

Rolling Pig | **Location Varies** ‒

Tejas Steak | **NE** ‒

Vegeria | **Alamo Hts** ‒

OFFBEAT

Beto's Comida | **North** 21

NEW Boehler's | **Near North** 19

Chris Madrid's | **Near North** 24

Chuy's | **North** 21

Cooper's BBQ | **New Braunfels** 25

Cove | **Near North** 23

El Bucanero | **East Side** ‒

NEW Esquire Tav. | **Downtown** ‒

NEW Feast | **Southtown** ‒

Josephine St. | **Near North** 25

Liberty Bar | **Southtown** 23

Madhatters | **Southtown** 22

Monterey | **Southtown** ‒

NEW Ocho | **Downtown** ‒

NEW Rest. Gwendolyn | 27
  Downtown

Welfare Café | **Boerne** ‐

Zinc Bistro | **Downtown** ‐

OUTDOOR DINING

(G=garden; P=patio; S=sidewalk;
T=terrace; W=waterside)

Ácenar | P, W | **River Walk** 22

Aldino | P | **Loop 1604** 21

Aldo's | G, P | **Medical Ctr** 24

Azúca | P | **Southtown** 22

Beto's Comida | P | **North** 21

🏿 Biga/Banks | T, W | 26
 River Walk

Big'z Burger | P | **Loop 1604** 23

Bin 555 | P, T | **N Central** 23

Boardwalk Bistro | P | 23
 Near North

🏿 Boudro's | P, W | **River Walk** 24

Cappy's | P | **Alamo Hts** 26

Chuy's | P | **North** 21

Ciao | S | **Olmos Pk** 24

Citrus | T | **Downtown** 26

Coco Chocolate | P | **N Central** 23

County Line | P | **River Walk** 21

El Jarro/Arturo | P | **North** 23

El Mirador | P | **Southtown** 22

🆕 Feast | P | **Southtown** ‐

Fig Tree | P, T, W | **River Walk** 24

Francesca's | T | **La Cantera** 26

Godai | P | **N Central** 28

🏿 Grey Moss Inn | P | **Helotes** 27

Josephine St. | P | **Near North** 25

La Fogata | P | **North** 22

La Frite | S | **Southtown** 26

La Gloria | P | **Near North** 23

La Hacienda/Los Barrios | P | 22
 North

La Margarita | P | **Market Sq** 24

🏿 Las Canarias | T | **River Walk** 26

Little Rhein | G, T, W | 21
 River Walk

Luce Rist. | P | **NW** 23

Lüke | P, S | **Downtown** 22

Madhatters | P | **Southtown** 22

Monterey | P | **Southtown** ‐

Paesanos | G, T, W | **multi.** 22

Paloma Blanca | P | **Alamo Hts** 25

Piatti | S | **Quarry** 24

Picnikins Patio | P | **N Central** 24

Roaring Fork | P | **Loop 1604** 24

Scenic Loop | P | **Leon Springs** 23

Tre Trattoria | P | **Near North** 24

20nine | P | **Quarry** 23

Welfare Café | P | **Boerne** ‐

Wildfish | P | **Loop 1604** 25

PEOPLE-WATCHING

Ácenar | **River Walk** 22

Aldino | **Loop 1604** 21

Barbaresco | **N Central** 19

Bistro Bakery/Café Artistes | 24
 Downtown

🆕 Boehler's | **Near North** 19

🏿 Bohanan's | **Downtown** 27

🏿 Boudro's | **River Walk** 24

Chris Madrid's | **Near North** 24

CIA Bakery | **Near North** 25

Coco Chocolate | **N Central** 23

🆕 Drew's | **Stone Oak** ‐

🆕 Esquire Tav. | **Downtown** ‐

🆕 Feast | **Southtown** ‐

La Fogata | **North** 22

La Frite | **Southtown** 26

La Gloria | **Near North** 23

Liberty Bar | **Southtown** 23

Lüke | **Downtown** 22

🆕 Med. Turkish Grill | 20
 N Central

Monterey | **Southtown** ‐

Myron's Prime | 28
 Churchill Estates

🆕 Ocho | **Downtown** ‐

Oma's Haus | **New Braunfels** ‐

Paesanos | **multi.** 22

Piatti | **Quarry** 24

Picnikins Patio | **N Central** 24

🆕 Rest. Gwendolyn | 27
 Downtown

🆕 Rolling Pig | **Location Varies** ‐

Sandbar | **Near North** 27

Taco Taco | **Olmos Pk** 25

🆕 Tejas Steak | **NE** ‐

Teka Molino | **Near North** ‐

Timbo's | **Near North** ‐

Tre Trattoria | **Near North** 24

20nine | **Quarry** 23

Zinc Bistro | **Downtown** ‐

POWER SCENES

Auden's Kitchen | **Stone Oak** 23

🏿 Biga/Banks | **River Walk** 26

Coco Chocolate | **N Central** 23

🆕 Drew's | **Stone Oak** ‐

🆕 Esquire Tav. | **Downtown** ‐

Grill/Leon Springs | **Leon Springs** 25

Il Sogno | **Near North** 27

Kirby's | **Loop 1604** 24

La Gloria | **Near North** 23

Liberty Bar | **Southtown** 23

Lüke | **Downtown** 22

Morton's | **Downtown** 26

Ounce | **Loop 1604** 22

SAN ANTONIO

SPECIAL FEATURES

Paesanos | **multi.** | 22
Palm | **Downtown** | 25
Piatti | **Quarry** | 24
Ruth's Chris | **Downtown** | 26
Sandbar | **Near North** | 27
Tre Trattoria | **Near North** | 24
Wildfish | **Loop 1604** | 25
Zinc Bistro | **Downtown** | -

QUIET CONVERSATION

Aldo's | **Medical Ctr** | 24
Z Biga/Banks | **River Walk** | 26
Bistro Bakery/Café Artistes | **Downtown** | 24
Z Bistro Vatel | **Olmos Pk** | 28
Z Bohanan's | **Downtown** | 27
Cappyccino's | **Alamo Hts** | 25
Cappy's | **Alamo Hts** | 26
Citrus | **Downtown** | 26
Coco Chocolate | **N Central** | 23
Cypress Grille | **Boerne** | 24
NEW Drew's | **Stone Oak** | -
18 Oaks Stkhse. | **NE** | 23
Francesca's | **La Cantera** | 26
Frederick's | **multi.** | 26
Z Grey Moss Inn | **Helotes** | 27
Grill/Leon Springs | **Leon Springs** | 25
India Oven | **N Central** | 24
Kirby's | **Loop 1604** | 24
Z Las Canarias | **River Walk** | 26
Little Rhein | **River Walk** | 21
Lüke | **Downtown** | 22
NEW Med. Turkish Grill | **N Central** | 20
Myron's Prime | **Churchill Estates** | 28
NEW Ocho | **Downtown** | -
Olmos Park | **Olmos Pk** | 28
Ounce | **Loop 1604** | 22
Palm | **Downtown** | 25
Perry's Steak | **La Cantera** | 26
NEW Rest. Gwendolyn | **Downtown** | 27
Sushihana | **Castle Hills** | 28
Tre Trattoria | **Downtown** | 24
20nine | **Quarry** | 23
NEW Vegeria | **Alamo Hts** | -
Welfare Café | **Boerne** | -

ROMANTIC PLACES

Aldo's | **Medical Ctr** | 24
Z Biga/Banks | **River Walk** | 26
Bistro Bakery/Café Artistes | **Downtown** | 24
Z Bistro Vatel | **Olmos Pk** | 28

Z Bohanan's | **Downtown** | 27
Citrus | **Downtown** | 26
Coco Chocolate | **N Central** | 23
18 Oaks Stkhse. | **NE** | 23
Fig Tree | **River Walk** | 24
Francesca's | **La Cantera** | 26
Z Grey Moss Inn | **Helotes** | 27
Grill/Leon Springs | **Leon Springs** | 25
Kirby's | **Loop 1604** | 24
Z Las Canarias | **River Walk** | 26
Little Rhein | **River Walk** | 21
Lüke | **Downtown** | 22
Myron's Prime | **Churchill Estates** | 28
Olmos Park | **Olmos Pk** | 28
Ounce | **Loop 1604** | 22
Perry's Steak | **La Cantera** | 26
NEW Rest. Gwendolyn | **Downtown** | 27
Z Silo | **multi.** | 27
Sushihana | **Castle Hills** | 28
Tre Trattoria | **Downtown** | 24
20nine | **Quarry** | 23
Welfare Café | **Boerne** | -
Zinc Bistro | **Downtown** | -

SINGLES SCENES

Ácenar | **River Walk** | 22
Aldino | **Loop 1604** | 21
Azúca | **Southtown** | 22
Barbaresco | **N Central** | 19
NEW Boehler's | **Near North** | 19
Z Bohanan's | **Downtown** | 27
Cibolo Moon | **NE** | -
Coco Chocolate | **N Central** | 23
NEW Esquire Tav. | **Downtown** | -
Fleming's Prime | **Quarry** | 25
Frederick's | **multi.** | 26
Grill/Leon Springs | **Leon Springs** | 25
La Gloria | **Near North** | 23
Max's | **Quarry** | 20
Monterey | **Southtown** | -
NEW Ocho | **Downtown** | -
Paesanos | **Loop 1604** | 22
Paloma Blanca | **Alamo Hts** | 25
Pappasito's | **NW** | 24
Roaring Fork | **Loop 1604** | 24
Rosario's | **Southtown** | 24
Stonewerks | **multi.** | 20
Timbo's | **Near North** | -
Wildfish | **Loop 1604** | 25
Zinc Bistro | **Downtown** | -

TRENDY

Ácenar | **River Walk** | 22
Auden's Kitchen | **Stone Oak** | 23
Azúca | **Southtown** | -

Barbaresco | **N Central** 19
☑ Biga/Banks | **River Walk** 26
☑ Bohanan's | **Downtown** 27
Coco Chocolate | **N Central** 23
☑ Dough | **N Central** 27
DUK | **Location Varies** –
NEW Esquire Tav. | **Downtown** –
NEW Feast | **Southtown** –
☑ Fogo/Chão | **Downtown** 25
Frederick's | **Churchill Estates** 26
Il Sogno | **Near North** 27
La Gloria | **Near North** 23
Liberty Bar | **Southtown** 23
Lüke | **Downtown** 22
Max's | **Quarry** 20
Monterey | **Southtown** –
NEW Ocho | **Downtown** –
Ounce | **Loop 1604** 22
NEW Rest. Gwendolyn | **Downtown** 27
Tre Trattoria | **multi.** 24
20nine | **Quarry** 23
Urban Taco | **Quarry** 20

VIEWS

Ácenar | **River Walk** 22
Aldaco's-Stone Oak | **Stone Oak** 20
☑ Biga/Banks | **River Walk** 26
Big'z Burger | **Loop 1604** 23
Bistro Bakery/Café Artistes | **Downtown** 24
☑ Bohanan's | **Downtown** 27
☑ Boudro's | **River Walk** 24
☑ Chart Hse. | **Downtown** 15
CIA Bakery | **Near North** 25
18 Oaks Stkhse. | **NE** 23
Fig Tree | **River Walk** 24
Francesca's | **La Cantera** 26
☑ Gristmill | **New Braunfels** 21
La Gloria | **Near North** 23
La Margarita | **Market Sq** 24
☑ Las Canarias | **River Walk** 26
Little Rhein | **River Walk** 21
Max's | **Quarry** 20
Mi Tierra | **Market Sq** 22
Paesanos | **River Walk** 22

Scenic Loop | **Leon Springs** 23
Welfare Café | **Boerne** –

WINE BARS

Bin 555 | **N Central** 23
Cypress Grille | **Boerne** 24
Fleming's Prime | **Quarry** 25
Huisache | **New Braunfels** 28
Max's | **Quarry** 20
Olmos Park | **Olmos Pk** 28
20nine | **Quarry** 23
Zinc Bistro | **Downtown** –

WINNING WINE LISTS

Aldo's | **Medical Ctr** 24
Auden's Kitchen | **Stone Oak** 23
☑ Biga/Banks | **River Walk** 26
Bin 555 | **N Central** 23
☑ Bohanan's | **Downtown** 27
☑ Boudro's | **River Walk** 24
Coco Chocolate | **N Central** 23
18 Oaks Stkhse. | **NE** 23
Fig Tree | **River Walk** 24
☑ Fogo/Chão | **Downtown** 25
Francesca's | **La Cantera** 26
Frederick's | **multi.** 26
☑ Grey Moss Inn | **Helotes** 27
Grill/Leon Springs | **Leon Springs** 25
Il Sogno | **Near North** 27
☑ Las Canarias | **River Walk** 26
Little Rhein | **River Walk** 21
Luce Rist. | **NW** 23
Morton's | **Downtown** 26
Myron's Prime | **Churchill Estates** 28
Ounce | **Loop 1604** 22
Paesanos | **Loop 1604** 22
Palm | **Downtown** 25
Perry's Steak | **La Cantera** 26
Ruth's Chris | **multi.** 26
Sandbar | **Near North** 27
☑ Silo | **Alamo Hts** 27
Sushihana | **Castle Hills** 28
20nine | **Quarry** 23
Two Bros. BBQ | **N Central** 19
Zinc Bistro | **Downtown** –

SAN ANTONIO

SPECIAL FEATURES

Wine Vintage Chart

This chart is based on a 30-point scale. The ratings (by U. of South Carolina law professor **Howard Stravitz**) reflect vintage quality and the wine's readiness to drink. A dash means the wine is past its peak or too young to rate. Loire ratings are for dry whites.

Whites	95	96	97	98	99	00	01	02	03	04	05	06	07	08	09	10
France:																
Alsace	24	23	23	25	23	25	26	22	21	22	23	21	26	26	23	26
Burgundy	27	26	22	21	24	24	23	27	23	26	26	25	26	25	25	–
Loire Valley	–	–	–	–	–	–	25	20	22	27	23	24	24	24	25	
Champagne	26	27	24	25	25	25	21	26	21	–	–	–	–	–	–	–
Sauternes	21	23	25	23	24	24	29	24	26	21	26	25	27	24	27	–
California:																
Chardonnay	–	–	–	–	22	21	24	25	22	26	29	24	27	23	27	–
Sauvignon Blanc	–	–	–	–	–	–	–	–	25	24	27	25	24	25	–	
Austria:																
Grüner V./Riesl.	22	–	25	22	26	22	23	25	25	24	23	26	25	24	25	–
Germany:	22	26	22	25	24	–	29	25	26	27	28	26	26	26	26	–

Reds	95	96	97	98	99	00	01	02	03	04	05	06	07	08	09	
France:																
Bordeaux	25	25	24	25	24	29	26	24	26	25	28	24	24	25	27	–
Burgundy	26	27	25	24	27	22	23	25	25	23	28	24	24	25	27	–
Rhône	26	22	23	27	26	27	26	–	26	25	27	25	26	23	27	–
Beaujolais	–	–	–	–	–	–	–	–	27	25	24	23	28	25		
California:																
Cab./Merlot	27	24	28	23	25	–	27	26	25	24	26	24	27	26	25	–
Pinot Noir	–	–	–	–	–	–	26	25	24	25	26	24	27	24	26	–
Zinfandel	–	–	–	–	–	25	24	26	24	23	21	26	23	25	–	
Oregon:																
Pinot Noir	–	–	–	–	–	–	26	24	25	24	25	24	27	24	–	
Italy:																
Tuscany	25	24	29	24	27	24	27	–	24	27	25	26	25	24	–	–
Piedmont	21	27	26	25	26	28	27	–	24	27	26	26	27	26	–	–
Spain:																
Rioja	26	24	25	22	25	24	28	–	23	27	26	24	24	25	26	–
Ribera del Duero/ Priorat	25	26	24	25	25	24	27	–	24	27	26	24	25	27	–	–
Australia:																
Shiraz/Cab.	23	25	24	26	24	24	26	26	25	25	26	21	23	26	24	–
Chile:	–	–	–	–	24	22	25	23	24	24	27	25	24	26	24	–
Argentina:																
Malbec	–	–	–	–	–	–	–	–	25	26	27	26	26	25	–	

Vote at zagat.com